Saving Our Constitution From the New World Order

by
Joseph Stumph

*Edited and Cover Design
by James Van Treese*

Printed by
Northwest Publishing Inc.
5949 South 350 West
Salt Lake City, UT 84107
801-266-5900

Copyright © 1993 NPI

Northwest Publishing, Inc.
5949 South 350 West
Salt Lake City, UT 84107

International Copyright Secured
All Rights Reserved

Reproductions in any manner, in whole or in part,
in English or in other languages, or otherwise
without the prior written permission of the
author and publisher is prohibited.
All rights reserved.

ISBN 1-56901-088-9

Printed In the United States of America

Dedication

Dedicated to that generation of courageous and generous Americans we call the Founding Fathers. And more specifically, to the 55 who dared to stand against the most powerful government on earth in 1776, and pledge their lives, their fortunes and their sacred honor to a high risk venture...the cause of liberty, when they signed the Declaration of Independence.

And to the 39 other great patriots who, eleven years later, signed the Constitution proposing union of the States into The United States.

And to all the brave men of valor who fought or died for America, from the tiny Army of George Washington to that powerful armada sent to oppose the tyrant of Iraq, Saddam Hussein. And to the wives and daughters who supported sons and brothers, and wept bitter tears of grief and whose hearts ached when their sons and husbands were returned to them in caskets, or left buried or unknown on foreign soil.

The Constitution they gave us, which is still the basic law of the land, is so powerful, the modern tyrants who are trying to destroy or replace it are succeeding, only because they have tirelessly worked to keep its teaching out of our educational structure, so that most of us are ignorant of its power. A recent poll found that only one-third of the American people knew that The Bill of Rights are the first Ten Amendments to the

Constitution.

Therefore, because *the people* and *the states* do not know about, nor understand how to use the power they have, these powers have lain dormant, for the most part, for several decades. As our Minuteman rockets tipped with nuclear warheads, have lain dormant in buried silos for over two decades, and could be launched immediately, if need be, so can the powers retained in the Constitution be exercised immediately by *the states* and *the people*, or we can completely withdraw all delegated powers from the federal government and eliminate its existence.

But all the efforts of the Founders and patriots have not been in vain. The Constitution they gave us has secured over 200 years of glorious liberty. We can show our appreciation by preserving it.

Acknowledgments

Our generation owes much to our fathers of former generations who established liberty on the American continent, and for many who have come after to sustain and defend that liberty.

The author wishes to especially give credit to Alexander H. Stephens, who after the Civil War wrote a book in two volumes brilliantly showing how the States established the Federal Union and the relationship they have to each other. Mr. Stephens served as the Vice President of the Southern Confederacy during the Civil War, or as he chose to call it, The War Between The States.

In this volume we quote extensively from the work of Mr. Stephens, who though he loved his country and the Constitution and counselled his countrymen against secession; nevertheless justified the secessionist States in their firing the first shots which started the Civil War. In this one instance he was wrong, but in establishing the lawful foundation, or the legal basis for the right of a State to secede from the Union, his research and historical documentation proves beyond a shadow of doubt that the South was right when 11 Southern States argued they had a legal right to leave the Union.

The author also wishes to thank Marvin Ashcroft of Logan, Utah who took his degree in history, for his help in researching the subject of secession.

The publisher, James Van Treese, has done a great service for the cause of liberty in being willing to publish a work such as this, for there are those who would suppress this type of education and suggested political action, and who rightfully view it as a threat to their plans to eliminate the Constitution and merge the United States into a one-world government. In many nations of the world any publisher who dared print such material as this work would quickly be put out of business or have his life put in jeopardy. And such is not unheard of even in the land of the free.

To my loyal and good wife LoLita who has for 33 years faithfully stood by and supported me, and who has been willing to sacrifice vacation time and many other hours we could otherwise have spent together, except for my researching and writing this work. Although I sometimes think she thinks, her mission in life is to keep me humble I express gratitude for a companion who is willing to always reveal her honest opinion, and for whose love and affection, which is unconditional, makes life worth living. I am grateful for her civilizing influence which she has in common with all good and virtuous women who manage to retain their beautiful and wonderful God-given femininity, in spite of the shrill cries and demands of the modern feminist movement.

To Tom Wood, attorney-at-law, who donated his time to professionalize the Ultimatum Resolution to dissolve the Union in Chapter 13.

And to Neva Funk of Manti, Utah who read the manuscript to improve punctuation and readability.

Contents

Dedication iii

Acknowledgments v

Definitions xi

Preface xxiii

Chapter

    1   Preparation—Key to Avoiding Bloodshed   1

    2   Lawful Secession—Remedy of Last Resort   17

    3   Treaties and Other Dangers   47

    4   13 Free, Sovereign and Independent Nations   85

    5   The Constitution—A Bloodless Revolution. Nine States Secede From Four States   149

    6   West Virginia. A Constitutional Outlaw. Double Standard and Hypocrisy of Abraham Lincoln   213

    7   Lincoln and the North—As Guilty as the South   233

8	Secession—Historical Precedents	241
9	The Kentucky and Virginia Resolutions	255
10	The Constitution is a Revokable Charter	279
11	The Supreme Court. "The Constitution Means What We Say It Means"	293
12	Jurisdiction. State vs. Federal	315
13	Model Ultimatum Resolution to Dissolve the Union. Resolution of Secession	373
14	Conclusion. What You Can Do	407

Appendix
    Secession Declaration of South Carolina, December 20, 1861   413

Saving Our Constitution From The New World Order

If ye love wealth better than liberty, the tranquility of servitude better than the animating contest of freedom, go home from us in peace. We ask not your counsels or arms. Crouch down and lick the hands which feed you. May your chains set lightly upon you, and may posterity forget that ye were our countrymen.

Samuel Adams, 1776

As long as the world shall last there will be wrongs, and if no man objected and no man rebelled, those wrongs would last forever. The objector and the rebel who raises his voice against what he believes to be the injustice of the present and the wrongs of the past is the one who hunches the world along.

Clarence S. Darrow, 1857-1938

No one wins when freedom fails. The best men rot in filthy jails. And those who cried appease, appease, are hanged by those they tried to please.

Author Unknown

x

DEFINITIONS

Sovereignty. The supreme, absolute, and uncontrollable power by which any independent state is governed, supreme political authority, the supreme will, paramount control of the constitution and frame of government and its administration, the self-sufficient source of political power from which all specific political powers are derived, the international independence of a state, combined with the right and power of regulating its internal affairs without foreign dictation, also a political society, or state, which is sovereign and independent.

The power to do everything in a state without accountability, to make laws, to execute and to apply them, to impose and collect taxes and levy contributions, to make war or peace, to form treaties of alliance or of commerce with foreign nations, and the like.

Sovereignty in government is that public authority which directs or orders what is to be done by each member associated in relation to the end of the association. It is the supreme power by which any citizen is governed and is the person or body of persons in the state to whom there is politically no superior. The necessary existence of the state and that right and power which necessarily follow is "sovereignty". By "sovereignty" in its largest sense is meant supreme absolute, uncontrollable power, the absolute right to govern. The word which by itself comes nearest to being the defintion of "sovereignty" is will or volition as applied to political affairs. City of Bisbee vs. Cochise County, 52 Ariz. 1, 78 p. 2d 982,986. Black's Law Dictionary.

In the United States *the people* are sovereign. *The people* created the States and delegated a portion of their sovereignty to State government. As *agents* themselves, *the states*, and *the people* created a *secondary agent*, the United States government, under a contract called the Constitution. *The people* gave each of their two agents certain specific authority to act *on behalf of* themselves, for the purpose of protecting their liberty, and to assure domestic tranquility. *The people* at all times retained, and do retain, *total sovereignty*. *The people* only temporarily delegated limited power to both of their agents, only so long as those *agents* responsibly exercise their delegated powers. *The people* can, at any time, *recall*, or *resume*, full sovereignty, and accordingly reduce or eliminate powers they temporarily assigned to one, or both of their agents. *The people* existed first, before either State or Federal governments. If *the people* choose to abolish or eliminate either one, or both of their *agents* of government, *the people* will continue to exist, and could establish new agents who might give more respect for the rights and liberty of *the people*. No Principal needs an agent who no longer respects or listens to him, or worse, attempts to defraud or bankrupt him.

Usurpation. The unlawful encroachment or assumption of the use of property, power or authority which belongs to another. An interruption or the disturbing a man in his right and possession.

The unlawful seizure or assumption of sovereign power. The assumption of government or supreme power by force or illegally, in derogation of the constitution and of the rights of the lawful ruler.   Black's Law Dictionary.

Principal. adjective. Chief; leading; most important or considerable; primary; original. Highest in rank, authority, character, importance, or degree. Ibid.
Principal. noun. The source of authority or right. A superintendent, as of a school. Ibid.

Agent. A person authorized by another (principal) to act for or in place of him; one entrusted with another's business. One who represents and acts for another under the contract or relation of agency...
One authorized to transact all business of principal, or all of principal's business of some particular kind, or all business at some particular place. Ibid.
Agent. One entrusted with the business of another; one who acts for another as his representative. Webster's Unabridged Dictionary.
Agency. A relationship between two persons, by agreement (contract, compact, constitution, etc. author) or otherwise, where one (the agent) may act on behalf of the other (the principal) and bind the principal by words and actions. Relation in which one person acts for or represents another by latter's authority either in the relationship of principal and agent, master and servant, or employer or proprietor and independent contractor...The relation created by express or implied contract or by law, whereby one party delegates the transaction of some lawful business with more or less discretionary power to another, who undertakes to manage the affair and render to him an account thereof...or relationship where one person confides the management of some affair, to be transacted on his account to another party. Or where one party is authorized to do certain acts for, or in relation to the rights or property of

the other...The consensual relation existing between two persons, by virtue of which one is subject to other's control...

Agency is the fiduciary relation which results from the manifestation of consent by one person to another that the other shall act on his behalf and subject to his control, and consent by the other so to act...   Black's Law Dictionary.

The United States government is merely an *agent* of the 50 States and *the people*, and an artificial agent at that, deriving its only power from a contract, the Constitution. The 50 State governments are also mere agents themselves, acting and existing at the pleasure of *the people*.

As Thomas Jefferson said in *the Declaration of Independence, the people,* at all times, retain the right to *change*, or to *abolish* their chosen forms of government, for government is merely an agent of *the people*.

Under the laws of contract, individuals and businesses by the thousands, daily create and abolish, add to or diminish, powers of agents. All in peace and according to law. Government, as an agent, is no different than a corporation, except in the case of government, *the people* delegate to it the *police power* for their protection. Protection is the main legitimate function of government. When government begins to abuse the *police power*, or any other power, on a national, state, or local level, *the people* merely have to withdraw the powers of agency.

It is a universally accepted law of nature, that an individual, a community, or a nation, has the right to defend and protect life, liberty and property against any unlawful aggressor. When government itself becomes that unlawful aggressor, history providing ample and numerous examples, it is the right of the individual, community, or nation to repel, or to destroy the aggressor. Historically, this has often been done by force of arms. However, it has often been accomplished peacefully as well. There is no reason for violence when *the people* choose to alter or abolish their form of government.

As Principal, *the people* at all times retain the right to use force if necessary, to abolish or withdraw powers they have delegated to their mere *agent*. History proves governments do not easily relinquish powers the people have delegated to them. That's why our Fathers so wisely insisted on the Second Amendment to the Constitution. To eternally guarantee the people's right to keep and bear arms, and to protect themselves from their own government; and, if they must, use their guns to withdraw the powers of agency from tyrannical government.

But any *responsible agent*, unless he has gone mad with arrogance and imagined grandeur, will peacefully surrender the powers of agency to his Principal upon demand. Particularly in the case of a corporation, for the corporation has no life, or existence of its own, except at the pleasure of the Principal.

Few responsible stockholders in any corporation would allow their agents, the officers and Board of Directors, to act in defiance of stockholder interests or to run continual deficits, or to operate in a manner detrimental to the long term interests of the stockholders. Few stockholders would allow the president of the company to burden their children and grandchildren with perpetual debt, while he and the Board of Directors personally enrich themselves and their friends. If the corporation appears to have become permanently unprofitable, stockholders with any sense at all, will dissolve the corporation and resume, or take back, all delegated power. This would only be good business. To allow one's agent to bind one's children down with perpetual debt, and in other ways infringe on the liberty of the Principal, or the Principal's children, would be foolish and irresponsible.

In dissolutions of corporations in the United States each day, either by direct action of the stockholders or through operation of laws of dormancy, violence plays no part.

Should 38 or more States decide to dissolve the corporate

structure of the United States government, violence should play no part. If *the people* withdraw the powers of agency from Washington, it is true, the president, the congress, the judges, and all other Federal employees would have to find new jobs. That's no big deal. Thousands, perhaps millions, of people have done it before when corporations have become unprofitable and have been dissolved.

Principals appoint or create agents for benefit of the Principal. If the agent does not do a good job, or exercises the powers of agency in a manner detrimental to the Principal, an intelligent and responsible Principal takes back to himself some, or all of his temporarily delegated powers. There is no reason for violence. There is no reason for war.

In fact, the failure of a Principal to withdraw the powers of agency in a timely manner can lead to war. If a Principal allows his agent to unlawfully bind him, and if the Principal knowingly and willingly allows his agent, over a long period of time, to usurp undelegated powers, the Principal by not acting, is by silence, agreeing to be bound by his agent.

If a Principal is ignorant, or does not consent to unlawful actions of an agent, the Principal is not lawfully bound. But if a Principal knows his agent is acting against the Principal's interests, lawfully or unlawfully, and does nothing, it is assumed the agent acted with consent of the Principal, and the Principal may discover he has allowed himself to be bound.

Secession, is the formal withdrawal from a political organizatlon, such as a state, empire, or federation. The term originated in ancient Rome, where on three occasions between 494 and 287 B.C. the oppressed Plebeians seceded from the republic by marching out of the city and refusing to return until their grievances were redressed. In modern times such action would be considered more of a strike or rebellion, for secession implies an attempt by a community or province to break away permanently from a larger organization and assume self government. Because political organizations normally do not recognize such a right, secession is *usually* a revolutlonary act. Emphasis added. Encyclopedia Americana.

Revolutions are not necessarily by force. They can be peaceful, as was the revolution when the Constitution of the United States replaced the Articles of Confederation.

Secession. The act of withdrawing from membership in a group.   Black's Law Dictionary

Secession. A going apart, separation. 1. An act of seceding; formal withdrawal or separation. 2. The withdrawal of a State from the Federal Union. 3. The act of withdrawing from fellowship and communion; retirement.

Secede. To go away, apart. 1. To withdraw from fellowship; to go into retirement. 2. To withdraw formally from membership in a group, association, organization, etc; to break off one's connection with others, as in a political or religious group.

Seceder. In Scotland, one of a body of Presbyterians who seceded from the Church of Scotland in 1733.

Webster's Unabridged Dictionary.

Revolution: A complete overthrow of the established government in any country or state by those who were previously subject to it. The word in its broadest significance is generally used to designate a sweeping change as applied to political change. It denotes a change in a method or system of government, or of the power which controls the government. It is frequently accomplished by or accompanied by violent acts, *but it need not be violent in its methods and it does not necessarily denote force or violence.* Emphasis added. *U.S. vs. Foster*, D.C.N.Y., 9 F.R.D. 367, 394. Black's Law Dictionary.

In the present United States (1993) if *we the people* act in a timely manner, we can preserve this Nation by a peaceful and lawful revolution. To delay, is to risk bloodshed. Today, we have the law on our side. Tomorrow it may be, that only blood revolution, if even that, will recover our lost liberty.

We will prove that the Constitution under which we presently live, was the result of revolution...a peaceful and bloodless revolution. The United States government was established in such a manner that it allows, by law and precedent, peaceful revolution by the States and/or the people.

Federal. A league or compact between two or more states, to become united under one central government. Black's Law Dictionary.

Federal. A league, treaty. 1. of or formed by a compact; specifically, designating or of a union of states, groups, etc. in which each member agrees to subordinate its power to that of the central authority in common affairs. 2. designating, of, or having to do with a central government of this sort. Webster's Unabridged Dictionary.

Compact. n. An agreement or contract between persons, nations or states. Commonly applied to working agreements between and among states concerning matters of mutual concern. A contract between parties, which creates obligations and rights capable of being enforced and contemplated as such between the parties, in their distinct and independent characters. A mutual consent of parties concerned respecting some property or right that is the object of the stipulation, or something that is to be done or forborne. Black's Law Dictionary.

Compact Clause. Article 1, Section 10, Clause 3, of U.S. Constitution provides: "No State shall, without the consent of Congress,...enter into any Agreement or *Compact* with another State..." Ibid.

Federation. A joining together of states or nations in a league or association; the league itself. Ibid.

League. An association or treaty of alliance between different nations, states, organizations, sports teams, or parties. Ibid.

Treaty. A compact made between two or more independent nations with a view to the public welfare.

An agreement, league, or contract between two or more nations or sovereigns, formally signed by commissioners properly authorized, and solemnly ratified by the several sovereigns or the supreme power of each state.

A treaty is not only a law but also a contract between two nations and must, if possible, be so construed as to give full force and effect to all its parts.

The term has a far more restricted meaning under U.S. Constitution than under international law. Emphasis added. Weinberger vs. Rossi, Dist. Col., 456 U.S. 25, 102 S. Ct. 1510, 1514, 71 L. Ed. 2d 715. Ibid.

New World Order. One-world government, the forerunner of which is The United Nations Organization headquartered in New York. The elimination of sovereignty of every nation on earth. This will include the United States. Under the New World Order, the Constitution of the United States will be eliminated. United Nations military forces will become the supreme military power replacing the military forces of all former nations.

Life, liberty and property of the individual will have little, if any, protection from the demanding and arbitrary tyranny of government. Property will be owned or controlled by government. Life and liberty will be allowed only to those who do not resist and do as they are commanded. *Author*

Corporation.

An artificial person or legal entity created by or under the authority of the laws of a state. An association of persons created by statute as a legal entity. The law treats the corporation itself as a person which can sue and be sued. The corporation is distinct from the individuals who comprise it (shareholders). Black's Law Dictionary.

Municipal Corporation.

A legal institution formed by charter from sovereign (i.e. state) power erecting a populous community of prescribed area into a body politic and corporate with corporate name...

Municipal corporation is a body politic and corporate, created to administer the internal concerns of the district embraced with its corporate limits,...Ibid.

John Marshall, chief justice of the U.S. Supreme Court, in a circuit court ruling held: "The United States is a government, and consequently a body politic and corporate, capable of attaining the objects for which it was created by the means which are necessary for their attainment. This great corporation was ordained and established by the American people, and endowed by them with great powers for important purposes." U.S. vs. Maurice, 2 Brock. 96, Federal Cases No. 15747. (1823). Quoted: in re Merriam's Estate, 36 NE 505. (1894).

Corporations are created for the benefits of the stockholders, or those who create it. Officers and directors of a corporation serve at the pleasure of the stockholders. Presidents and chief executive officers (CEO) can be fired by the stockholders. When corporate officers act in a manner which is fraudulent, or detrimental to the interests of THE PEOPLE, or stockholders, those officers can be dismissed and criminally prosecuted. When corporate officers waste corporate assets or live "high on the hog" with extravagant borrowing, they can all be fired by the shareholders; or the shareholders can DISSOLVE THE CORPORATION, whatever is their pleasure.

When corporate officers refuse to honor and obey the corporate charter, the stockholders can choose to discipline them, or destroy the corporation by dissolving the charter. The Constitution is the charter of the United States Corporation. Three-fourths of the states, 38, can lawfully dissolve the charter and automatically fire the President of the United States, 535 congressmen, nine supreme court justices and 3.1 million federal employees and keep for themselves some 1.5 trillion dollars annually which it is costing us to support the out-of-control nightmare in Washington.

If we were to accept the arguments of those liberals and socialists who say the United States is a Democracy, a simple majority of 26 States have the inherent right to dissolve the Union in total disregard of the Constitution. However, being a Republic, not a Democracy, we make the argument in this work that three-fourths of the States, not 26, can legally dissolve the Union.

Preface

It is not possible to retain the Constitution of the United States as the Supreme Law of the land, and at the same time, merge the sovereignty of the Federal government and the 50 States into a one world government under the United Nations, or *the New World Order*.

Slavery, though upheld by law and sustained by the Supreme Court, was an issue of irreconcilable difference. Its advocates had the law of the land on their side and refused to emancipate the slaves. The opponents of slavery had the moral law on their side, and could never, in good conscience, stand idly by without attempting to do something to free the black man.

Abortion, like slavery, has been upheld by law, and sustained by the Supreme Court, yet it must, and will, persist as an irreconcilable difference among our people.

Atheists and humanists have succeeded in getting the Supreme Court to take prayer and God out of the classroom, and are still working on removing every symbol of God or religion from public buildings and grounds.

The Bill of Rights was added to the Constitution as superfluous clarification, forbidding Federal encroachments on the rights of *the people* and *the states*. The Supreme Court, through clever rationalization, has twisted the Fourteenth

Amendment in such a way as to turn the Bill of Rights into prohibitions against the States as well as the Federal government. If accomplished properly, such prohibitions might be just and lawful, but done by usurpation, they become one more building block in constructing the fantasy under which we are presently governed; that the Federal government is the *master;* the States, the *servants*. If this illusion can be nurtured a little longer, it will allow the alleged *master* to merge us into a one world government, without the *states* and the *people* knowing they, all along, had the power to bring the madness of Washington under control.

The United States is loaded down with international treaties and agreements; loaded down with thousands of Executive Orders of the President; with numerous Supreme Court usurpations which are now the precedents for further usurpation; loaded down with socialist and freedom-sapping legislation, and we are crushing our children and grandchildren with a national debt, admitted and unfunded which may be approaching, if it has not already surpassed, the assets of personal and real property of the entire nation. And Congress continues to add to that debt some one billion dollars per day.

There appears to be only one way to settle the irreconcilable differences among us and to stop the mad rush of one world thinkers in their unlawful machinations to abolish the Constitution; only one way to eliminate the national debt and Federal entanglements; that is for *the states* and *the people* to take charge, crack the *State whip,* and either bring Congress, the President and the Federal Courts back under the *strict construction* of the Constitution, or send the whole bunch packing.

YES! Thirty-eight States acting together, can, if all else fails, abolish and dissolve the entire Federal Establishment, and along with it, the national debt and every other fraud perpetrated on the American people by a 200-year-old monster. If the States do this job themselves, they will retain the already established State Governments. They can retain the Constitution of the United States in the individual State governments, and after the "dust settles," those 50 *free, independent and sovereign states*, can if they wish, rejoin in Union, just as Nine States joined in a new union under the Constitution June 21, 1788, when abandoning the old Union under the Articles of Confederation.

If it appears impossible to get 38 States to work together to save the Constitution, one or more States may have to go it alone. This can be accomplished by secession, or separation from the United States, just as eleven States seceded prior to and after the beginning of the Civil War. But this time, we won't make the mistake made by the South. The law will be on our side and so will historical precedent.

The extreme action of secession, or Union dissolution, should not be necessary. But without giving due and thoughtful consideration to such lawful possible action, current trends in America indicate that Congress intends to permanently place the States and *the people* in a subservient position to the Federal government, and eventually, to a one-world government. If *the people* do not soon assert *their sovereignty* and put the Federal government in its place, and let Congress know it is dispensable, *we the people* are going to find our freedom has vanished and only bloodshed, if that, can recover it.

By bringing to the forefront the possibility of secession or Union dissolution, we put on notice the entire Federal establishment; we put on notice the Congress, the President and the Judiciary, that *we the people*, and each of the 50 States, have taken all the abuse and unconstitutional usurpations we intend to take. We turn on the lights for Congress and a President gone mad with power and grandeur, and bring them back down to earth so they realize their smallness and understand they truly are *public servants*, not kings or gods. We cause

Congress to reassess its role as a mere agent of *the people* and *the states*, and that if it persists in bankrupting the nation and ignoring the constitutional contract, the patience and endurance of *the people* is at an end. Washington must be brought to the realization that our destiny is in the hands of *the people*, not Washington.

Though it should be hoped by all that secession of one or more States, or dissolution of the Union itself by 38 or more States, will never be necessary, it is time we give serious consideration to such remedies. Without such a wake-up call, Congress, the President and the Courts are hell-bent on destruction of the Constitution, either by domestic corruption and usurpations and unpayable debt, or by merging us into the New World Order, or both. If Congress does not soon receive a jolt, or a wake-up call from *the people*; if Congress is not made to realize their insignificance in the true order of things, then Congress is going to bankrupt America, if it has not already done so, and lead us into total corruption and bondage. A little knowledge of history indicates to any person of average intelligence that we are in the last days of the enjoyment of liberty; that we have but a short time to act before the chains of dictatorship and tyranny assume their historical roles.

Fortunately, for the American people, we have almost 6,000 years of history as our guide. We have accumulated knowledge of the ages. We have numerous historical and legal precedents upon which to draw. In attempting to retain freedom for ourselves and our children, we need not proceed blindly, nor by trial and error as did our fathers who laid the necessary groundwork for us. We have, which material wealth allows us, time to get involved in bringing government under control.

If we lose our freedom, if we lose the Constitution, we have nobody to blame but our apathetic and pleasure-bent selves, for we have the power to either bring the Federal government back under control, or to destroy it.

Though preservation of the Union is most desireable, and appears to be the wiser course we should pursue, it may not be possible unless we are willing to go to the edge of the cliff; unless *we the people* take charge and let Congress and the President know in no uncertain terms, that we know our rights, we know the law, and we intend at any cost, to preserve our liberties, even if it means dissolving the Union and selling Washington, D.C. to the highest bidder. The possibility; the probability that *the people* will actually carry through on such a "threat," appears to be the only thing which will ever bring Washington under control.

It seems the world is at last beginning to learn that peaceful separation of people with major differences is far more preferable than war and bloodshed. Once again, on January 1, 1993, Czechoslovakia showed the world the way such separations, or secessions should work. The former Czechoslovakia peacefully became two new nations. Czechs and Slovaks split their 74-year-old homeland in two because of nationalism and their differences over post-Communist reforms. Bratislava is now the capital of Slovakia. Prague is the capital of the Czech Republic.

The newest nations in Europe were born peacefully.

There is some bitterness, but many gave thanks for the "velvet divorce" which was as peaceful as the "velvet revolution" that ended communist rule in 1989.

Some have asked what was gained by Slovak independence? If only peace was gained, and bloodshed avoided, was separation of the country not the best thing for these millions of people? It might just as well be asked, what is gained by millions of people staying together under one government, if by doing so, they must live together in continual violence and discontent?

Just before television went off midnight December 31,

1992, Czechoslovak Premier Jan Strasky thanked those who "have contributed to the fact that the state is dividing peacefully."

On the last day before the split, Ludovit Cernak, the Slovak economics minister, said in an interview: "The only thing I fear is that the nation will become nervous. If people massively begin to withdraw money from the banks and transfer it to Czech banks, everything would fall like a house of cards."

Prior to the split, most of the problems of separation had been settled. These two new nations had to divide "family" property. They will now have separate embassies with other nations. The two countries will maintain their common currency, at least for the time being. There will be no limit of movement of citizens for awhile, but there will be road and railroad border crossings beginning January 3, 1993, similar perhaps, to highway patrol stops required of the trucking industry in the United States, as trucks cross State borders.

Whether or not the United States splits into two, or into 50 separate nations in order to avoid bloodshed over several of our major differences, it is well for us to know separation is a lawful and viable option. It is well for us to understand that separation of nations into two or more parts is not historically unusual. It is right to consider the historical precedents of our own history beginning July 4, 1776, and realize that a breakup of the United States, even if not carried out, is an option which should receive calm and careful due consideration. Separation of man and wife, separation of gangs, separation of hateful or bitter people, separation of states or nations, is sometimes the only way to prevent eventual bloodshed and massive loss of human life and treasure.

Separation, divorce, secession, Union dissolution, therefore, should never be set aside as a no-no or as an unthinkable solution. History and experience and common sense teaches us, that sometimes to live apart, is the only way that both parties can continue to live. Often, living together means somebody dies.

Peace and happiness is the common goal of mankind. Without peace, without liberty, or at least the hope of attaining these, life is hardly worth living.

If peace and happiness is not possible living together, but both are attainable through separation, it is the height of foolishness to force ourselves to live together.

This world is big enough for everybody. If managed properly, the planet is capable of sustaining billions of more people. If certain blacks or whites cannot get along without hating each other, let them peacefully choose to live apart. They don't have to occupy the same land mass. If homosexuals and straights can't get along, let them separate and live in peace with their own kind. Who cares about another's sexual preferences, as long as it does not interfere with somebody else? Sure, homosexuality, adultery, fornication, burglary, thievery, murder are "sins" in various degrees among different people. Let each kind separate into its own community. If a man or woman wishes to sin, and does not interfere with my rights, his sins are between him and his God.

It is way past time when men stopped killing each other because they think differently. Let us realize that we are all different, and we all have an equal right to life, liberty and the pursuit of happiness. If we cannot attain these while living together, the solution is simple enough for any child to figure out. Agree to disagree, walk away from each other, separate, and let the other live in peace.

Whether for individuals or governments, the principle is the same. Separation in peace is preferable to living together, whatever its advantages, in violence, fear, or constant government intimidation.

XXX

Chapter 1

Preparation
Key to Avoiding Bloodshed
By J. Bracken Lee • Former Governor of Utah

If you say, "I don't believe in secession," then you must also say, "I don't believe in the Declaration of Independence. I don't believe in celebrating the 4th of July every year, nor the yearly massive displays of fireworks which take place all over America." To be consistent as a non-believer in secession, you must believe with King George and Great Britain, that George Washington, John Adams, Thomas Jefferson, and James Madison, our first four presidents, were all traitors and criminals worthy of death under the British Crown, for the Declaration of Independence they wrote, or adopted and sustained, is the greatest secession document of all time.

If you say, "I don't believe in secession," you must also say, "I don't believe in the Constitution of the United States. I don't believe the Constitution was inspired, for God would not sanction secession. I don't believe in the work of the Founding Fathers during the hot summer from May 25 through September 17, 1787."

The Constitution is, in addition to being the greatest document of liberty known to man, a Declaration of Secession. Nine States under it, unlawfully seceded from four States which were left outside. The nine had solemnly agreed with the four under the Articles of Confederation, that the thirteen States were to be a perpetual union, and in order to make any changes in their contract, or compact, or treaty, it would require the consent of all thirteen. But that compact was not only changed without unanimous consent, it was totally abandoned, and the four outsiders could stay out forever, or they could join if they wished. All eventually joined in the new compact, contract, or treaty, under the Constitution, but not for nearly two years.

If you say, "I don't believe in secession," you must also say, "I don't believe we should allow West Virginia to remain in the Union as a State. We should disqualify her senators and representatives in Congress and put her back under the jurisdiction, and within the boundaries of the State of Virginia."

West Virginia was carved out of about 38% of the land mass of Virginia, when the Western counties of Virginia seceded from Virginia at the beginning of the Civil War, without meeting the constitutional requirements for creating a new State.

If you say, "I don't believe in secession," you must also say, "We must give Texas back to Mexico and Panama back to Colombia. We must not recognize, as we have already done, Latvia, Lithuania and Estonia." For all of these were secessions of one people or one government from another. And if you don't believe in secession, something is drastically wrong in the former Soviet Union, for the remaining 12 republics have all gone their separate ways as one after another declared official secession from "Mother" Russia, as the world watched in shock and fascination

Secession is simply separating—whether a married couple, a couple living together outside marriage, a group, an association, a nation. When reconciliation and negotiation fail; when peace and harmony become impossible; when hatred and bitterness develop; when unrighteous dominion of one party over another becomes fixed, or permanent; when one attempts to become master, making another his servant; when differences become irreconcilable, separation is sometimes the best solution. Separation is sometimes the only solution in order to prevent the shedding of blood. When all else fails, there is nothing wrong with agreeing to disagree and walking away.

Secession has been a common historical occurrence. Separation, or divorce, which is the same thing, is so common in America, nobody gives it a second thought.

We may be approaching that time in America when gays and straights, pro-lifers and pro-choicers, liberals and conservatives, Christians and non-believers, black-hating whites, and white-hating blacks should just agree to disagree, go their separate but peaceful way, and divide the United States into sections or States into which each group would be invited to make his/her home.

This idea is especially attractive concerning the criminal element of mankind. Give all murderers an island of the sea away from everybody else, and let them live by themselves and govern themselves. Give all rapists a separate island. Give all thieves a separate island, etc. Such a separation of the criminal element from law abiding society would save billions of dollars we are presently forced to spend on maintaining numerous prisons. If separation of groups of criminals into a society where they were forced to live with their own kind became a reality, we would see a drastic drop in the crime rate. Such a system would truly become a deterrent to crime. No murderer would wish to be forced to live on an island of murderers under the law of the jungle. And we could eliminate the death penalty and the eternal arguments between proponents and opponents over the issue.

Serious thought will reveal the desireability of separation or secession as a remedy of last resort. When all else fails, peaceful secession is a most viable solution.

According to Samuel Sherwood, a constitutional scholar and teacher of the Constitution residing in Blackfoot, Idaho, when the American Colonists revolted against Great Britain in 1776, their "taxation without representation" amounted to .76 of 1% net effect on income. In the United States of 1992, net effect of total taxation on income is 53%. This means taxes today are 69.73 times higher than on our revolutionary fathers.

How long are the American people going to take these obscenely high taxes, with no end in sight, without following our fathers in revolution?

Probably not much longer. But we can avoid the bloodletting kind of revolution our fathers had to endure. If everybody will think it through, separation and secession is much more viable, much cheaper, more effective and far less stressful than war and bloodshed. Agreeing to disagree before we come to national blows and civil war, through peaceful secession, is the only rational approach to take in what we like to call this age of enlightenment.

* * * * * *

In January, 1790, George Washington delivered his first State of the Union address to Congress. One of the things he said was: "To be prepared for war is one of the most effectual means of preserving peace." On another occasion our first President wrote: "If we are wise, let us prepare for the worst; there is nothing, which will so soon produce a speedy and honorable peace as a state of preparation for war." To James McHenry. Fitzpatrick 25:151. (1782) Quoted from the book, The *Real George Washington*, p. 753, published by The National Center For Constitutional Studies.

In concluding World War II, the United States dropped atomic bombs on Hiroshima and Nagasaki, Japan.

Soon thereafter, the United States developed the hydrogen bomb, a weapon far more powerful than those dropped on Japan.

The Soviet Union succeeded in stealing our blueprints and built their own hydrogen bombs. This was followed by a massive buildup on both sides of nuclear weapons, so that by the 1960's it was possible for man to obliterate all life on earth, should the United States and the Soviet Union become involved in a nuclear war.

The United States adopted a policy known as MAD, or Mutually Assured Destruction. Under this policy the United States maintained a number of nuclear armed bombers in the air 24-hours a day, 365 days a year. A number of nuclear armed submarines roamed the oceans of the world. Deep underground silos protected nuclear missiles aimed at targets in the Soviet Union.

MAD was based on the theory that should the Soviet Union attack the United States, and even if such an attack should prove successful and destroy us, the Soviet Union would also be destroyed by our constantly alert retaliatory forces. Should the Soviets succeed in destroying our silo based missiles, sufficient numbers of our airborne hydrogen bombs, combined with missiles launched from undersea vessels, would still be able to annihilate the Soviet Union. Both nations would be destroyed should either attack the other.

Dangerous doctrine indeed, but it has worked so far. An uneasy peace has been maintained. Fortunately, no mad man has ever gained access to the nuclear trigger in the Soviet Union. And it must be admitted, knowing the designs of Soviet world conquest, that MAD was the best we could have done until, and unless, a system is ever developed to destroy attacking missiles in flight.

The thing which made MAD effective, and succeeded in discouraging the Soviet Union from launching an attack, was the United States made sure the Soviet leaders clearly understood the rules of the game. We made sure they knew we would hold nothing back should we be attacked. We made sure the enemy knew they would just as surely be destroyed as would the United States. Knowledge was power; like knowledge has always been power.

The United States hoped for the best; that nuclear war would never come; that Soviet leaders would never be so foolish as to fire that first nuclear missile. But at all times, we were prepared for the holocaust, and prepared to retaliate with everything that we had. Such a policy of "madness" has kept the peace, more or less, for several decades.

This book is a proposal for a domestic policy of MADness by one or more of the 50 States comprising the United States.

Unknown to most Americans, there are a number of silently approaching, possibly destructive scenarios developing which might attempt a "lawful" coup of the United States government. A violent, or unlawful coup is not out of the question. There are those who desire to eliminate, or suspend, or abolish, the Constitution of the United States, and merge us into a one-world government, a New World Order, or "Family of Nations."

If we are determined to maintain our constitutional liberties, we have the weapons to completely rout and "destroy" the enemies of America—to destroy them legally and lawfully, not literally. The law, historical precedent, right and truth, are all on the side of domestic MADness. Like our policy of MAD kept us out of nuclear war, this proposed domestic MAD should keep America's enemies from attempting to overthrow the United States government and abolishing the Constitution, if they know beforehand, their efforts are doomed to failure, and they will only succeed in bringing themselves to trial as traitors.

However, unlike our policy of nuclear MADness, domestic MADness will not, or should not cause bloodshed. It should be accomplished, if actually necessary to be implemented, with calm, reason and in peace, for it will be shown to be legal and lawful, viable and reasonable.

But to be successful, our enemies, as well as ourselves, must understand that in this game of governmental power, *we the people* have all the Aces. We have all the power. It is just a matter of whether or not we choose to use it. Leaders on both sides must know *the people* and *the states* will use our two domestic hydrogen bombs if there are those who would destroy our Constitution. By being willing to use these "bombs" it should never be necessary to actually do so. Just like it was never actually necessary to use our nuclear bombs against the Soviet Union.

In the United States we have, more or less, historically lived by the policy of President Theodore Roosevelt, "Walk softly, but carry a big stick." As a nation, like any wise government, the United States has maintained a policy that a strong military force keeps us out of war because it discourages any potential enemy from attacking us.

Nobody bothers the neighborhood bully, normally. The world has been fortunate that the United States has, for the most part, been a benevolent "bully." Because we have been powerful, few have dared to attack us.

Domestically, our leaders have forgotten who holds the real power in the United States. The real "bully," which is *the people*, has become ignorant, apathetic, rich, comparatively speaking, and lazy. This "benevolent bully" must be awakened, and those he has delegated as leaders must be put on alert that he is awake and ready to take action if he must.

Once the Federal government, especially the out-of-control Congress, realizes the bully might get them, and "destroy" them, all 535 of them are likely to come to their collective sense and attempt, in good faith, to straighten out the horrible mess they have created in this nation.

If they refuse, then we must use our "bombs" and "destroy" them.

                        signed
                        J. Bracken Lee
                        Former Governor of Utah 1949-1957
                        Salt Lake City, Utah

* * * * * *

It should be noted that we are aware of the possibility that the United States policy of MAD for the past several decades, might have been based on fraud and deception of the American people. Whether or not this policy may have been advanced for the purpose, among others, of draining trillions of dollars from the American taxpayers, we do not know.

It has recently come to light, that theoretically, nuclear devices can only be exploded at certain limited times, perhaps within a few seconds at certain times of the year, and there are certain areas on the earth where it is impossible to set off nuclear devices. According to this assertion, for example, there is a certain area in New Zealand which is known as a "nuclear free zone," where it is impossible to explode a nuclear bomb at any time. Allegedly, the sun must be in an exact position in relation to the earth in order for nuclear devices to work.

Bruce Cathie, in his book *The Bridge To Infinity, Harmonic 371244*, America West Publishers, Boulder, Colorado, says on page 170: "...The geometric trigger that caused the disruption of matter within the bomb was the spacial relationship between the Earth and the Sun at a given instant of time. This knowledge made it obvious to me that an all out atomic war would be impossible as each bomb would have to be detonated at a certain place at a certain time which could be precalculated years in advance by any proposed enemy. The whole process would be completely illogical...

"...As could be expected, once it became known that I had discovered the geometric nature of the bomb, I was contacted by personnel from various agencies and scientific establishments from around the world who tried their best to persuade me to keep quiet about it. I refused, as I believe the public have a right to know the truth about the geometric process involved."

Whether or not this is theory or fact is not relevant to the subject matter of this work. That must be left to others to research and write.

Regardless, it is a wise policy for nations, or a people, to plainly communicate to potential aggressive enemies, the fact that you are strong and have powerful weapons at your disposal, and that you have every intent of using those weapons to destroy that enemy and defend your country should you be attacked.

* * * * * *

"It is time to check and reverse the growth of government, which shows signs of having grown beyond the consent of the governed. It is my intention to curb the size and influence of the federal establishment and to demand recognition of the distinction between the powers granted to the federal government and those reserved to the states or to the people."
—Ronald Reagan
Inaugural Address, 1981

Whether or not President Reagan really tried to reduce the

size of government is not so important. After eight years in office, he had accomplished little so far as reshaping the bureaucracy toward his stated goal of smaller government. The enduring impact of liberals and socialists who came to power with Franklin D. Roosevelt in 1933 and with every presidential administration since then remains with us.

Numerous Federal agencies of one administration after another ever since the New Deal, have continually multiplied. Even under Reagan and George Bush, in spite of all their rhetoric about a government which is too big and spends too much, they didn't really try to restructure it.

While campaigning for President in 1980, Reagan said he would eliminate the departments of Education and Energy. He did neither. He actually participated in the creation of a new Cabinet department, Veterans Affairs.

It is true, the power of a president acting within the Constitution is limited and he cannot do as much as he would perhaps like to, without the cooperation of Congress.

If a Ronald Reagan cannot, or will not, bring Federal usurpation of power under control, and attempt to stop the frenzied spending of the Congress, there is little hope of preventing eventual financial collapse, resulting in chaos, bloodshed and overthrow of the government of the United States. Millions of uninformed and naive Americans refuse to believe it, but just such a collapse and destruction of the Constitution and our government is proceeding according to plan.

For the few millions, we hope, who have dug into the books and become informed about our imminent danger, we must provide them with an opposing plan by which law abiding Americans can effectively resist, and, it is hoped, defeat and throw off the forces of evil which have almost engulfed us.

Good stands on its own. Evil requires great effort and inexhaustible resources to sustain itself. Because liberty and the free agency of man is good, and because good, truth and liberty invite the assistance and blessing of almighty God, liberty can be maintained with a fraction of the resources and manpower which it takes to sustain evil and tyranny. Those on the side of limited government and human freedom should never lose hope. God is on our side, and the eventual outcome of the gigantic struggle for world power and dominion presently taking place is not in doubt. God will preserve liberty, even if only among a small remnant who are determined to live by His laws and give glory to His name, for it is but a short time until He comes in power and great glory to destroy the kingdoms of this world, and establish His own for a thousand years.

In the meantime, we are expected to do more than just sit around and pray for Him to come and deliver us. We are expected to do all we can do, without panic, and without fear. Then we can confidently look for Him to do the rest.

The following is quoted from the October 1992 issue of a letter by The National Center For Constitutional Studies, written by Andrew M. Allison, President.

"So where do we go from here? Even among 'conservatives' there is wide disagreement about how to address the country's woes. Some are hoping we can vote into the White House a modern George Washington who will single-handedly turn the government around. Others are 'withdrawing from the system' altogether (refusing to pay income taxes, etc.). A few are literally stacking up guns and ammunition, preparing for armed conflict with the 'new world order.' Still others are just wondering, grumbling, or throwing up their hands in despair.

"Personally, I don't believe that confrontation with the federal authorities or any other radical approach is the right answer. I believe we should obey the laws of the land—even unjust laws—while we urge our legislators to enact better ones. I also believe we have a moral obligation to identify and support good candidates, at all levels of government, who will wisely and honestly act on constitutional principles. God bless any candidate who will stand up for our Constitution.

"But what if our best efforts fail and the national government continues to plummet toward disaster?

"Just for the sake of discussion, let's consider an unthinkable extremity: the official abandonment of our Constitution by the United States government. Could that spell the end of America? No! America is not Washington, D.C.; it's tens of millions of individuals and families all across this great land from one ocean to another. We're not going to disappear. Of course, if our current system of government doesn't survive, it will be replaced by something else—but what?

"If our imagined scenario came true and our leaders in Washington actually discarded the Constitution, we can be sure that an elite group of 'master planners' (on the national and/or international level) would be diligently working to impose on us a much harsher form of government. And they might even prevail to some degree for a brief time.

"But remember that men aren't the only ones who make plans—so does God. And He always wins. As Benjamin Franklin wisely observed during the Constitutional Convention of 1787, 'God governs in the affairs of men.' Franklin then quoted a passage from the Old Testament: 'Except the Lord build the house, they labour in vain that build it.' (Psalm 127:1)

"The Almighty has a plan for America, and it has not yet been fulfilled. The Founders testified that this nation and its Constitution were established by the 'interposition of Heaven.' Surely the Lord did not provide His gracious guidance and protection merely to see this chosen Land of Liberty fall into the hands of tyrants! Our forefathers declared that God had consecrated America as a place of refuge for those who sought to worship and obey Him, and I believe that remains true today.

"So should we just sit back and wait for the Lord to put things right? Of course not—but what can we do?

"Our federal government has been on the wrong track for decades. It's currently racing down this track faster than ever, and we may not be able to correct its course before it plunges over the precipice. But we can begin, even now, to lay a new track. We can be more than 'freedom fighters' who expose and resist evil; we can work together as 'freedom builders' in laying a foundation for the literal rebirth of America.

"If it turns out that we can't save Washington, D.C., there are things we can save that are of far greater worth to us:

"Our relationship with God. We can strengthen our faith in the 'Author of liberty' by praying to Him, studying the holy scriptures, attending church, and keeping His commandments.

"Our families. We can express love to family members, work and play together, teach our children and grandchildren, store food and other needed commodities, and get out of debt.

"Our Constitution and the blessings of liberty. We can learn and then teach others how to apply the principles of freedom and self-government on which this nation was founded.

"The American way of life. Besides wielding our vote and our influence as citizens, we can 'rebuild the American culture of freedom and unity' through positive involvement with our neighbors in strengthening the communities where we live.

"Our Founding Fathers longed to establish a nation guided by the 'higher law' revealed from heaven. John Adams taught that if we would 'take the Bible for our only law book,' the result would be a 'paradise.' Many early Americans sought to help build the scriptural kingdom of God in that era.

"As we noted, their dream was only partially realized. But they had the assurance—and so do we—that 'the God of heaven shall set up a kingdom which shall never be destroyed...it shall break in pieces and consume all earthly kingdoms, and it shall stand forever.' " (Daniel 2:44, see also 7:14)

The suggestions above are all good. But we can do more.

God and our Fathers preserved for us, powerful tools with which to thwart the aggression of tyrants, in the framework of the Constitution. But our generation also has a tremendous advantage of being able to draw upon historical precedent, and thereby prove to the satisfaction of all law abiding men and women, the justness and legality of two major proposals outlining peaceful and lawful revolution in the United States of America.

This revolution can best be accomplished by three-fourths of the States, 38 or more, working together to resist, perhaps destroy, all efforts to suspend or abolish the Constitution. Failing this, the revolution can be accomplished, but with greater risk, by enough patriots coming together into one or more States, in sufficient numbers whereby they can control the electoral process and elect only constitutionalists as members of a State's legislature, and elect a governor and attorney general who would truly fight to preserve the Constitution within the boundaries of that State. Risk should be minimal in either case because the revolution will be one of law. But "there is safety in numbers." However, "one standing alone with God, is a majority."

Time may be very short, however, therefore we cannot wait for a large congregation of patriots to assemble. The plans outlined herein as Plan B, and Plan C, needs immediate coordination and implementation. All who wish to preserve the Constitution, if they agree with these plans, need to coordinate their efforts and work together. Then we will be fully prepared, just in case there are those who are going to try to overthrow the government of the United States and the Constitution; unless we take strong and bold action immediately to stop them.

This book is more than a plan. It is a legal brief which will convince the timid, and the most morally scrupulous adherents of law, that these proposals of revolution are lawfully sound, morally responsible, and have an extremely high probability of success. Successful implementation will not only preserve the Constitution and State governments, holding high the Constitution within State boundaries until the dust settles, but it will prevent certain bloodshed and unlawful revolution should we choose to "take our chances" and allow nature to follow its course. Certain bloodshed will follow implementation of a New World Order, and millions of Americans will have to be executed; in a "humane" way, of course.

With the results of the 1992 presidential and congressional elections, we find that, even with massive voter dissatisfaction, somehow we again elected numerous socialsts to Congress, and a President who is going to follow the same basic policies of the previous administration of reducing U.S. sovereignty and merging us into a command society in a one world government.

If we are going to preserve the Constitution, we must dare to be as bold as our fathers who established this nation some 200 years ago. Great victories are not won, and liberty is not preserved by timidity and ignorance. "The righteous are bold!" (Holy Bible, Proverbs 28:1)

To preserve the Constitution, we do not need massive numbers. We need men who love truth and righteousness, have the courage of their convictions, and who seek the guiding hand of God in their daily lives.

As the inspiring song says:

Give me some men, who are stout-hearted men,
Who will fight for the right they adore.

Start me with ten who are stout-hearted men,
And I'll soon give you ten thousand more, Oh

Shoulder to shoulder and bolder and bolder,
They grow as they go to the fore.

Then there's nothing in the world can halt or mar a plan.
When stout-hearted men, can stick together man to man.

> Stout-hearted Men
> By Oscar Hammerstein II
> Music by Sigmund Romberg

For the sake of those who do not realize the imminent dangers we face from traitors and one-worlders within our own ranks, we will briefly mention in this work a few dangers. However, our main effort is to point out the remedies which are available, and can be established by the States, before the fact, should we ever face a coup d'etat. All 50 governors, attorneys general, and all members of every State Legislature must be given an opportunity by their constituents to read and consider the plans outlined in this book. We must assume that some of them will be in the enemy camp, and will not cooperate, and will be working against us, for many sincerely believe the elimination of the Constitition and the establishment of a one world government is something which is desireable. We must assume some of our State leaders, especially from some of our larger, more liberal States, will actively be working "hand in glove" with the New World Order agents. Those who pretend to be for America and the Constitution, but who are actually working behind the scenes to destroy both, will not be pleased when they discover a viable and powerful plan of action actually exists which has the potential of stopping their one-world juggernaut in its tracks.

Nevertheless, the more widespread is the knowledge that actual power exists, and that a workable plan is being implemented to stop any attempted overthrow of the United States government, the greater chance we have of stopping potential traitors. If their chances of succeeding in an attempted coup appear to be precarious and uncertain, the less chance there is that they will even make the attempt.

Once the dark plans of traitors are exposed to the masses of the people, those traitors must succeed, or they face imprisonment or death. Therefore, if those who would betray our liberties are given to understand the people are fully prepared to resist and defeat them, they are likely to be discouraged from even making the attempt to destroy the Constitution. Traitors, criminals, even mad men, prefer to pursue their objectives in relative safety. When they see their course involves great risk to their personal safety, they are less heroes than cowards. Traitors shun the light and exposure, and will normally not advance against an informed and powerful enemy. Massive darkness is penetrated by a single lighted candle. Truth in the hands of an honest man, might overcome legions who are supported by lies and deception. And the enemies of freedom; the enemies of the Constitution are supported by lies and deception.

Everybody who becomes aware of, and agrees with the

ideas presented in this work, is encouraged to take action in his State, alone, or working with others of like mind. If you form a group in your own State, or wish to coordinate your efforts with ours, please write to the address near the back of this book on page 411.

Chapter 2

Lawful Secession
Remedy of Last Resort

As the presidential election of November 3, 1992 approached, rumor was rampant that the United States was headed for various national crises. Some said a collapse of our banking system was imminent, and only awaits the outcome of the election before those in power allow it to follow its natural course. Others said, and still say, in a banking collapse, or some other real, or imagined, national crisis, the President will declare a national emergency, institute martial law, and "temporarily" suspend the Constitution.

Still others fear the President might, at some uncertain future date, negotiate various treaties with the leading nations of the world, gain Senate ratification, and thereby, put the United States into a one-world government, or the New World Order or "family of nations," suspend or eliminate the Constitution, and thereby merge United States sovereignty into that of a one-world consolidation of power.

Some will say such ravings are "right-wing paranoia." But to totally discount such possibilities would be naive and foolish at best. To admit criminal conspiracies exist on a small scale, as we are continually reminded by the news media, and deny they exist in government and with elected officials, is to ignore history and abandon common sense.

Whether or not there is substance to current fears and rumors, the United States is, without doubt, headed for financial disaster. Unparalleled in the history of the world, we have accumulated a national debt of over 4 trillion dollars, and add to that debt currently about 1 billion dollars per day. This is only the admitted portion of our debt. Unfunded future obligations for Social Security, military pensions, pensions of some 3 million federal employees, etc. add many more trillions to this debt which can only be paid by ever-increasing tax burdens on our children, and our children's children into the infinite future.

In the early 1990's, the tax burden on the American worker is already so heavy, that millions of families, even with both husband and wife in a majority of these families working, are finding it more and more difficult to sustain themselves above the official poverty level. Single parent families have a harder time yet.

Just the interest on the current national debt has become the largest expenditure in the Federal budget, now approaching 1 billion dollars per day; over 300 billion dollars annually. In a few years, the interest alone is projected to absorb the total amount of money collected by the Federal government from the income tax.

It is anybody's guess as to the course the nation will be forced to take when, not if, but when, we are unable to pay the interest on the debt; when we can no longer meet the pension obligations of Social Security, Federal retirees and military pensions, and other numerous future obligations of the Federal government.

At the same time, pensions, bonding extravagance of the past and escalating social obligations of states, counties and cities are continally adding to future financial obligations we have and are putting on the shoulders of our children.

Already we are approaching, if we have not already surpassed, the outer limits of our ability to meet the tax burdens placed on us by our various governments. Even so, the spending spree of Federal and local governments continues unabated with no end in sight.

Our generation is doing on a massive scale, that which history teaches us destroys nations. We are wallowing in greed, extravagance and crime. We have millions on welfare "legally" plundering the productive workers. In a best case scenario, we have assured financial bondage for our children.

Anybody who has seriously considered where we are headed can see there is no possible way our children can meet the debt obligations we have placed upon them. We are quickly approaching the time, probably early in the next decade, when it will not be possible for our children to survive; it will not be possible for them to purchase food, clothing and shelter, and at the same time meet the obligations of pensions and other debt we have placed upon them.

Already we have some 44 million people drawing Social Security and Supplemental Security Income (SSI) checks every month. Another estimated 18.6 million people are employed by Federal, State and local governments, Federal employees alone, accounting for 3.1 million.

As welfare benefits have increased, the incentive to work, as compared to drawing welfare and "going fishing," has decreased the desire of those to work, who otherwise might do so, because they can make nearly as much, sometimes more, after taxes, by being on welfare than they can by working.

Our generation of greed and extravagance, has guaranteed a future economic war between the older and younger generations. Something will have to give as the percentage of people drawing government checks increase, and the percentage of productive workers decrease.

Human nature has not changed in some 6,000 years of recorded history. History, therefore, is a reliable guide by which we may anticipate the future. We can anticipate that in time of crisis, man made or natural, our Federal government might resort to drastic, radical, even unconstitutional methods and policies in attempting to remedy approaching crises.

A wise person, or people, will always prepare for the worst, while hoping for the best. Should the time ever come when our government is about to fall of its own excesses, or should our government attempt to suspend the Constitution, we will be wise if we have a plan at the State level which might sustain stability and the protections of organized government.

We can see trying times ahead. We will hope for the best; that our government will be able to straighten out the mess in Washington, get their spending under control, and start giving us responsible leadership; that they will get back to governing by the Constitution. We must hope that a majority of Congress will soon see that we are headed over the cliffs, and unselfishly seek remedies, hold the nation together and restore national harmony.

But, just in case, our leaders fail us, or refuse to come to their senses; just in case some of the current rumors about approaching national crises prove to be true; just in case there are men in power who intend to put the United States into a New World Order; just in case there are plans to suspend the Constitution; and just in case all the land and property and personal assets in the entire 50 States have been secretly pledged, and actually contracted, as collateral on the national debt and future United States financial obligations; just in case some of our national leaders who appear to be good guys, are really bad guys, and intend to do us in; just in case, mind you, there are government leaders secretly working to undermine the Constitution, it will be beneficial to the whole nation for a few of us to know the law, to know the Constitution, to know our rights so we will be able to effectively resist any attempted overthrow of the government of the United States. Just in case, our children will be thankful, and so will any American who cherishes his liberty, for those among us who are determined, no matter what happens, to sustain and defend the Constitution of the United States.

Just in case there are those who would sell us out, destroy the Constitution and the sovereignty of the 50 States, we must have a plan to foil such nefarious schemes of constitutional destruction.

The people and the states, have all the power in this United States of America. Our people do not realize this because the enemies of America have for decades, deliberately withheld much of our history and teachings of the Founding Fathers, and principles of the Constitution from our institutions of learning. The enemies of America know that it is impossible for an ignorant people, or an immoral people, or a lazy and apathetic people, to maintain their liberties. Therefore, for several decades, there has been deliberate, organized opposition to the teaching in the public schools and universities, of any sort of moral code, individual responsibility, and very little about the Constitution.

On the contrary, promiscuity and irresponsibility are encouraged. Refusal to accept blame for one's mistakes is widespread. Evil is called good, and good is called evil. In the 1960's prayer was taken out of the schools and replaced with increasing teenage pregnancy and violence, and out-of-control children.

Washington encourages all this. By threat of withholding federal funds from States and local communities which fail to comply with federal regulations and guidelines, Washington, with a small percentage of total dollars expended in education and many other areas, is able to dictate policy.

Yet, the original powers retained by the people and the states, remain with us even today. The people still have all the power. They only have to resume it or take it back; just reach out and claim it. That's what this book is about.

* * * * * *

Responsible leadership, whether corporate, government, small business, or the head of a family, will try to anticipate future problems. Government and business sometimes maintain complex and expensive intelligence networks for this purpose.

In the case of the United States government, it spends billions of dollars per year with the Central Intelligence Agency, (CIA) Federal Bureau of Investigation, (FBI) and other intelligence networks. Our agents in government know there are those who might conspire to weaken or overthrow our government, and we spend billions yearly to anticipate or eliminate problems before they materialize. It is common to see governments overthrown today, as well as historically.

Any responsible leadership, though it might hope for the best, will always be prepared for the worst. This is not paranoia. This is just good common sense. If one is prepared for the storm, and has everything secured, then one can go to bed and sleep comfortably at night. Preparedness brings peace of mind. To be unprepared for crisis brings paranoia, panic and fear.

We are going to assume a worst case scenario concerning the government of the United States. First we will discuss potential threats to our government, the Constitution and our way of life. Then we will outline options which are available to us to remedy such threats, should we be required to adopt one or more of our options in order to preserve the Constitution. We will follow with a lengthy discussion of the foundation in law and history which will sustain our rights, both moral and legal, to implement any one or more of the options we might find ourselves in need of pursuing.

Some of these options might be considered radical, impractical, illogical; even insane. Yet we will prove them to be historically sound and lawful. We may be accused of citing rebellion or sedition, yet we are merely advocating that which a free people have a right to do.

If everybody understands the rules of the game; if our leaders know that the people know the rules, we might well avoid the crisis. If there are those who might attempt to destroy the Constitution, yet they are well aware that the people have the knowledge and means of resisting and defeating them; when traitors know knowledge to defeat them is widespread, they are far less likely to attempt their criminal acts. If governors, attorneys general, and the legislatures of all 50 States are schooled and prepared in how to handle an attempted takeover of the Federal government, or a suspension of the Constitution, this alone will discourage the enemies of America from attempting to put their nefarious schemes into full force and effect.

Ignorance and liberty do not walk together. Our people

and our leaders must understand their rights and powers. We must know ahead of time that the course we intend to follow is moral, right and lawful.

A civilized and educated people believe in obeying, honoring, and sustaining the law. In our case we might qualify that by saying we believe in honoring, obeying and sustaining that law which is "In pursuance of the Constitution." All other laws "cometh of evil." Nevertheless, there are going to be bad laws sometimes, but there are usually ample means for their lawful remedy.

We will now outline possible dangers we face as a people. Further, how our form of government might be altered or abolished without the consent of the people. An outline of possible remedies will follow. After this, we will discuss in more detail the dangers, then in great detail, our options and remedies to these dangers.

Danger number one.

Treaties. This is one of the few areas of weakness in our Constitution. Through experience we have found we are vulnerable by way of the treaty making power we have delegated to our President and the Senate. Theoretically, the Constitution itself might be abolished through ratification of a treaty.

Danger number two.

A declaration of a national emergency by the President. This might be followed with a declaration of martial law under which constitutional civil rights might be "temporarily" suspended. Under martial law, the president assumes extraordinary powers just as he does in time of war.

For example, when Abraham Lincoln issued the famous Emancipation Proclamation, effective on January 1, 1863, he had no authority under the Constitution to free a single slave. But as Commander-in-Chief during time of war, he alleged that he had authority to do whatever he felt would advance the cause of the North in securing victory. Slavery was not actually abolished until after the Civil War with the adoption of the Thirteenth Amendment on December 18, 1865.

Danger number three.

Calling a Constitutional Convention of the States, allegedly to pass a Balanced Budget Amendment. It takes 34 States to do this. Thirty-two have petitioned, three of which have rescinded their petition, sensing the danger. The three rescissions might be ignored if two more States ask for a Convention. It was a Convention of 12 States in 1787 which went far beyond the purpose for which the Convention had been called, and ended up giving us our present Constitution. Like that 1787 Convention, a modern Convention could not be limited, contrary to what some alleged experts tell us. Such a Convention could propose an abolishment of our present Constitution, and the adoption of another which has been waiting "in the wings" for more than 15 years called The New States of America Constitution.

Danger number four.

Destruction of our industrial base, our mining industries and our ability to produce oil, by use of unreasonable, sometimes outrageous, Federal restrictions, bureaucratic red tape, radical environmental laws, and setting aside extravagantly huge tracts of land on which all commercial activities are forbidden. Huge reservoirs of oil lay untapped just off our Eastern, as well as our Western sea coasts, in Alaska and the surrounding sea. Mining activities are often discouraged by over-zealous Federal "guardians" of our national forests and other land tracts controlled by the Federal government.

The theory is, if we can be reduced to poverty on a national level, we can more easily be managed as a people, and merged into the long dreamed of one-world government. A poverty stricken people have to worry about survival. They do not have time to question and resist abuses by their government.

There are other dangers. Slavery simmered and festered for some 70 years under the Constitution, finally erupting in Civil War. We have serious differences among our people today, which might develop, longterm, into serious violence.

Slavery was an issue to which there may have been no peaceful solution. It existed as an irreconcilable difference. Its advocates refused to compromise. Its enemies could not compromise without violating their conscience, and violating their personal moral code. Compromise had been tried a number of times. It never worked. With hindsight, we know it could not work.

Like slavery, the issue of abortion is splitting the electorate of America. It appears to be an irreconcilable difference. It has already led to some violence. In some ways it parallels the evils of slavery. In 1857, the United States Supreme Court decided the case of Dred Scott, a negro slave who had been taken by his master into a free State, then returned to his home, a slave State. The Court held that slaves were property, not persons, under the law. They belonged to their owners just like any other piece of property.

In 1973, the United States Supreme Court made an equally momentous decision as that of Dred Scott. The Court, in Roe vs. Wade, held that prior to "viability," life in the womb is not a person, but is property belonging to the woman. As a mere blob of flesh, a woman may do with it as she pleases. She can choose to let it live, or she can choose to kill it by way of abortion. Though it cannot be denied that "the blob" is alive; even that it is a tiny human being, yet the Court rationalized and ruled that a woman can choose, as the "thing" is inside her body, and she can do what she will with her own body

This right to kill life in the womb, is rationalized by saying a pregnant woman, like anybody else, should not have her free agency suspended by the State. This is called pro-choice. By this same twisted reasoning we can justify almost any criminal act. The rapist has overpowering sexual urges which "are not his fault." The homosexual who takes advantage of children can't help it. He was "born that way." The heterosexual who abuses children, ditto. The murderer, the burglar, those who love violence; they are all exercising their free agency. They come from broken homes. They were raised with the disadvantages of poverty. They were abandoned as children. They were this, that and the other ad infinitum.

If the peaceable citizen has a right to be protected from the criminal element by the State, so does the unborn have the right to have its life protected by the State. It has nothing to do with church or religion, although these are valuable in giving one values which allow him to live in harmony with other people. But abortion concerns the civil right to live. When free agency infringes on the right of another to life, liberty or property, it must be held in check.

Those who opposed slavery said it was evil and immoral. It was against the laws of God and man. They refused to participate and worked ceaselessly to abolish it. Those who thought slavery was okay, and it was certainly legal under the Constitution, justified it by saying blacks were an inferior race. They were like children. Children must be guided, restrained and disciplined. Besides, God made the black man to be the servant of the white man, so they reasoned. The slaveholder was doing the black man a favor by giving him material security from the cradle to the grave. He was provided food, clothing and shelter, such as it was sometimes.

History tells us compromise was not possible.

Those who oppose abortion say it is evil and immoral. It is against the laws of God as well as the natural laws of man. That life in the womb, even prior to viability is a tiny baby; a little person; a human being. Therefore to abort it is to kill a human being. They say that the law and the Constitution; that the whole purpose of government is to protect life, liberty and property. Life in the womb has a right to be protected by government. To kill it borders on murder; if in fact, it is not murder.

Those who are for choice often say they are actually against abortion, "personally," but it should be up to the woman. It is a "matter of privacy." Many go far beyond the Supreme Court and advocate the right of the woman to abort up to the time just prior to actual birth of the baby.

Those who are pro-life might well make the case that in comparison to abortion, slavery was mild in its evils and immorality. Under slavery, the slave owner had no right to take the life of his slave. His life was protected by the law.

The fetus and embryo are being slaughtered wholesale, some 30 million since 1973.

There were only about 3.7 million blacks in the United States at the outbreak of the Civil War in 1861. Few of them were ever killed at the whim of their owner. Babies are being killed by the millions because they are inconvenient to carry to term, or care for after birth. Truly, which is the greater evil, slavery or abortion?

Like slavery, there appears to be no compromise possible with abortion. Those for "choice" claim a violation of conscience if the State bans abortion. Those for "life" claim a violation of conscience if the State allows abortion. In addition, anti-abortionists often believe God will hold them personally responsible at the final judgement if they do not do all in their power to educate and resist those who take life in the womb. Many slavery abolitionists believed likewise.

With abortion, like slavery, we are headed into trouble which cannot at present be clearly foreseen but it has a high probability of eventually ending in bloodshed, perhaps on a large scale.

We should not repeat the mistakes of our fathers. By studying history, we should be able to avoid their mistakes. We should be able to avoid bloodshed in facing any of the dangers which confront us. Our fathers ended up in Civil War. There was no excuse for that war. It could have been settled peacefully. Like then, though we have differences; there are peaceful remedies available to us.

We face other dangers. Homosexuals, who like to call themselves gay, in perverting a popular and positive perception, are similar to Southern slave owners who were demanding that their brethren who opposed slavery should cease calling slavery evil; cease opposing their right to capture run-a-way slaves, and peacefully acquiesce and accept the benefits of slavery to the economy. Gays, lesbians, pedophiles, demand that the "straight" community not only allow them to openly practice their sexual deviances, but that we smile as we give our approval and "admit" that such is normal. After all, they were born that way, weren't they?

Though we have major differences, birth has caused us to live with each other. Rather than settle our differences by the common method of bloodshed and warfare, let us explore history and discuss options which might avoid that drastic remedy. There are at least two which will work.

Now our options. Afterward, each option will be explored in greater detail. These options are presented as Plans A, B, and C. They are remedies which will work in case our national government attempts to eliminate the Constitution. Remedies for our domestic differences, for now, are a lower priority and will only be discussed briefly near the end of the book.

Plan A:

Plan A is more completely outlined in a little book by this author titled: *The Constitution Hanging By A Thread*. We will only review it here. This plan can and should be implemented by one or more of the 50 States, but a single State can accomplish it. And what one State does for itself, it will be doing for the other 49.

The Constitution, Article III, Section 2, paragraph 2 says: "In all cases...in which a state shall be party, the supreme court shall have original jurisdiction."

Our fathers, recognizing it would be beneath the dignity of one of the sovereign states to challenge Federal law or policy in a lower court, provided the states with this powerful tool of original jurisdiction. This eliminates time consuming and expensive appellate action. It also assures the aggrieved parties a final and widely respected decision, unlike normal litigation which reaches the supreme court only after working its way through the lower courts. Through normal procedures, the supreme court first decides whether or not it will hear a case. If it refuses to hear the case, it is sent back and the decision of the circuit court, or lower court, becomes the final decision. This is how it must be, for there is no way the supreme court could possibly have the time, even if it worked 24 hours a day, to hear every case presented to it.

Under Original Jurisdiction, an Attorney General of any one of the states may file a brief asking for a decision on a certain matter. The supreme court must hear the case.

Plan A is not an emergency measure, but it should, nevertheless, be implemented by one or more states immediately for it will begin putting the Federal government in its proper place, and perhaps preclude us from having to take more drastic measures sooner or later. The pursuit of plan A should cause little or no harm, and can do much good in getting us back to constitutional government.

Though some of these issues may already have been decided, more or less, by the Supreme Court, we should be demanding a rehearing with the Supreme Court acting as "the jury" under original jurisdiction. Because the Supreme Court has reversed itself dozens of times, we should force reconsideration of some past landmark decisions of more liberal courts. Right now, we have one of the best Supreme Courts in decades. It is a "strict constructionist" court more in line with the thinking of the Founding Fathers than we have had for many years. We must strike while "the iron is hot." This outstanding Court will not last forever. Under the Administration of President Bill Clinton we might assume appointment of the most socialist/liberal type of judges who have ever sat on the Court. We can only hope that Justice Rehnquist or any of the other conservatives will not resign from the bench during the Clinton Administration.

Under original jurisdiction we must find one Attorney General of a single state who will fight for the Constitution. A single victory by a State Attorney General in one of the following cases would be a fantastic victory for liberty and the Constitution.

Just a few of the issues we need to take before the Court in the very near future are:

1. Ask the Court to rule on the validity of the 14th Amendment. The history of this Amendment is covered in some detail later in this work. It should be abolished and

changed, then resubmitted to the States for possible lawful adoption. It was an outlaw Congress which gave us the 14th Amendment.

2. Ask to rule on the validity of the 16th Amendment, the Income Tax Amendment. Lengthy research indicates lawful ratification of three-fourths of the States was never attained. In alleged certifications of adoption, a number of States changed wording or punctuation in the Amendment as proposed and sent out by Congress. No changes can be made in the original proposal. Any change whatsoever legally voids any alleged certification. It would be like one party to a contract changing his copy after it had already been signed. Additions or deletions to a signed contract are null and void in a court of law. We need to present the 16th Amendment to the Supreme Court to be scrutinized according to law. If it was not lawfully ratified, we should resubmit it to the States. We should either follow the Constitution, or openly abandon it. If we are going to abandon it, let's do it properly and abolish the Federal government along with it. Without the Constitution, we have no Federal government. If the Federal government insists on operating outside the Constitution, we don't need a Federal government.

3. Reconsideration of cases involving the Federal Reserve System, and reconsideration of *Knox vs. Lee*, 1871, which made paper money equal with gold and silver. The Federal Reserve System is a monster which is "eating us alive." Allowing us to run up a debt which may cause this nation to eventually "self-destruct," and forcing us to pay hundreds of billions in interest on paper "money" created out of our own credit. Maybe the Federal Reserve System would be okay as a bank to handle our money, but it is the greatest fraud for us to be paying it interest on our own credit.

4. Demand the return of the Panama Canal to the United States. This multi-billion dollar property was stolen from us by President Jimmy Carter and the U.S. Senate, without the constitutionally required consent of the House of Representatives.

5. Ask for a ruling that the issue of citizen ownership of

firearms is a dead issue, the courts having no jurisdiction, and the Congress having no authority to interfere. There is no authority whatsoever in the Constitution for the Federal Government to have anything to do with firearms. Ask for an end to the endless debate about the meaning of the Second Amendment regarding the right to keep and bear arms. We don't even need the Second Amendment. It is superfluous. It is merely clarification that no authority exists, in the first place, anywhere in the Constitution for Federal interference regarding citizens ownership of firearms. Neither can States take guns away from law-abiding Americans.

Plan B:
Plans B and C must be held in reserve against that time when, and if, a worst case scenario develops in the United States. Either one should only be considered if it appears the demise of our Constitution, our national government, and our sovereignty is imminent. However radical they may at first appear, it should be kept in mind that most anything will be preferable to bloodshed or civil war. Our fathers did not consider revolution by blood too radical a step to take in preserving their liberties. Because of what they established for us under the Constitution, it is not necessary for us to resort to that last drastic step, unless all else fails.

Plans B and C are completely lawful and legal and will be proven so beyond a reasonable doubt to any rational mind. They are also in harmony with historical precedent, both in the history of our country, as well as others.

Rather than the necessary implementation of Plans B or C, it is to be hoped that by setting forth what we the people have a right to lawfully do, and what we the people intend to do, if we are pushed against the wall, and what we the people will actually do, if the traitors working within our borders and Washington, D.C. do not back off and leave us alone, will be sufficient to discourage our enemies from confronting us. It is hoped that our corrupt politicians in Washington will finally see the light, see that we mean business, and back off. When Washington sees that we know history, and we know the law, and that we have the power to dismantle the entire Federal apparatus, they will stop harassing us. When now ignorant congressmen and arrogant federal officials are made to understand we have the power to send them home on a permanent unpaid vacation without their lucrative pensions, and auction Washington, D.C. off to the highest bidders, we can hope they will finally get the message that the American people are fed up with their corruption and doubletalk and realize their fun and games are finished.

If Washington still refuses to get its act together after we clearly show them our options, then we will have no choice but to implement what we have clearly set before them. Tyrants never give up power easily. Neither can we expect Washington to shape up unless they know with a certainty that we have the knowledge and the power to not only call their bluff, but to actually beat them and send them packing.

Most of our leaders, though they are sworn to defend the Constitution, are ignorant of it and the nature of our government. By setting forth these plans so they, as well as we, understand the Constitution and the limited powers delegated, there should be no need for drastic action. Reason will dictate that everybody get back to playing by the rules of the game, which is the Constitution.

It was not the intent of our fathers to establish the Union with the idea of eventually dissolving it. Nevertheless, the possibility of dissolution is sewn right into the fabric of the Constitution. Article V reads: "The Congress, whenever two-thirds of both houses shall deem it necessary, shall propose amendments to this constitution, or on the application of the legislatures of two-thirds of the several states, shall call a convention for proposing amendments, which in either case, shall be valid to all intents and purposes, as part of this constitution, when ratified by the legislature of three-fourths of the several states, or by conventions in three-fourths thereof, as the one or the other mode of ratification may be proposed by the Congress..."

Through July, 1992, the Constitution has been amended 27 times. The Constitution says that three-fourths of the states can amend in any way they see fit. This amending power includes, if demanded by imminent necessity, the ability, and the right, to abolish the entire Constitution with all 27 amendments. That which can be put into the Constitution can be repealed.

The eighteenth amendment, prohibiting sale, transportation and manufacture of intoxicating liquors, was officially ratified January 16, 1919, and became effective one year later on January 16, 1920.

This amendment endured for almost 14 years. During this time amendments 19 and 20 were added to the Constitution. The States decided they were not happy with the results of prohibiting liquor. They decided the cure was worse than the sickness it was supposed to heal. The States decided to repeal the Eighteenth Amendment. On December 5, 1933, President Franklin Roosevelt proclaimed that three-fourths of the States had ratified the twenty-first amendment and it had been certified by the Secretary of State. Section I of the twenty-first amendment reads: "The eighteenth article of amendment to the Constitution of the United States is hereby repealed." Thus, the twenty-first amendment eliminated the eighteenth amendment.

If three-fourths of the States can eliminate one amendment, or make other changes in the Constitution, which changes have been made since the beginning, they could eliminate more amendments; they could eliminate them all. They could eliminate the entire Constitution if an emergency ever arose which might dictate such a course would be preferable to some alternative.

Abraham Lincoln was one of the greatest advocates for Perpetual Union. Under this theory, the Civil War was largely justified by Lincoln and the North. Yet even Lincoln admitted to the nation in his inaugural address as the new President on March 4, 1861: "If, by the mere force of numbers, a majority should deprive a minority of any clearly-written Constitutional right, it might, in a moral point of view, justify revolution; it certainly would, if such a right were a vital one..."

It is important to remember that revolution does not have

to cause bloodshed. Revolutions may be lawful, or they can be unlawful. If Americans should be required to take drastic steps to preserve their liberties and the Constitution, it will, perhaps, be considered revolutionary. Such a revolution should be accomplished through reason and calm consideration on all sides. Webster tells us the meaning of the kind of revolution to which Lincoln probably referred: "a complete or drastic change of any kind; as a revolution in modern physics."

So that bunch of good 'ol boys and girls in Washington really understand where the supreme power, or paramount power, or sovereignty lies in the United States of America, let's say just for the fun of it, that three-fourths of the States did decide that our Union is no longer workable; it is not practical; that if sinister traitors plan to suspend the Constitution anyway and eliminate our State governments, why don't we just do the job ourselves. That way, we at least retain our State governments intact, we eliminate the national debt, except that which we decide should rightfully be paid, and would get together again just like in 1787, and put everything back together again, if that is desireable. And just like our fathers in writing the Constitution made improvements in their former charter, the Articles of Confederation, we could make improvements where experience has shown us weaknesses in the Constitution our fathers gave us.

For instance, we might decide to limit the terms of congressmen and senators when we decided to put it all together again. We might decide to give the president a line-item veto so he could eliminate billions in pork barrel spending by Congress. We might limit the tenure of judges to something less than lifetime. We might write in more precautions when we allow treaties to take effect.

For the most part the Constitution has served us very well and will continue to do so, but if opportunity should present itself, we might wish to make a few minor changes.

Should the time come when our sovereignty is imminently threatened, and dissolution of the Union would be preferable to the alternative offered by a traitorous Congress and a traitorous President, three-fourths of the States can, and must, get together prior to any such emergency. Thirty-eight States must be willing to declare that the Union of the United States of America is hereby dissolved; the Constitution and the entire Federal apparatus which is authorized by it are eliminated; all Federal offices no longer exist, and the 50 States will each resume their original sovereignty. Should the Congress and/or the President ever attempt to abolish, eliminate, or suspend the Constitution, or in any manner whatsoever, attempt to eliminate the sovereignty of the states and the people, 38 States must be prepared to abolish the Federal Government by dissolving the Union.

At that point, all 50 States would resume original sovereignty which was held by the original thirteen States from July 4, 1776 through June 21, 1788. They would become self-governing with each of their governors, of course, remaining their Chief Executive, and assuming a "new" title of Commander in Chief of the Armed Forces, the State militia, which would now become an official Army. The national military forces could be automatically eliminated along with the Federal government, but that would not be desireable. More details on all this later. They would become 50 separate, sovereign, independent and free nations, exactly the same as the original 13 States prior to the adoption of the Articles of Confederation in 1781, and the adoption of the Constitution in 1788.

Without the Constitution, there would be no federal employees and no federal property.

Assets and lands controlled by the federal government would revert to the States. The States would take control of that which has always belonged to them, and the bullying of Washington concerning Western federal lands would come to an abrupt halt. Remaining obligations and problems, should the States implement Plan B, and dissolve the union, will take careful planning and a close working together of at least 38 States.

The Committee of 50 States will be working to get one, then two, and eventually we hope, 38 governors to see the wisdom of preparing beforehand to meet the crisis of a one world government coup of the United States. The way we are heading, it may not be too far in the future, even without a traitorous overthrow of the government, that 38 States may wish to dissolve the Union in order to start over without the socialistic baggage and foreign entanglements with which our present government is burdened. There appears to be no other way to eliminate numerous bad precedents of the Supreme Court, Executive Orders by the thousands, of several Presidents, and hundreds of Constitution-defying legislative Acts of Congress.

The practical way for this to work is to seek resolutions from the Legislatures of 38 States, saying that should a coup of the United States government take place, the Union is dissolved. See Ultimatum Resolution beginning on page 385.

Many and voluminous details would have to be worked out, of course, but this is an option which the States will only wish to implement if, and when all else fails, in their determination to maintain the Constitution. The Constitution would, at their option, remain the Supreme Law of each State until a new Union could be formed without all the baggage we presently carry, and among all States which wished to rejoin. Some States might wish to form a separate, more socialistic, perhaps godless Union. In the spirit of The Declaration of Independence, they should be allowed to do so. Let those who think alike go their separate ways and live apart in peace. The earth is large enough that we do not have to force philosophical opposites to live together. Divorce, separation, secession, is the best and logical solution for quarreling factions. Why haven't the Arabs and Jews come to this conclusion? Why don't they just agree to disagree, and separate like their ancient father Abraham, who gave his nephew Lot his choice of available real estate, and Abraham moved along to new land? (Genesis 13:1-12)

When the crisis occurs, the traitors attempting the coup might kidnap those appointed to meet i a Convention of the States, so that a meeting might not be possible. Perhaps thirty-eight States must simply resolve that in case of a coup, dissolution of the Union is automatic. Congress, the Judiciary and the Executive and all Federal employees are dismissed, and that a Convention of the States will be held as soon as practicable to work out all details.

Having 38 States call themselves into Convention is not the way to do it and be in compliance with the Constitution. The right way is for 34 States to petition Congress for a Convention of States, then whatever work that Convention does, submit amending proposals to the States. Then, ratification by three-fourths of the States would officially amend the Constitution, and could, by this process, abolish the Union.

However, we are anticipating traitorous abolition of the Constitution itself. In such an emergency, in which Congress itself has become part of a conspiracy to put us into a one-world government in which the Constitution is no longer recognized, there can be no doubt that three-fourths of the States acting in unison, as principals, might do that which their agent, Congress, refuses to do for them.

Allowing Congress to call a Convention of the States by petitions of two-thirds of member States, amounts to only a suggestion in Article V of the Constitution. This "requirement" to include Congress is a diplomatic nicety; a gentlemanly gesture by the States to include Congress in calling a convention of the States. But legally it is unenforceable and the Convention of 12 States of 1787 is the precedent proving that three-fourths of the States (actually only 9 of 13) could dissolve the Union.

Congress as a mere agent, and a mere one-third at that, has no power to dictate policy to its Principal, three-fourths of the States.

What if Congress refused to call a Convention even though two-thirds of the States demanded one? Would the States be barred from meeting? Of course not. Though there is no other provision in the Constitution, any principal can always do for himself, that which his agent might refuse to do for him. It would be absurd in the extreme to say that an agent might control the actions of the principal.

Logic, reason, law, tell us that three-fourths of the States acting in unison might lawfully dissolve the Union, even though they do not follow the constitutionally outlined procedure. If someone wishes to quibble over this, might we ask would there be any question concerning technical procedure if all 50 States agreed to meet in Convention without consulting Congress? If 50 could override the restrictions they themselves placed in the Constitution, could not three-fourths?

Barring an emergency, such as a coup d'etat, the 38 States, or more, should seriously consider dissolution of the Union and partititoning it off into two or more sections which could rejoin in a new confederation. These confederations might wish to maintain our military forces jointly. They would, no doubt, wish to continue commerce and trade with each other, but that could be done by treaty, whereas now, it is accomplished by many usurpations of the Constitution by Congress. When the 38 decide usurpations of undelegated powers have gone too far, and that 67 times the tax burdens placed on the colonists by King George is too heavy, the 38 have the option of a peaceful revolution. Bloodshed is not required. Secession or separation, has for our generation, been established in law and precedent. We have 6,000 years of history to guide us. We would be foolish indeed, if we insist on learning the lessons of history all over again, when our fathers have already made the mistakes for us. A wise man, or a wise generation learns by the mistakes of the past. He does not repeat them. It is not necessary for each generation to personally experience bloodshed to retain liberty.

Should it prove impossible to get 38 States to prepare for a worst case scenario as briefly outlined in Plan B, then each individual State must realize it has a lawful option to separate itself, and secede from the United States.

Plan C.
Plan C is the plan utilized by the eleven States which seceded from the Federal Union beginning with South Carolina, December 20, 1860. South Carolina was quickly followed by six additional States, and following the beginning of hostilities, four more States joined the Southern Confederacy, making a total of eleven which actually left the Union.

Most of us, if the thought has even occurred to us, make the assumption that secession by a State is illegal. In another book, this writer said: "The possibility of seceding from the Union, once a State joined, was not an option, or right the States retained to themselves. Thus the War between the States, the Civil War, was fought to enforce the theory of eternal union."

This statement is correct only from the viewpoint of the Northern States. The North won the Civil War, so it is natural that historians on the winning side of not only the Civil War, but any war, will slant history to show the winners in the more favorable light. Eternal union, "the union inseparable and forever," was the theme of the Civil War in the states which stayed with the Union. Abraham Lincoln used it as a means of maintaining loyalty to a doubtful cause, at the beginning of the war, and throughout as the people wearied of war.

But it was shocking to the author to discover this cry of Abraham Lincoln and the Northern Union had no legal foundation. It was empty rhetoric then, and it would be empty rhetoric if it should be used today.

Slavery as practiced in the Southern States until the end of the war in 1865 was evil and morally despicable, just as slavery at any time always has been. And those in the North, as well as many in the South who wished to see freedom for the black man, most certainly maintained the moral high ground. History judges the moral position of the abolitionist to be far more pure than that of those who maintained the inferiority of the black man as giving the white man the right to own him as a slave. All men, all races have their peculiar talents and abilities. These talents are obviously not equal, but it is equally obvious that race should not be a factor in the relations of men to each other or their governments. All should be equal before the law.

Secession for the South was an absolutely lawful remedy for its irreconcilable differences with the North. It was proper on constitutional grounds. It was proper also as the only viable remedy which stood a chance of averting bloodshed. It was the one way by which civil war could be avoided. Without separation, or secession, the forces of fate, history, and failed compromises of the past, were rapidly rushing headlong into an exploslon of civil war, which as it turned out, was not prevented even with separation of the contending forces.

If the South had not seceded, the North should have seceded itself. Such a secession by some of the Northern States had been threatened on a number of occasions, just as it had been in the South. It was widely held ever since the beginning of our Republic, up to the time of the Civil War, that States might leave the Union freely, just as they had joined it freely.

If secession was lawful in 1861, it is lawful in the 1990's. Nothing has been added to or taken away from the contract under which we live, the Constitution, since 1865 which would change our right to the same remedy which the South unsuccessfully attempted in 1860-61.

If secession was legal in 1860, why then did we end up in civil war? Why did the seven original seceding States not go their peaceful way, negotiate the loose ends regarding Federal properties in the seceding States and continue commerce as a separate confederacy? Why didn't the North, why didn't Abraham Lincoln and the Union just let them go in peace? If a divorce was not only the lawful remedy to their quarreling, but the proper ethical remedy, what in the world went wrong? Why did this nation allow itself to be sucked into such a bottomless pit of blood and horror, brother against brother, and squandered national treasure?

The answer to these questions are as pathetic and sad as they are simple! There was absolutely no excuse for the War between the States.

So we do not repeat our fathers' history of blood and horror, it appears crucially important that we understand the legal justifications of both sides of the conflict; who if anybody was right, and if we can discover the truth, if we today might rely on these truths should the need arise.

As stated above, the answer as to why the Civil War was fought is so simple, it is painful to now look back and see the absolute stupidity of those who were at fault. It makes one

Chapter 2

want to cry bitter tears, even now, to look back and see how a stupid miscalculation ended up killing more men by more than twice, than America suffered in World War II.

A tiny spark or a single match can start a fire which might turn into an uncontrolled holocaust. So it was with the Civil War.

Jefferson Davis, the newly elected President of the Southern Confederacy sent up orders to General P.G.T. Beauregard, one of his Southern Commanders, to "reduce the fort;" to open fire on Fort Sumter. This was the tragic and fatal mistake of the South. The initiation of offensive military action against property which had lawfully been ceded to the Union long ago. Not that this was the first abuse of common sense perpetrated against Northern property, but the firing on Fort Sumter was the match which started it all. Without the lighting of this match, there was no reason for war. There can be little doubt that the Southern Secession would have been successful. Abraham Lincoln had promised, "no bloodshed."

Jefferson Davis was a great patriot, as was Abraham Lincoln. Davis loved the Constitution of the United States. There is no intent to find fault with him, nor leaders of either side in the sad conflict of blood and tears. But Mr. Davis made the mistake of the nineteenth century by ordering the "reduction of Fort Sumter."

Perhaps we can discover the motivation for firing on Fort Sumter as we go more into this later.

If secession is, and always has been lawful, we need to know why sentiment for it was not universal. We also need to understand secession is an option which nobody wants to adopt except as a last resort. The Union has served us and our fathers quite well. It has made us the most powerful nation which ever existed on the planet, as well as the richest. It would be a shame to dismantle it.

However, liberty is more precious than life itself. If our options should be reduced to the point of losing our freedom, or dissolving the Union, the choice is clear. There is one thing even worse to consider, should all three, Plans A, B and C fail us.

Plan D.
And plan D is bloodshed, pure and simple. This plan will be discussed nowhere else in this work. All will hope it never comes to this. If it should, mass confusion and horror will reign supreme. Law and reason will be of little use. We will close discussion of Plan D with the words of Winston Churchill.

"Still, if you will not fight for the right when you can easily win without bloodshed; if you will not fight when your victory will be sure and not too costly; (Plans A, B and C) you may come to the moment when you will have to fight with all the odds against you and only a precarious chance of survival. There may even be a worse case. You may have to fight when there is no hope of victory, because it is better to perish than live as slaves."

To the informed and concerned mind who can see dark clouds gathering over America, the second two proposals , plans B and C, may, after awhile, appear not quite as radical and irrational as they may have at the first impression. As an alternative to State against State, brother against brother, Federal armies against State militias, such options are quite mild indeed, and are, at the least, worthy of serious and long consideration.

If somebody has better ideas, we are all ears.

Let us briefly mention the arguments of Plan C which will be covered in great detail later in this work, which detail will leave no doubt in any rational mind as to the legality of secession. It is the only practicable and viable solution, on those rare occasions, when a people find themselves betrayed by their leaders, or find they have irreconcilable differences which can be solved in no other way except by separation and living apart.

First, The Declaratlon of Independence which we still celebrate every July 4 and honor as heroes those who were actually traitors to the Central government, Great Britain. This Declaration was a document of secession, little if any different than the documents of Secession drawn up by the eleven seceding Southern States in 1860-61.

Second, we will consider the Articles of Confederation which governed the thirteen States from 1781 through 1788. These Articles declared the thirteen States to be in perpetual union. Yet, this document was ingloriously abandoned by nine of the States on June 21, 1788 when the nine joined in a new Union under our present Constitution, abandoning Virginia, New York, North Carolina and Rhode Island to drift as they chose; to join or not to join the new Union. The times demanded change, even though it meant breaking the solemn contract of perpetuity, so our fathers reasoned.

Third, we will examine in great detail the actual documents of ratification of each of the thirteen states as they, one by one, joined in the new Union. We will discover amazingly that some, particularly Virginia, reserved the right to resume her sovereignty, or to leave the Union if the time should come when she felt the Federal government was usurping undelegated powers or in any way abusing the States which created it. Secession was a reserved right. If one State reserved a certain right or privilege all States automatically reserve those same rights. And Virginia was not alone. This right of secession was not written in the Constitution, but it was understood. The Founders knew it would do no good to write into the Constitution the words "perpetual union," or that the States have no right to leave the Union, nor any other kind of prohibitory language. For these States were quietly, delicately, if not somewhat in embarrassment, in the very act of abandoning their old compact which they had specifically agreed would be perpetual, the Articles of Confederation.

Our fathers clearly understood that it is the right of the people to change and alter or abandon, any particular type of government by which they are governed. It had only been about 12 years since many of them had been involved in abolishing the ties with Great Britain in 1776.

Fourth. In 1861, Virginia became one of 11 States to secede from the United States. Forty-eight counties in the Western part of Virginia then declared their own independence from Virginia and formed their own provisional government. On May 13, 1862 these 48 counties calling themselves the Restored Government of Virginia gave their consent to the formation of a new State. The act of admission was approved by President Lincoln, December 31, 1862. These counties of Virginia were formally admitted into the Union June 20, 1863, as the new State of West Virginia.

This presents two extremely interesting points. The alleged purpose of Abraham Lincoln and the North in fighting the Civil War which at the moment of West Virginia coming into the Union was furiously raging, was to keep the Union together, and because secession was illegal. The whole basis for the war, or at least the major alleged reason, was that the Union was inseparable; the Constitution did not allow a State to leave the Union. The Northern 23 States refused to recognize the secession from the Union by the 11 Southern States. But what is this with 48 counties which had declared their secession from Virginia? This secession was not only being accepted as lawful by the Union and Abraham Lincoln, but these counties could now join the Union as a new State.

The second fascinating question about the creation of West Virginia is how in the world did the North justify this flagrant violation of the Constitution, in addition to its inconsistency on the question of secession? The Constitution plainly says, in Article IV, Section 3, "New states may be admitted by the Congress into this union; but no new state shall be formed or erected within the jurisdiction of any other state; nor any state be formed by the junction of two or more states, or parts of states, without the consent of the legislatures of the states concerned..."

Did Congress and the 48 counties have "the consent of the legislature" of Virginia to form this new State? Of course not. This act was blatantly unconstitutional. Alleged usurpation such as this was a major reason for Southern secession. If the Union were to argue it *was* constitutional, they, the Union, would have to admit Virginia had left the Union; that Virginia's secession was, after all, lawful; it was valid, and Virginia was in fact, as she declared, a separate nation at her moment of secession. If Virginia was in lawful secession, then it might be reasonably argued, Lincoln and the Union could, without being in violation of the Constitution, accept these counties as a new State in the Union.

Fifth. If the secession of the 11 Southern States was unlawful and in violation of the Constitution, then after the North won the war in the Spring of 1865, as the victor, she would, of course, arrest and try as traitors, the leaders of the "rebellion." Right?............Wrong!

The North did arrest the President of the Confederacy, Jefferson Davis, and Alexander Stephens, the Vice President, after the war was over. Stephens was kept in jail for about five months and released without trial, to go back to whatever life he chose. Jefferson Davis was kept in jail for some two years, all the while demanding trial, but the Union refused to try either man.

Why were these "traitors" never brought to trial? Because it appears the Union did not dare try these "rebels" and risk the possibility...no, the probability...perhaps the absolute certainty, that no court of law would convict these rebels for treason. The Union, in trials for war crimes, would have been confronted with trials by jury under the Constitution, and in those days, and up until the Sparf case in 1895, juries were informed of their right and duty, to not only judge the facts in trial, but to also judge whether or not the law itself, under which prosecution was brought, was just and fair, reasonable, and constitutional.

If the North had dared to try anybody for being traitors to the Union, and failed to get a conviction, there might have been another civil war in the North if a jury had made a formal declaration that these rebel "traitors" were innocent, because the secession they had attempted was lawful and according to the traditions of their fathers. The relatives, wives, daughters, sons of the 360,000 Union forces killed may have stormed Washington, D.C. themselves as they demanded, "if the Confederate States lawfully left the Union, for what purpose had this bloody war been fought?"

With the evidence presented in this book; with this legal brief, it will be plain that the secession of the South was absolutely legal and lawful in every respect. Proceedings of a court of law would clearly have established this truth. No way could the Union risk a court decision in favor of the South.

Sixth. We also will explore how we got Texas from Mexico. How we were involved in establishing Panama. All are very significant to the present case.

We will explore the "secession" in 1990 of Lithuania, Latvia and Estonia from the Soviet Union, and how the United States recognized their secession as lawful. We will consider the secessions of the remaining 12 Republics from the Soviet Union, until there was no longer any Soviet Union, only a loose Confederation.

We will show that history, law and precedent were on the side of the South when she seceded from the Union. And all these arguments are just as valid in the 1990's as they were in 1861. Unlike Jefferson Davis, we know there is no need to take offensive and unlawful military action.

If one or more States find that secession is all that is left, without caving into tyranny, we will not make the same mistake made by the Southern Confederacy. We need never, we will never, "fire on Fort Sumter."

Chapter 3

Treaties and Other Dangers

From the Constitution, Article II, Section 2, paragraph 2, referring to the President of the United States: "He shall have power, by and with the advice and consent of the senate, to make treaties, provided two-thirds of the senators present concur..."

The Constitution further declares in Article VI paragraph 2: "This constitution, *and the laws of the United States which shall be made in pursuance thereof*; and all treaties made, or which shall be made under the authority of the United States, shall be the supreme law of the land; and the judges in every state shall be bound thereby, anything in the constitution or laws of any state to the contrary notwithstanding."

Much has been written on the theoretical and practical applicability of treaty law. The full exploration of this subject would require hundreds of pages, but the intent of this work is merely to point out possible dangers to the Republic should we wake up some day and discover we have leaders at the helm of our Ship of State who might abuse the treaty power with which we have endowed them.

It was never intended by the Founders that the treaty power might be used in such a way as to actually override or nullify the Constitution itself. Indeed, such a probability appears to be remote. Nevertheless, as a worst case scenario, the possibility of a suspension or abolishment of the Constitution by Executive and Senate abuse of the treaty power, is worthy of reflection and, at least, due consideration. Especially so in view of this glaring weakness in the Constitution above in Article II. Treaties shall be valid and binding with the consent of the senate, *"provided two-thirds of the senators present concur."* This sentence was of major concern to many of the early fathers.

The United States has entered into many entangling treaties and executive agreements. To break free of these Constitution and sovereignty destroying agreements would be a formidable task, even should we be able to elect a majority to the Congress, and a President who was loyal to the Constitution and America's heritage of freedom. Given the current makeup of Congress and the Federal bureaucracy, and the bleak outlook for future change, chances of preventing a merger of the United States into a one-world government, and the elimination of the Constitution appear extremely remote indeed.

For example, on April 2, 1992, another U.N. treaty was skillfully orchestrated into Senate ratification by "one-worlders" in the Senate and Bush administration. This treaty is called the *International Covenant on Civil and Political Rights*. There was no debate during the closed door session and no roll call vote. Just a show of hands. As usual in actions of this kind, there was no mention of the action in the major media. Opponents of the treaty learned of the ratification only after the fact.

If such treaties are not harmful to the United States, why did our representatives refuse to take a roll call vote, so that each one is on record, and so that we, their constituents, will know how our senators voted? When a vote is taken by a show of hands, with no names recorded as voting yea or nay, it is not even possible to discover whether or not a quorum was present when the vote was taken. Lack of a quorum might well be the main reason non-recorded votes are taken in the Congress, in addition to the fact it becomes impossible for constituents to determine how their representatives voted on a treaty, or other issues of secrecy.

In the Constitution, Article I, Section 5, paragraph 1, it says, referring to the House and Senate: "...a majority of each shall constitute a quorum to do business..." There are 100 members in the Senate. As few as 51, therefore, may conduct business.

Two-thirds of 51 means that as few as 34 senators could bind us to a treaty, or other legislation for that matter.

Is it not wise to suppose that it might be possible to get 34 senators to conspire against their country, and in league with the President pass a treaty unfavorable to the United States?

Continuing with Article 1,5,1: "...but a smaller number may adjourn from day to day, and may be authorized to compel the attendance of absent members, in such manner, and under such penalties as each house may provide."

Is it unthinkable that this smaller number than a quorum, might "compel" only the attendance of the minimum 51 members, who they know to be in favor of the bad treaty, and fail to notify any of the other 49 members about their assembling to do business?

Dr. Edwin S. Corwin in his book, *The Constitution and What It Means Today*, said, "For many years the view prevailed in the House of Representatives that it was necessary for a majority of the members to vote on any proposition submitted to the House in order to satisfy the constitutional requirement of a quorum. It was the common practice for the opposition to break a quorum by refusing to vote. This was changed in 1890, by a ruling made by Speaker Reed, and later embodied in rule XV of the House, that members present in the chamber but not voting would be counted in determining the presence of a quorum."

We mention this only to show that rules of critical importance might be changed.

In continuing to quote from Dr. Corwin on House rules, it should be noted that the same applies to the Senate.

"So long as a quorum is present (at the opening of the day's business) it is sufficient to decide matters with a majority of those available to vote even though they do not constitute a majority of the entire membership of the House."

In the Senate, this means that if a quorum of only 51 members starts the session and then report to their committees or go back to their offices, the remaining members can go ahead and transact business. The Supreme Court has ruled, "A quorum once established is presumed to continue unless and until a point of no quorum is raised."

Dr. W. Cleon Skousen in his book, *The Making of America*, commenting on this point said: "A point of 'no quorum' would be raised if an important vote were about to be taken. Alert party whips or other interested members would demand a quorum and the whole House or Senate would be ordered to reassemble."

Dr. Skousen's commentary would, no doubt, be applicable in all ordinary circumstances. But in assuming a worst case scenario, it is possible to see how a few members who might have been "paid off," or who sincerely feel that the sacrifice of the Constitution "is really in the best interest of all mankind;" that these few members could possibly bind us to a treaty which a true quorum of the Senate might reject. How few might be able to sell us out is speculative. Might only three or four senators linger long into the night until everybody leaves, no quorum being called for, then vote to adopt a harmful treaty or other legislation?

In being cautious, it is well to remember confusion has arisen concerning this part of the Constitution: "And the judges in every state shall be bound thereby, (by treaties) anything in the constitution or laws of any state to the contrary notwithstanding." Does this mean judges must allow treaties to supercede the Constitution of the United States? Enemies of America might well attempt to argue, "yes, they do."

Some years ago it was argued by advocates of the United Nations Treaty that this provision allowed a treaty such as the United Nations Treaty to supersede our national Constitution, precisely what we are guarding against.

On a close reading of this provision one can see that it is

talking about the state constitutions, not the national Constitution.

First, this clause is directed at the judges of the States.

Second, it is referring to the "constitution or laws of any state."

Third, if this clause was referring to the national Constitution, it would be in contradiction and a violation of Article V, setting forth the amending process. If a treaty could amend or abolish the Constitution, or even change or alter it, it would make null and void and completely circumvent the entire amending process of Article V.

The Founders argued, and rightly so, that treaties must be supreme to the Constitutions of the States themselves. This is not an issue here. But the founders made it clear this provision did not mean treaties were to supersede the national Constitution.

Gilman Nicholas said, "They can, by this, make no treaty which shall be repugnant to the spirit of the Constitution, or inconsistent with the delegated powers. The treaties they make must be under the authority of the United States, to be within their province. It is sufficiently secured because it only declares that, in pursuance of the powers given, they shall be the supreme law of the land, notwithstanding anything in the constitution or laws of particular states." Elliot's debates 3:507. Mr. Nicholas was both a member of the Convention of States in Philadelphia in the summer of 1787, and a member of his own State delegation, New Hampshire.

Let us inquire further into the thinking of some of the Founders. We can perceive caution, but also a certain reliance on the integrity and virtue of those who would be entrusted to making treaties. They recognized possible danger, but some rationalized away this danger.

John Jay, in Federalist Paper number 64, in referring to selection of United States Senators by the State Legislatures: "...there is reason to presume that their attention and their votes will be directed to those men only who have become the most distinguished by their abilities and virtue...with such men the power of making treaties may be safely lodged... it was wise, therefore, in the convention, to provide not only that power of making treaties should be committed to able and honest men, but also that they should continue in place a sufficient time to become perfectly acquainted with our national concerns, and to form and introduce a system for the management of them...."

Over 200 years of experience has shown us that, in some respects, our fathers were, even in their extreme caution in guarding liberty, not perfect in their wisdom. They felt compelled on occasion, to trust the integrity and virtue of man, though they attempted in every way possible, to "bind him down with the chains of the Constitution."

With 200 years experience under the Constitution, we know we don't always get only the outstanding men of our States representing us in the Senate. We know we sometimes get scalawags or worse. We know we sometimes get even a majority who are willing to "go along to get along." We know even on occasion two-thirds will be willing, or allow themselves to be pressured into obvious violation of the Constitution. For example, when the Senate, without the constitutionally required consent of the House, gave away our Panama Canal under the Carter Administration, 1977-1981. And when both the House and Senate conspired to trash the constitutional requirement that: "No state shall...make anything but gold and silver coin a tender in payment of debts;..." Article I, 10, 1 of the Constitution which is supposed to still be binding, but which both State and Federal governments have flaunted and ignored for decades and the Supreme Court went along.

John Jay continued: "...It will not be in the power of the President and Senate to make any treaties by which they and their families and estates will not be equally bound and affected with the rest of the community; and having no private interests distinct from that of the nation, they will be under no temptations to neglect the latter..." Sorry, Mr. Jay. We honor and respect you, but you were wrong on this one.

"As to corruption, the case is not supposable. He must either have been very unfortunate in his intercourse with the world, or possess a heart very susceptible of such impressions, who can think it probable that the President and two thirds of the Senate will ever be capable of such unworthy conduct. The idea is too gross and too invidious to be entertained. But in such a case, if it should ever happen, the treaty so obtained from us would, like all other fraudulent contracts, be null and void by the laws of nations."

But, in your conclusions Mr. Jay, you are right on. Treaties, like contracts, if entered into fraudulently, are null and void at the option of the defrauded party.

But who decides if fraud is involved? If nobody challenges a fraudulent contract or a fraudulent treaty, it will stand regardless. It takes the decision of a court of law to release an injured party from a contract of fraud. This can be expensive and time consuming. The Supreme Court would have to decide if a treaty were contracted in fraud. This might take much time. In the meantime, the treaty could be implemented.

The protection of last resort must be the States themselves. The governors and attorney generals of each of the States should have the knowledge and courage to recognize a treaty as being fraudulent if the attempt should be made to use this means for suspending the Constitution. As a last resort, one or more governors must have the background, understanding and courage to be willing to proclaim: "the federal government has violated the trust of the people, the trust of the states, violated the contract (the Constitution) and all parties are automatically released from any duties or obligations under that contract. The contract now being null and void, this State (one or more of the 50 states) is exercising its option to no longer be bound. Therefore, not only the treaty contracted in fraud and deception is proclaimed to be not binding on this State, but we are exercising our lawful option to no longer be bound by the constitutional contract which has not only been violated in this particular instance, but on numerous other occasions as well." Violations and usurpations would then be listed.

Let us now consider an important Supreme Court decision, *Missouri vs. Holland* 252 U.S. 416; 40 S. Ct. 382; 64 L. Ed. 641 (1920). In commenting on this case we will be quoting extensively from the book *Cases in Constitutional Law* by Robert E. and Robert F. Cushman but such will not be acknowledged in quotation marks, as these authors themselves are quoting at length from the decision of the Court. Theirs and the authors comments will be intermingled.

In discussing the implied powers of Congress it is important to bear in mind that they may be derived not merely from the specific grants of power to Congress but also from the clause of the Constitution which authorizes Congress "to make all laws which shall be necessary and proper for carrying into execution the foregoing powers, and all other powers vested by this Constitution in the government of the United States, or in any department or officer thereof." Among these "other powers" vested in the departments or officers of the government is the treaty-making power, which resides in the President and Senate.

Thus Congress may derive legislative authority from the power to carry out the provisions of a treaty when it could not derive it from any of the specific grants of legislative power enumerated in Article I. That such treaties are, as the Constitution says, "the supreme law of the land," was made clear as early as 1796 in *Ware vs. Hylton*, 3 Dall. 199, reaffirmed in *Hauenstein vs. Lynham*, 100 U.S. 483 (1880), both cases in which the Court held invalid a Virginia Statute denying an alien rights which the federal government had guaranteed him by a treaty with his native land.

These early decisions appear to be sound and proper. Mass confusion and injustice would result if aliens visiting the country had to submit themselves to the various State Statutes without the umbrella protection of the Central government given to them by treaty with their own country.

In 1913, Congress passed an act forbidding, save under strict regulations, the killing of migratory birds. The control of bird life is not one of the powers which the Constitution grants to Congress, and two lower federal courts held the law unconstitutional: *United States vs. Shauver*, 214 Fed. 154 (1914); *United States vs. McCullagh*, 221 Fed. 288 (1915). These cases have been generally regarded as correct.

A short time later, in 1916, we entered into a treaty with Great Britain, the terms of which bound the United States and Canada to protect migratory birds, and proposed legislation for that purpose. Might we suppose our government "conspired" to do by treaty, that which the courts had so recently ruled it could not do with domestic legislation?

In 1918, Congress passed such a law, much more elaborate than the act of 1913, forbidding the killing, capturing, or selling of the birds included within the provisions of the treaty except in accordance with regulations set by the Secretary of Agriculture. The Secretary of Agriculture promulgated suitable regulations, and the State of Missouri, on the ground that her reserved powers were invaded by the act, brought action to enjoin a game warden of the United States from enforcing the provisions of the act and the rules established by the Secretary of Agriculture. The decision of the Court makes it clear that Congress may regulate bird life as a means of carrying into effect the provisions of a treaty when it could not regulate it as an independent exercise of legislative power.

Certain questions arise in connection with the treaty power. First, is a treaty "self-executing" or is a statute of Congress necessary before it goes into effect? Marshall answered this question in *Foster vs. Neilson*, 2 Pet. 253 (1829), when he said: "Our Constitution declares a treaty to be the law of the land. It is, consequently, to be regarded in courts of justice as equivalent to an Act of the Legislature, whenever it operates of itself, without the aid of any legislative provision. But when the terms of the stipulation import a contract—when either of the parties engages to perform a particular act—the treaty addresses itself to the political, not the judicial department; and the Legislature must execute the contract before it can become a rule for the Court."

Whether or not a treaty is self-executing is a question for the Courts to decide. Public attention was focused on this question when a California court held that the state's Alien Land Law had been nullified by our adherence to the United Nations Charter, an interpretation which was rejected by the state's supreme court; see *Fujii vs. California*, 38 Cal. 2d 718 (1952).

An important problem raised by *Missouri vs. Holland* is the extent to which, if at all, Congress was free to make treaties which limited the rights of citizens guaranteed them by the Constitution. If Congress was freed from the restrictions of the Tenth Amendment, as the Court in the present case held, was it also freed from the limitations of the Bill of Rights? Despite Mr. Justice Holmes' reassuring statement that the migratory-birds treaty "does not contravene any prohibitory words to be found in the Constitution," there was no firm decision on this important point. Speaking for four members of the Court in *Reid vs. Covert*, 354 U.S. 1; 77 S. Ct. 1222; 1 L. Ed. 2d 1148 (1957), Mr. Justice Black emphasized that the "obvious and decisive answer to this, of course, is that no agreement with a foreign nation can confer power on the Congress, or on any other branch of government, which is free from the restraints of the Constitution."

In 1957, Girard, an American soldier, was turned over to the Japanese authorities for trial on charges of having killed a Japanese woman. A United States district court ordered the military authorities not to turn Girard over to the Japanese, and the Supreme Court, in a percuriam opinion, reversed this order. The Court pointed out that "a sovereign nation has exclusive jurisdiction to punish offenses against its laws committed within its borders" and nothing in the Constitution or subsequent legislation was found to nullify the provision in our security treaty with Japan (a Status of Forces Agreement) under which we would give "sympathetic consideration" to a request that we relinquish our jurisdiction in such cases. *Wilson vs. Girard*, 354 U.S. 524 (1957).

Mr. Justice Holmes delivered the opinion of the Court, saying in part: ..."As we have said, the question raised is the general one whether the treaty and statute are void as an interference with the rights reserved to the states."

To answer this question it is not enough to refer to the Tenth Amendment, reserving the powers not delegated to the United States, because by Article II, section 2, the power to make treaties is delegated expressly, and by Article VI, treaties made under the authority of the United States along with the Constitution and laws of the United States, made in pursuance thereof, are declared the supreme law of the land. If the treaty is valid, there can be no dispute about the validity of the statute under Article I, section 8, as a necessary and proper means to execute the powers of the government. The language of the Constitution as to the supremacy of treaties being general, the question before us is narrowed to an inquiry into the ground upon which the present supposed exception is placed.

It is said that a treaty cannot be valid if it infringes the Constitution, that there are limits, therefore, to the treaty-making power, and that one such limit is that what an act of Congress could not do unaided, in derogation of the powers reserved to the states, a treaty cannot do. An earlier act of Congress that attempted by itself and not in pursuance of a treaty to regulate the killing of migratory birds within the states had been held bad in the district court...Those decisions were supported by arguments that migratory birds were owned by the states in their sovereign capacity for the benefit of their people, and that under cases like *Geer vs. Connecticut*, 161 U.S. 519, this control was one that Congress had no power to displace. The same argument is supposed to apply now with equal force.

Whether the two cases cited were decided rightly or not, they cannot be accepted as a test of the treaty power. Acts of Congress are the supreme law of the land only when made in pursuance of the Constitution, while treaties are declared to be so when made under the authority of the United States. It is open to question whether the authority of the United States means more than the formal acts prescribed to make the convention. We do not mean to imply that there are no qualifications to the treaty-making power; but they must be ascertained in a different way. It is obvious that there may be matters of the sharpest exigency for the national well-being that an act of Congress could not deal with, but that a treaty followed by such an act could, and it is not lightly to be assumed that, in matters requiring national action, "a power which must belong to and somewhere reside in every civilized government" is not to be found...We are not yet discussing the particular case before us, but only are considering the validity of the test proposed. With regard to that, we may add that when we are dealing with words that also are a constituent act, like the Constitution of the United States, we must realize that they have called into life a being the development of which could not have been foreseen completely by the most gifted of its begetters. It was enough for them to realize or to hope that they had created an organism; it has taken a century and has cost their successors much sweat and blood to prove that they created a nation. The case before us must be considered in the light of our whole experience, and not merely in that of what was said a hundred years ago. The treaty in question does not contravene any prohibitory words to be found in the Constitution. (It should be noted here that the reasoning of Mr. Holmes is slippery and deceptive like that of many others who have weakened the Constitution, when he uses the word *prohibitory*. The Constitution is a document *delegating powers* from the States, *not* a document allowing the Federal government to do anything not prohibited. Just because something is not prohibited in the Constitution, does not mean those things are allowed.) The only question is whether it is forbidden by some invisible radiation from the general terms of the Tenth Amendment. We must consider what this country has become in deciding what that amendment has reserved. (The Tenth Amendment is clear and unambiguous. All powers not delegated are reserved to the States and the People. We don't need the Supreme Court to explain it.)

Continuing with Justice Holmes: The state, as we have intimated, founds its claim of exclusive authority upon an assertion of title to migratory birds,—an assertion that is embodied in statute. No doubt it is true that, as between a state and its inhabitants, the state may regulate the killing and sale of such birds, but it does not follow that its authority is exclusive of paramount powers, (the states are paramount in all things not delegated). To put the claim of the state upon title is to lean upon a slender reed. Wild birds are not in the possession of anyone; and possession is the beginning of ownership. The whole foundation of the state's rights is the presence within their jurisdiction of birds that yesterday had not arrived, tomorrow may be in another State and in a week, a thousand miles away. If we are to be accurate, we cannot put the case of the state upon higher ground than that the treaty deals with creatures that for the moment are within the state borders, that it must be carried out by officers of the United States within the same territory, and that, but for the treaty, the State would be free to regulate this subject itself.

As most of the laws of the United States are carried out within the states, and as many of them deal with matters which, in the silence of such laws, the state might regulate, such general grounds are not enough to support Missouri's claim. Valid treaties, of course, "are as binding within the territorial limits of the states as they are elsewhere throughout the dominion of the United States, ...No doubt the great body of private relations usually fall within the control of the state, but a treaty may override its power..."

Here a national interest of very nearly the first magnitude is involved. It can be protected only by national action in concert with that of another power. (If the Court can construe migratory birds to be important in the first magnitude, we may find the court's ability to rationalize, almost infinite, should they be asked to decide the validity of a treaty of a subject far more important than birds. The court is here putting its stamp of approval on the hanky panky of Congress doing by treaty, that which it failed to do with domestic legislation.) The subject matter is only transitorily within the state, and has no permanent habitat therein. But for the treaty and the statute, there soon might be no birds for any powers to deal with. We see nothing in the Constitution that compels the government to sit by while a food supply is cut off and the protectors of our forests and our crops are destroyed. (It is obvious, the Court majority are wearing blinders. Are the good justices suggesting that Missouri will eventually kill all the birds of the earth? Absurd)! It is not sufficient to rely upon the states. The reliance is vain, and were it otherwise, the question is whether the United States is forbidden to act. We are of the opinion that the treaty and statute must be upheld... Decree affirmed. Mr. Justice Van Devanter and Mr. Justice Pitney dissent. End of intermingling commentary.

In this early case, the environmentalists had hardly begun their attacks on the Constitution, State's Rights, and our industrial and manufacturing institutions. The environmental movement is a far greater threat today.

Many pretended environmental dangers are constantly being thrown at the American people by a constitutionally hostile national media. We are told that the ozone of the earth is being depleted. That the earth is warming. A few years ago, the danger was reversed; the earth was cooling. For all of the imagined environmental problems, the New World Order people have a pat answer. Delegation of more power to government and consolidate all governments into a single world unit under the United Nations Organization. This means more and more treaties.

At the 1992 Earth Summit in Rio de Janeiro, Senator Steve Symms, Republican of Idaho, was a member of the 11-member U.S. Senate delegation. In responding to a reporter's question about the possibility of Senate ratification of a treaty concerning climate change, Symms responded: "...once a President goes for a treaty... the record shows that few treaties have failed." A special report of *The New American* magazine, 1992, page 54. 770 Westhill Boulevard, Appleton, Wisconsin 54915.

The United States is bound to numerous international agencies and quasi-governmental supranational organizations, many under the authority of the United Nations Organization. Others, such as the World Bank, the International Monetary Fund, and the Bank for International Settlements, have great power and are all chipping away at United States sovereignty, and selling out the rights and freedom of Americans to these one-world agencies. Whole industries such as banking and securities are subjected to global, not just national regulation.

The problem of treaties superseding the United States Constitution is one which has been recognized for decades, if not from the beginning of our Republic. In the early 1950's, we had a number of statesmen in the U.S. Senate who clearly understood the spider's web of sovereignty destoying international entanglements we were getting ourselves into even in that early day. In February, 1952, Ohio's Senator John Bricker introduced into the Senate, the Bricker Amendment to the Constitution, known as Senate Joint Resolution 130. After many months and being watered down from the original proposal, it failed to pass the Senate by a single vote in the needed two-thirds majority, and only after furious lobbying and pressure by the globalists. The Bricker Amendment, if it had been added to the Constitution, woud have made null and void any conflict a treaty might have with the U.S. Constitution.

Our Founding Fathers, though brilliant and inspired, did not reach perfection in writing the Constitution. The portion concerning treaties is weak.

The Bricker Amendment would have solved this weakness in the Constitution. It reads:

Section 1. A provision of a treaty which conflicts with this Constitution shall not be of any force or effect.

Section 2. A treaty shall become effective as internal law in the United States only through legislation which would be valid in the absence of the treaty.

Section 3. Congress shall have power to regulate all executive and other agreements with any foreign power or international organization. All such agreements shall be subject to the limitations imposed on treaties by this article.

Section 4. The Congress shall have power to enforce this article by appropriate legislation.

By 1954, after months of spirited national debate, the Senate voted, and the Senate failed, to protect America from the potential tyranny of treaties. Why would anybody who wishes to preserve the Constitution vote against such a proposal to protect our national interests and strengthen the Constitution? Dare we suggest there might be those in high places who might have long-term plans to undermine, and eventually destroy, the Constitution and the liberty which Americans have for so long taken for granted? You better believe it! If you are still ignorant about numerous historical conspiracies of small groups of criminals who have attempted, and who have often succceded, in taking over and controlling governments, you need to hit the books. Dozens of such books document the evidence and the facts. Many books readily available, detail the fact that the government of the United States is not only in process of being merged into a one-world government in which the Constitution we know and cherish will be eliminated, but we are perhaps, in the last years or months of our life as a constitutional republic.

Frank Chodorov, writing in Human Events during debate on the Bricker Amendment said, the "nation is threatened by invasion, not by a foreign army, but by its own legal entanglements. Not soldiers, but theoreticians and visonaries attacking its independence and who aim to bring its people under the rule of an agglomeration of foreign governments."

The Eisenhower administration and our State Department did all in their power to defeat the Bricker Amendment. Our Secretary of State, John Foster Dulles led the charge. This same John Foster Dulles only two years before said: "the treaty power is an extraordinary power, liable to abuse." He warned, "Treaties can take power away from the Congress and give them to the President. They can take powers from the states and give them to the federal government or to some international body and they can cut across the rights given to the people by their constitutional Bill of Rights."

When the treaty power is admitted by men of such stature as Mr. Dulles to be a danger to our Bill of Rights protections, why have successive administrations and our U.S. Senate refused for 40 years, to give us the protection of the Bricker Amendment? Why, unless sometime "down the road," the Bricker Amendment would stand in the way of implementing a one-world socialist government under a new United Nations treaty which would abolish and supersede the Constitution?

The Supreme Court of the United States has upheld the supremacy of treaty law, as we have seen.

To quote from The Free Market, September 1992 issue, published by the Ludwig von Mises Institute, Auburn, Alabama 36849, an article written by Justin Raimondo: "Are we going to let global bureaucrats run the economy and preside over a worldwide redistribution of America's dwindling wealth?

"When George Bush went to war against Saddam Hussein, the first step was to seek United Nations sanction. What could be more indicative of the power shift and the direction we are headed? Only after securing the approval of that August body did the President of the United States deign to ask for congressional approval. Surely the process should have been reversed.

"The United Nations seeks to promulgate international standards of child rearing, substance use, banking contracts, and even allowable speech. According to one U.N. declaration, worlds that inflict 'mental harm' on minorities ought to be outlawed.

"Ensconced in tax-free and taxpayer subsidized splendor, globalist bureaucrats sit in their offices at the U.N., the World Bank, and the International Monetary Fund, spinning webs of rules, regulations, proclamations, and other edicts, covering everything from education to labor relations to the environment. From the General Agreement of Tariffs and Trade (GATT author) to the hundreds of executive agreements entered into by an administration obsessed with foreign affairs, we are so entangled in the web that it will take nothing less than a constitutional amendment to cut us free.

"As Frank E. Holman, president of the American Bar Association, and the spark plug of the Bricker Amendment movement wrote, 'However long the fight for an adequate Constitutional Amendment on treaties and other international agreements, it will and must be won. This will be the history of the Bricker Amendment as it has been the history of all other great issues and causes.'

"Holman's comments were published in 1954 as *The Story of the Bricker Amendment* (The First Phase)—a title which we can only hope is prophetic. For it seems that now, more than ever, some bulwark against the new globalism is needed. In these days of the 'New World Order' the time is now to bring back Bricker and begin the second phase."

To the globalist, or Centralist, *more government* is always the answer to problems of society, if not to problems of individuals as well.

There is a powerful truth which we the people need to make sure our governors, attorney generals and all members of the 50 State legislatures understand, so they will at least have the knowledge, and we hope, the courage to resist, if not defy, future Federal coercion and usurpation of undelegated constitutional powers. That is, if an action of government is inconsistent with the Constitution it is unlawful, illegal, null and void.

An unconstitutional treaty, legislative act, or Executive Order, can be defined as usurpation, therefore, invalid and unlawful, and leads to tyranny. If government officials act without authorization, the individuals, though acting under color of law, are no different than any other common criminal.

In America, no government official has any authority to act outside of, against, or in violation of the Constitution, even in times of war, or declared national emergency. If elected or appointed public officials act without authority of law, or in violation of law, it is impossible for them to be acting as agents of the people, and their acts make them lawbreakers or outlaws. They are no different than any other lawbreaker and should just as readily be prosecuted to the full extent of the law.

DANGER NUMBER TWO

We will not dwell on this danger but briefly. A volume could easily be written outlining a potential coup by a traitorous President.

Most Americans would probably agree that Abraham Lincoln was a great man, and a good President. On his day of inauguration, March 4, 1861, he took office under circumstances more trying than any President of the United States before, or since his administration. Seven States had already seceded from the Union and several others were threatening to do so. President James Buchanan, Lincoln's predecessor, did not know what to do. Neither did anybody else. Some on both sides wanted war. Most, on both sides, saw no reason for war. Indeed, there was no reason for war, and they were willing to allow time to peacefully settle the issue.

Concerning the integrity of Abraham Lincoln, there can be little doubt, he was an honest man. He also understood and loved the Constitution of the United States.

Had he lived, there can be little doubt that in the Reconstruction of the South after the war, Lincoln would have treated the South more as errant brothers than vanquished traitors and rebels.

But even under Abraham Lincoln, the Constitution was flagrantly violated during that time of "national emergency" the Civil War. If a man of Lincoln's stature felt compelled, rightly or wrongly, to violate his oath of office by not, at all times, abiding by strict constitutional procedures, what might we expect from politicians in the 1990's who appear to be men far less exemplary than Lincoln? Corruption and extravagance in Washington, D.C. is running rampant and is common knowledge. When have we had a President who even comes close to "honest Abe?" Recent Presidents are far more suspected, than respected.

If Lincoln disregarded the Constitution because of extraordinary circumstances, might we expect far greater violations in some real...or pretended..."national emergency" as we approach the year 2,000?

Abraham Lincoln instituted martial law, which has been described as "no law at all." Martial law is the exercise of governmental powers by military forces within domestic territory. During the Civil War martial law was declared, not only in the secessionist States, but in many places in the North. Martial law usually includes the suspension of the writ of habeus corpus which means "to bring a party before a court or judge." The primary function of the writ is to release from unlawful imprisonment. Under habeas corpus, an independent proceeding is instituted to determine whether a defendant is being unlawfully deprived of his or her liberty. When habeas corpus is suspended, as under martial law, a person might be held indefinitely without charges being filed against him and without trial. This was a common occurrence during the Civil War and it was official policy under the Lincoln administration. Arbitrary arrests were numerous. Some people were held only a short time and then released. Others were held for many months, sometimes on mere suspicion of being rebel sympathizers.

Under martial law, if a commander disregards the usual guarantees of constitutional rights, makes summary seizures, arrests and imprisonments, his proceedings may ultimately be held justifiable, but he takes a risk. His actions are reviewable by the courts, and decisions of commanders acting by authority of martial law were sometimes reversed during and after the Civil War. But numerous injustices were never rectified.

Between the firing on Sumter, April 12, 1861, and the assembling of Congress in a special session called by the President on July 4, 1861, President Lincoln took several measures to defend the nation and prosecute the war against the Confederacy. Why Lincoln did not immediately summon a special session of Congress is not immediately apparent, but he may have had doubts of being supported before the fact, in some of the unconstitutional actions he took during this interval.

Many people of boldness, including presidents and children, will sometimes operate under the theory that "it is easier to get forgiveness, than it is consent." Or, "it is easier to get consent, after a foul deed has been committed, because it is too late to do anything about it, or once deeply committed, it is difficult to withdraw." The theory is, if there is doubt about getting consent or permission to do something, go ahead and just do it. If afterward you are told you did wrong, you can beg for forgiveness, apologize and promise "never to do it again." If one chooses to operate in such a manner, he accomplishes what he set out to do without violating an order, or having been told no. With appropriate feigned humility, one can usually obtain forgiveness after the fact, if one acted with disapproval, and cordial relations will continue on a normal basis. Whereas, if one attempts to gain consent before the fact, and consent is refused, one will be found in rebellion if he proceeds with open disobedience toward the forbidden goal or object. Consent before the fact might be impossible. If sought after the fact, at least, "I have a chance."

On July 4, 1861, a national holiday in remembrance of our birth of liberty, Congress was faced with a "fait accompli;" a fact or deed accomplished, presumably irreversible. If this was President Lincoln's idea of getting Congress to back his war effort against the South, it worked.

"In referring to his proclamation of May 4, 1861, calling for enlistments in the regular army far beyond the existing legal limits, Lincoln himself frankly admitted that he had overstepped his authority." Nicolay and Hay, Works, Vl, 308.

"The alleged 'unconstitutionality' of this conduct of President Lincoln was urged as a leading argument by those who contended that the whole process by which the 'war' began was illegal. This matter was elaborately threshed out before the Supreme Court in the Prize Cases..." 67 U.S. 635. From the book, Constitutional Problems under Lincoln by James G. Randall, Ph.D., 1926, page 52.

The Supreme Court agreed that from July 13, 1861, when Congress officially recognized a state of war, the President became invested with the war power, and the legal foundations of a state of war were in force. They divided, with the Chief Justice in the minority, on the question of the President's power and of the legality of the war before that time.

An important point covered in this decision was the legal effect of the action of Congress approving the President's war measures. The language of the act in which Congress ratified the President's acts is as follows: "...be it...enacted, that all the acts, proclamations, and orders of the President... (after March 4, 1861, inauguration day,) respecting the army and navy of the United States, and calling out or relating to the militia or volunteers from the States, are hereby approved and in all respects legalized and made valid...as if they had been issued and done under the previous express authority and direction of the Congress of the United States.

"What was the force of this subsequent ratification of acts which many claimed to be unconstitutional? Having held that the President's course in meeting the emergency with warlike measures was entirely legal in itself, the court was under the necessity of proceeding *circumspectly* in dealing with a legislative provision which seemed to imply some defect in the measures taken by the executive, *and which was denounced as creating a war 'ex post facto...'

"The Supreme Court upheld this ratifytng measure, but at the same time prudently refused to admit that it was necessary. 'If it were necessary to the technical existence of a war that it should have a legislative sanction,' said the court, 'we find it in almost every act passed at the extraordinary session of 1861,...and finally,...we find Congress...passing an act approving, legalizing and making valid all the acts...of the President, as if they had been issued and done...under the previous express authority and direction of the Congress.' 67 U.S. 670-671. The position of the court was that there was no defect in the action of the President, but that, if such defect had existed, this subsequent legislation of Congress would have sufficed to cure it." Ibid p. 56.

The Supreme Court found itself, as did Senator Sherman, after the fact, in the same position Congress found itself, after the fact, almost of necessity, of having to rule in favor of the President. Could the Court rule that the President was acting unconstitutionally, when he was in the act of prosecuting a war, over the issue of another allegedly unconstitutional act, that being a State separating itself, or seceding from the Union? Should the Court have ruled the other way and said the

---

*Senator Sherman, while vindicating the President, assumed that his acts were illegal. "I am going to vote," he said, "for the resolution (to approve and confirm thc President's acts, and I am going to vote for it upon the assumption that the different acts of the Administration recited in this preamble were illegal...l am willing to make them as legal and valid as if they had the previous sanction of Congress." Quoted in Upton, Military Policy of the United States, 231.

President had acted in violation of the Constitution on one or more occasions from April, 12, 1861, until Congress met on July 4, the war might then and there have come to a screeching halt while Northern leadership got down to seriously debating whether, after all, "is it worth pursuing a bloody civil war with our Southern brethren?" And, "what business have we in going to war because we, the North, say secession is unconstitutional, and at the same time we are violating the Constitution in our prosecution of the war?"

Lincoln called for a special session of Congress on April, 15. Why did he not schedule such a session immediately, instead of waiting 80 days? This is a very troubling question. If Lincoln did this in order not to have his hands tied with congressional legalities, and to get the war off "to a flying start," it makes one wonder whether his accusers were right on another matter. Did Lincoln "sucker" the South into firing on Sumter? Or was he really acting in good faith and merely attempting to supply troops with food and supplies?

In examining the four years of Lincoln's administration and the numerous violations of the Constitution which took place during that time, we cannot help but question his motivations for the war. Was he determined to free the slaves regardless of the cost? Or was a civil war so constitutionally complex that nobody else could have done any better?

Regardless, precedents were set by Lincoln which might be used as precedent today should President Clinton declare a national emergency, followed by a declaration of martial law. If Lincoln could violate the law in fighting to "save the law," might not a lesser man do the same?

"As interpreted by President Lincoln, the war power specifically included the right to determine the existence of rebellion and call forth the militia to suppress it; the right to increase the regular army by calling for volunteers beyond the authorized total; the right to suspend the habeas corpus privilege; the right to proclaim martial law; the right to place persons under arrest without warrant and without judicially showing the cause of detention; the right to seize citizens' property if such seizure should become indispensable to the successful prosecution of the war; the right to spend money from the treasury of the United States without congressional appropriation; *the right to suppress newspapers; and the right to do unusual things by proclamation especially to proclaim freedom to the slaves of those in arms against the Government. These were some of the conspicuous powers which President Lincoln exercised, and in the exercise of which he was as a rule, though not without exception, sustained in the courts.

"Analyzing the President's war power further, we find that besides the executive power which during the war expanded enormously, there was a considerable amount of 'presidential legislation' (for in many cases it virtually amounted to that), and there were also notable instances of presidential justice.

"...President Lincoln issued 'regulations' for the enforcement of the Militia Act of 1862 which established conscription for the first time during the war. The act itself did not specifically authorize conscription at all, and so far as the draft was used in 1862 (in Indiana, Wisconsin, and other States) it rested upon these executive regulations..."

Even under the Constitution the President has large discre-

---

* In reporting to Congress various measures taken to meet the national emergency, Lincoln stated that early in the war he gave large powers to certain trusted citizens who were to make arrangements for transporting troops and supplies and otherwise providing for the public defense. Doubting the loyalty of certain persons in the government departments, he directed the Secretary of the Treasury to advance two million dollars of public money without security to John A. Dix, George Opdyke, and Richard H. Blatchford of New York, to pay the expenses of certain "military and naval measures necessary for the defense and support of the Government." This would seem to have been in violation of that clause of the Constitution (Art. 1, sec. 9, par. 7) which provides that "no money shall *be drawn from the Treasury but in consequence of appropriations made by law."* Lincoln confessed the irregularity of this procedure when he said, *"I am not aware that a dollar of the public funds thus confided without authority of law to unofficial persons was either lost or wasted." (Lincoln's message to Congress, May 28, 1862: Nicolay and Hay, Works, VII, 189-194.)*

tionary power. This power assumes great importance in times of domestic emergency, as well as war time. If not authorized to assume the role of dictator, he is at least clothed with latent powers which in time of war or national emergency are capable of wide expansion.

In league with the governor of a State, the President can send in hundreds, or thousands of troops or federal marshalls, to do just about anything they wish, including murdering private citizens and confiscating or destroying private property. Some think the Randy Weaver case in Northern Idaho in the summer of 1992, wherein a mother and wife with an 8-month old baby in her arms was shot in the head by federal agents, was a trial run. Why else would Cecil Andrus, Governor of Idaho, invite and acquiesce in the entrance of hundreds of federal agents into his State with accompanying heavy military armor, allegedly to arrest a single human being on an alleged minor firearms violation?

Some say the Los Angeles riots of 1992, after the acquittal of four policemen, was another trial run in preparation for numerous simultaneous riots in cities all over the United States. When the appropriate time arrives the President might declare martial law, followed by a *proclamation*, or some sort of *declaration*, that the Constitution is *temporarily suspended*. Should that day arrive, we will discover that temporary means permanent, as we are eased into The New World Order.

One other dangerous precedent showing how the Federal Executive, Legislative and Judiciary will act in concert in obvious violation of the Constitution, should be mentioned.

Shortly after the Japanese attack on Pearl Harbor, December 7, 1941, tens of thousands of Japanese American citizens were forced out of their homes and "temporarily" placed in detention camps. The Supreme Court in Korematsu vs. United States, 323 U.S. 214, 65 S. Ct. 193, 89 L.Ed. 194 (1944), squirmed and twisted, but affirmed the guilt of Mr. Korematsu in violating the "law." This law was Exclusion Order No. 34, one of a number of military orders and proclamations, which was based on an Executive Order of the President, No. 9066, 7 Federal Register 1407, which was based on an Act of

Congress of March 21, 1942, 56 Stat. 173, 18 U.S.C.A., 97a.

In giving its blessing to a blatant violation of the Constitution, the Court acknowledged: "...we are not unmindful of the hardships imposed by it upon a large group of American citizens...But hardships are part of war, and war is an aggregation of hardships. All citizens alike, both in and out of uniform, feel the impact of war in greater or lesser measure. Citizenship has its responsibilities as well as its privileges, and in time of war the burden is always heavier. Compulsory exclusion of large groups of citizens from their homes, except under circumstances of direct emergency and peril, is inconsistent with our basic governmental institutions. But when under conditions of modern warfare our shores are threatened by hostile forces, the power to protect must be commensurate with the threatened danger..."

This case illustrates again, the tendency of judges to acquiesce in, and go along with their brothers in Congress and the Executive branches of the Federal government and sanction gross violations of the Constitution in times of "emergency" or national stress, or war. Judges, after all, are mere men, and are subject to pressure of their peers. Few men indeed, are capable of resisting pressure by their peers to "go along, in order to get along," whether they are of the lowest or of the highest rank in society. From children to old men, few are able and willing to do that which is right, regardless of the consequences, or regardless of peer pressure to go along with the crowd.

In the Korematsu case justices Roberts, Murphy and Jackson dissented. In his dissent Justice Jackson said: "Korematsu was born on our soil, of parents born in Japan. The Constitution makes him a citizen of the United States by nativity and a citizen of California by residence. No claim is made that he is not loyal to this country. There is no suggestion that apart from the matter involved here, he is not law-abiding and well disposed. Korematsu, however, has been convicted of an act not commonly a crime. It consists merely of being present in the state whereof he is a citizen, near the place where he was born, and where all his life he has lived..."

Justice Roberts in his dissent said: "...it is the case of convicting a citizen as a punishment for not submitting to imprisonment in a concentration camp, based on his ancestry, and solely because of his ancestry, without evidence or inquiry concerning his loyalty and good disposition towards the United States. If this be a correct statement of the facts disclosed by this record, and facts of which we take judicial notice, I need hardly labor the conclusion that Constitutional rights have been violated..."

In concluding his dissent Justice Jackson said: "My duties as a justice as I see them do not require me to make a military judgment as to whether General DeWitt's evacution and detention program was a reasonable military necessity. I do not suggest that the courts should have attempted to interfere with the Army in carrying out its task. But I do not think they may be asked to execute a military expedient that has no place in law under the Constitution. I would reverse the judgment and discharge the prisoner."

Even if the minority opinion of the Court had prevailed, the damage had been done to these tens of thousands of Japanese men, women and children for the Supreme Court decision was not handed down until 1944 and these American citizens had been rounded up and detained in 1942.

If the President and Congress conspire to abolish the Constitution and install the New World Order, you can bet your boots the Supreme Court will go along. Two more cases at the end of this book will be cited to show that the Court has historically "gone along." After all, the Court, Congress and the President are on the same team. They are the three branches of Federal entity. They tend to protect their turf from each other, but they join as a team, quite often, when it comes to "them against us;" them against the people and the States. The Feds are jealous of their artificial power, because down deep, they know they don't have any power at all, except at the pleasure of the States. Therefore, when one is weak, he operates with bluff and bluster. The coward who is afraid of exposure, will rant, rave, threaten and try to intimidate. But call his bluff, and he runs like a yellow dog.

The Federal government has us bluffed out, and Americans are running scared. We must call the Federal bluff before it is too late.

Millions of trusting Americans are indifferent and unconcerned. Like generations past, prior to man-made or natural disasters, they argue that nothing out of the ordinary will ever take place. "All things continue as from the beginning."

The Spotlight, a weekly Washington newspaper reports in its issue of September 28, 1992: "The Spotlight has learned some top military officers—fed up with President George Bush's treasonous disregard for the Constitution...have mulled the idea of seizing power through a coup d'etat....

"These military leaders claim the United States has grown too close to the U.N. under the current administration. Many claim their sworn duty to 'defend the Constitution' is threatened by this country's cozy relationship with a foreign entity.

"The president swears to 'preserve, protect and defend the Constitution of the United States,' before taking office...

"Despite his pledge, Bush....now threatens to relinquish control of the U. S. military to the U.N...

"The New York Times...blatantly declared in an editorial: 'The army of tomorrow is not the U.S. Army...Peace will be secured by U.N. forces patrolling the turbulent globe.'

"Many (military officers) have reportedly expressed outrage at Bush's New World Order and attacks aimed at American sovereignty. In fact, some appear ready to label the president a domestic enemy.

"The final straw in what many officers reportedly see as 'treason' on the part of the president is plans for a U.N. army. 'In effect officers are being asked to violate (their) oaths by taking orders from the U.N.,' a source said..."

In another Spotlight article of November 30, 1992 by James P. Tucker, Jr., it is reported:

"President-elect Bill Clinton is just as strongly committed to the Bilderberg program for world government as President George Bush and would take a giant step toward that goal by establishing a global army under the United Nations.

"The plan is to introduce a world army so gradually that

Americans will be unaware of this surrender of sovereignty until the force is in place and empowered to intervene at the whim of the U.N. Security Council, in domestic affairs of the United States.

"The U.N. hopes to act on establishing a world army at 'a special meeting of the (Security) Council next spring, at the latest,' according to a U.N. document dated October 29, 1992.

"'Member states' are to make available to the Security Council 'appropriately experienced military or civilian staff, for a fixed period of time, to help with work on peace-keeping operations,' the document said. "In bureaucratic jargon, 'fixed period' means permanently.

"Prior to the election, U.N. bureaucrats in Washington and New York expressed complete confidence the United States will both finance and make itself subservient to a world army whether Bush or Clinton had been elected....

"U.N. personnel were in no way concerned about the necessities of American politics. While Bush and Clinton both supported an expanded larger 'peacekeepinq force,' they stopped short of publicly backing a permanent world army during the election season.

"This was mere political expediency, the U.N. operatives said, the purpose of which was to 'appease the electorate's nationalistic instincts.' Bush, however, in his speech to the U.N. on September 22, called for a 'new emphasis on peacekeeping' and 'to strengthen' U.N. 'peacekeeping operations.'

"Clinton bluntly called for a permanent U.N. 'rapid deployment force' in a speech to the Los Angeles World Affairs Council.

"A Clinton adviser on the U.N., Richard Gardner, a professor of international law, has drafted a plan for a world army of 30,000 men. Each of the five members of the Security Council would contribute 2,000 troops, and 30 other nations would provide up to 750 each.

"Under Gardner's plan—now the president-elect's—the world army could interfere anywhere without regard to 'provincial nationalism.' It would enter once-sovereign nations to 'protect human rights' as defined by the world government.

"They envision the day when, after Americans are accustomed to seeing the world army intervene in troubled African nations, they would welcome its appearance on U.S. soil on such occasions as the riots in Los Angeles.

"That would mark the moment when Americans accept the superiority of a world government over their own.

"There is strong resistance by military officers in the Pentagon and elsewhere to placing American soldiers under the command of a foreign leader to carry out military missions at the direction of the U.N.

"It was military pressure that caused Bush to pull back from an outright commitment to surrender U.S. troops to a global army; Bilderberg operatives in the State Department had urged the step. U.N. operatives said they understood the 'political necessities,' and a global army will be in place on schedule.

"In additlon to long subservience to the world shadow government, the president-elect has a personal reason for surrendering his role as commander in chief, the U.N. functionaries said.

"While Bush had an honorable record of combat service in World War II, Clinton dodged the draft during the Vietnam War. Once, in a campaign speech, Clinton suggested sending troops into Bosnia. The next day, Gen. Norman Schwarzkopf said there would be a 'morale problem' if a draft dodger sent soldiers into combat.

"Under the new order, no U.S. president ever has to send Americans into combat,' one source said. 'The secretary-general of the U.N. would do that."

If President Clinton and the Congress should, say, in 1993, 1994, or whenever, by legislation, or even by Executive Order of the President acting alone, under some alleged "national emergency," order the United States army, or United Nations troops within our borders, to "confiscate by house to house search, all firearms, including rifles and shotguns," would any governor or State Legislature dare oppose such an order? Not very likely, unless they have prepared ahead of time and are backed up by large numbers of citizens who understand what is coming down.

Who, or what, could stop such a blatant violation of the Constitution and the Second Amendment? Not the Supreme Court. It would probably take at least two years for an appeal by any private citizen to reach the Supreme Court, just as in the Korematsu case. Even then, would the Court dare to rule justly and correctly?

The skeptic will say such an order to confiscate firearms is more right wing paranoia. Nevertheless, wisdom and experience and history teach people who wish to remain free, to always assume a worst case scenario and be prepared to meet it...*just in case*. Don't unduly worry, and don't ever panic, but *always be prepared* for men in power to act for their personal best interests, and against the interests of *the people* at large.

DANGER NUMBER THREE

Calling a Constitutional Convention of the States, allegedly to pass a Balanced Budget Amendment.

Congress refuses to balance the budget. In fiscal year 1992, the admitted deficit was some 300 billion dollars, not counting who knows how many billions were spent "off budget." In November, 1992 the national debt is around 4 trillion, l00 billion dollars ($4,100,000,000,000), not counting another 12-15 trillion in future military, congressional, federal employee pensions, Social Security obligations, etc. for which nothing has been set aside. The interest alone, some $300 billion in 1992, is rapidly escalating where it will soon take the entire income tax of the American people to pay it.

Since the debt and Congress is out of control, and there appears to be no possibility of Congress containing the debt, the idea has been suggested that the States must do the job.

Under Article V of the Constitution, "The Congress...on the application of the legislatures of two-thirds of the several states, shall call a convention for proposing amendments, (to the Constitution) which...shall be valid to all intents and purposes, as part of this constitution, when ratified by the legislatures of three-fourths of the several states, or by conventions in three-fourths thereof.."

It has been proposed, that under this article the States amend the Constitution which will require Congress to balance the budget. Two-thirds of the States, or 34 States, can force a Convention. Thirty-two have petitioned Congress for such a Convention, but three have rescinded their petitions, leaving twenty-nine in place. Should two more new States, however, petititon Congress for a Convention, a corrupt government in Washington is likely to ignore the three rescissions and go ahead with a Convention. The three rescinding States seem to have sensed the danger to the Constitution of a modern day Convention.

Contrary to what some of the "experts" tell us, a Constitutional Convention could not be limited in its work. The Convention of 1787, consisting of delegates from 12 of the 13 States met for the mere purpose of revising the "Constitution" of that day, the Articles of Confederation. Instead the Convention proposed the abolishment of the Articles of Confederation and the adoption of an entirely new system of government under our present Constitution. A modern day Convention of States would have far more authoritative prestige than the one in 1787. That Convention had no lawful procedure for proposing a new form of government. Our present Constitution does provide such lawful procedure. If a Convention of the l990's proposed to abolish our present Constitution and adopt an entirely different form of government, or proposed to abolish the Constitution and merge the United States into a single one-world government, there is nothing anybody could do to stop such a radical proposal.

However, three-fourths of the States would have to agree with any proposal which came out of the Convention. This requirement has sucked some patriots into supporting the internationalist scheme to call such a Convention. The danger here is, that Congress might designate State "Conventions" to ratify proposed amendments, rather than the legislatures of the States. It is conceivable that these special ratifying conventions could be stacked by those who favor the destruction of the Constitution.

Based upon years of intensive research, working closely with constitutional scholars well versed on the issue, a Washington institution known as Liberty Lobby concluded that the proposed amendment is a smoke screen for an insidious scheme to convene a Constitutional Convention in order to scrap the Constitution and set in place a new form of government. Liberty Lobby reports, "a seemingly endless number of political 'leaders' and Establishment newspaper columnists continue talking about 'gridlocked government' coupled with the suggestion that America needs a new form of government." A Constitutional Convention would be a first step in that direction.

A new Constitution has actually been written and has been waiting "in the wings" for more than 15 years. It is called The New States of America Constitution.

The following is taken from a Review and Commentary on Rexford G. Tugwell's book *The Emerging Constitution*, by Colonel Curtis B. Dall and E. Stanley Rittenhouse. Rittenhouse is an author. Dall was a well-known author and lecturer, and a former investment banker who was connected with the federal banking-political complex at the highest levels. He was also the son-in-law of President Franklin D. Roosevelt.

"In 1964, the writing of a new constitution for America began, at a tax-exempt foundation with the misleading name, Center for the Study of Democratic Institutions.

"The people who took it upon themselves to write this new constitution on our behalf were, of course, not elected representatives, or in any other way our representatives. As a tax-exempt foundation, they were able to do political work on what amounts to a subsidy taken from your taxes, but you and I were never asked if we wanted a new constitution written. Indeed, only a very tiny fraction of the people of the United States even know that it exists: it has been made known to practically no one except a select category of influential people whose views and interest generally coincide with those of the people who wrote it. The American people as a whole are still in the dark about it, and this situation is deliberate. It is therefore truly a 'secret' constitution.

"This model constitution took ten years to write, drawing upon the efforts of more than 100 people. A preliminary version was published in 1970 and given exposure in limited circles. But in 1974, an essentially final version was quietly published in a book entitled '*The Emerging Constitution*' by Rexford G. Tugwell (Harper Row, $20), the man who directed the formulation of the new constitution. It is the fortieth draft. During most of the time that their constitution was being written, the Center for the Study of Democratic Institutions was lavishly funded to the tune of $2,500,000 annually."

The new Constitution would have the form and appearance of the old. It is merely a form to pacify those still remembering the liberty that the old Constitution guaranteed. The new Constitution "is a bridge, a part of the hopefully peaceful transition from a Constitutional Republic to an oligarchic world dictatorship."

This new constitutional bridge leading to world dictatorship admittedly will be in effect only 25 years...at most. From Article XI, Section 2. "When this Constitution shall have been in effect for twenty-five years, the Overseer shall ask, by referendum, whether a new Constitution shall be prepared. If a majority so decide, the Council, making use of such advice as may be available, and consulting those who have made complaint, shall prepare a new draft for submission at the next election. If not disapproved by a majority it shall be in effect. If disapproved, it shall be redrafted and resubmitted with such changes as may be then appropriate to the circumstances, and it shall be submitted to the voters at the following election.

"If not disapproved by a majority, it shall be in effect. If disapproved, it shall be restudied and resubmitted."

How many times would the people have to say no before the government would stop calling for more elections? And why, after just 25 years, would the people want another new Constitution...unless, of course, the new Constitution was to be the final step in establishing a one-world government without any sovereignty whatsoever to be left to the American people?

When the first new Constitution becomes effective, Article XII, Section 4, Paragraph 3 says: "The President shall cause to be constituted an appropriate commission to designate existing laws inconsistent with this Constitution, and they shall be void; also the commission shall assist the President and the legislative houses in the formulating of such laws as may be consistent with the Constitution and necessary to its implementation."

The President, alone, through his personally appointed "commission," will abolish existing laws according to his whim, and in the same manner establish new laws. If you thought a nine-man Supreme Court was occasionally dictatorial, "you ain't seen nothing yet," if we adopt this new Constitution. Any ten-year old should be able to detect the makings of a dictatorship in this Article.

The full text of The New States Constitution, analysis and commentary may be ordered from Liberty Library, 300 Independence Avenue, S.E., Washington, D.C. 20003.

DANGER NUMBER 4

The Federal government has gone to the extreme in using the environment as an excuse to control, undermine and destroy American industry. Because of unreasonable, often outrageous, Federal regulations and restrictions, the United States is heavily dependent on foreign oil, while we have huge untapped reserves off both the Atlantic and Pacific coasts, and even more in the Northern seas off the Alaskan coast. Huge Federal tracts consisting of millions of acres have been set aside with all commercial activities banned.

Americans are getting used to the idea that a liberal Congress, bent on comfortably merging the United States into a single world government, can do just about anything it wishes if done in the name of environmentalism. No end is in sight unless the States take the bull by the horns and tell the Federal government enough is enough. Timid State leaders cannot do the job. Only governors and attorneys general of the States who understand the relationship between the States and the Central government, and who have the backbone to stand up and fight the entrenched bureaucracy, have the slightest chance of curbing Federal usurpations. And it probably can only be done by three-fourths of the States acting in concert, with the very real threat that they WILL dissolve the Union if that is what it takes.

An exhaustive study of various dangers to the Constitution is not the intent of this work. Neither is the amplification of major differences among our people, such as abortion, prayer in school, race relations and many other differences.

The main thrust of this writing is to suggest that splitting up the United States of America into 50 separate independent, free and sovereign nations might be the best solution to many of our problems. Let those who think alike separate themselves from those who differ. Splitting up might very well be the only possible solution in defeating a determined and powerful clique who are determined to overthrow the government of the United States and put us into a one-world government.

Men and women who marry, and later find they are not suited to one another, more often than not, end up getting divorced. Many divorces end in friendship. Some in bitterness. But when two people find they are simply too different to happily live together, society thinks nothing of them getting a divorce.

Why should it be any different in relations between communities and nations? The Union of The United States of America is not sacred. It was not established in perpetuity. Alliances, associations, confederations of nations; treaties, compacts and all sorts of agreements among states and nations are sometimes long-lasting, sometimes short. One generation has no moral or legal right to bind following generations to contracts or debt from which that generation will get little or no benefit.

Who can blame the children of the next generation in America, when finding themselves burdened with overwhelming and unpayable Federal debt, revolt and repudiate the debt and profligacy of their fathers? Common sense, and justice herself, would denounce as fools, the generation which follows ours, if they should acknowledge and attempt to pay, even the interest, on the debt which our immoral and selfish generation left them.

If our children have any collective sense, they will revolt and refuse to pay to the government the trillions of dollars which will be necessary to meet all the pension obligations of Social Security, Federal, State and military pensions, and other future financial burdens which we are leaving them.

Our children may be only too glad, once they discover there is a bloodless way to accomplish it, to rid themselves of these trillions in debt, by dissolving and abolishing the Federal government. If there is another way, or a better way, let us try to find it before America is destroyed by traitors, criminals, riot and revolt, as our people self-destruct along with their political leaders in a mad binge of humanistic corruption.

President John Adams and other early American Founders knew whereof they spoke when they said, "this Constitution was made only for a religious people," meaning an honest and law-abiding people. If the humanistic anti-God element among us continues to increase their numbers and their influence, the Constitution can only be saved if the honest and upright among us come together and establish an island of safety where we live the moral law, and where we hold high the Constitution as the Supreme Law among a remnant who respect and honor our Creator.

If separation of a State, or States from the Union is the best answer to differences, and as a last resort remedy to those who would carry out a coup, let us examine the lawful basis for such remedies.

Chapter 4

13 Free, Sovereign, and Independent Nations

The Constitution of the United States has served us very well for most of the past 200 years. There have been several instances of abuse and usurpation, but until recent years, the general tendency of elected officials and the courts was to honor and sustain the law according to the Constitution in the tradition of the Founding Fathers. In other words, the Constitution was interpreted according to its actual wording and the intent of those who wrote it, just as any contract should be interpreted.

This should be the first requirement of any person appointed, or elected, to be a judge, especially when that appointment is to sit as one of the nine justices of the United States Supreme Court; they should be advocates of *strict construction.*

When President George Bush nominated Clarence Thomas to replace the retiring Thurgood Marshall in the summer of 1991, many Americans, generally known as conservatives, were greatly pleased because Thomas was perceived to be a strict constructionist. Many other Americans, generally known as liberals, or socialists, opposed the seating of Clarence Thomas as a justice of the Supreme Court, because he was perceived to be a strict constructionist. Thus, the closeness of the Senate vote for the confirmation of Thomas; 52 for, 48 against.

America is now enjoying the blessing of an additional strict constructionist judge, but only after his opponents threw every possible roadblock in his path. America was not so fortunate when another strict constructionist some four years earlier, Robert Bork, was nominated to the Supreme Court by President Ronald Reagan. Bork was defeated 58 to 42. Every conceivable excuse to oppose his confirmation was used against him, but like Clarence Thomas, the real reason for liberal opposition was that he believed in interpreting the Constitution in its original intent and according to the actual wording.

In America today, conservatives generally favor the strict construction view of the Constitution. Liberals generally oppose strict construction. Strict construction impedes "social progress," and consolidation of power into fewer hands. This difference of opinion and policy has been with us from the beginning of the Republic. Thomas Jefferson, one of the giants of profound importance and influence in establishing our Republic, was totally of the strict constructionist school. Alexander Hamilton, the first Secretary of the Treasury in the administration of George Washington, and John Adams, who followed Washington as President, though great men in many ways, were advocates of *implied powers* in the Constitution. Adams and Hamilton were *Nationalists* at first, roughly equivalent to the modern liberal. They were for consolidating power in the Federal government. Jefferson was similar to the modern conservative. He was a strong advocate of States' Rights, the sovereignty of the States, and the sovereignty of *the people*. Those who thought like Jefferson were known as *Federalists* during, and prior to the Constitutional Convention of 1787. Because the *Nationalists* views of consolidating power were not popular by the time John Adams became President in 1797, the *Nationalists* had appropriated to themselves the name of *Federalists*, but continued to follow their theories of consolidating power in the Federal government. The true

Federalists of the earlier days came to be known in the 1790's as the Republican Party, of which Thomas Jefferson is considered the founder. This Republican Party should not be confused with the Repubican Party which was reorganized in 1854, and elected Abraham Lincoln as President in 1860. The Republican Party of Thomas Jefferson was later called the Democratic-Republican party, and eventully the Democratic party.

Like Jefferson, the Republicans favored a limited central government which respected states' rights and allowed for broad citizen participation.

The philosophical differences between the Federalists and the Republicans were destined to exert an immeasurable influence on American politics for generations.

Today the names are changed or twisted, but the basic differences between these opposing views of consolidation and centralism on the one hand, and limited government and states' rights on the other, are still with us.

Today, those who believe in consolidating power in the Federal government are known as liberals, socialists, and one-worlders. But today those who would consolidate power have set their sights on the ultimate goal. Their beliefs have evolved to where they will be satisfied with nothing less than total power in a one-world consolidation of all people on the planet being ruled by a single world government.

Those from the Jefferson school of limited government and states' rights are called conservatives or populists, or libertarians. They advocate a strict constructionist view of the Constitution, and believe, because it was designed to control the tendency of human nature to abuse power and authority, that the Constitution for the most part, is as valid today as it was in 1787. "Times change," but human nature remains the same since Adam and Eve.

The liberals and socialists, on the other hand, view the Constitution as out of date and of little value in a modern world. They want judges who will rule according to a certain social agenda, and who will twist the original meaning and intent of the Constitution to suit their current political agenda.

What they really want is to eliminate the Constitution entirely. To this end, they have written the proposed *New Constitution for the New States of America.*

The views of Thomas Jefferson and James Madison, fondly called the Father of the Constitution, and other early American patriots who established this nation, attempted to delegate only that amount of power necessary to insure the happiness, peace, and domestic tranquility of the people. Their views have proven valuable and workable and worth sustaining for the happiness of ourselves, our children, and future generations.

To insure against the success of the liberals and socialists eventually being able to dismantle and entirely destroy the Constitution, it is essential for elected officials in both State and Federal governments to understand the legal relationship between *the people*, the *states*, and the *Federal* government. It is desireable that every citizen understand how this nation is put together under the contract by which we are governed, the Constitution.

The leaders of those who wish to eliminate the Constitution and consolidate power recognize the value of ignorance of the masses. Thus, the deliberate lowering of the educational standards of the public schools in America today. And the intended mass destruction of the nation's moral structure; the intended corruption we see taking place at every level of government and in the private lives of millions of Americans. Ignorance, corruption and immorality are the ingredients which lead to consolidation of government power. At a certain advanced state, things get so bad that the people, in crying out for law and order against the anarchy of the streets, will demand what the socialists have been seeking all along; a powerful central government which will rule with a rod of iron. Unknown to the masses, until it will be too late, the people wake up to find they have shackled themselves with tyranny from which there will be little likelihood of escape.

The Founders of America knew and taught the value of education and morality if a people expected to live in freedom. John Adams, though a disappointment as President, nevertheless, recognized what it takes to sustain liberty. He said: "our Constitution was made only for a moral and religious people. It is wholly inadequate to the government of any other." *

To clearly understand the relationship of the States, the Federal government and *the people*, let's start at the beginning.

It is a self-evident fact that every man and woman, rich or poor, ignorant or educated, black, white, brown, yellow or red, poor manners or good, should be equal before the law, or under the law. Thomas Jefferson in *The Declaration of Independence*, put it this way: "We hold these Truths to be self-evident, that all Men are created equal, that they are endowed by their Creator with certain inalienable Rights,...." Some quibble over this statement in the Declaration of Independence, but we all know what was meant. It is equally self-evident that all men are not created equal in abilities, talents, physical attributes, mentalities, etc. Jefferson meant we are all equal before God and man in our absolute right to equal treatment, equal justice, equal mercy under the laws of God and man. In the final judgment, we can be assured that God will be color-blind and status-blind in dispensing justice and mercy; that previous wealth or status or honor of men will be irrelevant. Ideally, this is the way the laws of man should also operate. This is the way men deserve to be equal with each other.

Jefferson went on to say in the Declaration, that among the rights of men are,..."Life, Liberty, and the Pursuit of Happiness—that to secure these rights, governments are instituted among men, deriving their just powers from the consent of the governed."

If we lived in a society of just men, where everybody truly loved everybody else and sought the happiness of his neighbor

---

* As quoted by John R. Howe, Jr., *The Changing Political Thought of John Adams*, Princeton, N.J.; Princeton Univ. Press, 1966, p. 185.

as well as that of himself, there might be no need for government. A state of anarchy, or no government might work just fine. Perhaps some sort of corporate structure would be needed to adjust honest differences of opinion among men, but not an instrument of force. Government is force. We have found it to be absolutely necessary to domestically control the criminal element which always exists among men. We have found it to be absolutely necessary nationally to protect us from the criminal element of other nations which might attack our borders were we to leave ourselves defenseless without the police protection of a standing army.

Not too long after Columbus "discovered" America, many people began migrating here for opportunity and freedom. Many came to escape the oppression of kings and tyrants. At first, some of these emigrants governed their own little groups. Since there were no other people, except Indians, who also operated with little government, if any, self-government was the only government possible. This was the status of the Pilgrims who landed at Plymouth in 1620.

By 1776, the population of the Colonies had reached approximately 2,500,000. Each of the thirteen Colonies had their own separate colonial governments, but the Crown of England presided over them all. As all governments tend to do with age, King George was becoming more and more oppressive.

During the ten years preceding 1776, things had gotten so bad, many of the colonists decided they had taken enough of the abuses and oppression of England and something had to be done. All thirteen Colonies sent representatives to Philadelphia to figure out the best course to follow.

From this assembled delegation, on July 4, 1776, the Colonies sent King George a powerful message telling him they would no longer allow England to preside over them. They declared themselves to be free and independent States, or Nations, in that well known and revered document officially known as *The Declaration of Independence*.

From that time forward, those thirteen little States, or little Republics, or Nations, were in fact, independent, sovereign, self-governing Nations. There was a problem of course. King George and Great Britain did not take kindly to these colonial rebels and their Declaration of Independence. The Colonies were revolting so far as the king was concerned. The leaders of this rebellion were traitors to the Crown and would suffer accordingly. *Secession*, or separation, would not be allowed.

War and bloodshed followed. For over 200 years, we have honored the patriots who fought the Revolutionary War in their *secession* from England.

More than five years later, the British General, Cornwallis, surrendered to George Washington on October 19, 1781. This, in effect, ended the Revolutionary War and the Colonies made valid and binding the independence they had so bravely declared five years earlier.

Except for a few minor skirmishes in the South, an unproclaimed truce was in effect after the Cornwallis surrender at Yorktown. The war, however, did not officially end until a final agreement was reached. Official recognition was not given by England until the signing of the Treaty of Paris on September 3, 1783.

The settlements negotiated in this Treaty were complicated by considerations involving France, Spain, and the Netherlands, as well as British and American interests.

The first article of the treaty, and the most important, recognized the former colonies to be ***"free, sovereign, and independent states."***

The Colonies declared themselves to be independent on July 4, 1776. It became official, and recognized by the world September 3, 1783. Nothing has changed since then. The original thirteen States, or Nations, have been joined by thirty-seven more States bringing the total to fifty. But all still remain *free, sovereign and independent states.*

After July 4, 1776, the Colonies were proud of their newly independent status, though British opposition made future independence far from certain. The Colonies, now claiming Statehood, realized they must work together if they were going to succeed against King George. To this end, after months of haggling, wrangling and much stress, representatives in Congress assembled, on November 15, 1777, and finally agreed on what were called the *Articles of Confederation.*

These Articles were a weak compact between the thirteen sovereign states. The document made it clear that they were to remain supreme, independent, and largely disunited. They emphasized *perpetual union*, but did not consolidate their thirteen sovereignties into a general union. In this form, the Articles of Confederation were sent to the states for ratification.

The States debated the ramifications of a central government for years. The last State, Maryland, did not adopt the Articles until March 1, 1781.

Meanwhile, George Washington and his small army were desperately trying to fight the war for independence. The States, through the Congress, operated under the Articles of Confederation all through the war though they were not formally and officially ratified until the war was almost over.

Though the Articles of Confederation emphasized perpetual union, what happened to this agreement, this contract...this *treaty*, between the thirteen states of early America? This question is of utmost importance in considering laws, agreements, contracts, or treaties between nations.

Following the Revolutionary War, the States found themselves continually quarreling and wrangling with each other over such things as commerce, tarriffs, and trade, etc. England and Spain expected the United States to collapse. So did many Americans. Internal revolts and civil war were threatened. Independence from Great Britain was nice, but there was definitely more to governing themselves than those early Americans had realized. The governing document, the Articles of Confederation, simply was not working out and something had to be done.

By the Spring of 1787, preparations were being made to again have the States send representatives to Philadelphia to revise the Articles of Confederation, so as to make them more effective in reducing tensions between the States.

Beginning in May, 55 representatives of most of the States

eventually showed up out of 73 who had been appointed. All the States except Rhode Island had representatives at this Constitutional Convention at some time. Forty-two delegates remained to see the work finished, of which 39 actually signed the proposed Constitution to unite the 13 States on September 17, 1787.

> From the record of that day:
> "In Convention, Monday September 17th, 1787.
> "PRESENT
> "The States of New Hampshire
> Massachusetts
> Connecticut
> Mr. Hamilton from New York
> New Jersey
> Pennsylvania
> Delaware
> Maryland
> Virginia
> North Carolina
> South Carolina
> Georgia
>
> "RESOLVED,
> "That the preceding Constitution be laid before the United States in Congress assembled, and that it is the opinion of this Convention, that it should afterwards be submitted to a Convention of Delegates, chosen in each state by the people thereof, under the recommendation of its Legislature, for their assent and ratification; and that each Convention assenting to, and ratifying the same, should give notice thereof to the United States in Congress assembled.
> "Resolved, That it is the opinion of this Convention, that as soon as the Conventions of nine States shall have ratified this Constitution, the United States in Congress assembled, should fix a day on which electors should be appointed by the States which shall have ratified the same, and a day on which the electors should assemble to vote for the President, and the

time and place for commencing proceedings under this Constitution. That after such publication, the electors should be appointed and the Senators and Representatives elected: That the electors should meet on the day fixed for the election of the President, and should transmit their votes certified, signed, sealed and directed, as the Constitution requires, to the Secretary of the United States in Congress assembled, that the Senators and Representatives should convene at the time and place assigned; that the Senators should appoint a President of the Senate, for the sole purpose of receiving, opening and counting the votes for President; and that after he shall be chosen, the Congress, together with the President, should without delay, proceed to execute this Constitution.

"By the unanimous order of the Convention,
George Washington, President.
William Jackson, Secretary."

It should be remembered that the Constitution at this time was a mere proposal to Congress, which Congress would then submit to the States for either their rejection or adoption. And this Congress was operating under the weak authority of the Articles of Confederation, which all the States had agreed would be *perpetual,* but which now, it was proposed, would be by implication, abandoned, eliminated, or done away with entirely. Some features of the Articles of Confederation would be retained, but the new proposed Constitution was radically different, though it remained merely a contract, or compact, between independent and sovereign states.

The following commentary along with the above quoted Resolution and the Constitution itself were submitted to Congress.

"In Convention, September 17, 1787

"Sir,

"We have now the honor to submit to the consideration of the United States in Congress assembled, that Constitution which has appeared to us the most adviseable.

"The friends of our country have long seen and desired, that the power of making war, peace and treaties, that of levying money and regulating commerce, and the correspondent executive and judicial authorities should be fully and effectually vested in the general government of the Union: but the impropriety of delegating such extensive trust to one body of men is evident—hence results the necessity of a different organization.

"It is obviously impracticable in the foederal(sic) government of these States to secure all rights of independent sovereignty to each, and yet provide for the interest and safety of all individuals entering into society, must give up a share of liberty to preserve the rest. The magnitude of the sacrifice must depend as well on situation and circumstance, as on the object to be obtained. It is at all times difficult to draw with precision, the line between those rights which must be surrendered and those which may be reserved; and on the present occasion, this difficulty was encreased(sic) by a difference among the several states as to their situation, extent, habits, and particular interests.

"In all our deliberations on this subject, we kept steadily in our view that which appears to us the greatest interest of every true American, the consolidation of our Union in which is involved our prosperity, felicity, safety, perhaps our national existence. This important consideration, seriously and deeply impressed on our minds, led each State in the Convention to be less rigid on points of inferior magnitude, than might have been otherwise expected; and thus the Constitution, which we now present, is the result of a spirit of amity, and of that mutual deference and concession which the peculiarity of our political situation rendered indispensible.

"That it will meet the full and entire approbation of every State is not perhaps to be expected; but each will consider, that had her interests been alone consulted, the consequences might have been particularly disagreeable or injurious to others, that it is liable to as few exceptions as could reasonably have been expected, we hope and believe, that it may promote the lasting welfare of that country so dear to us all, and secure her freedom and happiness is our most ardent wish.

"With great respect,
We have the honor to be,

> Sir,
> Your Excellency's most
> Obedient and humble servants,
> George Washington, President.
>
> By unanimous order of the Convention.
> His Excellency
> The President of Congress."

Eleven days later the following resolution was passed by Congress.

"*The United States* in Congress Assembled, Friday, September 28, 1787:

"Present—New Hampshire
>   Massachusetts
>   Connecticut
>   New York
>   New Jersey
>   Pennsylvania
>   Delaware
>   Virginia
>   North Carolina
>   South Carolina
>   Georgia
>   and from Maryland, Mr. Ross"

(Again, Rhode Island did not participate)

"Congress, having received the Report of the Convention, assembled in Philadelphia,

"Resolved Unanimously,

"That the said report, with the Resolutions and Letter accompanying the same, be transmitted to the several Legislatures, in order to be submitted to a Convention of Delegates, chosen in each State by *the People* (emphasis added) thereof in Conformity to the Resolves of the Convention, made and provided in that Case.

"Charles Thomson, Secretary"

The proposed contract, agreement, treaty, trust or compact; whatever we might choose to call the Constitution, for it is all of these, would only become effective if at least nine states agreed to adopt it. If only one or two, or eight States ratified this proposal, it would have no effect; it would be as if no proposal had ever been submitted. The Articles of Confederation would remain in effect, and in fact, was the governing document through all of 1787 and part of 1788 insofar as eleven States were concerned; perhaps through May 29, 1790, for Rhode Island, which is the date she finally joined the Union.

Following ratification by the ninth State, New Hampshire, on June 21, 1788, the nine ratifying States, at this point, had abandoned the *perpetual union* of the Articles of Confederation. The four remaining States, under the *perpetual* Articles of Confederaton, until they ratified the new Constitution, retained the legal right to be governed, and to make any rightful, lawful, demands under the Articles of Confederation to which they might have need.

Virginia ratified the new Constitution June 25, 1788. During this four day period, from when the new Union was officially formed on June 21, Virginia was not part of the Union. Virginia stood alone, outside this new Union, as did the three remaining former Confederate sister States. These four were now on their own as free, independent and sovereign nations, exactly as was France, Spain, Great Britain or any other sovereign nation. New York did not join the new Union until July 26, 1788. North Carolina was undecided whether or not to join for 17 months, but finally committed November 21, 1789. Rhode Island waited for almost two years but came in May 29, 1790.

June 21, 1788, the day New Hampshire joined eight other States in adopting the new Constitution, which on that historic day, joined nine of the thirteen States in a *brand new Union*, was a day of great celebration by the nine. Delaware, Pennsylvania, New Jersey, Georgia, Connecticut, Massachusetts, Maryland, South Carolina, and at last, New Hampshire. This fulfilled the requirement of the proposed contract, the Constitution, that upon the acceptance of any nine of the thirteen, those nine would form a new Union. The name would remain the same as the old Union, *the United States*, but it was a new, and very different union, under a very different contract. And the name of the contract was changed. The old contract was called *the Articles of Confederation*, the new contract was called a *Constitution*. The old contract specifically stated, in *four places*, that the old union shall be "*perpetual*." The new contract said nothing about perpetual union.

The Articles of Confederation did not become binding on any State until all thirteen had ratified, or agreed to adopt them. The new contract only required nine of the thirteen States to become effective.

The new Constitution only required that three-fourths of member States need agree in order to amend, change, or even abolish and abandon the Federal government. The Articles of Confederation required unanimous consent of all thirteen in order to amend, abolish, abandon, or change in any way. To quote from Article XIII: "And the Articles of this confederation shall be inviolably observed by every state, and the union shall be perpetual; nor shall any alteration at any time hereafter be made in any of them unless such alteration be agreed to in a congress of the united states, (note united states was not capitalized) and be afterwards confirmed by the legislatures of every state."

Whoa! Perpetual? Unanimous consent to change? Was not the new Constitution itself an abandonment of the Articles of Confederation; an elimination, or discarding of that Union which had been agreed only some six years before, was to be perpetual? Now under this new proposed Constitution, they were agreeing that only nine could not only change the Articles of Confederation, they were saying that only nine States could abandon, or *secede* from the other four. Nine States could separate themselves from the remaining four in violation of their solemn compact, the Articles of Confederation.

The Constitution of 1787 was an *unlawful* proposal of *revolution*.. It was an open and direct violation of established law, as a proposal, and it was *secession*, or separation from the four States which were left out, after nine States joined under the new proposal. The Constitution was secession, little different than the Colonies *secession* from England with the Declaration of Independence of July 4, 1776. The Constitution was secession, little different from that of South Carolina on December 20, 1860, and the other ten States which followed her in 1861.

On June 21, 1788, nine States *seceded*, separated, abandoned, left to fend for themselves, their four sister States, Virginia, New York, North Carolina and Rhode Island. June 21, 1788, marked perhaps one of the greatest revolutions of all time, yet one of the most quiet and peaceful revolutions imaginable. It was a strange revolution. It was violation of established law by men, and States, which men for the most part, were men of high moral character, and men who believed in honoring, obeying and sustaining the law. Yet nine States, led by men of great character, with little apparent shame, openly violated the old contract, and said to the four outsiders, "join us or stay out; we nine are going to operate under a new contract called the Constitution."

What if one or more of the four States which had been abandoned, or *seceded* from, should insist on maintaining the old Union under the Articles of Confederation? What if one or more of these four States refused to *ever* join the new Union?

What if Rhode Island, which refused to even send delegates to Philadelphia to so much as discuss the revision of the Articles of Confederation, should attempt to hold all the States to the old contract? If Rhode Island would not discuss revision, what in the world would she think of the more radical proposal of complete abandonment of the Articles of Confederation?

Rhode Island, by not participating, could feel very secure that no matter what the other 12 states did in Philadelphia during that hot summer of 1787, no revisions changes or amendments, and certainly no abandonment of the Articles of Confederation was possible without her participation and consent. At least according to law! Might we suppose Rhode Island was outraged when she heard of this new Constitution proposal, the adoption of which would require only nine States?

It is true, Virginia quickly joined the first nine States in this revolution only four days later on June 25, 1788, and New York came in just one month later, July 26, 1788. But North Carolina and Rhode Island were still out of the new Union when George Washington took the oath of office as our first President on April 30, 1789, and there was some question whether or not these two States might ever join in adopting the Constitution. North Carolina voted it down the first time.

The legal questions of adopting the Constitution, while quietly abandoning the Articles of Confederation, were subtle and somewhat embarrassing to our fathers. In pursuing these questions, there is no intent to defame or ridicule them. On the contrary, they are held in highest esteem by this writer. We are dwelling on these matters to point out that *secession*, even though at first shocking to the average person as a serious modern proposal, is historically sound, has strong precedents in the history of the United States, and is more lawful, should it be needed as a remedy today, than it was when our fathers adopted the Constitution we now honor as the Supreme Law of the land.

James Madison touched slightly on the matter of the nine States adopting the Constitution, which would leave out four States. In the Federalist Papers, number 43, part 9, near the end of this long essay, he quotes Article VII of the *new* Constitution which says: "The ratification of the conventions of nine States shall be sufficient for the establishment of this Constitution between the States, ratifying the same."

Now let's follow the reasoning of Madison, one of the greatest of the Founding Fathers. He says, "This article speaks for itself. The express authority of the people alone could give due validity to the Constitution. To have required the ratification of the thirteen States would have subjected the essential interests of the whole to the caprice or corruption of a single member..."

This statement is somewhat amusing, yet a sad commentary on the weakness of human nature. This was a blatant rationalization by a great and honest man, that "well, in this particular case, we can't be bothered with the technicalities of the law...well, yes, the law, the Articles of Confederation, do say all thirteen States must agree to any changes, but after all, it just isn't practical."

Even Mr. Madison dredged up a bogeyman as justification for not complying with the law. He was saying, one State might subject the other twelve to "caprice or corruption." Nevertheless, was that not in accordance with their original contract?

Speaking of the lawful necessity of all thirteen States agreeing to abandon, or change, the Articles of Confederation, Mr. Madison continues: "...It would have marked a want of foresight in the convention, which our own experience would have rendered inexcusable."

Mr. Madison continues: "Two questions of a ***very delicate nature*** (emphasis added) present themselves on this occasion: 1. On what principle the Confederation (Articles of Confederation) which stands in the solemn form of a compact among the States, can be superseded without the unanimous consent of the parties to it? 2. What relation is to subsist between the nine or more States ratifying the Constitution, and the remaining few who do not become parties to it?

"The first question is answered at once by recurring to the absolute necessity of the case; to the great principle of self-preservation; to the transcendent law of nature and of nature's God, which declares that the safety and happiness of society are the objects at which all political institutions aim and to which all such institutions must be sacrificed..."

Such twisted rationalization. In other words, "the end justifies the means," which is an argument all honest men normally reject when reaching for an excuse to justify their actions.

Continuing: "...Perhaps also an answer may be found without searching beyond the principles of the compact itself. It has been heretofore noted among the defects of the Confederation that in many of the States it had received no higher sanction than a mere legislative ratification. The principle of reciprocality seems to require that its obligation on the other States should be reduced to the same standard..."

WOW! Now we are being told, the Articles of Confederation really didn't amount to anything anyway. After all, they were held in such low esteem and the Articles were not adopted by the people themselves, but were the result of "mere legislative ratification." In other words, the State legislatures, mere agents of *the people*, not *the people* themselves, ratified the Articles of Confederation. And since such lowly ratification by *some* of the State legislatures made the contract legal, all parties, or all States, were to be bound equally, one State not being bound to a higher standard than that of the lowest.

This concept is based on true principles. For example, some states entered the Union under certain congressional restrictions which had not been required of others, yet once accepted as a State of the Union it should be argued that all States are equal. Congress has, on occasion, forced compliance with its views within the Constitution of the new State. However, once a member of the Union, any coercive congressional restrictions written in the new State's Constitution might be deleted or changed according to the will of the people of that State. *Coyle vs. Smith*, 221 U.S. 559; 31 S. Ct. 688; 55 L. Ed. 853 (1911).

It is almost inconceivable that Mr. Madison and our fathers could have resorted to such outlandish reasoning to justify an unlawful proposal to abandon the Articles of Confederation. The logic was a desperate attempt to give the appearance of acting in accordance with law, when in fact, they were proposing an overthrow of, or revolution against, established law and established government.

What is so amazing is, the tortured reasoning of Mr. Madison was not really necessary. The Declaration of Independence, then only 12 years old, they all accepted as justification for their *secession* from Great Britain. Their current proposal of *secession*, the Constitution, was not anticipating war or bloodshed. And the Declaration of 1776 spelled out very clearly how it is the right of a people to change one form of government for another.

Perhaps Mr. Madison and others were troubled by the fact they had written in the phrase *perpetual union*, not once, but four times, in the Articles of Confederation. But did they not all understand this was more for show than it was as law? They all knew the impossibility of actually binding sovereign nations to the terms of a treaty, compact, or contract. Did they not insert the phrase *perpetual union* in the old contract four times, the more to impress *Great Britain*, that if she continued against one or more of the thirteen States, she would have to fight them all?

It is apparent that *perpetual union* was intended as a bluff, as the thirteen Colonies played their revolutionary hand against Great Britain. Perhaps such a bluff would contribute to the remote possibility that King George would see their determination and be more willing to compromise if he thought he was up against "Perpetual Union" and a group of rebels who obviously were not going to back down.

If perpetual union was a bluff, it didn't work. Neither did it work as law. Neither was there any precedent for such high and mighty sounding aspirations, or pretended loyalties. One generation cannot lawfully, ethically, morally, or in any other way, bind succeeding generations. The fathers of one generation might attempt to hand down law and values of their own to their children and grandchildren, but the succeeding generation is free to either accept or reject the wisdom and law of their fathers.

No confederacy of states or nations can ever be said to be perpetual. Divorce between the sexes and between nations is universal, and common. Such divorces are accomplished peacefully sometimes; at other times with bitterness and long-lasting hatreds.

When humanity finally matures, divorce of all kinds will be accomplished with calm, reason and negotiation, and in peace. There is no reason for hostility, bitterness or war. Everybody recognizes that every man and woman is different than every other person on the planet. When we discover it is impossible to live together in peace, we should simply *agree to disagree*, and separate from each other. But why not do it in peace? Why try to destroy another person or another nation? What is accomplished by bitterly trying to hurt, or destroy, another person or nation? Everybody loses when energy is expended in destruction of lives or property. War reduces a certain percentage of the earth's wealth; it destroys millions, or billions of man hours previously spent in production of goods and commodities. And such utter foolishness, when that which is sought by all people, happiness, can much more easily be reached through calm reason and negotiation.

When all else fails, sometimes separation, or *secession* is the most logical, the most reasonable solution. Why James Madison did not make this simple case, is not readily seen. Nevertheless, it is the case we make in this writing.

But to continue with the amazing line of reasoning of the great Madison: "...A compact between independent sovereigns founded on ordinary acts of legislative authority, can pretend to no higher validity than a league or treaty between the parties. (The Articles of Confederation and the Constitution can both be defined as a league, a treaty, a compact. All are contracts, or agreements among one or more nations, or states.) It is an established doctrine on the subject of treaties that all the articles are mutual conditions of each other; that a breach of any one article is a breach of the whole treaty; and that a breach, committed by either of the parties, absolves the others, and authorizes them, if they please, to pronounce the compact violated and void..."

Here Mr. Madison is hinting that "nobody really paid much attention to the Articles of Confederation anyway." He is resurrecting, very subtly, skeletons in the common closets of the thirteen States. He is saying, "all of us violated the Articles of Confederation. All of us are sinners...no matter which nine of the thirteen States might eventually adopt the new Constitution, those nine can then remind the remaining four States of their violations; their breaking of the law, and thus making null and void, the old Articles of Confederation."

This time, Mr. Madison is using a valid and reasonable argument in his rationalizations, but isn't it amazing how we, as human beings, will let things slide, unless and until the time comes that we can turn a thing to our own advantage?

Mr. Madison continues: "Should it unhappily be necessary

to appeal to these delicate truths for a justification for dispensing with the consent of particular States to a dissolution of the federal pact, will not the complaining parties find it a difficult task to answer the multiplied and important infractions with which they may be confronted?"

Yes, indeed he was speaking of delicate truths. The Constitution, if adopted, would be *dissolving the union*, in violation of their own law. Somehow, "we must find justification for this *revolution*," though peaceful it was likely to be.

The Father of the Constitution continued: "The time has been when it was incumbent on us all to veil the ideas which this paragraph exhibits. The scene is now changed, and with it the part which the same motives dictate."

In other words, in the past we kept quiet, veiled, hid, and did not broadcast the numerous open violations of all thirteen States and the disrespect which we held for the Articles of Confederation. We all just sort of "went along to get along," to at least maintain some sort of cooperative union, though it was violated and broken at will by all, without any sort of enforcement mechanism.

How could any one of the four States which might refuse to ratify the Constitution complain? If one or more of them should attempt to argue *perpetuity* of the old contract, and the illegality of the new Constitution without the unanimous consent of all thirteen States, we *nine*, "will have to remind our errant and sinning sister States, that all thirteen of us committed numerous violations of the old contract. Therefore, under the laws of contracts, all thirteen are released from further obedience or obligation." Now we are relying on the law to justify the violation of another law.

"Times had changed." If non-joining States should complain, the *nine* would simply be forced to air all the dirty linen of any State which might object to the adoption of the Constitution.

Now let us consider the second question brought up by Mr. Madison above which was: "What relation is to subsist between the nine or more States ratifying the Constitution, and the remaining few who do not become parties to it?"

In answer: "The second question is not less delicate; and the flattering prospect of its being merely hypothetical, forbids an over-curious discussion of it. It is one of those cases which must be left to provide for itself. In general, it may be observed that although no political relation can subsist between the assenting and dissenting States, yet the moral relations will remain uncanceled..."

Mr. Madison here clearly exhibits the moral high ground to which our Fathers attempted on most occasions to adhere. Though no political ties will remain between the first nine States which might adopt the new Constitution, and the four remaining outside the new Union; even though a political and lawfully questionable separation, or secession, will have taken place, yet the nine States will retain moral obligations to the four outsiders. For example, should one or more of the four outside States be attacked militarily by a foreign power, the nine States then operating under the new Constitution would be morally bound to come to their defense. Though Mr. Madison doesn't say it, the obligations were greater than moral. Can there be any doubt that should this issue ever be debated in a court of law, that these obligations here put forth as moral, would actually be legal obligations under the lingering ties of the Articles of Confederation?

Mr. Madison concludes Federalist No. 43 with: "The claims of justice, both on one side and on the other, will be in force, and must be fulfilled; the rights of humanity must in all cases be duly and mutually respected; while considerations of a common interest, and above all, the remembrance of the endearing scenes which are past, and the anticipation of a speedy triumph over the obstacles to *reunion,* will, it is hoped, not urge in vain *moderation* on one side, and *prudence* on the other. Emphasis added.

Here is an admission that the Constitution was proposed *secession*, but it was "anticipated" the obstacles to reunion would not take too long.

The same would be true today. Should 38 or more States find it necessary to dissolve our present Union, it will be hoped a speedy reunion might thereafter be accomplished.

Remembering that all thirteen States had fought as brothers in the Revolutionary War, these and other "endearing scenes" should not be forgotten. The first nine States to join in the new Union should resort to "moderation" and not try to force or coerce any of the four States which might decide to remain outside this new Union, if in fact nine should actually decide to join. On the other hand, the four or fewer States which might decide the new Union is not for them, but prefer to hold and force all thirteen States to abide by and honor the original Articles of Confederation, which could not lawfully be changed without the dissenting States' consent; in these States, or State, Mr. Madison was urging "*prudence*." In other words, if you don't wish to join our new Union, "don't push your luck," or we may be forced to bring up those "delicate truths" of former violations under the Articles of Confederation. You four, "as sinners yourselves, don't get too pushy."

The old history books show our generation clearly that James Madison and most of the Founding Fathers of our nation, were honest and honorable men. The lesson for us today is, if even the greatest men among us will, on occasion, resort to weak rationalizations to accomplish what appears to be worthwhile and honorable ends, what will those who we might elect today do, who we might assume to be less honorable and honest, to accomplish what appears to them to be a great and worthy goal; a one-world government in which we scrap, or abandon, the Constitution of the United States?

Is it not conceivable if such great men as James Madison could rationalize the unlawful scrapping of the Articles of Confederation, American leaders in the 1990's might rationalize the unlawful scrapping of the Constitution in favor of what they perceive to be the necessity and desireability of a single world government in a *new world order*?

Madison and the other Founders were seeking a "more perfect Union." They were attempting to bring about increased "domestic tranquility," a more workable and efficient system of free trade among themselves, and a united single power to deal with other nations in commerce, and in case of war, a single military force under a single "commander in chief."

Our Fathers always retained the objective of maximizing individual freedom and minimizing the powers of government to maintain that freedom.

The objective of a *new world order* under the *United Nations* is to force the entire human family into compliance with the views and dictates of a few elite and "more intelligent" men. These perceive themselves to be superior to the rest of us and they, by right of their superior intelligence and greater wealth, which they succeeded in confiscating from *the people* through such massive deceptions as *The Federal Reserve system*, will force their will upon whatever remains of the human family after they eliminate millions, perhaps billions of undesireables and potential resisters. Unlike the Founding Fathers, the New World Order will maximize government power as it seeks to rule the planet with a *rod of iron*.

Should the New World Order succeed in doing away with our Constitution, it is probable that over half of America's 250 million people will have to be killed. Americans are more "spoiled" by freedom than any other nation on the earth. We therefore, pose the greatest threat, both before and after the "insiders" take over the world. Because we have grown up with the sweet fruits of liberty, we will give the greatest resistance to the power brokers who lust for control of humanity. The New World Order will have one answer for those of us who resist them. Death! And terror as they consolidate power!

Although the Constitution says nothing about abandoning the Articles of Confederation which were supposed to be perpetual, it appears that all parties, more or less, simly let go, abandoned, or assumed the Articles were no longer valid or binding.

As there was no war, or any sort of national emergency, from June 21, 1788, until Rhode Island joined in 1790, none of the four States outside the new Compact of Union appeared to have any need to make demands on the others who had abandoned the Articles of Confederation and adopted the new Constitution.

But what if Rhode Island or North Carolina had been

attacked by a foreign power during this interval, say by France, Spain, or even by King George who might have had second thoughts about granting independence to his former Colonies? These States would have, no doubt, called upon their former Confederate sisters for assistance in defending themselves, and no doubt, would have received it.

And since the old Articles were supposedly perpetually binding, they would have been able to make a powerful case of being *entitled* legally to full cooperation and military assistance. In fact, if they had decided to stay out of the new Union established by the new Constitution forever, would the old Articles of Confederation remain binding on those States which abandoned the Articles and joined themselves together under the new Constitution?

It appears from a legal standpoint both the Articles of Confederation and the Constitution were in effect during this time of June 21, 1788 through May 29, 1790. Would the States making up the new Union have honored the old Articles of Confederation had an emergency arose during this time frame? Yes! Mr. Madison recognized, at the least, "a moral obligation."

If the Articles of Confederation which had sewn within the fabric, the phrase of perpetual union, and yet it was quickly dissolved and replaced by the Constitution; and since the Constitution makes no such pretention of claiming perpetuity by saying nothing , is it reasonable to claim the United States, as presently constituted, is a nation of perpetual union? Of course not!

Perpetual union, like other unworkable parts of the Articles of Confederation, was a phrase which contradicted the history of nations and their dealings and treaties with each other. It should not be so, but Lenin was correct when he said, "treaties are like pie crusts, made to be broken." Lenin was merely making this remark as a student of history. Some nations are more honorable than others in keeping treaties and other agreements between them. Lenin and Soviet leaders who have followed him, have proved to be faithful disciples of this doctrine as they have broken treaties with the United States almost as quickly as they were signed.

Perpetual union was, and is, a contradiction of that great document which our Fathers, and we, revere most highly, and the adoption of which we remember as one of our most important national holidays, which we still celebrate every July 4, the Declaration of Independence. This grand document was more than an official statement telling King George and Great Britaln the Colonies were severing the ties of government between them. It was a declaration of *"secession,"* or a breaking away from, similar to the secession of 11 Southern States which seceded from the Union in 1860-61.

But the Declaration was adopted by men of high principle; men with a keen sense of right and wrong. Their collective conscience demanded of them that should their declaration lead to bloodshed, they must be able to morally justify the stand they had taken. The great character of these men would not allow them to go to war unless they felt they were justified in the eyes of any impartial judge. In their own eyes, they would only invite war if they were certain they held the moral high ground. The Declaration of Independence was an explanation of why the Colonies were morally justified in becoming independent little nations.

Fifty-five great men signed the Declaration of Independence on July 4, or shortly thereafter.* They declared, "...whenever any form of Government becomes destructive..., it is the Right of the People to alter or to abolish it..." It continues: "...Prudence, indeed, will dictate that Governments long established should not be changed for light and transient causes...But when a long train of abuses and usurpations, pursuing invariably the same object, evinces a design to reduce them under absolute despotism, it is *their right, it is their duty to throw off such government...*" Emphasis added.

---

*There were officially 56 signers of the Declaration of Independence. But the name of Thomas McKean of Delaware was not included in the list of signers printed by order of Congress on January 18, 1777, as he did not sign the engrossed copy until some time thereafter, probably in 1781.

Many of these abuses the colonists suffered under the King were listed. Few just men could argue with our Fathers. King George truly had been abusive, and they were justified in throwing off his attempts to force them to submit to his will.

If we really believe that which we say we revere, no government can ever be considered perpetual, so long as man, along with his weaknesses of the flesh is in charge. If, as Thomas Jefferson and the Founders declared in 1776, it is a *right* and a *duty* to throw off despotic government, that right and duty is eternal. What was true in 1776 was right for the South...or for the North, in 1861. It is true in the United States of America in 1993 and beyond.

Men of peace and goodwill tend to suffer oppression for a time, appealing to their oppressors by lawful and peaceful methods for justice and right. But when all else fails, Thomas Jefferson sadly observed: "The tree of liberty must be refreshed from time to time with the blood of patriots and tyrants. It is its natural manure." Journals of Continental Congress by Ford, Vol. 4:467.

It is very clear then, prior to the Constitution becoming effective with its ratification by the ninth State, New Hampshire, June 21, 1788, each of the thirteen States were *free, independent, and sovereign*. Thirteen separate nations; little Republics. Did the adoption of the Constitution change this status? Yes, but only to the extent that these thirteen little nations delegated certain limited and specified powers of their own to their new creation, the Federal or Central government. They did only that which any principal in a contract has a right to do. As the principal, they delegated to their newly created *agent* certain specified rights and duties.

The Constitution established an *agent* and *principal* relationship. In the laws of nations, or the laws of contracts, if an agent usurps more authority than was delegated by the principal, or if the agent becomes abusive or attempts to take advantage of his trusted position as agent, the principal at all times retains the right to recall part, or all, of any authority he has delegated. In such cases the principal remains in command and for valid reason, sometimes for no reason at all, has the right to make null and void any rights which he had temporarily delegated to his agent.

The Constitution is also a contract wherein the States agreed to delegate certain of their rights to a central authority which would speak and act for all in dealing with other nations, and to settle internal matters among themselves wherein the services of an unbiased third party would act as a final arbiter.

In the constitutional contract, the Founders did their best to limit the possibility their new creation of a central government might usurp undelegated authority, or might become abusive of its own creators. But the States of 1788 also understood, that even with their best efforts, it might be possible for their new creation to turn into a Frankenstein monster. In some States the vote on whether or not to join the Union was very close. For instance, Rhode Island and Providence Plantations ratified with 34 yeas and 32 nays, and then only after the Union had already been in existence for almost two years.

It is unlikely that even the required nine States would have joined in Union had they not been assured that a *Bill of Rights* would be added to the Constitution as Amendments. This was accomplished December 15, 1791 when Virginia ratified the first 10 Amendments and completed the required three-fourths of the States.

The *people* of those early days in America jealously guarded their liberties, and ours, when they so cautiously delegated just a few limited powers. To be sure the new President of the Union they would choose, the Congress they would elect, and the judges who would be seated understood their positions as *servants of the people* not masters, they adopted a catch-all Amendment which could not be more clear or unambiguous. This was the last and Tenth Amendment. It says: *"The powers not delegated to the United States by the Constitution, nor prohibited by it to the States, are reserved to the States respectively, or to the people."*

The States are still, in modern America, sovereign, free, and independent. So what happens if the President of the

United States usurps undelegated authority, not authorized in the Constitution? What happens if Congress and the President conspire together to usurp undelegated powers and infringe on the rights of the States or the People? Normally, the Supreme Court will be appealed to for a decision, and all parties will respect and comply with that decision, though all parties will not necessarily be pleased with decisions of the Supreme Court.

What if the Supreme Court flagrantly violates the Constitution by rendering a decision in obvious contempt of the Constitution, or takes jurisdiction in a case which should obviously remain in a State court?

The States are sovereign in all areas except where they have specifically delegated power to the Federal government. The Federal government is sovereign in those few areas for which the States made it responsible. What happens when the State and Federal governments disagree on an area of responsibility? What happens when both Federal and State governments claim it is their right to govern, or rule in a given situation? What happens when two sovereigns clash and there is no third party to appeal to for final arbitration? What happens when two sovereigns meet with irreconcilable differences?

Historically, these questions have been settled by resorting to force of arms, and the sovereign with the more powerful army settles the question in his favor.

Is this what, in the final analysis, our Fathers left us with when they gave us the Constitution of the United States? Does the Constitution guarantee us any more safety and peace, if we meet an irreconcilable difference, than nations and civilizations before us have secured? Is there no way man can avoid bloodshed, in the long run, in his attempts to live in peace and liberty?

These are hard questions and our Fathers did not answer them all.

When they adopted the Constitution, they, in fact, built right into the very structure, an irreconcilable difference with which many of our greatest statesmen, patriots, and lovers of liberty wrestled for decades. This issue was slavery. The best minds in America were unable to peacefully resolve the issue.

The words slave, or slavery, are not found in the Constitution. But representation and direct taxes were apportioned among the states by a formula which counted slaves as three fifths of "all other persons." Indians were not counted for purposes of taxes or representation. Article I, Section 2, paragraph 3.

Again, Article I, Section 9, Par. 1, says: "The migration or importation of such persons as any of the states now existing shall think proper to admit, shall not be prohibited by the Congress prior to the year one thousand eight hundred and eight, but a tax or duty may be imposed on such importation, not exceeding ten dollars for each person." This was a direct reference to the importation of slaves, and the Constitution itself prohibited such importation from Africa, or anywhere else, after the lapse of 20 years. This prohibition, it was hoped by many of the Founders, would gradually cause the demise and eventual elimination of slavery from the United States.

It would seem that to many of the writers of the Constitution, perhaps all, that down deep, even those who were advocates of the slave system, knew it was not right and did not want to soil, or encumber the Constitution with the actual word slave. Perhaps it was thought when succeeding generations should be able to accomplish that which they could not, the total abolishment of slavery, the words slave or slavery would not then be found within the pages of this grand and historical document of human liberty. Perhaps succeeding generations would not think too unkindly of their fathers, or be reminded of this black mark which they felt compelled to include in the Constitution for the sake of Union.

If Union of the thirteen States was to be possible, those of our Fathers who despised slavery and recognized its inconsistency with the principles of human liberty for which they had been willing to die, knew they must allow its continuance. If Union was to be possible, abolishment of slavery at that time was impossible.

Those of our Fathers who would, in their hearts, have no

part of slavery, truly found themselves to be the victims of that great biblical truth recorded by Moses: "for I the Lord thy God am a jealous God, visiting the iniquity of the fathers upon the children unto the third and fourth generation of them that hate me." Deuteronomy 5:9, Exodus 20:5.

The evil of slavery was deeply entrenched in American society when the Constitution was written in 1787. If Union of the 13 States was to be accomplished, and the majority considered Union desireable, those who opposed slavery with their heart and soul still felt compelled to have its protection and perpetuation written into the Supreme law of the land, the Constitution. Those who opposed slavery clearly seeing its hypocritical advocacy by many of their brethren, who insisted on their own right to be free, did succeed in gaining a compromise of sorts. This was, of course, importation of slaves would be banned forever after 20 years.

Things did not work out as the abolitionists had hoped. The irreconcilable difference of slavery persisted and intensified as the years and decades passed. Those who opposed slavery on moral grounds could not possibly compromise their conscience. Yet they found themselves in the position of having to defy the Constitution in part, though they loved it, and in the case of elected officials were sworn to uphold and defend it. Sixty-two years later, in 1850, and Union having proven beneficial to all the original thirteen States as well as additional States, slavery was still a matter of great agitation.

Slaves were continually running away and entering the borders of States which had abolished slavery, known as free States. Northern abolitionists were known to go into the South and deliberately stir up the slaves to rebel against their masters. The slave States complained to the Federal government, and to the governments of free States, that under the Constitution and laws passed to enforce it, they were bound by the law to arrest and return to their owners any slave found within the borders of the free States.

The Territories, which by 1850 included huge tracts of midwest and far west land which would eventually become a number of new States, were constitutionally regulated by

Congress. The Southern States insisted they had the constitutional right to take their "property," their slaves, into these territories, retain ownership, and work them just as they had in their previous home State. The Northern States were equally adamant that slavery would not be allowed in the territories.

With 20th century hindsight, we know who was morally right. But who was in the right legally? If you were the judge, what would you decide, and how could you legally, and constitutionally, justify your decision? Truly, "the chickens were coming home to roost." The sins of those early white Dutch, and those early black African slave traders, had harnessed their children and grandchildren to this evil monstrosity from which there appeared to be no escape. If there was any solution to slavery, it had escaped the best minds of the eighteenth and nineteenth centuries.

As early as 1820, the Congress accomplished what was considered to be a milestone. Congress passed a major Act, which proved to be a temporary pacifier, known as The Missouri Compromise, and it settled, somewhat, the question of slavery for some 30 years. The compromise provided for the admission of Missouri into the Union as a slave state but prohibited slavery in the rest of the northern Louisiana Purchase territory. It went into effect through an act of Congress signed by President James Monroe, March 6, 1820.

Before the Missouri Compromise was adopted, the issue of slavery extension was passionately debated for a year in Congress and by *the people* nationwide. Speeches and writings revealed the sectional differences that would eventually tear the Union asunder. Thomas Jefferson, who was now almost 77 years old, wrote: "This momentous question, like a fire bell in the night, awakened and filled me with terror." John Quincy Adams called it ". . .a mere preamble, a title page to a great, tragic volume."

In February, 1819 the House of Representatives considered a bill authorizing the territory of Missouri to frame a constitution (the first step toward statehood).In the past, territories south of the Ohio River and the Mason and Dixon

Chapter 4

Line had been automatically made slave states. Most of Missouri is north of that line, but many of its citizens were slaveholders.

A bill to permit slavery in Missouri on a temporary basis, but prohibiting further entry of slaves, passed the House but was rejected by the Senate. The matter was left unsettled until the next session of Congress. In the meantime, Alabama had been admitted as a slave state, making the number of slave and free states 11 each. If Missouri was admitted, the balance in the Senate, where each state had two votes, would be upset.

The Solution

The House passed a bill, March 1, 1820, requiring Missouri to be a free state. The Senate dropped the anti-slavery provision and added an amendment proposed by Senator J.B. Thomas of Illinois. The amendment provided that Missouri would be a slave state, but that slavery would be prohibited in the Louisiana territory north of 36° 30', the southern border of Missouri. This amendment was the heart of the compromise; it was made possible because Maine had applied for statehood as a free state and the admission of both Missouri and Maine would maintain the balance between free and slave states.

The Missouri constitution was presented to Congress for approval in 1821. It included a paragraph requiring the legislature to prevent the immigration of free Negroes into the state. The anti-slavery faction in Congress objected to this provision and a compromise bill, often called the Second Missouri Compromise, was passed on March 2, 1821. This measure required the Missouri legislature to pledge that it would never pass a law limiting the rights guaranteed to all citizens by the Federal government. Missouri was admitted on August 10, 1821.

Some of the above is taken from or directly quoted from the New Standard Encyclopedia, pages 443-444.

Thirty years later, in 1850, passions concerning slavery, still burned, perhaps more fiercely than ever. If the Union was to be maintained, another major compromise became essential. The Compromise of 1850 consisted of five separate statutes which became law in September, 1850. These statutes resulted from nine arduous months of debate over the issue of the extension of slavery into the Western territories. The sudden death in July of President Zachary Taylor, whose veto had been feared by the compromisers, and the willingness of many Northern and Southern leaders to relinquish their sectional differences to avert war, contributed to the final passage of the acts. The five bills were debated and voted on separately from September 9 to 20. At best, the Compromise of 1850 was a temporary truce between the slave and free states. Four years later its value was negated by the Kansas-Nebraska Act.

Part of this act provided: "...further, that when admitted as a state, the said territory, or any portion of the same, shall be received into the Union, with or without slavery as their constitution may prescribe at the time of their admission."

Once a territory was admitted as a State, it was on an equal basis, legally, with the thirteen original States, and the Constitution of a State can be changed at any time by the people of said State following the outlined procedure for amending it. Abolitionists fervently hoped for a day when every State would amend their constitutions and laws abolishing slavery forever. The slave-holding States feared the day might come when the sentiment of three-fourths of the States might be against slavery, and it would then be possible to amend the Federal Constitution banning slavery nationwide once and for all.

Perhaps the most important part, or act, of the five acts comprising the Compromise of 1850 was prefaced: "An act to amend, and supplementary to the act entitled, 'An act respecting fugitives from justice and persons escaping from the service of their masters,' approved February 12, 1793." In effect, the Act of 1850, was sort of an update of a 57-year-old law dating back to the beginning of the Union, insofar as fugitive slaves were concerned.

Section 4 of the act reads: "And be it further enacted, that the commissioners above named shall have concurrent jurisdiction with the judges of the Circuit and District courts of the United States...to take and remove such fugitives from service or labor, under the restrictions herein contained, to the state or territory from which such persons may have escaped or fled."

Section 5. "And be it further enacted, that it shall be the duty of all marshalls and deputy marshalls to obey and execute all warrants and precepts issued under the provisions of this act when to them directed; and should any marshall or deputy marshall refuse to receive such warrant, or other process, when tendered, or to use all proper means diligently to execute the same, he shall, on conviction thereof, be fined in the sum of $1,000, to the use of such claimant, on the motion of such claimant, by the Circuit or District Court for the district of such marshall; and after arrest of such fugitive by such marshall or his deputy, or while at any time in his custody under the provision of this act, should such fugitive escape, whether with or without the assent of such marshall or his deputy, such marshall shall be liable, on his official bond, to be prosecuted for the benefit of such claimant, for the full value of the service or labor of said fugitive in the state, territory, or district whence he escaped."

The assured self destruction of this Act and guaranteed anxiety and agitation of *the people*, perhaps only with 20th century hindsight, is obvious in the extreme.

Section 5 continues: "And the better to enable the said commissioners, when thus appointed, to execute their duties faithfully and efficiently, in conformity with the requirements of the Constitution of the United States and of this act, they are hereby authorized and empowered, within their counties respectively, to appoint, in writing under their hands, any one or more suitable persons, from time to time, to execute all such warrants and other process as may be issued by them in the lawful performance of their respective duties; with authority to such commissioners or the persons to be appointed by them, to execute process as aforesaid, *to summon and call to their aid the bystanders*, or posse comitatus of the proper county, when necessary to ensure a faithful observance of the clause of the Constitution referred to, in conformity with the provisions of this act; *and all good citizens are hereby commanded to aid and assist in the prompt and efficient execution of this law whenever their services may be required, as aforesaid, for that purpose;* Emphasis added.

Good citizens are supposed to respect and uphold the law. This is what we are taught. This is what we believe. The law and the Constitution required all people, not just those who believed in slavery, to assist the marshalls, or sheriffs, or other legally constituted officers of the law to help in the arrest of runaway slaves.

Section 6. "And be it further enacted, that when a person held to service or labor in any state or territory of the United States has heretofore or shall hereafter escape into another state or territory of the United States, the person or persons to whom such service or labor may be due, his, her, or their agent or attorney...may pursue and reclaim such fugitive person...and remove such fugitive person back to the state or territory whence he or she may have escaped as aforesaid. *In no trial or hearing under this act shall the testimony of such alledged fugitive be admitted in evidence...*" Emphasis added.

Slaves were not citizens. They were entitled to life and humane treatment from the slave owner, and the necessities of life, but that was about all.

Section 7 continues: " And be it further enacted, that any person who shall knowingly and willingly obstruct, hinder, or prevent such claimant, his agent or attorney, or any person or persons lawfully assisting him, her, or them, from arresting such a fugitive from service or labor, either with or without process as aforesaid, or shall rescue, or attempt to rescue, such fugitive from service or labor, from the custody of such claimant, his or her agent or attorney, or other person or persons lawfully assisting as aforesaid, when so arrested, pursuant to the authority herein given and declared; or shall aid, abet, or assist such person so owing service or labor as aforesaid, directly or indirectly, to escape from such claimant, his agent or attorney, or other person or persons legally authorized as aforesaid; or shall harbor or conceal such fugitive, so as to prevent the discovery and arrest of such person, after notice or knowledge of the fact that such person was a fugitive from service or labor as aforesaid, shall, for either of said offenses, be subject to a fine not exceeding $1,000 and imprisonment not exceeding six months, by indictment and conviction before the District Court of the United States for the district in which such offense may have been committed, or before the proper court of criminal jurisdiction, if committed within any one of the organized territories of the United States; and shall moreover forfeit and pay, by way of civil damages to the party injured by such illegal conduct, the sum of $1,000 for each fugitive so lost as aforesaid, to be recovered by action of debt in any of the District or Territorial courts aforesaid, within whose jurisdiction the said offense may have been committed."

Section 9. "And be it further enacted, that, upon affidavit made by the claimant of such fugitive,...it shall be the duty of the officer making the arrest to retain such fugitive in his custody and to remove him to the state whence he fled, and there to deliver him to said claimant....And to this end, the officer aforesaid is hereby authorized and required to employ so many persons as he may deem necessary to overcome such force, and to retain them in his service so long as circumstances may require. The said officer and his assistants, while so employed to receive the same compensation and to be allowed the same expenses as are now allowed by law for transportation of criminals, to be certified by the judge of the district within which the arrest is made, and paid out of the Treasury of the United States."

Thus, those who hated slavery; those whose conscience told them slavery was evil; those whose religion taught them slavery was ungodly, were not only compelled by law to assist in recovering runaway, or fugitive slaves, they were compelled through taxation, to share in the expenses of recovery.

This was supposed to be a great compromise, but to the sincere abolitionist, the situation was unbearable in the extreme. How does one react when one's conscience clashes with the law of the land? With the benefit of history, would we be capable of passing legislation superior, more appropriate, or effective, or fair, than that which was passed by our Fathers, as bad as it was, in 1850?

All the while the slaveholder stood solidly on the legal foundation of the Constitution, and there was no way to lawfully dislodge him except by appealing to his conscience.

In a compromise, both sides have to receive something as well as give. Those who opposed slavery made some headway in suppressing the slave trade in the District of Columbia with the Compromise of 1850.

This part of the Statute said: "Be it enacted by the Senate and House of Representatives of the United States of America in Congress assembled, that from and after January 1, 1851, it shall not be lawful to bring into the District of Columbia any slave whatever for the pupose of being sold, or for the purpose of being placed in depot, to be subsequently transferred to any other state or place to be sold as merchandise. And if any slave shall be brought into the said District by its owner, or by the authority or consent of its owner, contrary to the provisions of this act, such slave shall thereupon become liberated and free." Source: Statutes IX, pp. 446-458, 462-465, 467-468, as reprinted in the 1968 edition, The Annals of America, Volume 8, Encyclopaedia Britannica, Inc.

William H. Seward was a staunch abolitionist Senator from New York. He made the claim, there is a "higher law than the Constitution," in his attempts, like other Northerners, to justify their resistance to the Fugitive Slave Act. He urged his fellow Senators to consider not only the constitutional, but also the moral implications of slavery when they ruled on the status of the new territories.

Ralph Waldo Emerson, commenting on the Fugitive Slave Law in a speech delivered in New York on March 4, 1854, called it, "This filthy enactment." He said, "I will not obey it..."

In defying the law and the Constitution, the abolitionists established a vast interstate network which became known as the "underground railroad." This network assisted slaves in escaping to freedom. Southern Indiana and Ohio, free states, were major players in this "railroad."

A leader in this underground railroad, Levi Coffin left for posterity a fascinating, yet sad record of black men yearning to be free, and being helped along the way by white brothers who were willing to risk their own freedom to liberate slaves.

Mr. Coffin says: "Our house was large and well adapted for secreting fugitives. Very often slaves would lie concealed in upper chambers for weeks without the boarders or frequent visitors at the house knowing anything about it....

"The fugitives generally arrived in the night and were secreted among the friendly colored people or hidden in the upper room of our house. They came alone or in companies, and in a few instances had a white guide to direct them.

"...Sometimes slaves would manage to accumulate a little money by working at making baskets at night or on the Sabbath, and when they had saved a few dollars they were very willing to give it all to some white man in whom they had confidence, if he would help them across the river and direct them how to reach the Underground Railroad." Reminiscences, 2nd edition, Cincinnati, 1880, 298-311.

It is uncertain how effective, or how many negroes actually gained their freedom in this operation, but Southern outrage continued to mount, as abolitionists of the North invented one means after another in their never-ending determination to overcome slavery, even though they were flaunting the law and mocking the Constitution.

According to the law, Southern outrage was justified. If they obeyed the law when it was of benefit to others, they had the right to expect others to obey the law when it was of benefit to the South. All men of intelligence and common sense understand the necessity of obedience to law. In a government of law, individuals and States do not have the right to obey only those laws with which they agree. If every man obeyed only those laws which meet with his personal approval, chaos and anarchy would prevail. Organized government cannot exist for long in such a society.

According to the moral law that man should be free to live according to the dictates of his own conscience, the Northern position of resistance to slavery was justified. It would seem that the wisdom of Solomon himself would not have been sufficient to solve the impending crisis of the United States in the 1850's.

The irresistible force of moral law in the North was destined to explode in fury against the immovable object of constitutional law which stood like the rock of Gibraltar on the side of the South.

There was one possible remedy which might deny the grim reaper his harvest of blood, carnage and treasure. But fate would insist that the generation of Americans who would be living in 1861, would finally have to pay for the sins of their fathers who had brought slaves to the American Continent some 200 years before.

The one remedy which might have worked, if cooler heads had prevailed, the only possible remedy available, which might and could have prevented the bloodshed and horror of the Civil War was a separation, a divorce of the free States from the States which wished to maintain legal slavery. The legal term was *secession.*

In human relationships there occasionally comes a time when even honest and sincere men must agree to disagree in order to live in peace.

In marriage, a common ground for divorce in modern America, is irreconcilable differences. In some of these divorces, husband and wife, even though their irreconcilable differences are impossible to overcome, they retain respect, sometimes even love for each other, and occasionally even remarry one or more times. Separation between people, or nations does not have to be permanent, depending on the circumstances. The marriage contract is usually officially annulled by a Judge, but sometimes the separation takes place by one or both parties simply walking away forever.

People of all races religions and philosophies generally choose to associate with their own kind. This is nature. A man who is faithful to his wife does not usually choose friends who are having affairs. The local bar fly does not spend time with advocates of abstinence from liquor. Homosexuals do not enjoy being around those who condemn their practices as sinful. Most people prefer to marry their own race and in their own religion.

In spite of the best efforts of Washington for the past three decades to force mix the races in America, blacks still prefer the company of blacks, whites and other races ditto, as a general rule.

The point is, people can choose to live separately, or apart and still remain friends. Agreeing to disagree does not mean hatred or bitterness must accompany the disagreement. Divorce among nations does not, and should not have to mean war.

Rational people, especially educated, religious people of sound mind and reason, should be able to live in peace and harmony with each other. Observation and experience teaches all of us that great differences exist in the thinking and desires and policies of individuals, communities and nations. Life itself forces a certain amount of temporary integration from day to day. Nations find it advantageous economically to trade and barter, regardless of differences in national policy.

"Marriage for many people is a terrible form of physical and/or psychological bondage and the only healthy way out of it is divorce. But, as with marriage, divorce (as an option) 'should not be entered into lightly....' " 1992 Marlin Industrial Division, Inc., North Haven, Ct. Neither should alliances or confederacies of states or nations be broken lightly.

Governments should not, and usually cannot, force people to continue in the married state. It should be just as impossible to force nations, states, or communities to live together under one constitution if they have differences which are irreconcilable. To apply force or coercion in either case would not be right. And to apply force in the case of nations or states, which is likely to cause war, is madness and amorality, unless it is a case of a people rising up against tyranny.

Many statesmen in our early history, including Abraham Lincoln, recognized that the United States could not permanently endure half slave and half free. One or the other would eventually have to prevail if they were to remain under one government, or under one roof.

A "divorce" of one or more States from the Union had been threatened a number of times. Not just many in the South, but many in the North by 1860, felt separation was the only possible solution to slavery and other differences.

With hindsight, it is clear that secession of the South from the North, or vice versa, was the only possible solution to slavery in 1861. Secession was the right remedy, insofar as preventing war. It would not have freed the slaves, but the war was not begun for that purpose anyway. Secession was the only remedy which could have prevented bloodshed. Secession was threatened for decades, again and again, even by some in the North when they were forced to help round up runaway slaves to send them back to their masters.

Finally South Carolina did it. South Carolina gave notice and declared her independence from the Union, December 20, 1860. See Appendix, page 413.

If secession was the right remedy for irreconcilable differences, what went wrong? Why didn't it work out? Why did it result in the Civil War? Were our fathers, by the fate of being born in the United States and inheriting the problem of slavery, doomed to shed the blood of each other to the extent of one million men? (total killed and wounded in the Civil War. Actually killed on both sides, about 620,000. Estimates do not agree, but roughly 360,000 were killed on the side of the North, and 260,000 of the South. These estimates do not include civilian casualties).

The question of secession is as relevant today, as it was in 1860-61. The Civil War and the reasons it came about is a fascinating and sad part of the history of this great land which most of us cherish, and of which we are proud to be known as free born citizens.

Because the question of secession is still important, it seems prudent to examine closely, the nature of State and Federal governments, and the legal basis on which the eleven seceding Southern States built their case. Why did the South feel justified in leaving the Union? Did they attempt to justify their position legally? If so, were their legal arguments logical, and sound? If the North disagreed with the legality of secession, did they offer alternatives, or attempt to dissuade any of the Southern States from leaving the Union? Last of all, was secession allowed by the contract, or compact of Union, or the Constitution? Did the Constitution say anything at all about a State leaving the Union?

The main reason for this book is to explore the answer to these questions and determine, should the need ever arise, if secession of one or more States is a viable option in 1993 and beyond. Should the need arise, if secession should be an option chosen by one or more States, would it have a solid legal foundation? Or, as many would no doubt argue, would such an attempt simply be rebellion, and need to be put down by the President by sending in the United States army?

Since 1861, we have added Amendments thirteen through twenty-seven to the Constitution, but none of them address the question of secession. If secession was legal and lawful in 1860-61, it is legal and lawful in 1993 and beyond.

In addressing this monumental question of secession, there is no intent, nor desire, to bring about dissolution of the Union of the United States of America. There is no desire to harm our beloved country in any manner. On the contrary! In setting forth the legal arguments for secession, not emotional nor subjective arguments, it is hoped that those who would abandon, or destroy, or suspend the Constitution, if such there are, will reconsider their nefarious schemes of world domination. It is hoped, if there should happen to be a conspiracy to destroy the Constitution, the perpetrators will see the futility of their efforts, at least from a lawful perspective, and abandon any hopes or dreams they may have to bluff the American people into submission.

Secession was considered radical in 1861. It would be considered radical today. It is something which has never been considered, even by most patriots. Secession is an option which has not even entered the mind of most modern Americans. If the thought ever entered the mind, it was immediately dismissed with the thought that the Civil War settled that question for all time. The theory of eternal union is just that, a theory. It is an assumption with little, or no legal foundation. The Articles of Confederation which governed the United States previous to the adoption of the Constitution boldly stated that union of the 13 original States was to be in perpetuity. Eternal union under the Articles was not theory. It was plainly written in the contract itself.

Yet, what happened? As soon as it was seen the Articles of Confederation were unworkable, twelve of the thirteen States sent delegates to a convention, and the result was an abandonment of their perpetual union.

Our own history, in setting forth the case for secession, sets powerful precedents in making the case for dissolution of the United States in 1993 and beyond. But it must always be kept in mind, dissolution of our Union, like the dissolution of a marriage, should not take place for light or transient reasons.

If the old Union of the 1780's established in "perpetuity" was abandoned peacefully without a whimper, does it not seem reasonable, if circumstances should arise which leave free men no other reasonable choice, that one or more States might determine for themselves to leave the Union today, when the Constitution makes no claim to Perpetuity?

Our present Constitution says nothing about secession. If the old Union could break up and start over, when the contract specifically stated their Union was permanent, is it not reasonable to assume our present Union might also have a separation of one or more states, when the present contract does not even address the question? Of course! Reason alone tells us *sovereign, free and independent states* retain their sovereignty regardless of temporary compacts, treaties, or agreements they might make with other states, or nations. That any Sovereign State has a moral, as well as a legal right, to abandon an unworkable agreement, to abandon an agreement whose people have become so different it is no longer enjoyable to live together, or to abandon a contract which is being violated by one or more of the other contracting parties. Even though the contract is more than 200 years old, it is still only temporary, not perpetual, even if it said within the contract that it was perpetual, which it does not.

One generation cannot morally, ethically, or legally bind the next; nor is it even practical to attempt to do so. Without informed consent, without knowledge, without free choice, without even being born, it is impossible under contract law to legally bind an individual, or a nation, to an agreement of any kind.

If there is no other legal or viable solution to a problem jointly faced by two or more sovereigns, separation, or agreeing to disagree, or "divorcing" is not only the best remedy, it is the lawful and logical remedy. When bloodshed or war seems to be imminent otherwise, peaceful separation should be considered by far the better remedy.

When eleven Southern States seceded from the Union in 1860-61, law and reason was on their side. There was no reason for war. War would not have come if reason and patience had prevailed.

When thirteen Colonies seceded from their Union with Great Britain in 1776, law and reason was on their side, though not nearly so strongly, from a legal standpoint, as was the later secession of the South. War should not have come. But King George was a tyrant, and he was not about to lose all that real estate without a fight. But in law, the Colonies, like the South, were legally in the right.

Thomas Jefferson made the arguments best in the *Declaration of Independence*. In declaring the rights of men to be free, Jefferson's arguments are eternally valid. His reasoning makes as much sense today as it did in 1776.

If one or more of the 50 States choose to separate from the United States in 1993 or beyond, or if 38 States choose to dissolve the Federal government and sell Washington D.C. to the highest bidder, let us start with the same arguments we all revere, hold high, and celebrate every July 4, the Declaration of Independence. Let's bring Thomas Jefferson back, and let him make our arguments for us.

> "In Congress, July 4, 1776,
> A Declaration
> By the representatives of the
> United States of America
> in General Congress Assembled.

"When in the course of human events, it becomes necessary for one people to dissolve the political bands which have connected them with another, and to assume among the powers of the earth, the separate and equal station to which the Laws of Nature and of nature's God entitle them, a decent respect to the opinions of mankind requires that they should declare the causes which impel them to the separation."

Jefferson is not arguing legal necessity, he simply says common courtesy suggests they should declare their reasons for separation.

"We hold these truths to be self-evident, that all men are created equal, that they are endowed by their Creator with certain unalienable rights, that among these are life, liberty, and the pursuit of happiness."

It was understood then, and it is understood now, that when Jefferson said men were created equal, he meant equal before the laws of God and man. Our fathers undertood as well as we do, that men are not equal in mental and physical abilities, and those who would argue this point show the absurd lengths to which they will go in their attempts to make the Founding Fathers look bad.

Continuing with the same sentence: "That to secure these rights, Governments are instituted among men, *deriving their just powers from the consent of the governed* that whenever any form of government becomes destructive of these ends, it is the right of the people to alter or to abolish it, and to institute new government, laying its foundation on such principles, and organizing its powers in such form, as to them shall seem most likely to effect their safety and happiness. Emphasis added. Prudence, indeed, will dictate that governments long established should not be changed for light and transient causes; and accordingly, all experience hath shewn that mankind are more disposed to suffer, while evils are sufferable, than to right themselves by abolishing the forms to which they are accustomed. But when a long train of abuses and usurpations pursuing invariably the same object, evinces a design to reduce them under absolute despotism *it is their right, it is their duty, to throw off such government, and to provide new guards for their future security*. Emphasis added. Such has been the patient sufferance of these Colonies."

Such has been the patient sufferance of these 50 States for the last several decades as the Supreme Court, Presidents, more or less, from Franklin Roosevelt to the present time, and Congress have worked hand in hand to eliminate one constitutional protection after another, and to relegate *"states' rights"* to the garbage bin of history.

Continuing with the same sentence: "and such is now the necessity which constrains them to alter their former Systems of Government. The history of the present King of Great Britain is a history of repeated injuries and usurpations, all having in direct object the establishment of an absolute tyranny over these states. To prove this, let facts be submitted to a candid world."

The history of the Federal government from the passage of The Federal Reserve Act in 1913, and the adoption of the Income Tax by way of the 16th Amendment, also 1913, to the present time, "is a history of repeated injuries and usurpations, all having in direct object the establishment of an absolute tyranny over these states and *over the entire world*," Jefferson would need to add, if he were alive today.

"He has refused his Assent to Laws, the most wholesome and necessary for public good."

Our problem today is not a lack of laws out of Washington, our problem is the continual and never ending flow of laws, regulations and Executive Orders coming from Washington.

"He has forbidden his Governors to pass laws of immediate and pressing importance, unless suspended in their operation till his assent should be obtained; and when so suspended, he has utterly neglected to attend to them."

If our Fathers felt compelled to separate from their union with Britain because the King would not pass enough laws, how much more should Americans today feel justified in separating themselves from the Federal government when our liberties are threatened by too many, not too few laws?

"He has refused to pass other laws for the accommodation of large districts of people, unless those people would relinquish the right of representation in the Legislature, a right inestimable to them, and formidable to tyrants only."

Washington today, and for several years, has refused to release hundreds of millions, perhaps billions of dollars in Federal gas tax revenues back to the states, unless the states agreed to violate their constitutional sovereignty, and legislate laws on the State level, which met with the approval of the Federal government. For instance, in the 1970's, Washington said, "unless you reduce maximum speed limits to 55 miles per hour on all State roads, as well as freeways, we will withhold all Federal highway funds." By 1992, this restriction is still in place, but the Federal government now "allows" the States to increase the speed limit to 65 miles per hour on certain highways. Other forms of Federal punishment was threatened if a certain percentage of states did not pass laws compelling their citizens to wear seat belts when driving an automobile.

"He has called together Legislative Bodies at places unusual, uncomfortable, and distant from the depository of their public records, for the sole purpose of fatiguing them into compliance with his measures."

Washington has called together committees and authorized innumerable studies, deliberately hampered and stopped extension and increase of our industrial capacity, by wearing out and fatiguing entrepreneurs into compliance with its measures.

"He has dissolved representative houses repeatedly, for opposing with manly firmness his invasions on the rights of the people."

Washington has abused the judicial system, dissolving the rights of the people, and sending them to prison for opposing with manly firmness unjust laws, or "laws that never were" because they were unconstitutional "on their face," and were in obvious and direct contradiction of the Constitution.

"He has refused for a long time, after such Dissolutions, to cause others to be elected; whereby the Legislative Powers, incapable of annihilation, have returned to the people at large for their exercise; the state remaining, in the mean time, exposed to all the dangers of invasion from without and convulsions within."

We have no similar complaint today, but Jefferson makes

a powerful point in stating the truth that when there is no legislature, or organized government, the legislative powers remain in the people themselves. Only as the people delegate authority to elected officials, do they give up said authority...temporarily. For *the people*, can resume, or retake any authority which they have temporarily assigned to an agent.

"He has endeavoured to prevent the population of these states, for that purpose of obstructing the laws for naturalization of foreigners, refusing to pass others to encourage their migrations hither, and raising the conditions of new appropriations of lands."

Washington has allowed tens of thousands of illegal aliens, some say two to three million, to cross our borders and remain here on a permanent basis, often sapping our generous welfare systems, and other disgraceful government handouts.

"He has obstructed the administration of justice by refusing his assent to laws for establishing judiciary powers."

Washington has obstructed the administration of justice by prosecuting and imprisoning many who demand their rights under the Constitution.

"He has made Judges dependent on his Will alone, for the tenure of their offices, and the amount and payment of their salaries."

Presidents and the Senate have attempted, and sometimes succeeded, in "packing the Supreme Court," and lower courts, with liberal or socialist judges who will rule, not according to the *strict construction* of the Constitution, but according to their personal ideas of what is good for society and what appears to be politically expedient at the moment.

"He has erected a multitude of new offices, and sent hither swarms of officers to harrass our people and eat out their substance."

If Jefferson thought they had swarms of officers harrassing them in 1776, he would be astounded if he could take a look at the Internal Revenue Service and dozens of other Federal agencies which Washington has turned loose on our people today. One Congressman, George Hansen of Idaho, wrote a book about Internal Revenue abuses titled, *To Harass our People*. As a result, "he had to go," and accordingly, appropriate powers were brought to bear against him and he was soon defeated in his effort to maintain his seat in Congress. As an appropriate warning to those of us of lesser rank, George Hansen was also prosecuted on trumped up charges and sent to prison. Shades of King George!

"He has kept among us, in times of peace, standing armies without the consent of our Legislatures."

Since the end of World War II, we have maintained huge armies, navy and air force stationed around the world. To some extent, these may have been justified, but America cannot be the policeman for the world, and when we act as such, the very least we should have demanded, and should still demand, is payment in the billions of dollars for military services rendered, especially from Germany and Japan; who while we were protecting them, were investing billions of their own money into increasing their industrial and productive capacity in order to more effectively compete with the incredibly efficient industry and production facilities of America.

"He has affected to render the military independent of and superior to the civil power."

This has not happened to us...yet. Just in case the President of the United States should ever attempt it, is one of the reasons this book was written.

"He has combined with others to subject us to a jurisdiction foreign to our Constitution, and unacknowledged by our Laws, giving his assent to their acts of pretended Legislation:"

My how times never change! Jefferson could easily be referring to the United Nations Organization established in 1945 following World War II, and the World Court which the planners hope to eventually have take jurisdiction for the United Nations of the world. President George Bush, when he decided to take military action against Iraq and Saddam Hussein, sought first the blessing of the United Nations, after which he asked our own Congress for its consent; pretending the United Nations is more important than the Constitution.

Chapter 4

Nevertheless, though the U.N. gave its consent, if Congress had failed to go along and make appropriations, the President would have been limited in what he could have done.

We are overwhelmed with national and international laws, treaties, regulations, etc., many of them only "pretended," insofar as being constitutional. But unless they are challenged, they stand, and become permanent chains on our liberties.

"For quartering large bodies of armed troops among us:

"For protecting them by a mock trial, from punishment for any murders which they should commit on the inhabitants of these states:"

These murders are not uncommon in the present decade. The nation, insofar as it was not suppressed by the controlled media, was a witness in the summer of 1992 to such murders in Northern Idaho. One Vickie Weaver, wife of Randy Weaver, was shot, allegedly with babe in arms by Federal agents who were determined at all costs to get this family. The Federal agents also shot her teenage son, but the main person they were after was the husband Randy who allegedly sold a shotgun to an undercover Federal agent, the barrel of which was allegedly a fraction of an inch shorter than allowed by law. Depending on the reports one reads, or hears, there were apparently at least 200 Federal agents, possibly as many as 500, appropriately armed who surrounded the house of the Weavers. There is little doubt the whole family would have been murdered except for the intervention of many people in the local community and one presidential candidate running on the Populist Party ticket, Bo Gritz.

"For cutting off our trade with all parts of the world:

"For imposing taxes on us without our consent:"

The evidence is powerful that the income tax, by way of the 16th Amendment is not legal because the required three-fourths of the States never properly ratified it. This Amendment should be challenged by at least one State Attorney General under the *original jurisdiction* clause of the Constitution before the Supreme Court.

If Jefferson thought taxes were high without their consent,

he should be here to see how much higher they have become *with* our alleged consent. If rebellion and secession were justifiable on taxation alone, we would have split with the Federal government long ago, for our taxes are many times as much as the Colonists were paying in 1776.

"For depriving us, in many Cases, of the Benefits of Trial by Jury:"

We are subjected to almost the same abuse today. Yes, we do get a trial by jury if we demand it, but the jury is misinformed by the judges of the land, and told by those judges: "Your job in this case is to decide the facts. I will instruct you as to the law." If according to the law, as told the jury by the judge, a person is found guilty by facts presented, the jury is supposed to return a guilty verdict. The jury is not informed they have the right to decide whether or not they think the law is fair, just, or to what degree it might actually apply. They are not told they have the right, truly the duty, if they think the law is unjust, or unfair, they can completely disregard the judge's instructions. To ignore the judge would perhaps, seldom be wise, but juries have this power if they wish to exercise it. An informed jury is 100% in control in a criminal trial. It can even ignore all the facts, as well as the law, and find the defendant not guilty, even though it is obvious he is guilty. This would not be right either, but it has been known to happen in the United States, especially in the early days of the Republic.

If a jury chooses to ignore the judge's instructions and go against him, there is not a thing he, or anybody else can do about it. For more information on the power of the jury see, *Citizens Rule Book,* published by Liberty Library, 300 Independence Ave., SE, Washington, DC 20003. $1.00 per copy.

Jefferson continues: "For transporting us beyond seas to be tried for pretended offences:" (sic)

This is not yet a common occurrence, but if, and when, the New World Order replaces the Constitution, this will become a common method of securing guilty verdicts against those who protest too loudly against increasing encroachments on individual liberty under the one world government.

It appears that we are in the beginning stages of this future horror with what might be considered a trial run, though this particular case is not necessarily the first instance of the United States conspiring with a foreign nation to unjustly prosecute a U.S. citizen.

A retired Cleveland autoworker, Mr. John Demjanjuk, was accused of Nazi war crimes in World War II. He was spirited out of the United States with the blessing of our State Department and put under the jurisdiction of the Israeli courts. He was, expectedly, found guilty and sentenced to death. The verdict is, in the fall of 1992, on appeal with the Supreme Court of Israel. Fortunately, it appears facts which our government attempted to cover up which would have cleared Mr. Demjanjuk of any offense have come to light, and the Supreme Court of Israel may yet find in behalf of this U.S. citizen.

"For abolishing the free system of English Laws in a neighboring Province, establishing therein an arbitrary Government, and enlarging its Boundaries, so as to render it at once an example and fit instrument for introducing the same absolute rule into these Colonies:"

For establishing the United Nations building in New York following World War II, wherein spys, secret police, etc. of the nations of the earth are allowed diplomatic immunity and can thereby be given numerous opportunities to penetrate more easily our security systems and silently work to weaken us from within.

"For taking away our Charters, abolishing our most valuable laws, and altering fundamentally the forms of our Governments:"

For working to eliminate State boundaries and putting the States in a regional government of ten regions, instead of the 50 States, continually weakening our Constitution, with the intent to eventually abolish, or suspend it, and altering fundamentally the form of our government, so as to "comfortably" merge us into a one world government.

"For suspending our own Legislatures, and declaring themselves invested with power to legislate for us in all cases whatsoever."

For gradually causing our State legislatures and governors to become subservient to the Federal will, and largely ineffective in preserving "the separation of powers and States' rights," elected and unelected Federal officers now hold the states by the throat and dictate much of state policy and legislation by intimidation and threat of cutting off Federal funding for highways, schools, parks, research, etc. State highway speeds of 55 and 65 mph, and the adoption of State seat belt laws are only two of dozens of examples where Federal policy has, in effect, suspended our legislatures as effectively as did King George.

"He has abdicated Government here, by declaring us out of his protection and waging war against us."

Washington has abdicated government *by the people, for the people, of the people*, and has so far as it has dared, abolished the Constitution, and is waging secret war against the states and the people.

"He has plundered our seas, ravaged our coasts, burnt our towns, and destroyed the lives of our people."

Washington has plundered our treasury, ravaged our children and grandchildren for many generations to come by loading them down with a national debt which is so large it can never be paid, and continued to increase the tax load in a pretended effort to reduce a rocketing deficit, currently at approximately $1 billion per day.

"He is, at this time, transporting large armies of foreign mercenaries to complete the works of death, desolation, and tyranny already begun with circumstances of cruelty and perfidy, scarcely paralleled in the most barbarous ages, and totally unworthy the head of a civilized nation.

"He has constrained our fellow citizens taken captive on the high seas to bear arms against their country, to become the executioners of their friends and brethren, or to fall themselves by their hands."

Washington has sent our fighting men around the globe to fight in undeclared wars in Korea and Vietnam in which we suffered tens of thousands killed. Pretended offenses against our "national security" is used as an excuse for us to enter military ventures and international schemes which weaken the Constitution.

The war against Iraq and Saddam Hussein is the latest example, wherein the Ambassador of the United States to Iraq, April Glaspie, tells Hussein the United States has no interest in his ventures in that part of the world. Within days Hussein attacks and takes over the country of Kuwait. Suddenly we do have an interest and proceed to slaughter tens of thousands of Iraqi soldiers and civilians. Critics believe the entire affair was orchestrated to strengthen the United Nations, set a precedent for the United Nations to dictate policy to a sovereign Nation, and to take a major step toward implementing the New World Order.

"He has excited domestic insurrections amongst us, and has endeavoured (sic) to bring on the inhabitants of our frontiers, the merciless Indian Savages, whose known Rule of Warfare is an undistinguished destruction of all ages, sexes and conditions."

Washington has excited domestic insurrections and race riots by legislating and encouraging the mixing of the races, forcing integration of blacks and whites by busing children out of their natural school boundaries, causing havoc and hatred between races by giving preference to blacks and other "minorities," not only in Federal hiring, but through legislation and intimidation, forcing the states and private employers to also give preference to minorities in jobs. Even judges are now appointed, sometimes, based almost solely on the color of their skin or gender. Affirmative Action (skin color) is in, qualified and competent is secondary, or not applicable. White male is out, black female is in and "politically correct."

Washington has caused and encouraged an increase in crime and burgeoning prison populations through distribution nationwide of generous welfare handouts to millions, who not having to work for a living have nothing better to do than pillage, rape, murder, and raise hell in general. To further increase and encourage this criminal scene, Washington continually attempts to undermine and destroy the law abiding citizen's desire and ability to defend themselves by making it difficult, eventually impossible, for them to buy and own firearms with which to protect themselves. Criminals' rights are foremost. Victims are on their own.

Washington continually stirs up trouble between the races through educational efforts to convince this generation of blacks that somehow they are entitled to preference and privilege because hundreds of years ago the white man held his black fathers in bondage. Little is said about their black fathers in Africa rounding up their fellow blacks and selling them to the white man for profit.

White Washington politicians pretend to have personal and endless compassion for the black man, and will spend endless amounts of taxpayer dollars promoting black welfare. They force blacks to go to white schools, whites to go to black schools, and send their own children to private schools, and exempt themselves from the unjust laws they legislate and force the rest of us to live by, all for the sake of securing and maintaining themselves in perpetual office and to gain the vote of the black man. They have little time or sympathy for a much worse off minority, the American Indians who still live in conditions of poverty which make the average black man appear to be living like a king in comparison.

Jefferson continued: "In every stage of these oppressions we have petititoned for redress in the most humble terms: Our repeated petitions have been answered only by repeated injury. A Prince, whose character is thus marked by every act which may define a tyrant, is unfit to be the ruler of a free people."

For decades, at every stage of our oppressions, we have petitioned Congress and the President for redress in the most humble terms. Our repeated petitions have been answered only by repeated increases in taxes, laws more oppressive than ever before, increased catering to multiplying hoards of special interest groups willing to trade their votes for billions of taxpayer dollars, and attempting to put the next generation in financial bondage by burdening them with debt so large, that even now the time is rapidly approaching when it will be impossible to pay the interest on it. A President, and Congress whose character is thus marked by every act which may define a tyrant is unfit to be the rulers of a free people.

"Nor have we been wanting in attentions to our British brethren. We have warned them from time to time of attempts by their Legislature to extend an unwarrantable jurisdiction over us. We have reminded them of the circumstances of our emigration and settlement here. We have appealed to their native justice and magnanimity, and we have conjured them by the ties of our common kindred to disavow these usurpations which would inevitably interrupt our connections and correspondence. They too have been deaf to the voice of justice and of consanguinity. (The relation or connection of persons descended from the same ancestor; blood relationship. close relationship. Websters) We must, therefore, acquiesce in the necessity, which denounces our separation and hold them, as we hold the rest of mankind, enemies in war, in peace, friends."

We have succeeded from time to time in throwing some of the rascals out of Congress, but for the most part, Congress and the President continue to exercise unwarrantable jurisdiction over us. We remind them once again that it was *the people* who created the *states*, and it was the *states* which sent delegates to write the Constitution, and it was again the *states* which adopted that same Constitution, and by said Constitution, created the present Federal government which did not exist until at least nine *states* agreed to so create it, the ninth, New Hampshire, so agreeing on June 21, 1788. Prior to June 21, 1788, there was no Federal government and if the States should so decide in 1993 or beyond, that the Federal government is more trouble than it is worth the *states* can just as readily dismantle the Federal government and cause it to cease to exist, just as they created it in the first place. The Federal government was created by peaceful agreement; it can also be dismantled by peaceful agreement of the States.

We further remind Washington that such a dismantling is not out of the question in terms of practicality and neither is it rebellion. It is an option which the states might exercise lawfully and legally, according to the laws of nations, according to the laws of contracts, according to the laws of principal and agent, according to treaty law, and according to the *Declaration of Independence* of July 4, 1776.

We also remind Washington the main reason the original thirteen *states* united in 1776, was for purposes of national defense against the aggression of Great Britain. We remind Washington there is nothing impractical about dismantling Washington if it does not cease its abuses and usurpations. The State governments will still be organized and in place with their militias and armed citizens, for Congress has not succeeded in disarming *the people*. And these *50 states* could renew their Union again, if necessary, for purposes of national defense. They could, in fact, agree after dismantling the Federal government with its millions of employees to establish a corporate structure with a Board of Directors and a Chief Executive Officer whose only purpose of existence would be to defend the *50 States* from enemy attack by a foreign power. This one corporation would largely serve the purpose for which we originally created a Federal government. By dismantling the Federal government the *50 states* would be free to start over again, free from the numerous foreign entanglements and treaties, free from trillions of phony debt on which we are presently forced to pay hundreds of billions just in interest annually, free from numerous unconstitutional usurpations, and free to reunite, one by one, State by State, if each individual State could see advantages to itself for again coming together as States United under a Constitution.

We must, therefore, remind Washington that the *states* as creators of the Federal government are the masters, and that the District of Columbia is owned by the 50 States each entitled to a pro-rated percentage of the value should they decide to dismantle Washington, D.C. and sell it and resume their original independence and sovereignty, and resume each and every authority they delegated to the Federal government in the Constitution. We must remind Washington that *the States*, as *the Master*, expects Washington to play its part as an obedient servant, and to cease and desist from attempting to play the role of master.

In fantasyland, created objects may end up controlling their creators. In fiction, Frankenstein monsters may become more powerful than the scientist who created them but not so in the real world of the United States today. It may take a firm hand. It may even take bloodshed, though legally, there is no need for it, but we must demand that Washington retreat from its stance of agression against these 50 Sates and our people. And if all negotiations and reason should fail us, we have the lawful right to dismantle the entire Federal apparatus and return to our original position; separate, independent and free States.

Jefferson concluded: "We, therefore, the Representatives of the *United States of America*, in General Congress Assembled, appealing to the Supreme Judge of the world for the rectitude of our intentions, do in the name, and by authority of the good people of these Colonies, solemnly publish and declare, that these United Colonies, are, and of right ought to be, free and independent states; that they are absolved from all allegiance to the British Crown, and that all political connection between them and the State of Great Britain, is and ought to be totally dissolved; and that as *free and independent states*, (Emphasis added) they have full power to levy war, conclude peace, contract alliances, establish commerce, and to do all other acts and things which *independent states* may of right do. And for the support of this Declaration, with a firm reliance on the protection of divine providence, we mutually pledge to each other our lives, our fortunes, and our sacred honor."

"Signed by order and in behalf of the Congress,
John Hancock, President.
Attest,
Charles Thomson, Secretary.
Philadelphia"

The Declaration of Independence was agreed to and eventually signed by 56 representatives of each of the thirteen *free and independent states* of:

New Hampshire
Massachusetts Bay

Rhode Island and Providence Plantation
Connecticut
New York
New Jersey
Pennsylvania
Delaware
Maryland
Virginia
North Carolina
South Carolina
Georgia

England agreed with her former Colonies position stated in the Declaration of Independence when she signed the Treaty of Paris on September 3, 1783, wherein the former thirteen Colonies were recognized as *free, sovereign and independent states.* On that date, the rest of the world essentially, along with Great Britain, recognized that thirteen new nations, little Republics, were now officially part of the brotherhood of nations of planet earth.

The *secession* of July 4, 1776, now had the approval of the world.

Historically, secession, or separation of groups, states, or nations from official and unofficial ties and agreements have been accomplished both peacefully and by force of arms.

Thomas Jefferson, and those who assisted him in putting the final touches on the Declaration of Independence believed God was on their side. They merely wished to be left alone to live their lives in peace without harassment or intimidation from government. The Founders were outstanding students of history. Madison, Jefferson and others had access to, or had purchased numerous volumes of history, including the Holy Bible. And the Bible does place God on the side of liberty and the Founders. "...proclaim liberty throughout all the land unto all the inhabitants thereof:..." Leviticus 25:10. "Is not this the fast that I have chosen? To loose the bands of wickedness, to undo the heavy burdens, and to let the oppressed go free, and that ye break every yoke?" Isaiah 58:6. "...to proclaim liberty to the captives and the opening of the prison to them that are bound;..." Isaiah 61:1 "Therefore thus saith the Lord; Ye have not hearkened unto me in proclaiming liberty, every one to his brother, and evey man to his neighbor:..." Jeremiah 34:17. For failure to proclaim liberty as God had commanded, God proclaimed to the people in the days of Jeremiah that he would send them the sword, pestilence, famine and scatter them into all the nations of the earth. Jesus said: "And ye shall know the truth, and the truth shall make you free." John 8:32. "...where the spirit of the Lord is, there is liberty." 2 Corinthians 3:17. James 1:25 refers to liberty as the perfect law.

The Declaration of Independence, standing alone, gives us a powerful legal foundation, if in 1993 or beyond, the usurpations and abuses of the Constitution by the Federal government should become so bad *the people* and *the states* are unwilling to tolerate further abuse. One or more States have every right to resume original sovereignty and separate itself, or themselves, from the United States of America. This right, under the Constitution, is far more defendable, and right from a legal standpoint, in 1993 or beyond, than was the position of Jefferson and our Fathers on July 4, 1776, though their position was also very solid legally.

If all 50 States wished to act in concert, or even if just three-fourths, or 38 States, wished to get together in a Convention, they could legally and lawfully abolish...eliminate the entire Federal apparatus. The States could, if things get too bad or out of hand, abolish the Federal government, and along with that, they would automatically abolish the Internal Revenue Service, The Federal Reserve System and its two or three trillion dollars in debt which makes up a huge portion of our national debt. After that the States could tell President Clinton and the 435 members of the House of Representatives, and the 100 members of the Senate they are fired, gone, outta here; "get out of Washington and don't ever come back. And by the way, your exorbitant million dollar pensions are cancelled, your perks and privileges are eliminated and you are on your own. You will either start making an honest living or you can starve; we really don't care which you choose."

After eliminating the Congress and the Executive departments, the States might wish to retain the services of the nine Supreme Court justices and their staffs to still be the final arbiter of differences, but the States could just as easily tell the Supreme Court to get lost along with the rest of Washington.

The States could then, if they chose, put up for sale that block of real estate known as Washington, District of Columbia, and let it go to the highest bidder, piece by piece, building by building, or to some large corporate group in a single piece.

The States would then divide the proceeds among themselves.

This same procedure could be followed with all the national parks, other Federal property, military bases, etc.

It is up to the States. It is up to the *people*. They retain the option to do anything they wish, at any time, with that Federal Frankenstein monster in Washington, D.C. That Washington monster supposes it has switched roles with its creators. But an out of control and arrogant bunch of 535 congressmen and women can be readily tamed and brought to heel, or even fired with the stroke of the pen of 38 States.

After the 38 States destroyed the fire-breathing monster, they would be free to start over again without all the chains, and much of the financial bondage with which we, our children, and our children's children ad infinitum, are now burdened. We would be free, without bloodshed, to organize some sort of new Union for purposes of national defense, or free, perhaps, to simply organize some sort of private corporation with the delegated responsibility to protect the States from attack by any foreign power.

This option the States have to dismantle the Federal government may quickly become very attractive to us if the Federal noose continues to be tightened around the necks of the States and the people as it has been since the 1930's. This option may become extremely attractive should the Federal government attempt, in some manner, to "temporarily" suspend or make the Constitution null and void.

Federal usurpation of constitutional powers reserved to the States cannot get much worse before the point is reached where the only answer the *people* have is to resort to bloodshed. Already such rumblings by some of the *people* are being heard as their rights are being trampled far worse, especially in the matter of taxation, than were the rights of colonial subjects of King George in 1776.

Bloodshed is imminent unless Federal officers and elected officials, as well as the legislatures, governors, and attorneys general of the 50 States have a clear understanding of how this government is put together, and how the States, and the *people*, not Washington, are in control and have *all* the power if they wish to exercise it.

Ignorance of the structure and nature of the government of the United States prevails on a massive scale, and disaster and bloodshed in the streets of American cities can only be averted if the leaders of the American people on State and Federal and County levels understand who holds real power under the Constitution.

By simply understanding the way the game can potentially be played, will hopefully, be sufficient to cause Congress and the President to wake up and realize their smallness; to realize that they are only pawns with little real power, and can be squashed, eliminated at any moment the Kings, Queens, Rooks, Bishops and Knights choose to eliminate and take *their* pawns out of the game.

But if Washington persists in the unrelenting path it is following in destroying the Constitution, the States must prepare to "take the bull by the horns," and rather than allowing bloodshed to take place in our cities and streets, they must be prepared to dissolve our Union and start over with some new form of central government, or corporate structure. The States must be prepared, since they and *the people* they represent hold all the real power to do whatever is necessary to protect *the people* from losing the liberties they inherited, from either foreign or domestic enemies.

We can thank Thomas Jefferson for giving us a Declaration of Independence which applies to 20th century government just as readily as it applied in 1776. This Declaration is our first argument in support of our lawful right to free the

States and *the people* from the increasing usurpations of Washington. It is our first argument in setting forth the legal and lawful right of the People to sever or to destroy the ties created by the States as *principal,* and the Federal government as the *agent*, if the States choose to do so.

But there is much more than the Declaration of Independence. A number of powerful arguments will now follow which will establish beyond a shadow of doubt the legal and lawful right of a State, or States, to leave the Union, or dismantle it altogether, although the Declaration of Independece, by itself, firmly establishes that right, even if no other legal arguments were available.

Chapter 5

**The Constitution—A bloodless revolution.
Nine States secede from four States.**

The next argument showing the superior power of the States over the Federal government, and showing the States' right to withdraw from the Union freely, as they freely joined, requires that we investigate the historical record regarding the action taken by each of the original *free, independent and sovereign states*; by each of these *independent nations*. Let us see what these nations did when the *proposed* Constitution was submitted to them by the Congress, as requested by the Convention of Philadelphia. Let us see how this proposed Constitution which proposed to join at least nine of a possible thirteen in Union, was understood by the States, and what construction was put upon it by its supporters and advocates. Let's inquire whether adoption of the Constitution was considered by the States as a surrender of their sovereignty, or simply as a new Contract, Compact, or Agreement under which they would join forces for purposes of defense against foreign agression, and certain limited internal regulation of commerce, and a few other things which could be handled better by a central authority.

We will look at the documents of ratification in the order in which each of the first nine States agreed to join in Union, and follow this with a few which later joined the first nine.

For the following record and some of the commentry, the author wishes to give credit to Alexander H. Stephens, Vice President of the Southern Confederacy from 1861-1865, and the book he wrote in 1868 titled: *A Constitutional View of the Late War Between the States*. To eliminate confusion, only the ratifying documents of each of the States will be shown with quotation marks, as is shown in Mr. Stephens record, or where he, himself, is quoting another. Most of the commentary will be from Mr. Stephens book, but will not be shown with quotation marks. These records, though not the Stephens book, are widely available at State and National archives and many public libraries.

First, Delaware

The Legislature of the State of Delaware called a Convention of her people to consider the Constitution and the action upon it, according to the request of Congress. In the Convention of this State, there seems to have been no division and no discussion. At least none of the debates in that body, if any were had, have been preserved. Here is the action of the Convention.

"We, the Deputies of the People of the Delaware State in Convention met, having taken into our serious consideration the Federal Constitution, proposed and agreed upon by the Deputies of the United States, in a General Convention held at the City of Philadelphia, on the seventeenth day of September, in the year of our Lord one thousand seven hundred and eighty-seven, have approved, assented to, ratified, and confirmed, and by these presents do, in virtue of the power and authority to us given, for and in behalf of ourselves and our constituents, fully, freely, and entirely approve of, assent to, ratify, and confirm the said Constitution.

"Done in Convention at Dover this seventh day of December in the year aforesaid, and in the year of the Independence of the United States of America, the twelfth." Elliot's Debates, vol. 1, p. 319.

In this very act of ratification, we see it styled by the Sovereign people of Delaware, "The Federal Constitution." Indeed, no one can doubt for a moment, from the course of her delegates in the Philadelphia Convention, that the People of Delaware understood the Constitution as they here style it, to be Federal in its character, and that the Sovereignty of the State was still retained.

Mr. Stephens, in the above paragraph, emphasizes the Constitution was *Federal* in nature. Two hundred years ago Federal clearly meant the States were sovereign and independent, whereas those who would eliminate State sovereignty, or reduce it, tried to claim our central government was *National* in character. In its broadest sense, a National government of the United States would have eliminated the States altogether and consolidated them into a single central government. A National government would have meant one consolidated whole; a single head, without all the "inefficiency" and bother of separate State units.

Whether the United States is a *National* government or a *Federal* government was a subject of heated and prolonged debate among some of our early statesmen for several decades after the Union was formed. This debate probably reached a climax in early 1833. Two great patriots who both loved the Constitution and loved America went at it on the floor of the United States Senate. Daniel Webster, the greatest orator of his day and a leader in the Senate for nearly 30 years, and one who was not easily bested, took the floor in an extremely long speech on February 16, 1833. Webster attempted to make the case that the Constitution was a compact but that the States were not sovereign, the position of the *Nationalists*. Webster's arguments were weak at best, for he was attempting to prove as fact, that which was not true.

Ten days later, Senator John C. Calhoun took the floor and argued the *Federalist* position. Calhoun so demolished the arguments of Webster, that Webster had little to say in rebuttal, and in later years appeared to have been converted to Calhoun's position that our government is Federal in nature, not National. Webster's conversion was quite clearly shown in a case he argued before the Supreme Court in January 1839, six years after his "debate" with Calhoun. The case the Court had under consideration was, *The Bank of Augusta* vs. *Earle*. In this case, the nature of the General Government and the nature of the State Governments in their relations to each other, came up for adjudication, and Webster took the *Federal* position.

Second, Pennsylvania

The next State in order was Pennsylvania. In this, as in the case of Delaware, let us look first into the action of the State and then into the debates, as far as we have them, to see what light they throw upon this action. First, then the action of the Convention is in these words.

"In the name of the people of Pennsylvania.

"Be it known unto all men, that we, the delegates of the people of the Commonwealth of Pennsylvania, in General Convention assembled, have assented to and ratified, and by these presents do, in the name and by the authority of the same people and for ourselves, assent to and ratify the foregoing Constitution for the United States of America. Done in Convention at Philadelphia, the twelfth day of December, in the year of our Lord one thousand seven hundred and eighty-seven, and of the independence of the United States of America the twelfth. In witness whereof, we have hereunto subscribed our names." Elliot's Debates, vol. 1, p. 319.

No allusion in this is made to the character of the instrument or of the understanding of the members of the Convention of it, farther (sic) than their styling it a "Constitution for States United," and not for the whole mass of the people of these States in the aggregate. This of itself is quite enough to show that they considered it Federal or Federative in its character!

But we are not left in doubt or to inference on this point. The debates in the Convention of Pennsylvania have been in part preserved. We have the speeches of Mr. Wilson, who had been in the Federal Convention that framed the Constitution, and who was also in the State Convention that ratified it. These, it is true, are all of the debates that we have, but they throw much light upon the subject.

Mr. Wilson, recollect, was one of the ablest and most zealous of the Nationals in the Federal Convention. But when their plan failed, he, as Hamilton, Morris, King, and Madison, gave the Constitution agreed upon his warm support. What he said, therefore, in the State Convention, touching the character, or nature of the Constitution, which was finally agreed upon, is entitled to great weight, and particularly all his disclaimers, as to its being a Consolidation of the whole people of the country into one single grand National Republic. Let us then, in the second place, see what was his judgment of it as given to the Pennsylvania Convention. In opening the deliberations of that body, he said:

"The United States may adopt any one of four different systems. They may become consolidated into one Government in which the separate existence of the States shall be entirely absolved. They may reject any plan of Union or association and act as separate an unconnected States. They may form two or more Confederacies. (two possible reasons for two or more confederacies, might have been for the slave States to form a separate Union from the free States. Or the large States might have formed a separate Union, and the small States formed themselves together). They may unite in one Federal Republic." (This is the one we have).

After giving his opinion against the first three, he concludes thus:

"The remaining system which the American States may adopt is a Union of them under one Confederate Republic. It will not be necessary to employ much time, or many arguments, to show that this is the most eligible system that can be proposed. By adopting this system, the vigor and decision of a wide spreading monarchy may be joined to the freedom and beneficence of a contracted Republic. The extent of territory, the diversity of climate and soil, the number, and greatness, and connection of lakes and rivers with which the United States are intersected, and almost surrounded, all indicate an enlarged Government to be fit and advantageous for them.

"If those opinions and wishes are as well founded as they have been general, the late Convention were justified in proposing to their constituents one *Confederate Republic* as the best system of a National Government for the United States." Elliots Debates, Vol. 2, p. 418.

In another speech, on 1st December, 1787, as the discussion progressed he said: "We have heard much about a consolidated Government. I wish the honorable gentleman would condescend to give us a definition of what he meant by it. I think this more necessary, because I apprehend that the term, in the numerous times it has been used, has not always been used in the same sense. It may be said, and I believe it has been said, that a consolidated Government is such as will absorb and destroy the Governments of the several States. If it is taken in this view, the plan before us is not a consolidated Government, as I showed on a former day, and may if necessary, show further on some future occasion. On the other hand, if it is meant that the General Government will take from the State Governments their power in some particulars, it is confessed and evident that this will be its operation and effect."

Again on the 4th of December, he said, "The very manner of introducing this institution by the recognition of the authority of the people is said to change the principles of the present Confederation and to introduce a consolidating and absorbing government.

"In this Confederated Republic, the Sovereignty of the States it is said, is not preserved. We are told that there cannot be two Sovereign powers, and that a subordinate Sovereignty is no Sovereignty.

"It will be worth while, Mr. President, to consider this objection at large. When I had the honor of speaking formerly on this subject, I stated, in as concise a manner as possible, the leading ideas that occurred to me to ascertain where the Supreme and Sovereign power resides. It has not been, nor I presume, will it be denied, that somewhere there is, and of necessity must be, a Supreme, absolute, and uncontrollable authority. This I believe, may justly be termed the Sovereign power; for, from that gentleman's (Mr. Findley) account of the matter, it cannot be sovereign unless it is supreme; for, says he a subordinate Sovereignty is no Sovereignty at all. I had the honor of observing that if the question was asked where the Supreme power resided, different answers would be given by different writers. I mentioned that Blackstone would tell you that, in Britain, it is lodged in the British Parliament; and I believe there is no writer on this subject, on the other side of the Atlantic, but supposed it to be vested in that body. I stated further, that if the question was asked of some politician, who had not considered the subject with sufficient accuracy where the Supreme power resided in our Government, he would answer that it was vested in the State Constitutions. This opinion approaches near the truth, but does not reach it; for the truth is, that the Supreme, absolute, and uncontrollable authority *remains with the people*. I mentioned also, that the practical recognition of this truth was reserved for the honor of this country. I recollect no Constitution founded on this principle; but we have witnessed the improvement and enjoy the happiness of seeing it carried into practice. The great and penetrating mind of Locke seems to be the only one that pointed towards even the theory of this great truth.

"When I made the observation that some politicians would say the Supreme power was lodged in our State Constitutions, I did not suspect that the honorable gentleman from Westmoreland (Mr. Findley) was included in that description; but I find myself disappointed, for I imagined his opposition would arise from another consideration. His position is that the Supreme power resides in the States, as Governments; and mine is that it resides in *the people*, as the fountain of Government; *that the people have not—that the people meant not—and that the people ought not—to part with it to any government whatsoever*. In their hands it remains secure. They can delegate it in such proportions, to such bodies, on such terms, and under such limitations, as they think proper. I agree with the members in opposition, that there cannot be two Sovereign powers on the same subject. * * * This, I say, is the inherent and unalienable right of the people; and as an illustration of it I beg to read a few words from the Declaration of Independence, made by the Representatives of the United States and recognised (sic) by the whole Union.

"'We hold these truths to be self-evident, that all men are created equal; that they are endowed by their Creator with certain inalienable rights; that among these are life, liberty, and the pursuit of happiness; that to secure these rights, Governments are instituted among men, deriving their just powers from the consent of the governed; that, whenever any form of Government becomes destructive of these ends, it is the right of the people to alter, or abolish it, and institute a new Government, laying its foundation on such principles, and organizing its powers in such forms, as to them shall seem most likely to effect their safety and happiness.

"This is the broad basis on which our independence was placed: on the same certain and solid foundation this system is erected..."

It is to be regretted that no part of these debates has been preserved but the speeches of Mr Wilson, from which these extracts have been read. From these, however, it abundantly appears that the nature and character of the Government to be instituted under the Constitution of the United States was thoroughly discussed. It appears clearly, that there was strong opposition to many of its features, but what is of very great importance in our investigation, it is equally clear that Mr. Wilson and the majority who acted with him in that Convention, held the Constitution to be strictly Federal, and that the Government instituted by it was a Federal Government, or Confederated Republic. Whatever may have been his original views as to a consolidation of the States into one National Republic, he distinctly and frankly avowed that the Constitution which had been agreed upon did not affect that result. He declared further, that according to his understanding of the Constitution, the State Governments, as States under it, would enjoy as much power and more dignity, happiness, and security, than they had done before. He insisted that no cause of distrust should arise from apprehensions on that score; for the powers of the Federal Government, said he, with emphasis, were as well defined in the Constitution as under the Articles of Confederation. His whole powers seem to have been put forth to demonstrate that it was not a Consolidated Government, as the opponents of it argued that it would be construed to be. (These opponents were attempting to defeat the Constitution in the Pennsylvania Convention because they feared loss of State Sovereignty). He declared that it was not treating the Constitution with decency to make such insinuations against it. These speeches of Mr. Wilson, without doubt, controlled the majority of the Pennsylvania Convention, who gave the Constitution their sanction. They show clearly what must have been the understanding of the friends and advocates of the Constitution as to its nature, and as to the nature of the Union thereby established, when they started it, in their ordinance of ratification, "a Constitution for States." These speeches of Mr. Wilson were also extensively published in the newspapers of the day. They were widely circulated in other States and, Mr. Curtis says, had great influence on the action of other State Conventions.

Third, New Jersey

The Legislature of this State called a Convention of her people, to which the Constitution was referred. That Convention came to the following resolutions and ordinance. Elliot's Debates, vol. 1, p 320.

"In Convention of the State of New Jersey, 18 December, 1787.

"Whereas, a convention of delegates from the following States, viz.: New Hampshire, Massachusetts, Connecticut, New York, New Jersey, Pennsylvania, Delaware, Maryland, Virginia, North Carolina, South Carolina, and Georgia, met at Philadelphia, for the purpose of deliberating on, and forming a Constitution for the United States of America, finished their session on the 17th day of September last, and reported to Congress the form which they had agreed upon in the words following, viz.:

"And whereas, Congress, on the 28th day of September last, unanimously did resolve, 'That the said report, with the Resolutions and letter accompanying the same, be transmitted to the several Legislatures, in order to be submitted to a Convention of Delegates, chosen in each State by the people thereof, in conformity to the resolves of the Convention made and provided in that case;'

"And whereas, the Legislature of this State did on the 29th day of October last, resolve in the words following, viz.: 'Resolved, unanimously, that it be recommended to such of the inhabitants of this State as are entitled to vote for Representatives in General Assembly, to meet in their respective counties on the fourth Tuesday in November next, at the several places fixed by law for holding the annual elections, to choose three suitable persons to serve as delegates from each county in a State Convention, for the purposes hereinbefore mentioned, and that the same be conducted agreeably to the mode, and conformably with the rules and regulations, prescribed for conducting such elections;

"Resolved unanimously, That the persons so selected to serve in State Convention, do assemble and meet together on the second Tuesday in December next, at Trenton, in the county of Hunterdon, then and there to take into consideration the aforesaid Constitution, and if approved of by them, finally to ratify the same in behalf and on the part of this State, and make report thereof to the United States in Congress assembled, in conformity with the resolutions thereto annexed.

"'Resolved, That the sheriffs of the respective counties of this State shall be, and they are hereby required to give as timely notice as may be, by advertisements to the people of their counties, of the time, place and purpose of holding elections as aforesaid.'

"And whereas, The Legislature of this State did also, on the 1st day of November last, make and pass the following act, viz.: 'An Act to authorize the people of this State to meet in convention, deliberate upon, agree to, and ratify the Constitution of the United States proposed by the late General Convention, be it enacted by the Council and General Assembly of this State, and it is hereby enacted by the authority of the same, that it shall and may be lawful for the people thereof, by their Delegates, to meet in Convention to deliberate upon, and if approved of by them, to ratify the Constitution for the United States proposed by the General Convention held at Philadelphia, and every act, matter, and clause therein contained, conformably to the resolutions of the Legislature passed the 29th day of October, 1787, any law, usage, or custom to the contrary in any wise notwithstanding;'

"Now be it known, That we, the Delegates of the State of New Jersey, chosen by the people thereof for the purposes aforesaid, having maturely deliberated on and considered the aforesaid proposed Constitution, do hereby, for and on the behalf of the people of the said State of New Jersey, agree to ratify and confirm the same and every part thereof.

"Done in Convention by the unanimous consent of the members present, this 18th day of December, in the year of our Lord 1787, and of the independence of the United States of America, the twelfth."

There was no opposition to the Constitution in the Convention of New Jersey. It was unanimously adopted. But the action of the convention shows how they understood it. They agreed to and ratified it as "a Constitution *for*, not *of*, the United States of America."

Fourth, Georgia

"In Convention, Wednesday, January 2nd, 1788.

"To all to whom these presents shall come, greeting:

"Whereas the form of a Constitution for the Government of the United States of America, was on the 17th day of September, 1787, agreed upon and reported to Congress by the Deputies of the said United States, convened in Philadelphia, which said the Constitution is written in the following words, to wit:

"And whereas, the United States in Congress assembled did, on the 28th day of September, 1787, resolve unanimously, 'That the said report, with the resolutions and letter accompanying the same, be transmitted to the several Legislatures in order to be submitted to a Convention of Delegates chosen in each State by the people thereof, in conformity to the resolves of the Convention made and provided in that case.'

"And whereas, the Legislature of the State of Georgia did, on the 26th day of October, 1787, in pursuance of the above recited resolution of Congress, Resolve, that a Convention be elected on the day of the next general election and in the same manner that representatives are elected; and that the said Convention consist of not more than three members from each county; and that the said Convention should meet at August, (Sic) Georgia, on the fourth Tuesday in December then next, and as soon thereafter as convenient, proceed to consider the said report and resolutions, and to adopt or reject any part or the whole thereof;

"Now know ye, that we, the delegates of the people of the State of Georgia, in convention met, pursuant to the resolutions of the Legislature foresaid, having taken into our serious consideration the said Constitution, have assented to, ratified, and adopted, and by these presents do, in virtue of the powers and authority to us given by the people of the said State for that purpose, for and in behalf of ourselves and our constituents, fully and entirely assent to, ratify, and adopt the said Constitution.

"Done in Convention, at August, (Sic) in the said State, on the 2nd day of January, in the year of our Lord, 1788, and of the independence of the United States the twelfth."

In the Georgia Convention there was no opposing voice. The Constitution was unanimously assented to, ratified, and adopted as "a Constitution for the Government of the United States of America." A Government of States. A Federal Republic.

Fifth, Connecticut

"In the name of the People of the State of Connecticut. We, the Delegates of the people of said State, in General Convention assembled, pursuant to an Act of the Legislature in

October last, have assented to, and ratified, and by these presents do assent to, ratify, and adopt the Constitution reported by the Convention of Delegates in Philadelphia on the 17th day of September, A.D., 1787, for the United States of America.

"Done in Convention at Hartford, this 9th day of January, A.D., 1788. In witness whereof, we have hereunto set our hands."

Oliver Ellsworth was a prominent member of the Connecticut ratifying Convention. He was afterwards Chief Justice of the Supreme Court of the United States. He and Roger Sherman were delegates in the Philadelphia Convention which wrote the Constitution. After the adjournment of the Federal Convention they wrote a letter to the governor of Connecticut stating distinctly that the sovereignty of the States was retained. Ante. p. 154.

Under the Articles of Confederation, Congress had no power to collect taxes. Congress could merely request the States to pay their fair share of the amount of money needed to run the Federal government. The States were not always prompt in paying these requests of Congress, to say the least. Part of the reason for needing the Constitution was to remedy this weakness of the Articles of Confederation. The Constitution provided for direct taxation of *the people*, not the States.

In the Connecticut Convention, Mr. Ellsworth made the following comments in regard to this matter.

"Hence, we see how necessary for the Union is a coercive principle. No man pretends the contrary; we all see and feel this necessity. The only question is, shall it be a coercion of law, or a coercion of arms? There is no other possible alternative. Where will those who oppose a coercion of law come out? Where will they end? A necessary consequence of their principles is a war of the States, one against the other. I am for coercion by law—that coercion which acts only upon delinquent individuals. This Constitution does not attempt to *coerce sovereign bodies, states, in their political capacity*. No coercion is applicable to such bodies but that of an armed force. If we should attempt to execute the laws of the Union by sending an armed force against a delinquent State, it would involve the good and bad, the innocent and guilty, in the same calamity. But this legal coercion (the Constitution) singles out the guilty individual and punishes him for breaking the laws of the Union." Elliot's Debates, vol. 2, p 197.

Mr. Ellsworth was not speaking of only taxes in this speech. He was speaking of the great advantage that would result from delegating to the Congress power to pass laws that would operate directly upon the people and not upon the States in their corporate capacities. This, he maintained, would be a great improvement in the federal system over what was then operative, the Articles of Confederation.

But he, like many others, were careful to point out that under the Constitution the States would remain sovereign just as they had been under the Articles.

Sixth, Massachusetts

It is tedious to go through with all these dry, musty records, but it is essential to show the intent and understanding of the Fathers of our country. They are the title-deeds of our political inheritance of Constitutional Liberty.

"Commonwealth of Massachusetts.

"The Convention having impartially discussed and fully considered the Constitution for the United States of America, reported to Congress by the Convention of Delegates from the United States of America, and submitted to us by a resolution of the General Court of the said Commonwealth, passed the 25th day of October, last past, and acknowledging with grateful hearts, the goodness of the Supreme Ruler of the Universe in affording the people of the United States, in the course of his providence, an opportunity, deliberately and peaceably, without fraud or surprise, of entering into an explicit and solemn compact with each other, by assenting to and ratifying a new Constitution in order to form a more perfect Union, establish justice, insure domestic tranquility, provide for the common defence,(sic) promote the general welfare, and secure the blessings of liberty to themselves and their posterity, do, in the name and in behalf of the people of the Commonwealth of Massachusetts, assent to and ratify the said Constitution for the United States of America.

"And as it is the opinion of this Convention that certain amendments and alterations in the said Constitution would remove the fears and quiet the apprehensions of many of the good people of this Commonwealth, and more effectually guard against an undue administration of the Federal Government, the Convention do therefore recommend that the following alterations and provisions be introduced into the said Constitution:"

This was followed by the proposal that nine amendments or a Bill of Rights should be added to the proposed Constitution. The first, and most important proposed amendment was: "That it explicitly declare that all powers not expressly delegated by the aforesaid Constitution are reserved to the several States to be by them exercised."

This proposal was, in fact, later made a part of the Constitution and is known as the Tenth Amendment, but reads somewhat differently than proposed by Massachusetts.

"And the Convention do, in the name and in behalf of the people of this Commonwealth, enjoin it upon their representatives in Congress, at all times, until the alterations and provisions aforesaid have been considered agreeably to the fifth article of the said Constitution, to exert all their influence and use all reasonable and legal methods to obtain a ratification of the said alterations and provisions in such manner as is provided in the said article."

The fifth article referred to above is, of course, the process for amending the Constitution. It should be noted here that it was an unspoken understanding, at least with many among these State ratifying Conventions, that should amendments not later be added to the Constitution, as Massachusetts was proposing, Massachusetts could as easily withdraw from the Union, just as she was joining with the stipulation that nine amendments be added to the Constitution, or at least, amendments must be added sufficient to calm the fears of many that too much power was being given up to the new central government. It was understood, as the Virginia Convention actually formalized in writing, that as sovereign States, should this Constitution not be adopted in good faith, a State was as free to leave the Union as it was to now join.

Massachusetts had great opposition to the Constitution in its Convention, as did Pennsylvania. Massachusetts voted to ratify with 187 yeas. But almost as many delegates opposed. The nays were 168. Many of our Fathers were determined to keep government small and easy to overthrow, should politicians let power go to their heads. They were determined to delegate to any proposed central government, only the minimum powers necessary to govern themselves efficiently.

"And that the United States, in Congress assembled, may have due notice of the assent and ratification of the said Constitution by this Convention, it is resolved, That the assent and ratification aforesaid be engrossed on parchment, together with the recommendation and injunction aforesaid, and with this resolution; and that his Excellency, John Hancock, Esqr., President, and the Hon. William Cushing, Esqr., Vice President of the Convention, transmit the same, countersigned by the Secretary of the Convention, under their hands and seals, to the United States in Congress assembled." Elliots Debates, vol. 1, pp. 322, 323.

Seventh, Maryland

"In Convention of the Delegates of the people of the State of Maryland, April 28, 1788.

"We, the Delegates of the people of the State of Maryland, having fully considered the Constitution of the United States of America, reported to Congress, by the Convention of Deputies from the United States of America, held in Philadelphia on the 17th day of September, in the year 1787, of which the annexed is a copy, and submitted to us by a resolution of the General Assembly of Maryland, in November Session, 1787, do for ourselves, and in the name and on behalf of the people of this State, assent to, and ratify the said Constitution.

"In witness whereof, we have hereunto subscribed our names."

In this State there was no material division of sentiment. There was little or no discussion. The vote on it was 63 to 11. It was simply assented to and ratified as the "Constitution of the United States of America." The Convention of Maryland styled it a Constitution of States.

Eighth, South Carolina

"In Convention of the people of the State of South Carolina by their representatives, held in the City of Charleston on Monday, the 12th day of May, and continued by divers adjournments to Friday, the 23rd day of May, Anno Domini, 1788, and in the twelfth year of the independence of the United States of America.

"The Convention, having maturely considered the Constitution, or form of government, reported to Congress by the Convention of Delegates from the United States of America and submitted to them by a resolution of the Legislature of this State, passed the 17th and 18th days of February last, in order to form a more perfect Union, establish justice, insure domestic tranquility, provide for the common defence, (sic) promote the general welfare, and secure the blessings of liberty to the people of the said United States, and their posterity, do, in the name and behalf of the people of this State, hereby assent to and ratify the said Constitution.

"Done in Convention the 23d day of May, in the year of our Lord, 1788, and of the Independence of the United States of America the twelfth.

"And whereas, it is essential to the preservation of the rights reserved to the several States and the freedom of the people, under the operations of a General Government, that the right of prescribing the manner, time, and places of holding the elections to the Federal Legislature, should be forever inseparably annexed to the Sovereignty of the several States, This Convention doth declare that the same ought to remain to all posterity, a perpetual and fundamental right in the local, exclusive of the interference of the General Government, except in cases where the Legislatures of the States shall refuse or neglect to perform and fulfill the same, according to the tenure of the said Constitution. *This convention doth also declare, that no section or paragraph of the said Constitution warrants a construction, that the states do not retain every power not expressly relinquished by them and vested in the general government of the Union.* Emphasis added.

"Resolved, That the General Government of the United States ought never to impose direct taxes, but where the moneys arising from the duties, imposts, and excise are insufficient for the public exigencies, nor then until Congress shall have made a requisition upon the States to assess, levy, and pay their respective proportions of such requisitions; and in case any State shall neglect or refuse to pay its proportion, pursuant to such requisition, then Congress may assess and levy such State's proportion, together with interest thereon, at the rate of six per centum per annum from the time of payment prescribed by such requisition.

"Resolved, That the third section of the sixth article ought to be amended by inserting the word 'other' between the words 'no' and 'religious.'

"Resolved, That it be a standing instruction to all such delegates as may hereafter be elected to represent this State in the General Government, to exert their utmost abilities and influence to effect an alteration of the Constitution conformably to the aforegoing resolutions.

"Done in Convention the 23d day of May, in the year of our Lord, 1788, and of the Independence of the United States of America the twelfth." Elliots Debates, vol. 1, p. 325

There was an express declaration that the Constitution had been assented to and ratified, with the understanding that no section or paragraph of the Constitution warranted a construction that the States did not retain every power not expressly relinquished by them. These declarations forever fixed the understanding of the State with which she had entered into the Compact, and the understanding with which her ratification was accepted by the other States.

Let us consider some of the debates. Very few speeches made in this Convention have been preserved. No one disputed the character of the Government. The speeches related mostly to particular powers delegated. From one of them we perceive, however, that there was spirited opposition made by a respectable minority. This was headed by Patrick Dollard of Prince Fredericks. He said, "My constituents are highly alarmed at the large and rapid strides which this new Government has taken towards despotism. They say it is big with political mischiefs, and pregnant with a greater variety of impending woes to the good people of the Southern States, especially South Carolina, than all the plagues supposed to issue from the poisonous box of Pandora!" South Carolina ratified, however, 149 to 73.

The most important debate in South Carolina on the Constitution was in the Legislature, on the proposition to call a Convention to take it into consideration. In this body, as in the Convention, there was a respectable and spirited minority against the Constitution, though the call for a Convention was unanimous. In the debate on that question, Hon. Rawlins Lowndes concluded his speech by saying he wished for no other epitaph than to have inscribed on his tomb, "Here lies the man that opposed the Constitution because it was ruinous to the liberty of America!"

These apprehensions and forebodings were, doubtless, awakened by the utterance of such sentiments as those which fell from General Pinckney in the discussion which Judge Story quotes. He did maintain that the States, severally, were never Sovereign, but in this position he was not sustained either by the Legislature or the Convention as we have seen by the Protocol of the latter.

Ninth, New Hampshire

"In Convention of the Delegates of the People of the State of New Hampshire, June the 21st, 1788.

"The Convention, having impartially discussed and fully considered the Constitution for the United States of America, reported to Congress by the Convention of Delegates from the United States of America, and submitted to us by a resolution of the General Court of said State, passed the 14th day of December last past, and acknowledging, with grateful hearts, the goodness of the Supreme Ruler of the Universe in affording the people of the United States, in the course of His providence, an opportunity, deliberately and peaceably, without fraud or surprise, of entering into an explicit and solemn compact with each other, by assenting to and ratifying a new Constitution in order to form a more perfect Union, establish Justice, insure domestic tranquility, provide for the common defence,(sic) promote the general welfare, and secure the blessings of liberty to themselves and their posterity, Do, in the name and behalf of the people of the State of New Hampshire, assent to and ratify the said Constitution for the United States of America. And as it is the opinion of this Convention that certain amendments and alterations in the said Constitution would remove the fears and quiet the apprehensions of many of the good people of this State, and more effectually guard against an undue administration of the Federal Government, The Convention do, therefore, recommend that the following alterations and provisions be introduced in the said Constitution

Here New Hampshire listed twelve proposed amendments to the Constitution, only one of which we will reproduce. It was number one, and it was similar to the first proposed amendment of Massachusetts. It is: "That it be explicitly declared that all powers not expressly and particularly delegated by the aforesaid Constitution, are reserved to the several States to be by them exercised."

The Constitution, even without this proposal which became the Tenth Amendment, was clear and unambiguous. The Federal government had only the authority expressly delegated to it. Our Fathers were wisely skeptical anyway, and they insisted their intent be made doubly clear by adding this amendment. Even with the Tenth Amendment, look how far we have allowed tyranny to advance with a Federal government which assumes more power continually, and has grown so large, it is essentially an uncontrollable monster bent on devouring both our liberty and the entire wealth of the whole people. Its debt, the admitted 4 trillion dollars, plus unfunded future obligations, is approaching, if it has not already surpassed, the total appraised value of the entire land mass of the United States, the buildings, the cities, the mines, all the personal property of the entire 250 million people of the United States, and anything else of value we might have.

"And the Convention do, in the name and in behalf of the people of this State, enjoin it upon their representatives in Congress, at all times, until the alterations and provisions aforesaid have been considered agreeably to the fifth article of the said Constitution, to exert all their influence, and use all reasonable and legal methods to obtain a ratification of the said alterations and provisions in such manner as is provided in the article.

"And that the United States, in Congress assembled, may have due notice of the assent and ratification of the said Constitution by this Convention, it is Resolved, that the assent and ratification aforesaid be engrossed on parchment, together with the recommendation and injunction aforesaid, and with this resolution; and that John Sullivan, Esqr., President of the Convention, and John Langon, Esqr., President of the State, transmit the same, countersigned by the Secretary of Convention and the Secretary of State, under their hands and seals to the United States in Congress assembled." Elliot's Debates, vol. 1, pp. 325-327.

When New Hampshire on this historic June 21, 1788, joined with her eight preceding sister States, the nine States met the requirements of Union to which representatives of 12 States had agreed in Convention the previous September 17. Article 7, the Constitution.

When word reached the other eight States, there must have been dancing in the streets. These nine States, whether or not the other four ever joined them, would now have a central government sufficiently strong to settle their individual differences, but they were retaining all sovereignty, except that specifically delegated. They were retaining their independence.

Should any or all of the remaining States decide to join them, they would now be joining an existing Union of nine States. However, if the four chose not to join, they would be recognized as sovereign, free and independent States, or Nations, by the Union of nine, as well as other nations of the earth.

Since the nine States had now adopted the Constitution as their governing charter, the former charter, the Articles of Confederation, their former contract of *perpetual union*, was now to be unceremoniously abandoned, at least by the nine. Four days later, it was also abandoned by Virginia as she became the tenth to join the new Union. The final three States, of course, eventually abandoned the old *perpetual union*, opting to adopt the Constitution which said nothing about Union in perpetuity. In fact, the next State to join, Virginia, made it very clear the Union she was joining this time was definitely *not* necessarily, a *perpetual union.*

Tenth, Virginia

We come now to Virginia, the mother of States, as she has properly been called.

First, we will look into her action, then into the debates.

The words of her ratification are as follows:

"We, the Delegates of the people of Virginia, duly elected in pursuance of a recommendation from the General Assembly, and now met in Convention, having fully and freely investigated and discussed the proceedings of the Federal Convention, and being prepared as well as the most mature deliberation hath enabled us to decide thereon, Do, in the name and in behalf of the people of Virginia, declare and make known, that the powers granted under the Constitution, being derived from the people of the United States, **may be resumed by them whensoever the same shall be perverted to their injury or oppression**, (emphasis added) and that every power not granted thereby remains with them, and at their will; that therefore, no right of any denomination can be cancelled, abridged, restrained, or modified, by the Congress, by the Senate or House of Representatives, acting in any capacity by the President, or any department or officer of the United States except in those instances in which power is given by the Constitution for those purposes; and that, among other essential rights, the liberty of conscience, and of the press, cannot be cancelled, abridged, restrained, or modified, by any authority of the United States. With these impressions, with a solemn appeal to the searcher of all hearts for the purity of our intentions, and under the conviction that whatsoever imperfections may exist in the Constitution ought rather to be examined in the mode prescribed therein, than to bring the Union into danger by a delay with a hope of obtaining amendments previous to the ratifications, We, the said Delegates, in the name and in behalf of the people of Virginia, do, by these presents, assent to and ratify the Constitution recommended on the 17th day of September, 1787, by the Federal Convention, for the Government of the United States, hereby announcing to all those whom it may concern, that the said Constitution is binding upon the said people according to an authentic copy hereto annexed in the words following:

"Done in Convention, this 25th day of June, 1788." Elliot's Debates, vol. 1, p. 327.

It is to be noted that the Virginia Convention expressly declare and make known that the powers granted under it may be resumed by them whensoever they may be perverted to their injury. Virginia hurried her ratification, rather "than bring the Union into danger by a delay with a hope of obtaining amendments previous to the ratifications,..." but by reserving her right to leave the Union, she knew there was no risk, for if the other States refused to adopt amendments, or a Bill of Rights, she could simply leave the Union, just as they had all left the Union under the Articles of Confederation, and previous to that, they had all left Great Britain in 1776.

This business of leaving, or separating or seceding from the Union, was no big deal. Sovereign States abandoning their compacts of agreement to join in Union was historically, and for these 13 States, nothing unusual, nor illegal. "Everybody does it," if things don't work out.

Virginia in inserting the clause to resume her sovereignty in her ratification certification was actually doing overkill. This clause was superfluous. Even without it, the right to resume her sovereignty would always exist. There was not then, and no Amendments have been added since, to change it. There is nothing in the Constitution saying a State cannot secede from the Union. Nothing which remotely refers to a State either leaving or permanently remaining in the Union. Since the Constitution says nothing about leaving the Union, some argue this means the Union is perpetual. It can never be broken up. A State, or States, "do not have the option to abandon the Union." These arguments have no basis, no substance. They are without a legal foundation, and the history and laws of nations are against such fantasies.

On the contrary, Virginia, or any other State, freely joined in Union. They had the right to leave just as freely. This was understood. It did not have to be in writing. Virginia was just being super cautious. The States in adopting the first ten Amendments, the Bill of Rights, were again being super cautious. Many of the Founders argued against a Bill of Rights because it was obvious, "they were superfluous; they were not needed because the States retain all powers not specifically delegated."

Nevertheless, our Fathers, understanding the tendency of all government toward tyranny, insisted on adding a Bill of Rights to the Constitution, and Virginia insisted on putting in writing that which all understood she and the other States were retaining; the right to resume their sovereignty, if their child, their creation, their agent, the new Federal government should get out of hand and get too big for its britches.

All parties understood that since they were abandoning their own Articles of Confederation, which specifically stated the *Union was to be perpetual;* that it was useless, a waste of time, a lot of hot air, a historical contradiction to write into any agreement among sovereign nations or states that it is to be perpetual. The words *perpetual union* were probably inserted in the Articles of Confederation more for show than for substance.

Nevertheless, we cannot fault Virginia for putting the right to resume her sovereignty right in her certification of ratification. It eliminates any possible basis in law for those who might later claim that the Union of the United States is one in perpetuity.

At this time when Virginia entered the Union, it was slightly less than 12 years since she and her 12 sister Colonies had adopted The Declaration of Independence, "seceding" from Great Britain. She and the other 12 States had made it very clear that at all times, "...whenever any form of government becomes destructive...it is the right of the people to alter or to abolish it."

In reserving in writing, though unnecessary, her right to resume sovereignty, or leave the Union, Virginia automatically reserved the same right to every other State. These first ten States, and all States joining later, being equally bound, were equally entitled to rights which might be stipulated by any one State. Once a State becomes a part of the Union, it is equal in every respect to every other State in the Union.

Should there remain any doubt as to Virginia's assertion of her right to resume sovereignty, let us refer to the Fifth Article of the Constitution. The States retained under this Article, in the broadest sense of the amending process, the right to abolish the entire Federal government; to abolish the Congress, the Supreme Court and fire the President if three-fourths of them decided to get together and eliminate, or destroy, their entire creation. If the States chose to take this action, the world would not end. The sovereign, independent, and free State governments would still exist and continue to maintain law and order. This is as true today as it was 200 years ago.

The delegation of powers was by the States separately. Whoever delegates can resume. The right to resume or recall attends all delegations of all sorts. It is similar to one delegating authority to one's attorney at law. Any of us understand we have a right to authorize an attorney, or lawyer, or anybody else for that matter, to act for, or on behalf of ourselves. This is legally done with what we call a *Power of Attorney*. But, just as we can give another person a power of attorney, we can withdraw the power of attorney and the person who had it temporarily will no longer have that authority. Our right to withdraw a power of attorney is an option we can exercise at any time we choose to do so.

Let us consider the debates in the Virginia Convention if there should be any doubt as to the understanding we should have on this point.

In Virginia, as in Massachusetts, the Constitution underwent a thorough discussion. The Convention was in session nearly a month. Many of the ablest men of the State were members of it. Men who had first put the rebellion against Great Britain in motion. Patrick Henry was there. George Mason, Bushrod Washington, Henry Lee of Westmorland, George Nicholas, Edmund Pendleton, Edmund Randolph, James Monroe, James Madison, *The father of the Constitution*, and John Marshall. A brighter galaxy of talent, statesmanship and oratory was never assembled in this Republic. The debates fill a large volume by themselves. Let us glean from these discussions the leading ideas of the advocates as well as the opponents of the Constitution in our main point, that is, the nature and character of the government instituted by it. As in Masschusetts, so in Virginia, the opposition was able and formidable. The greatest orator of the age headed it.

"This proposal of altering our Federal Government," said Patrick Henry, "is of a most alarming nature! Make the best of this new Government—say it is composed by any thing but inspiration—you ought to be extremely cautious, watchful, jealous of your liberty, for instead of securing your rights, you may lose them forever.

"I have the highest veneration for those gentlemen; but sir, give me leave to demand, what right had they to say, '*we, the people?*' My political curiosity, exclusive of my anxious solicitude for the public welfare, leads me to ask, who authorized them to speak the language of, 'we, the people,' instead of, 'We, the States?' States are the characteristics and the soul of a Confederation! If the States be not the agents of this Compact, it must be one great, consolidated, National

Government of all the States!"

It might be noted here that Patrick Henry, in his zeal of opposition, was doing a little nit-picking. He was making a mountain out of a mole hill. But his point is well taken. Like others, he was determined that this government was not to be national, but federal in nature. None were going to allow a consolidation of the States and the people into a single national governing body.

Edmund Pendleton, President of the Convention, answered Patrick Henry. "'*We, the people*,' possessing all power, form a government, such as we think will secure happiness, and suppose in adopting this plan, we should be mistaken in the end; where is the cause of alarm on that quarter? In the same plan we point out an easy and quiet method of reforming what may be found amiss. No, but, say gentlemen, we have put the introduction of that method in the hands of our servants who will interrupt it from motives of self-interest. What then? We will resist, did my friend say? Conveying an idea of force. Who shall dare to resist the people? *No, we will assemble in Convention;* **wholly recall our delegated powers,** *or reform* them so as to prevent such abuse. Emphasis added.

"This is the only Government founded in real Compact. There is no quarrel between Government and liberty; the former is the shield and protector of the latter."

"This Constitution is said to have beautiful features," said Mr. Henry, subsequently, "but when I come to examine these features, sir, they appear to me horribly frightful! Among other deformities, it has an awful squinting; it squints towards monarchy, and does not this raise indignation in the breast of every true American?

"We are told," said he, "that this Government, collectively taken, is without an example; that it is National in this part, and Federal in that part, etc. We may be amused, if we please, by a treatise of political anatomy. In the brain it is National; the stamina are Federal; some limbs are Federal, others National. The Senators are voted for by the State Legislatures; so far it is Federal. Individuals choose the members of the first branch; here it is National. It is Federal in conferring general powers, but National in retaining them. It is not to be supported by the States; the pockets of individuals are to be searched for its maintenance. What signifies it to me that you have the most curious anatomical description of it in its creation? To all the common purposes of legislation, it is a great Consolidation of Government. You are not to have the right to legislate in any but trivial cases; you are not to touch private contracts; you are not to have the right of having arms in your own defence; you cannot be trusted with dealing out justice between man and man. What shall the States have to do? Take care of the poor, repair and make highways, erect bridges, and so on, and so on? Abolish the State Legislatures at once. What purposes should they be continued for? Our Legislature will, indeed, be a ludicrous spectacle—one hundred and eighty men marching in solemn, farcical procession, exhibiting a mournful proof of the lost liberty of their country without the power of restoring it. But, sir, we have the consolation that it is a mixed Government; that is, it may work sorely on your neck, but you will have some comfort by saying that it was a Federal Government in its origin.

"I beg gentlemen to consider: lay aside our prejudices. Is this a Federal Government? Is it not a consolidated Government for almost every purpose? Is the Government of Virginia a State Government after this Government is adopted? Grant that it is a Republican Government, but for what purposes? For such trivial domestic considerations as render it unworthy the name of a Legislature. I shall take leave of this political anatomy by observing that it is the most extraordinary that ever entered into the imagination of man. If our political diseases demand a cure, this is an unheard of medicine. The honorable member, I am convinced, wanted a name for it. Were your health in danger, would you take new medicine? I need not make use of these exclamations, for every member in this committee must be alarmed at making new and unusual experiments in Government."

Mr. Lee answered, "But, sir, this is a Consolidated Government," he tells us, and most feelingly does he dwell on the imaginary dangers of this pretended Consolidation. I did suppose that an honorable gentleman, whom I do not now see (Mr. Madison), had placed this in such a clear light that every man would have been satisfied with it.

"If this were a consolidated Government, ought it not to be ratified by a majority of the people as individuals and not as States? Suppose Virginia, Connecticut, Massachusetts, and Pennsylvania, had ratified it; these four States, being a majority of the people of America, would by their adoption, have made it binding on all the States had this been a Consolidated Government. But it is only the Governments of those seven States who have adopted it. If the honorable gentleman will attend to this, we shall hear no more of Consolidation."

This same argument can be used in modern America against that great and widely believed lie, that the United States is a Democracy. We are not a Democracy, we are a Republic and the two are worlds apart. But the moderns who work for *consolidation* of our government into a single whole, would like all to believe we are a Democracy, because democracy leads to Consolidation, to bigger government, and more powerful. But that is another story.

"I say that this new system shows, in stronger terms than words could declare, that the liberties of the people are secure. It goes on the principle that *all power is in the people*, and that rulers have no powers but what are enumerated in that paper. When a question arises with respect to the legality of any power, exercised or assumed by Congress, it is plain on the side of the governed: *Is it enumerated in the Constitution?* If it be, it is legal and just. It is otherwise arbitrary and unconstitutional. Candor must confess that it is infinitely more attentive to the liberties of the people than any State Government.

Mr. Lee then said, that under the State Governments the people reserved to themselves certain enumerated rights, and that the rest were vested in their rulers; that, consequently, the powers reserved to the people were but an inconsiderable exception from what were given to their rulers; but that in the Federal Government the rulers of the people were vested with certain defined powers, and that what were not delegated to those rulers were retained by the people. The consequence of this, he said, was that the limited powers were only an exception to those which rested in the people, and that they knew what they had given up, and could be in no danger. He exemplified the proposition in a familiar manner. He observed that if a man delegated certain powers to an agent, it would be an insult upon common sense to suppose that the agent could legally transact any business for his principal which was not contained in the commission whereby the powers were delegated; but that if a man empowered his representative or agent to transact all his business except certain enumerated parts, the clear result was that the agent could lawfully transact every possible part of his principal's business, except the enumerated parts, and added that these plain propositions were sufficient to demonstrate the inutility and folly (were he permitted to use the expression) of Bills of Rights."

Like others, Mr. Lee was contending the Constitution did not need a Bill of Rights.

Governor Randolph, who had favored a National Government in the Convention at Philadelphia, replied as follows: "The liberty of the press is supposed to be in danger. If this were the case, it would produce extreme repugnancy in my mind. If it ever will be suppressed in this country, the liberty of the people will not be far from being sacrificed."

The Founders did not seem to anticipate that a free press might be a controlled press, nevertheless. Could they, or anybody else, have anticipated the three major television networks, and all major newspapers and most magazines of today, would be owned, controlled, or manipulated as they are, so *the people* receive only the information necessary to maintain complacency, yet remain in ignorance of what is really going on? Governor Randolph continues: "Where is the danger of it? He says that every power is given to the General Government that is not reserved to the States. Pardon me if I say the reverse of the proposition is true. I defy any one to prove the contrary. Every power not given it by this system is left with the States."

We must remember this argument was put forth prior to

the adoption of the first ten amendments, the tenth amendment specifically setting forth this reservation of powers to the States.

Also in reply to the seeming paranoia of Patrick Henry, John Marshall (afterwards Chief Justice of the Supreme Court), said: " We are threatened with the loss of our liberties by the possible abuse of power, nothwithstanding the maxim that those who give may take away. *It is the people that give power, and can take it back.* What shall restrain them? They are the masters who give it, and of whom *their servants* hold it." Emphasis added.

Patrick Henry should always be held in highest esteem for his immortal "liberty or death" speech in the Virginia Convention of March 23, 1775, and as one of our greatest Founding Fathers, but in this Convention of constitutional debate, he was far outclassed because he was in error, and his opponents had the truth on their side.

George Nicholas said: "But it is objected to for want of a Bill of Rights. It is a principle universally agreed upon, that all powers not given are retained. Where, by the Constitution, the General Government has general powers for any purpose, its powers are absolute. Where it has powers with some exceptions, they are absolute only as to those exceptions. In either case, the people retain what is not conferred on the General Government, *as it is by their positive grant that it has any of its powers.* (Emphasis added) In England, in all disputes between the king and people, recurrence is had to the enumerated rights of the people to determine. Are the rights in dispute secured? Are they included in Magna Charta, Bill of Rights, etc.? If not, they are, generally speaking, within the king's prerogative. In disputes between the Congress and the people, the reverse of the proposition holds. *Is the disputed right enumerated? If not, Congress cannot meddle with it.*" Emphasis added.

Mr. Nicholas concluded, by making a few observations on the general structure of the government and its probable happy operation. He said that it was a government calculated to suit almost any extent of territory. He then quoted the opinion of the celebrated Montesquieu from volume 1, p. 9, where that writer speaks of a Confederate Republic as the only safe means of extending the sphere of a Republican Government to any considerable degree.

Mr. Madison said: "The powers of the General Government relate to external objects and are but few. But the powers in the States relate to those great objects which immediately concern the prosperity of the people. Let us observe also, that the powers in the General Government are those which will be exercised ***mostly in time of war***, (emphasis added) while those of the State Governments will be exercised in time of peace. I should not complete the view which ought to be taken of this subject without making this additional remark, that the powers vested in the proposed Government are not so much an augmentation of powers in the General Government, as a change rendered necessary for the purpose of giving efficacy to those which were vested in it before. It cannot escape any gentleman, that this power, in theory, exists in the Confederation (under the Articles of Confederation, under which these gentlemen and the States were governed only a few days or weeks before this speech) as fully as in this Constitution. The only difference is this—that now they tax States, and by this plan they will tax individuals. There is no theoretic difference between the two. But in practice there will be an infinite difference between them. There is an ineffectual power; (meaning the Articles of Confederation with no power to force States to pay their fair share of taxation) the other (Constitution) is adequate to the purpose for which it is given. This change was necessary for the public safety.

"Let us suppose, for a moment, that the acts of Congress requiring money from the States had been as effectual as the paper on the table, suppose all the laws of Congress had complete compliance, will any gentleman say that, as far as we can judge from past experience, the State Governments would have been debased, and all consolidated and incorporated into one system? My imagination cannot reach it. I conceive that had those acts that effect, which all laws ought to have, the States would have retained their Sovereignty."

George Mason, in opposition said: "The objection was, that too much power was given to Congress—power that would finally destroy the State Governments more effectually by insidious, underhanded means, than such as could be openly practiced."

How far-seeing were the fears of our Fathers, and how prophetic they could hardly have imagined. How could they possibly have anticipated that the People would ever fall into such ignorance and apathy as we have in modern America? That Congress, the President and the Courts would combine against *the people* so that Congress does today control State governments to a significant degree by threatening to withhold "Federal money" from the States and *the people* who fail to comply with the wishes and fantasies of Congress; Federal money which came from the people in the first place. The Fathers could hardly have imagined that the blessings of liberty they were handing to their children on a silver platter, would bring such wealth and prosperity, that those children would become so bent on pleasures and accumulation of property, they would stand in danger of, and possibly lose the greatest gift of God to man in this world...*human liberty*. We are letting Congress "by underhanded means," as feared by the Founders, destroy this once great Nation.

Mr. Marshall replied: "When the Government is drawn from the people, and depending on the people for its continuance, oppressive measures will not be attempted, as they will certainly draw on their authors the resentment of those on whom they depend. On this Government, thus depending *on ourselves for its existence*, I will rest my safety, nothwithstanding the danger depicted by the honorable gentleman. I cannot help being surprised that the worthy member thought this power so dangerous."

Mr. Marshall and others did not foresee the year 1913 when a private bank would be established, *The Federal Reserve System*, which would be authorized by Congress to print our money, create billions or trillions of dollars in credit, charge *the people* interest on this, the people's own credit, then use this massive money machine to eliminate constitutional protections.

Mr. Marshall did not anticipate how inneffective the public schools and universities of America would become in less than 200 years; that the masses of the people would allow themselves to be manipulated, coerced and intimidated by their State, as well as this proposed new Federal government, because of massive ignorance of their history, the Constitution, and having little understanding of the perpetual sovereignty of *the people*, not only in this government, but in any government on earth.

But the point Mr. Marshall was making was valid then and it is valid today. The Federal government of the United States *is dependent on the people for its existence*. The *sovereign people*, and the *sovereign states* can always, if they choose, take the Federal Government out of existence just as they were about to bring it into existence. The Federal Government was created by the *states*, it could be destroyed by the *states*. And if the States should choose to so destroy at any given time, all the States would resume their original position of *free, independent*, and *sovereign states*. The world would not come to an end, and the *state* governments would continue to function as they always had before.

And after the States destroyed their creation they could at some future date again join in yet another Union if it suits their purpose.

There was nothing sacred about the ties the Colonies had to King George in 1776. There is nothing sacred about the Federal government more than 200 years later, that the States should not dismantle it piece by piece and eliminate its usurpations and assumptions of undelegated powers, and its planned destruction of the Constitution itself.

It will be far better to destroy the Federal Government of the United States than to allow the Federal Government to destroy the Constitution. If this becomes the final choice, there is no question that the *states*, acting in concert, must eliminate or abolish the Federal structure and resume their own sovereignty.

Mr. Marshall then concluded: "the power of governing the

militia was not vested in the States by implication, because being possessed of it antecedent to the adoption of the Government, and not being divested of it by any grant or restriction in the Constitution, they must necessarily be as fully possessed of it as ever they had been. And it could not be said that any of the States derived any powers from that system, but retained them, though not acknowledged in any part of it."

This point is extremely important for we often read in the newspapers and hear in other media, that the Federal Government is *allowing the states* to do such and such, or *allowing the states* to have a say in a certain matter. This indicates the long term objective of conditioning the people to believe that *the states* are mere pawns in their relationship to the Federal government, when we have shown, the opposite is the actual fact.

Mr. Henry again spoke as follows: "A bill of rights may be summed up in a few words. What do they tell us? That our rights are reserved. Why not say so? Is it because it will consume too much paper? Gentlemen's reasoning against a bill of rights does not satisfy me—without saying which has the right side, it remains doubtful. A bill of rights is a favorite thing with the Virginians and the people of the other States, likewise. It may be their prejudice, but the Government ought to suit their geniuses; otherwise its operation will be unhappy. *A Bill of Rights, even if its necessity be doubtful, will exclude the possibility of dispute; and with great submission, I think the best way is to have no dispute.* (Emphasis added.) In the present Constitution they are restrained from issuing general warrants to search suspected places or seize persons not named, without evidence of the commission of a fact, etc. There was certainly some celestial influence governing those who deliberated on that Constitution; for they have with the most cautious and enlightened circumspection, guarded those indefeasible rights which ought ever to be held sacred!"

Mr. George Nicholas, in answer, said: "That though there was a declaration of rights in the Government of Virginia, it was no conclusive reason that there should be one in this Constitution; for if it was unnecessary in the former, its omission in the latter could be no defect. They ought, therefore, to prove that it was essentially necessary to be inserted in the Constitution of Virginia. There were five or six states in the Union which had no bill of rights, separately and distinctly as such; but they annexed the substance of a bill of rights to their respective Constitutions. These States, he further observed, were as free as this State, and their liberties as secure as ours. If so, gentlemen's arguments from the precedent were not good. In Virginia, all powers were given to the Government without any exception. It was different in the General Government, to which certain special powers were delegated for certain purposes. He asked which was the more safe. Was it safer to grant general powers than certain limited powers?"

He continued: "A bill of rights is only an acknowledgement of the pre-existing claim to rights in the people. They belong to us as much as if they had been inserted in the Constitution. But it is said that, if it be doubtful, the possibility of dispute ought to be precluded. Admitting it was proper for the Convention to have inserted a bill of rights, it is not proper here to propose it as the condition of our accession to the Union. Would you reject this Government for its omission, dissolve the Union and bring miseries on yourselves and posterity? I hope the gentleman does not oppose it on this ground solely. Is there another reason? He said that it is not only the general wish of this State, but all the States to have a bill of rights. If it be so, where is the difficulty of having this done by way of subsequent amendment? We shall find the other States willing to accord with their own favorite wish. The gentleman last up says that the power of legislation includes everything. A general power of legislation does. But this is a special power of legislation. Therefore, it does not contain that plenitude of power which he imagines. They cannot legislate in any case but those particularly enumerated. No gentleman, who is a friend to the Government, ought to withhold his assent from it for this reason."

Mr. Henry continued his strenuous opposition in the following language: "The Honorable gentleman (Governor Randolph), who was up some time ago, exhorts us not to fall into a repetition of the defects of the Confederation. He said we ought not to declare that each State retains every power, jurisdiction, and right, which is not expressly delegated because experience has proved the insertion or such a restriction to be destructive and mentioned an instance to prove it. That case, Mr. Chairman, appears to me to militate against himself. They can exercise power, by implication, in one instance as well as in another. Thus, by the gentleman's own argument, they can exercise the power, though it be not delegated. We have nothing local to ask. We ask rights which concern the general happiness. Must not justice bring them into the concesssion of these? The Honorable gentleman was pleased to say that the new Government, in this policy, will be equal to what the present is. If so, that amendment will not injure that part.

"He speaks of war and bloodshed. Whence do this war and bloodshed come? I fear it, but not from the source he speaks of. I fear it, sir, from the operation and friends of the Federal Government. He speaks with contempt of this amendment. But whoever will advert to the use made repeatedly in England, of the prerogative of the King, and the frequent attacks on the privileges of the people, notwithstanding many Legislative acts to secure them, will see the necessity of *excluding implications*. Nations who have trusted to logical deductions have lost their liberty!

"The worthy member who proposed to ratify has also proposed that what amendments may be deemed necessary should be recommended to Congress, and that a committee should be appointed to consider what amendments were necessary. But what does it all come to at last? That it is a vain project, and that it is indecent and improper! I will not argue unfairly, but I will ask him if amendments are not unattainable? Will gentlemen then lay their hands on their hearts and say that they can adopt it in this shape? When we demand this security of our privileges, the language of Virginia is not that of respect! Give me leave to deny! She only asks amendments previous to her adoption of the Constitution.

"He tells you of the important blessings which he imagines will result to us and mankind in general from the adoption of this system. I see the awful immensity of the dangers with which it is pregnant! I see it! I feel it! I see beings of a higher order anxious concerning our decision! When I see beyond the horizon that bounds human eyes and look at the final consummation of all human things, and see those intelligent beings which inhabit the ethereal mansions, reviewing the political decisions and revolutions which, in the progress of time, will happen in America, and the consequent happiness or misery of mankind, I am led to believe that much of the account, on one side or the other, will depend on what we now decide! Our own happiness alone is not affected by the event! *All nations are interested in the determination! We have it in our power to secure the happiness of one half of the human race!* (Emphasis added). Its adoption may involve the misery of the other hemisphere."

Just at this point in Mr. Henry's speech, the heavens blackened with a gathering tempest, which burst with so terrible a fury as to put the whole house in such disorder that he could proceed no further! It was the last speech that Patrick Henry made in that Convention! "Here a violent storm arose which put the House in such disorder that Mr. Henry was obliged to conclude." Reporter. Elliot's Debates, volume 3, p 625.

Did Patrick Henry receive inspiration, or revelation from Deity, which allowed him to see into the future and understand better the workings of political systems controlled by human passion, more so than any of his many great and equally patriotic colleagues in that renowned body of sages and statesmen? Did he see further into the future than Pendleton, Madison, or Marshall when he said, 'I see it, I feel it?' Did he get glimpses of the terrible scenes of the Civil War? Or of the potentially more horrible wars yet ahead of us in the year 2,000?

We know the skepticism of Patrick Henry was well justified by our history of the last 200 years, especially the last five decades. Nevertheless, he was wrong in supposing the amendments known as the Bill of Rights would never be adopted. The fears of Patrick Henry may well yet prove prophetic, but the power is still in *the people*, if they will only use it to keep his fears from coming to pass, as pointed out in the reply of Mr. Nicholas.

He argued that the language of the proposed ratification would secure everything which gentlemen desired, as it declared that all powers vested in the Constitution were derived from the people, and might be resumed by them whensoever they should be perverted to their injury and oppression; and that every power not granted thereby remained at their will. No danger whatever could arise; for says he, these expressions will become a part of the contract. The Constitution cannot be binding on Virginia, but with these conditions. If thirteen individuals are about to make a contract, and one agrees to it, but at the same time declares that he understands its meaning, signification, and intent to be, what the words of the contract plainly and obviously denote, that it is not to be construed so as to impose any supplementary condition upon him, and that he is to be exonerated from it whensoever any such imposition shall be attempted, we ask whether, in this case, these conditions on which he has assented to it, would not be binding on the other twelve? In like manner, these conditions will be binding on Congress. They can exercise no power that is not expressly granted them.

Virginia ratified the Constitution by a vote of 89 in favor, 79 against.

Immediately afterwards the amendments which had been agreed upon to be proposed were taken up and adopted without opposition. They were twenty in number. Very similar, in many respects to those incorporated by Massachusetts in her ratification. The first, and most important, was:

"1st. That each State in the Union shall, respectively, retain every power, jurisdiction, and right, which is not by this Constitution delegated to the Congress of the United States, or to the departments of the Federal Government." This, of course, is the Tenth Amendment as we know it today.

These proceedings conclusively show how the Convention of Virginia understood the Constitution. That is, that it was *Federal* in its character, and that the Government under it was to be a Federal Government, one founded upon Compact between Sovereign States. The Constitution was merely a contract, or treaty. The Federal Government, a mere corporate creation of sovereign principals.

Not a member of the Convention advocated the Constitution upon any other principles. The opposition of Patrick Henry, George Mason, and others was altogether argumentative, and sprung mainly from apprehensions that the Constitution would not be construed as its friends maintained that it would be, and that powers not delegated *would* be assumed by construction and implication. In hindsight, we know these fears were well founded.

These proceedings also show clearly that Virginia understood by the declaration in her ratification that her people had the right to resume the powers that they had delegated in case these powers, in their judgment, should be perverted to their injury. In doing so, no resort to force or war was anticipated. Virginia was joining the Union of her own free will; she could and would leave also, on her own free will if she, in her judgment alone, felt it necessary or advisable to do so.

Eleventh, New York

Here is the ratification of New York.

"We the delegates of the people of the State of New York, duly elected and met in Convention, having maturely considered the Constitution for the United States of America, agreed to on the 17th day of September, in the year 1787, by the Convention then assembled at Philadelphia, in the Commonwealth of Pennsylvania (a copy whereof precedes these presents), and having also seriously and deliberately considered the present situation of the United States,—Do declare and make known,—

"That all power is originally vested in, and consequently derived from the people, and that Government is instituted by them for their common interest, protection, and security.

"That the enjoyment of life, liberty, and the pursuit of

happiness are essential rights which every Government ought to respect and preserve.

"That the powers of Government may be re-assumed by the people, whensoever it shall become necessary to their happiness; (emphasis added) that every power, jurisdiction, and right, which is not by the said Constitution clearly delegated to the Congress of the United States, or the departments of the Government thereof, *remains to the people of the several States, or to their respective State Government* to whom they may have granted the same; and that those clauses, in the said Constitution, which declare that Congress shall not have or exercise certain powers, *do not imply that Congress is entitled to any powers not given by the said Constitution;* (emphasis added) but such clauses are to be construed either as exceptions to certain specified powers, or as inserted merely for greater caution.

"That the people have an equal, natural, and unalienable right, freely and peaceably, to exercise their religion, according to the dictates of conscience; and that no religious sect, or society, ought to be favored or established by law in preference to others.

"That the people have a right to keep and bear arms; that a well regulated militia, *including the body of the people capable of bearing arms,* is the proper, natural, and safe defence of a free State. Emphasis added.

"That the militia should not be subject to martial law, except in time of war, rebellion or insurrection.

"That standing armies, in time of peace, are dangerous to liberty, and ought not to be kept up, except in cases of necessity, and that at all times the military should be under strict subordination to the civil power.

"That, in time of peace, no soldier ought to be quartered in any house without the consent of the owner, and in time of war only by the civil magistrate, in such manner as the laws may direct.

"That no person ought to be taken, imprisoned, or disseized of his freehold, or be exiled, or deprived of his privileges, franchises, life, liberty, or property, but by the process of law.

"That no person ought to be put twice in jeopardy of life or limb, for one and the same offense; nor unless in case of impeachment, be punished more than once for the same offense. That every person restrained of his liberty is entitled to an inquiry into the lawfulness of such restraint, and to a removal thereof if unlawful; and that such inquiry, or removal, ought not to be denied or delayed except when, on account of public danger, the Congress shall suspend the privilege of the writ of Habeas Corpus. That excessive bail ought not to be required, nor excessive fines imposed, nor cruel or unusual punishments inflicted.

"That (except in the government of the land and naval forces, and of the militia, when in actual service, and in cases of impeachment) a presentment, or indictment by a grand jury ought to be observed as a necessary preliminary to the trial of all crimes cognizable by the judiciary of the United States; and such trial should be speedy, public, and by an impartial jury of the county where the crime was committed; and that no person can be found guilty without the unanimous consent of such jury. But in cases of crimes not committed within any county of any of the United States, and in cases of crimes not committed within any county in which a general insurrection may prevail, or which may be in the possession of a foreign enemy, the inquiry and trial may be in such county as the Congress shall by law direct; which county, in the two cases last mentioned, should be as near as conveniently may be to that county in which the crime may have been committed— and that, in all criminal prosecutions, the accused ought to be informed of the cause and nature of his accusation, to be confronted with his accusers and the witnesses against him, to have the means of producing his witnesss, and the assistance of counsel for his defence; and should not be compelled to give evidence against himself.

"That every freeman has a rignt to be secure from all unreasonable searches or seizures of his person, his papers, or his property; and therefore, that all warrants to search suspected places, or seize any freeman, his papers, or property, without information upon oath, or affirmation of sufficient cause, are grievous and oppressive; and that all general warrants (or such in which the place or person suspected are not particularly designated) are dangerous, and ought not to be granted.

"That the people have a right peaceably to assemble together, to consult for their common good, or to instruct their representatives, and that every person, has the right to petition, or apply to the Legislature, for redress of grievances.

"That the freedom of the press ought not to be violated or restrained. (The New York delegation did not, apparently, anticipate the press might one day join hands with the government and conspire to keep *the people* in ignorance, and that the *New York Times* of the 20th century would be a leading advocate of publishing all the news *that's fit to print*, and *only* that news which the government and media know will keep the people in the dark about what the government is *really* doing)

"That there should be once in four years, an election of the President and Vice President, so that no officer who may be appointed by the Congress, to act as President, in case of the removal, death, resignation, or inability of the President and Vice President, can in any case continue to act beyond the termination of the period for which the last President and Vice President were elected.

"That nothing contained in the said Constitutution is to be construed to prevent the legislature of any State from passing laws at its discretion from time to time, divide such state into convenient districts, and to apportion its representatives to and amongst such districts.

"That the prohibition contained in the said Constitution against ex post facto laws, extends only to laws concerning crimes

"That all appeals in causes determinable according to the course of the common law ought to be by writ of error, and not otherwise.

"That the Judicial power of the United States, in cases in which a State may be a party, does not extend to criminal prosecutions, or to authorize any suit by any person against a State.

"That the judicial power of the United States, as to

controversies between citizens of the same State, claiming lands under grants from different States, is not to be construed to extend to any other controversies between them, except those which relate to such lands, so claimed under grants of different States.

"That the jurisdiction of the Supreme Court of the United States, or of any other Court to be instituted by the Congress, is not in any case to be increased, enlarged or extended, by any faction, collusion, or mere suggestion; *and that no treaty is to be construed so to operate as to alter the Constitution of any State*. Emphasis added.

"Under these impressions, and declaring that the rights aforesaid cannot be abridged or violated, and that the explanations aforesaid are consistent with the said Constitution, and in confidence that the amendments, which shall have been proposed to the said Constitution, will receive an early and mature consideration. We, the said delegates, in the name and in the behalf of the people of the State of New York, do, by these presents, assent to, and ratify the said Constitution. In full confidence, nevertheless, that until a Convention shall be called and convened, for proposing amendments to the said Constitution, the militia of this State will not be continued in service out of this State for a longer term than six weeks without the consent of the Legislature thereof; that the Congress will not make or alter any regulation in this State, respecting the times, places, and manner of holding elections for Senators or Representatives, unless the Legislature of this State shall neglect or refuse to make laws or regulations for the purpose, or from any circumstance, be incapable of making the same; and that in those cases, such power will only be exercised until the Legislature of this State shall make provision in the premises; that no excise will be imposed on any article of the growth, production, or manufacture of the United States, or any of them within this State, ardent spirits excepted; and that Congress will not lay direct taxes within this State, but when the moneys arising from the impost and excise shall be insufficient for the public exigencies, nor then, until Congress shall first have made a requisition upon this State to assess, levy, and pay the amount of such requisition, made agreeably to the census fixed in the said Constitution, in such way and manner as the Legislature of this State shall judge best; but that in such case, if the State shall neglect or refuse to pay its proportion, pursuant to such requisition, then the Congress may assess and levy this State's proportion, together with interest, at the rate of six per centum per annum, from the time at which the same was required to be paid.

"Done in Convention at Poughkeepsie, in the county of Duchess, in the State of New York, the 25th day of July in the year of our Lord 1788."

As Virginia, New York accompanied her ratification with the express declaration that *the powers of Government may be resumed by the people whensoever it shall become necessary to their happiness*, etc.

Possible future *secession* from the Union was specifically reserved and made part of the *contract*.

Hamilton failed to see our day, when Congress, through the *power of the purse*, would intimidate and control the legislatures of the States. He failed to see our day when our State legislators, governors, and attorneys general, would become so ignorant of the very structure of our government that they would allow Congress to nearly destroy the Constitution; that they would let Congress spend this nation into near oblivion and run up a debt so gigantic that generations to come, to infinity, will be unable to pay it.

Nevertheless, Hamilton and many others who supported ratification of the Constitution knew they were giving future generations the tools, if they were not ignorant of their use, to put Congress, the Executive and the Courts in their rightful and minor place any time they chose to do so.

Again Hamilton said: "The gentlemen are afraid that the State Governments will be abolished. But sir, their existence does not depend upon the laws of the United States. *Congress can no more abolish the State Governments, than they can dissolve the Union.* The whole Constitution is repugnant to it, and yet the gentleman would introduce an additional useless provision against it."

Hamilton should have mentioned that on the contrary, the States could abolish the Congress along with the entire Federal Government. Though this was understood by our Fathers, perhaps it was thought ungentlemanly, or too provocative to mention it.

Again he said: "The State Governments possess inherent advantages which will ever give them an influence and ascendancy over the National Government, and will forever preclude the possibility of federal encroachments. That their liberties, indeed, can be subverted by the Federal head, is repugnant to every rule of political calculation. Is not this arrangement then, sir, a most wise and prudent one?..."

In the l990's, Mr. Hamilton, we must answer yes, yes, yes! You are absolutely right from a legal and technical standpoint. Your arguments were sound and powerful. Now we must find the will to put them into effect. Mr. Hamilton, sir, we thank you for your efforts in helping our generation to understand that *we, the people*, and *the States*, are still in control if we have the will and the knowledge to take charge.

Mr. Hamilton: "I insist that it never can be the interest or desire of the National Legislature to destroy *the States Governments*." He really missed the boat on this piece of speculation. In fact, later in the Administration of George Washington, he did his share toward reducing sovereignty of the States. "It can derive no advantage from such an event; but on the contrary, would lose an indispensable support, a necessary aid in executing the laws and conveying the influence of Government to the doors of the people. The Union is dependent on the will of the State Governments for its Chief Magistrate, (President) and for its Senate. (The Senate is now elected by direct popular vote. Changed by the 17th Amendment) The blow aimed at the members must give a fatal wound to the head, and the destruction of the States must be at once a political suicide..."

"The States can never lose their powers till the whole people of America are robbed of their liberties. These must go together; they must support each other, or meet one common fate. Elliot's Debates, vol. 2, p. 282, 296, 355

"With regard to the *jurisdiction* of the two governments, I shall certainly admit that the Constitution ought to be so formed as not to prevent the States from providing for their own existence; and I maintain that it is so formed, and that their power of providing for themselves is sufficiently established. This is conceded by one gentleman, and in the next breath the concession is retracted. He says Congress have but one exclusive right in taxation—that of duties on imports; certainly then their other powers are only concurrent. But, to take off the force of this obvious conclusion, he immediately says that the laws of the United States are supreme; and that where there is one supreme, there cannot be concurrent authority; and further, that where the laws of the Union are supreme, those of the States must be subordinate, because there cannot be two supremes. This is curious sophistry. That two supremes cannot act together is false. They are inconsistent only when they are aimed at each other, or at one indivisible object. The laws of the United States are supreme as to all their proper, constitutional objects; the laws of the States are supreme in the same way. These supreme laws may act on different objects without clashing, or they may operate on different parts of the same object with perfect harmony. Suppose both Governments should lay a tax of a penny on a certain article: had not each an independent and uncontrollable power to collect its own tax? The meaning of the maxim, there cannot be two supremes, is simply this—two powers cannot be supreme over each other. This meaning is entirely perverted by the gentleman. But it is said disputes between collectors are to be referred to the Federal courts. This is again wandering in the field of conjecture. But suppose the fact certain, is it not to be presumed that they will express the true meaning of the Constitution and the laws? Will they not be bound to consider the concurrent jurisdiction; to declare that both the taxes shall have equal operation; that both the powers, in that respect, are Sovereign and co-extensive? If they transgress their duty, we are to hope that they will be punished. Sir, we can reason from probabilities alone. When we leave common sense, and give ourselves up to conjecture, there can be no certainty, no security in our reasonings.

"I imagine, I have stated to the committee abundant reasons to prove the entire safety of the State Governments and of the people."

The debates in the New York Convention lasted more than a month. The vote was close, 30 yeas, 27 nays. Hamilton's arguments in debate are particularly important because, at heart, he was more of a *Nationalist*, not a *Federalist*.

His copious and elaborate speeches abundantly show that he considered the plan, the Constitution, finally adopted by the Philadelphia Convention, to be a Federal one. And his greatest efforts were put forth against those who argued that a different construction might be put upon it. In one of his speeches he styled the Union a Confederacy; that is a league, or alliance, of two or more nations or states in support of some common act or enterprise. As such, he gave it his zealous support, though it was not such a one as he wished to see organized. Nor was it one in which he had much real confidence. The idea on which it was based was not his own. Failing in his own, he patriotically took the plan adopted and threw his whole soul in its support as an experiment.

Fortunately, Hamilton's ideas of greater consolidation of power in the Federal Government were not written into the Constitution at Philadelphia, or liberty, as our generation has known it, probably would have ended long ago.

Even with the separation of powers written into the Constitution, and limited delegated powers, we are in a death struggle with men of great wealth, power and intellect who are determined to eliminate State Sovereignty and the sovereignty of *the people* in a gigantic world wide consolidation of governmental power. But as Hamilton correctly argued in the New York Convention, it is not possible for such a consolidation to legally come about. The States, and *the people*, were retaining, and still retain, all the real power!

Twelfth, North Carolina

Before looking at the certification of ratification of North

Carolina, let us consider the fact that she remained outside the new Union for precisely 17 months, almost a year-and-a-half. New Hampshire ratified June 21, 1788, as the ninth State, making the new Union effective, or operative, or so it could lawfully function among the nine States which had signed the *contract*. North Carolina remained outside until November 21, 1789. Just as Virginia and New York were outside the Union, except for a much shorter period of time.

During this seventeen month time frame, the eleven States which had already joined in union under the new Constitution had, in fact, *seceded* from the Union to which North Carolina and Rhode Island still belonged, under the old Articles of Confederation which had become effective in March 1781. In theory, at least, North Carolina and Rhode Island still clung to the old Union under the Confederation by themselves. The other eleven States had not just *seceded* from that Union; they had "overthrown" an existing government and left North Carolina and Rhode Island to fend for themselves. From the point of view of North Carolina and Rhode Island, had not the other eleven States committed treason against them? Was not the purpose of the new Constitution, in fact, the overthrow of an existing government under the old Articles, as well as a "more perfect Union?"

Yet, this "overthrow" of an existing government; this *secession*, or separation, took place peacefully, as it should. Jefferson had said in The Declaration of Independence, "it is the right of the people to alter or abolish, and to institute new Government," whenever as to them shall seem most likely to effect their safety and happiness.

After the bitter battle Hamilton and Jay waged against Governor Clinton of New York, and the governor's men, New York became the "eleventh pillar" of the new Union. James Wilson then wrote to his wife: "Last night they fired thirteen cannon...over the funeral of the Confederation, and this morning they saluted the new government with eleven cannon."

If Jefferson was right, as we affirm he was every July 4, the separation of the first eleven States under the Constitution from North Carolina and Rhode Island, was nothing to get excited about—no reason for war. Everybody was just doing their own thing. Why not do it in peace? People have a right to govern themselves in small groups or large. Wars to determine the size of territory to be governed by a select group are such a terrible waste of life and resources. These thirteen little nations peacefully separated on June 21, 1788, and by May 29, 1790, all thirteen had again joined peacefully in a completely new Union under the Constitution.

Though this new Union was to endure for more than 200 years, there was, and is, nothing which forbids, legally, ethically, or any other way, future separation of one or more States, if the people should choose to so separate for whatever reason. And then like the original thirteen States, they might rejoin in Union if, and when, grievances and differences can be negotiated to the satisfaction of all parties.

The ratification of North Carolina is in these words:

"In Convention:

"Whereas, the General Convention which met in Philadelphia in pursuance of a recommendation of Congress, did recommend to the citizens of the United States a Constitution, or form of Government, in the following words, namely: Resolved, That this Convention, in behalf of the freemen, citizens, and inhabitants of the State of North Carolina, do adopt and ratify the said Constitution and form of Government.

"Done, in Convention, this twenty-first day of November, one thousand seven hundred and eighty-nine."

Having waited so long to join this new Union, nevertheless, the proceedings in North Carolina were short. In the debates, Mr. Davie, said:..."The act of the Convention (at Philadelphia) is but a mere proposal, similar to the production of a private pen. I think it a Government which, if adopted, will cherish and protect the happiness and liberty of America; but I hold my mind open to conviction. I am ready to recede from my opinion if it be proved to be ill-founded...The weakness and inefficiency of the old Confederation produced the necessity of calling the Federal Convention. Their plan is now before you; and I hope, on a deliberate consideration, every man will see the necessity of such a system. It has been the subject of much jealousy and censure out of doors. I hope gentlemen will now come forward with their objections, and that they will be thrown out and answered with candor and moderation...A consolidation of the States is said by some gentlemen to have been intended. They insinuate that this was the cause of their giving this power of elections. If there were any seeds in this Constitution which might, one day produce a consolidation, it would, sir, with me, be an insuperable objection, I am so perfectly convinced that so extensive a country as this can never be managed by one consolidated Government. The Federal Convention were as well convinced as the members of this House, that the State Governments were absolutely necessary to the existence of the Federal Government. They considered them as the great massy pillars on which this political fabric was to be extended and supported; and were fully persuaded that, when they were removed, or should moulder down by time the General Government must tumble into ruin. A very little reflection will show that no department of it can exist without the State Governments.

"Let us begin with the House of Representatives. Who are to vote for the Federal Representatives? Those who vote for the State Representatives. If the State Government vanishes, the General Government must vanish also. This is the foundation on which this Government was raised, and without which it cannot possibly exist.

"The next department is the Senate. How is it formed? By the States themselves. Do they not choose them? Are they not created by them? And will they not have the interest of the States particularly at heart? The States, sir, can put a final period to the Government, as was observed by a gentleman who thought this power over elections unnecessary. If the State Legislatures think proper, they may refuse to choose Senators, and the Government must be destroyed."

This argument was weakened, perhaps, by adoption of the Seventeenth Amendment which was declared to have been ratified by 36 States, which "constitute three fourths," on May 31, 1913. Under constitutional theory, the Founders had given the Senate the responsibility of representing the States. The Senate was supposed to, in theory, stand guard over *states' rights*. Their duty was to keep taxes low, balance the budget, "temper the radicalism of the House," and serve as the "elder statesmen" of the Congress. So senators could remain above the popular issues of the day, prior to the Seventeenth Amendment, they were appointed by the State Legislatures, rather than being elected directly by the people of the State.

The Seventeenth Amendment, theoretically, changed all this. It made the Senate, as well as the House, a reflection of the popular will, and weakened the sovereign interests of the States. It was the States, however, which forced the adoption of the Seventeenth Amendment. The Senate had resisted this change from the beginning, and only capitulated when nearly two-thirds of the state legislatures had voted for a constitutional convention to pass the amendment, and knew the amendment was going to be added to the Constitution with, or without, the Senate's blessing.

"The final blow came in 1911 when the Chicago Tribune revealed that Senator William Lorimer (R. Ill.) has literally purchased his appointment by wholesale bribery of the state assembly. The Senate not only refused to seat Lorimer, but the incident broke down all remaining resistance to the passage of the Seventeenth Amendment." Book, *Making of America*, by W. Cleon Skousen.

The North Carolina Convention recommended six amendments to the Constitution. We will quote only the first, which like other States' proposed amendments, eventually was edited to what became the Tenth Amendment.

"1. Each State in the Union shall respectively retain every power, jurisdiction, and right, which is not by this Constitution delegated to the Congress of the United States, or to the departments of the General Government; nor shall the said Congress, nor any department of the said Government exercise any act of authority over any individual in any of the said States, but such as can be justified under some power particularly given in this Constitution; but the said Constitution shall be considered at all times a solemn instrument defining the extent of their authority and the limits of which they cannot rightfully in any instance exceed." Elliot's Debates, vol. 4, pp. 21-23, 58, 249. The vote of North Carolina was, 194 yeas, 77 nays.

Thirteenth, Rhode Island

Even after the new Union had been in effect almost two years, Rhode Island entered with extreme caution on May 29, 1790. Their delegation's vote was a close, 34 yeas, 32 nays. With the closeness of the vote, one might imagine the passion and fire of her debates. Her proceedings were voluminous. Their very length shows how completely Federal, not National, they were, and how they were guarding against every possible danger to the Sovereignty of their State.

Here is the document of ratification.

"We the Delegates of the people of the State of Rhode Island and Providence Plantations, duly elected and met in Convention, having maturely considered the Constitution for the United States of America, agreed to on the seventeenth day of September, in the year one thousand seven hundred and eighty-seven, by the Convention then assembled at Philadelphia, in the Commonwealth of Pennsylvania (a copy whereof precedes these presents), and having also seriously and deliberately considered the present situation of this State, do declare and make known,—

"I. That there are certain natural rights of which men, when they form a social compact, cannot deprive or divest their posterity, among which are the enjoyment of life and liberty, with the means of acquiring, possessing and protecting property, and pursuing and obtaining happiness and safety.

"II. That all power is naturally vested in, and consequently derived from, *the people;* (emphasis added) that magistrates, therefore, are their trustees and agents, and at all times amenable to them.

"III. That the powers of Government **may be resumed by the people whensoever it shall become necessary to their happiness.** (In other words, secede, separate, leave the Union as freely as they were then joining). That the rights of the States respectively to nominate and appoint all State officers, and every other power, jurisdiction, and right, which is not by the said Constitution clearly delegated to the Congress of the United States, or to the Departments of Government thereof, remain to the people of the several States, or their respective State Governments to whom they may have granted the same; and that those clauses in the Constitution which declare that Congress shall not have or exercise certain powers, do not imply that Congress is entitled to any powers not given by the said Constitution; but such clauses are to be construed as exceptions to certain specified powers, or as inserted merely for greater caution.

"IV. That religion or the duty which we owe to our Creator, and the manner of dischargIng it, can be directed only by reason and conviction, and not by force and violence; and therefore, all men have a natural, equal, and unalienable right to the exercise of religion according to the dictates of conscience; and that no particular religious Sect, or Society, ought to be favored or established by law in preference to others.

"V. That the legislative, executive, and judiciary powers of Government should be separate and distinct; and that the members of the two first may be restrained from oppression by feeling and participating in the public burdens, they should, at fixed periods, be reduced to a private station returned into the mass of the people, and the vacancies be supplied by certain and regular elections, in which all, or any part of the former members to be eligible or ineligible, as the rules of the Constitution of Government and the laws shall direct.

"VI. That elections of representatives in Legislature ought to be free and frequent, and all men having sufficient evidence of permanent common interest with, and attachment to, the community, ought to have the right of suffrage; (right to vote) and no aid, charge, tax, or fee can be set, rated, or levied upon the people, without their own consent, or that of their representatives so elected, nor can they be bound by any law to which they have not in like manner consented for the public good.

"VII. That all power of suspending laws, or the execution of laws, by any authority, without the consent of the representatives of the people in the Legislature, is injurious to their rights, and ought not to be exercised.

"VIII. That in all capital and criminal prosecutions, a man hath the right to demand the cause and nature of his accusation, to be confronted with the accusers and witnesses, to call for evidence, and be allowed counsel in his favor, and to a fair and speedy trial by an impartial jury in his vicinage, without whose unanimous consent he cannot be found guilty, (except in the government of the land and naval forces,) nor can he be compelled to give evidence against himself.

"IX. That no freeman ought to be taken, imprisoned, or disseized of his freehold, liberties, privileges, or franchises, or outlawed, or exiled, or in any manner destroyed, or deprived of his life, liberty, or property, but by the trial by jury, or by the laws of the land.

"X. That every freeman, restrained of his liberty, is entitled to a remedy to inquire into the lawfulness thereof, and to remove the same if unlawful, and that such remedy ought not to be denied or delayed.

"XI. That in controversies respecting property, and in suits between man and man, the ancient trial by jury, as hath been exercised by us and our ancestors from the time whereof the memory of man is not to the contrary, is one of the greatest securities to the rights of the people, and ought to remain sacred and inviolable.

"XII. That every freeman ought to obtain right and justice, freely and without sale, completely and without sale, completely and without denial, promptly and without delay; and that all establishments, or regulations contravening these rights are oppressive and unjust.

"XIII. That excessive bail ought not to be required, nor excessive fines imposed, nor cruel or unusual punishments inflicted.

"XIV. That every person has a right to be secure from all unreasonable searches and seizures of his person, his papers, or his property; and, therefore, that all warrants to search suspected places, to seize any person, his papers, or his property without information upon oath or affirmation of sufficient cause, are grievous and oppressive; and that all general warrants (or such in which the place or person suspected are not particularly designated) are dangerous, and ought not to be granted.

"XV. That the people have a right peaceably to assemble together, to consult for their common good, or to instruct their representatives; and that every person has a right to petition or apply to the Legislature for redress of grievances.

"XVI. That the people have a right to freedom of speech, and of writing, and publishing their sentiments That freedom of the press is one of the greatest bulwarks of liberty, and ought not to be violated.

"XVII. *That the people have a right to keep and bear arms; that a well regulated militia, including the body of the people capable of bearing arms, is the proper, natural, and safe defence of a free State;* that the militia shall not be subject to martial law, except in time of war, rebellion, or insurrection; that standing armies, in time of peace, are dangerous to liberty, and ought not to be kept up, except in cases of necessity; and that, at all times, the military should be under strict subordination to the civil power; that in time of peace no soldier ought to be quartered in any house without the consent of the owner, and in time of war only by the civil magistrates in such manner as the law directs.

"XVIII. That any person religiously scrupulous of bearing arms ought to be exempted upon the payment of an equivalent to employ another to bear arms in his stead.

"*Under these impressions*, and declaring that *the rights aforesaid* cannot be abridged or violated, and that the explanations aforesaid are consistent with the said Constitution, and in confidence that the amendments hereafter mentioned will receive an early and mature consideration, and conformably to the fifth article of said Constitution, speedily become a part thereof,—We, the said Delegates, in the name and in the behalf of the people of the State of Rhode Island and Providence Plantations, do by these presents, assent to and ratify the said Constitution. In full confidence, nevertheless, that until the amendments hereafter proposed and undermentioned shall be agreed to and ratified, pursuant to the aforesaid fifth article, the militia will not be continued in service out of this State for a longer term than six weeks without the consent of the Legislature thereof; that the Congress will not make or alter any regulation in this State respecting the times, places, and manner of holding elections for Senators or Representatives unless the Legislature of this State shall neglect or refuse to make laws or regulations for the purpose, or from any circumstance be incapable of making the same; and that in those cases such power will only be exercised until the Legislature of this State shall make provision in the premises; that the Congress will not lay direct taxes within this State but when the moneys arising from impost, tonnage, and excise, shall be insufficient for the public exigencies, nor until the Congress shall have first made a requisition upon this State to assess, levy, and pay the amount of such requisition, made agreeably to the census fixed in the said Constitution, in such way and manner as the Legislature of this State shall judge best; and that Congress will not lay any capitation or poll tax.

"Done in Convention at Newport, in the County of Newport, in the State of Rhode Island and Providence Plantations, the twenty-ninth day of May, in the year of our Lord one thousand seven hundred and ninety, and in the fourteenth year of the Independence of the United States of America."

We have now gone through with the action of all the first thirteen States upon the Constitution. We have examined the records themselves. In them we see the Union was first formed by separate and distinct Colonies for the common maintenance of the chartered rights of each. When this failed, it became a Union of separate, distinct States, by Articles of Confederation for the support and maintenance of the Independence and Sovereignty of each. The absolute right of local Self Government, or State Sovereignty, was the principal and leading idea throughout. We have seen that these States, as Sovereign, responded to a call of a General Federal Convention to revise the first Articles of Confederation. The Constitution which we still honor after 200 years, was the result of their labors.

We have seen that it was submitted to the Legislatures of each State, in their separate state organizations, to be referred by them to a Convention in each State, of the people thereof, that they, *the people*, in their Sovereign majesty, might approve or reject each, separately, for themselves as States and that it was to be established between such States only as should ratify it, and then only in case as many as nine should so ratify.

If fewer than nine should have ratified the Constitution, there never would have been a House of Representatives, a Senate, a President, nor a Supreme Court, a Cabinet, a CIA, IRS, FDS, FCC, TVA, etc. etc. ad nauseum.

We have seen that the State Conventions did so act upon the proposal to adopt the Constitution separately and severally, and adopt it as a Constitution *for the states*, so to be united thereby, each believing it to be a Federal Constitution and that all powers not delegated were reserved to the States.

The absence of a bill of rights from the Constitution became the major obstacle for ratification by the States. The notion had been proposed in committee but was voted down as unnecessary. Most of the delegates reasoned, "how could the government exceed the specific enumeration of powers?" In vain, did Madison and Hamilton argue the case: A bill of rights was absurd, redundant, unnecessary. "Why declare that things shall not be done, which there is no power to do?"

James Wilson attacked from another angle. He said, the very act of detailing rights would have the effect of limiting them. "Who will be bold enough to enumerate all the rights of the people? And...if the enumeration is not complete, everything not expressly mentioned will be presumed to be purposely omitted." Even Washington agreed. Liberty was too precious to be defined by the limited forethought of man. But Jefferson took the side of the "radicals." He said: "A Bill of Rights is what the people are entitled to against every government on earth, general or particular."

Wilson, Madison, Hamilton and others were technically and legally correct. If a power is not delegated, why declare the Federal government has no power to exercise such power?

Why, for example, do we need the Second Amendment declaring the right of the people to keep and bear arms shall not be infringed, when no authority whatsoever is delegated to the Federal government regarding guns. It is not even mentioned in the Constitution, therefore, the right to keep and bear arms is automatically reserved to *the States*, or to *the people*. Reference, Tenth Amendment, which itself should not have been necessary.

But Jefferson and Patrick Henry and those who demanded a Bill of Rights were also right. Just as they feared, we have evolved to where the Supreme Court itself, following the early precedents of the Federalist Chief Justice John Marshall, 1801-1835; it is the position of the Supreme Court that, "whatever is not prohibited" by the Constitution is allowed, the exact opposite of all early constitutional theory.

This 180 degree usurpation by all three departments of the Federal government, in assuming all powers *not prohibited* by the Constitution, is sufficient in itself for three-fourths of the States to *dissolve the Union* and start over, or it is sufficient reason for one or more States to secede from a Union which has assumed and usurped powers far beyond those which were delegated. If the Federal goverment, acting as the mere *agent* of the *States*, refuses to abandon its accumulated usurpations of power, the States have only one option left to them. Their lawful and reserved right *to dissolve or secede from the Union*. The right to destroy that which they created and *resume* the individual sovereignty, independence and freedom held by each of the original thirteen States.

Those who wanted Union finally realized that without the inclusion of a Bill of Rights, the Constitution would not be ratified. Those who desired Union promised to amend the Constitution once the new government was elected and placed in office. In some States this point was bitterly contested. "Fistfights broke out in the Pennsylvania legislature when the Federalists forcibly kept those opposed in the hall in order to fix a quorum." Harvard Magazine, May-June 1987 by Robin U. Russin.

By Federalists, in this quote, it must be understood, were

those most strongly seeking union. The Nationalists, those for consolidating the states themselves into a single National Union, had already lost in the Philadelphia Convention.

These views for and against a Bill of Rights are important to our generation. Washington, Madison and Hamilton, and many other great statesmen, said the Bill of Rights were overkill. Totally unnecessary. Their views were correct then, and those views are valid today. Any time we undertake to pursue our rights under the Constitution, we should at first, forget all about the Bill of Rights and insist that those who would usurp undelegated powers show us in the Constitution where this usurpation is authorized. If they cannot point to an authorizing clause in the Constitution, that should be the end of any argument. Case closed. The end.

Only if usurpers might cast doubt on the strength of our position from the body of the Constitution should we ever resort to use of the Bill of Rights in asserting our rights. Actually the Bill of Rights are redundant, as advanced by many of the Founders.

For example, we don't need the Second Amendment to validate the right of the people to "keep and bear arms." Patriots are always telling liberals and socialists in Washington and the State Capitols, that firearms legislation is a violation of their Second Amendment rights. This is a defensive stance we are assuming. It is stupid of us to resort to use of the Second Amendment in defending our right to buy, own and protect ourselves with all kinds of firearms, until we have exhausted all our arguments, and exhausted the enemies of the Constitution, by demanding to be shown where there is any authority in the Constitution for State or Federal governments to place controls of any kind on the *people's* rights to firearms. There is no such authorization. Therefore, we should be putting the burden of proof on the liberals and socialists; on those who would, if they could, register, and eventually confiscate, all the firearms of all the *people*.

But only when all else fails, need we resort to use of the Second Amendment, or any of the other Amendments which make up the Bill of Rights. Washington, Hamilton and Madison were right. The Bill of Rights are overkill.

But fortunately, Jefferson's arguments for a Bill of Rights prevailed. With over 200 years hindsight, these Amendments have come in handy in the cause of liberty on many occasions. But they have made us lazy. By assuming the defensive position, we have lost much of our understanding that it should always be us who are determined to sustain the Constitution, who should be forcing the socialists into a defensive stance. Make them prove under what constitutional authority they make proposals for legislation, or policy. Where is their authority when they pass laws to force the States into compliance? From which part of the Constitution does the President draw the authority to enforce his Executive Orders? If they cannot cite their authority from the Constitution, it does not exist. Federal officers are all sworn to uphold and defend the Constitution. It is absurd for *we, the people*, to allow the innumerable usurpations of Congress and the President to continue, when they cannot show by what authority they have acted.

We don't need the Bill of Rights, but we should be glad we have them...*just in case, we, the people*, find ourselves in need of them as backup arguments when we are proving the Federal government is limited to only that authority spelled out in the Constitution. But that should be rare when everybody understands that the Constitution is specific delegation of powers, not an enumeration of rights, as some misguided court decisions attempt to tell us. We need more lawyers who better understand the Constitution when arguing constitutional issues before the courts.

We have gone into the debates in the several State Conventions, and seen what were the leading ideas of both friends and opponents as to the nature and character of the Constitution. While many apprehended danger to the sovereignty of the separate States from *constructions* and *implications*, yet on all sides it was *universally* admitted that the Constitution is *Federal* in nature, not *National*. It was with this understanding of its nature, by every advocate and supporter it had in every State in the Union, even by Hamilton, Morris, Wilson, King,

Madison and Randolph, who had favored a *National Government* proper in the Federal Convention. The leading idea in all the Conventions was that a Confederate Republic was to be established by the Constitution upon the model set forth by Montesquieu (1689-1755) the great French political philosopher who wrote, *The Spirit of the Laws*, published in 1748, and which is one of the greatest political treatises ever written. The Founders were well acquainted with his work.

According to the model of Montesquieu, an artificial State is created for foreign or national, as well as interstate purposes, and these, only by several small Republics, thus confederating for their common defense and happiness; each retaining its separate *sovereignty*, and the artificial State so created by them being, at all times, subject to their will and power.

That this artificial State so created may be dissolved, and yet the separate Republics survive, retaining at all times their State organization and sovereignty.

This model of a Confederate Republic by Montesquieu was the leading idea with the advocates of the system as it appears from the debates in every State where we have access to them.

As shown by the history of its formation, the Constitution created, as Washington styled it, "a Confederated Republic," bound together by a Compact of Union between Sovereign States.

It is hoped, with wide dissemination of these views of the nature of the American Republic, we might begin to eliminate from our national media such twisted views as that expressed in a recent newspaper item. It said: "Legislation to increase consumers' access to their credit reports and make it easier for them to correct errors has effectively died after the House refused to **let states** (emphasis added) adopt more stringent requirements." Deseret News, Salt Lake City, Utah, September 25, 1992.

Here is one more example of the tail wagging the dog from an editorial of Scripps Howard News Service.

"The great debate over how much health care we can afford and who should be covered is moving into the hard-choices stage, with Oregon leading the way.

"Starting next year, Oregon will stop making Medicaid payments on procedures it considers ineffective or optional. Instead, it will use the money saved to provide basic health care to 120,000 poor people who currently have no medical coverage."

Here comes the kicker. Another of thousands of current examples of blatant, outrageous, infuriating usurpations of undelegated powers by the Federal government. "The five-year experiment was given the green light by the Clinton administration last week with the proviso that Oregon's priorities be reviewed to make sure they comply with federal law." From reprint, Deseret News, March 23, 1993, p. A8.

Who cares whether Oregon's priorities comply with Federal law? The roles of agent and principal have been reversed, and an ignorant people don't know the difference. Constitutionally, we are so ignorant, that Washington tells us tails wag dogs and we believe it. Washington says "jump," and the States say "yes sir," and "how high sir?" In modern America, Alice in Wonderland is not fantasy; it is real life.

Before Oregon, or any other State worries about complying with Federal law, they should be questioning and challenging every Federal law which might have the appearance of infringing on State powers. This could easily and inexpensively be done by any State Attorney General by filing legal actions directly with the U.S. Supreme Court under the power of *original jurisdiction*. Constitution, Article III, Section 2, Paragraph 2.

Our liberal media are bombarding the American people with the idea that the States are subservient to the Federal government; when in fact the reverse is true, as is clearly seen from the above. If we fail to reinstitute the teaching of the Constitution and how it was established in our educational systems, our children are going to find themselves without its protection, and living with far less freedom under some sort of New World Order.

The thought that the House, Senate or the President will *let the states* do something, is repulsive and arrogant. This is akin to one saying, in all seriousness; "Today as I was walking down the street, I noticed a tail wagging several large and powerful dogs." Or a father commenting on procedures in his home: "My child tells me what I can or cannot do. As the father, I don't have the authority to do anything on my own." Or the assembly line worker telling the Chairman of the Board at General Motors Corporation: "You do what I tell you to do or you will pay hell."

How absurd and laughable would be such assertions. Yet in dealing with the Federal government, this is how far we have gone astray in allowing Federal usurpation of undelegated powers.

Fortunately, we can still correct the course of the old Ship of State without bloodshed. But it is going to take a lot of work with elected officials in the State governments.

Chapter 6

West Virginia. A Constitutional outlaw. Double standard and hypocrisy of Abraham Lincoln.

Now we will explore a most amazing and fascinating precedent in our history which, by itself, shows the right of *secession, or revolution* by a people when they and their peers have major differences on which there is no possible agreement. It shows how separation is sometimes the only viable solution. It is a precedent which is cemented in our history, perhaps by the divine hand, for specific use in our day when evil and conspiring men would attempt to destroy the Sovereignty of the 50 States along with the Constitution.

That precedent is the entry into the Union of our 35th State, West Virginia in the middle of the Civil War, June 20, 1863.

To fully understand the significance of West Virginia being accepted into the Union, we need to give a short review of the Civil War and the friction between States leading up to it.

Agitation between slave holders and abolitionists was not the only issue leading to the Civil War, but it was the major issue. Tariffs on manufactured goods was a detriment to the South while it helped Northern industry to compete with manufacturing in other nations.

Though Abraham Lincoln did not, in the beginning, take up arms to free the slaves, emancipation of the slaves finally became a major objective of the North. Emancipation was a sort of, "as long as we are fighting this war anyway, we might as well free the slaves."

But in the beginning of the war, Abraham Lincoln justified the war's prolongation under the theory that, at all costs, "*the Union must be preserved.*" He said there was no provision in the Constitution for a State to secede from the Union; that attempted secession by Southern States was unlawful, and was, in fact, rebellion against constituted authority. "The Union," cried Northern radicals, "was perpetual." Some in loud mockery of our own history said, "Union now and forever, inviolate."

The American Civil War was a four-year conflict between 11 Southern States and 23 Northern States, not counting West Virginia, and counting Kansas which came into the Union under the Administration of President James Buchanan on January 29, 1861, about 5 weeks prior to the inauguration of Abraham Lincoln. Perhaps the most accurate name for this war was put forward by Alexander H. Stephens, Vice President of the Southern Confederacy. He called it The War Between the States. Others called it the War for the Union, the War for Southern Independence, and the War of the Rebellion.

It began the early morning of Friday, April 12, 1861. Within the walls of the unfinished Fort Sumter, in the harbor of Charleston, South Carolina were stationed 76 soldiers and 7 officers of the Union Army under the command of Major Robert Anderson, along with some 45 civilians.

Their food would last only about three more days and Abraham Lincoln had sent word to the governor of South Carolina he intended to bring in provisions.

The seceding states had already demanded, and received one way or the other, control of most Federal forts, and other military facilities or Federal property within their borders. Blood had not been required in these takeovers by either North or South.

James Buchanan had attempted to provision Fort Sumter

two months before when he sent the ship, Star of the West, into Charleston Harbor. But it was turned back when it was fired on by a Confederate shore battery. After that, President Buchanan decided to let things ride and allow his successor to handle this secession problem.

Lincoln claimed, and rightly so, Sumter was Federal property. He did not recognize secession, but even if he had, title to Federal properties had long ago been ceded by the States to the Federal government. Lincoln said, "Sumter is our property and we don't intend to let our men be forced out by starvation," or words to that effect.

Fort Sumter was of grave concern to both sides. Jefferson Davis, after consulting with his newly formed cabinet, made the fatal decision. His secretary of state, Robert Toombs of Georgia, was far wiser than the President. He warned: "The firing upon that fort will inaugurate a civil war greater than any the world has yet seen... You will wantonly strike a hornet's nest which extends from mountains to ocean, and legions now quiet will swarm out and sting us to death. It is unnecessary, it puts us in the wrong, it is fatal." Stovall's Life of Toombs, p. 226, quoted from A History of The United States by John Fiske, p. 376 (1894).

The warning of Toombs as recorded by another writer: "It is suicide, murder, and will lose us every friend in the North." American Political and Social History by Harold Underwood Faulkner, 1941, p. 337. Toombs was so obviously right. "That first gun at Sumter brought all the free States to their feet as one man." Lowell.

Sumter electrified the North. It eliminated Northern indecision. Secession was not the cause of the war. It was the foolish attack; it was the taking of offensive military action against lawfully held Federal property, Fort Sumter. Just because South Carolina had seceded from the Union, gave her no right to assume command and take over Federal property. In due time perhaps, Sumter and other Federal properties might have been purchased, or otherwise negotiated away from the Union, but to attempt to take them by force was not only illegal and unlawful, it was the height of folly. The side which fires the first shot is almost always put at a psychological disadvantage. Those attacked unjustly are usually more emotionally committed to "fight to the death."

The South knew law, precedent and history were on their side. They had a right to leave the Union. But the firing on Fort Sumter had to lead to lingering doubts in the Southern mind as to the justness and validity of the war. Only by sustaining the fantasy that Lincoln, in attempting to provision Fort Sumter, was the one who really started the war, could the South justify their position. Whether or not Lincoln intended military reinforcement, as well as supplies, is irrelevent. By law, Lincoln had a right to reinforce and defend Fort Sumter.

Robert Toombs came close to becoming the President of the Confederacy, rather than Jefferson Davis. If he had, secession probably would have been successful for the South, and the Civil War probably would have been avoided.

After the meeting with his cabinet, Jefferson Davis sent word to General Beauregard to demand the evacuation of Fort Sumter, "or reduce it."

At 3:20 a.m. the commander of some 7,000 Confederates, Brigadier General P.G.T. (Pierre Gustave Toutant) Beauregard, sent word to Major Anderson he would open fire on the fort in one hour unless the fort was evaucated. Anderson refused and became a hero of the North. At 4:30 a.m. Beauregard gave the order and the first shot was fired.

Bombardment of the fort continued for some 32 hours. Early afternoon the next day, Major Anderson accepted the generous terms of surrender of General Beauregard, and the following day, Sunday, April 14, he and all his men walked out and boarded ship which safely carried them away.

Robert Toombs could not have been more right. The South fired first. Abraham Lincoln had every right to defend Federal property. He was on the defensive. He now had every justification to "put down this rebellion." Jefferson Davis made the mistake of the century. Many hotheads in the South were itching for a fight against "those cowardly Northern Yankees."

The lawful course the seven seceding States had taken in

leaving the Union was nullified by their stupid blunder in firing on Fort Sumter. Now Northern radicals could, with some justification, demand Southern blood.

Fort Sumter was such a blunder, why did Jefferson Davis order the attack? His rationalization was that Lincoln actually started the war by bringing supply ships to, not only supply Sumter, but "to bring in reinforcements."

But what difference did it make whether it was food, or food and arms? Besides the 7,000 Confederate troops were sufficient to see that nothing but food and necessary supplies were brought in. Beauregard could have prevented military reinforcements from entering the fort.

And Abraham Lincoln had not only promised, "no blood would flow unless his hand was forced," he was too smart to *fire the first shot*. There was already too much Southern sentiment in the North. Too many people of influence, as well as many of the common people, found nothing illegal about secession. Lincoln was a brand new *minority* president. He had received not quite 40% of the popular vote. James Buchanan, the sitting President during the time in which seven States had already seceded, dared do nothing, or felt there was nothing he lawfully could do about States declaring their independence of the Union. And he was right! If Buchanan, who probably had a much stronger support base than Lincoln, felt there was nothing he could do, how could Lincoln possibly have had the nerve to take offensive action; to *fire the first shot?*

As Lincoln said, if war was to come, it would come by initiation of the South.

Lincoln had a hard time sustaining popular sentiment for the war as it was. If he had fired the first shot, it is probable the entire Union, North as well as South, would have splintered asunder.

If war came, it was a "family" fight and in order for Lincoln to have any chance, all things considered, he had to be sure he was in the right. He had to be sure his actions were defensive, not offensive.

It appears there was some urgency by the seven seceding

States by this late date of April 12, to force the hand of the other slave-holding States to join in the secession. It had been over two months when the last of the seven, Texas, had seceded on February 1. The more States to join the Confederacy the better. They would particularly like to have Virginia join them, but Virginia was undecided to stay in the Union or go with the South. Nothing was happening and a lot of people were becoming impatient.

By firing on Fort Sumter, the South may have reasoned, "we will force the hand of the other slave States, and at the same time, show the yellow yankees we mean business."

Sure enough, April 15, Abraham Lincoln asked for 75,000 volunteers to put down the rebellion and four more States joined the Confederacy bringing the total to 11. Virginia seceded April 17 and was followed in May by Arkansas, Tennessee and North Carolina.

But frighten the "cowardly North?" Such Southern foolishness. Fort Sumter solidified Northern support for Abraham Lincoln against the "slaveholders."

Before that first shot was fired, there was great support in the North for Southern secession. Really, "It was the answer to our decades of quarreling over slavery and other matters." The feeling was growing in the North that the Southern states should be allowed to withdraw peacefully. There were affectionate farewells of Southern Senators and Congressmen in Washington to their Northern colleagues, and the moving responses helped increase this departing spirit of, "Let's just peacefully agree to disagree." This, in spite of the firing on the supply ship, Star of the West in Charleston harbor on January 9th, which had constituted an act of war, but President Buchanan did nothing. "Why not let Lincoln handle this hot potato?"

Horace Greeley, editor of the New York Tribune, a Lincoln Republican, as influential in party circles as Seward and Lincoln, favored peaceful secession. He said: "If the cotton states shall decide that they can do better outside of the Union than in it, we insist on letting them go in peace...We hope never to live in a republic whereof one section is pinned to the residue by bayonets."

"This was, after all, good American respect for the democratic right to self-government. Great lawyers insisted that it was good constitutional law, as well...." From, A Complete History of the United States, p. 292, by Clement Wood, 1941.

When the South bombarded Fort Sumter for almost a day-and-a-half, there was no hope for further negotiation or compromise. The dye was cast. But there was only two ways to solve the slave issue. War or secession. Secession could have worked; it should have worked! But the South pushed its luck. Law and history was on the side of the South, but the right to self defense was on the side of the North.

There was a possible third way to end slavery, but many decades of effort prior to the Civil war had proven that this possibility was remote. That was through education and appeal to Christian principles.

After secession of the first seven States, negotiations might have continued for those seven to rejoin the Union after settling their differences, if such were possible. Compromise on slavery had been attempted several times, however, and since peace on this issue had never been lasting, it was not likely that seceding States would ever have come back into the Union until they had given up slavery.

With those who sought to abolish slavery it was a moral issue; a matter of conscience. Honest men can compromise on administration or policy. But they cannot compromise conscience. Even with successful secession, the sincere abolitionist would have to continue to make some effort, at least, toward eventually freeing the black man.

With the advantage of 20th century hindsight, it is still hard to understand the reasoning of the South in resorting to military action when they had already accomplished that which they had every legal right to do, leave the Union.

The new President Lincoln and the North were faced with a fait accompli, and there could be little said by the North which could justify the initiation of force against their Southern brethren. And there was little Northern sentiment to take up arms, against their "erring sisters." Yes, slavery was terrible; it was sometimes inhumane; it was evil and satanic, and it was incomprehensible to many, how one could profess the love of Christ and to follow Him, yet argue in behalf of slavery.

But in the United States in 1861, it was legal. It was sewn into the Supreme Law of the land. There was nothing anybody could legally do about it, except appeal to the empathy of the slaveholder, and hope to eventually educate him, shame him, or outlaw slavery by amending the Constitution.

For the South to go on the offensive through force of arms was foolish and excessive. The tiny match they lit at Fort Sumter set off the holocaust.

The United States was understood from its founding in 1788 under the Constitution, to be a *new experiment* in the governing of free men. Even some of the Founders wondered whether it would, or could, last very long. Benjamin Franklin, on emerging from the Convention in Philadelphia on September 17, 1787, on being asked what the delegates had produced, reportedly replied: "A republic...if you can keep it."

The Union was now in its 74th year and had come close before to splitting apart. Secession had been threatened by States in the North, as well as the South, a number of times, almost from the beginning. It was common knowledge that some of the original thirteen States had specifically reserved the right to leave the Union and *resume their sovereignty* should "this new experiment" fail to work as well as everybody hoped it would. Virginia could not have made herself more clear in this regard.

By April 12, 1861, secession by seven States was a fact. The decades long threat had actually been carried out. Now time was needed to let the dust settle, and to let people and politicians alike calmly ponder "where do we go from here?" There was no hurry. Major Anderson and his men should have been treated as "foreign diplomats," for such they were under the Southern theory that the seceded States were now back in their original position of 1776 and 1787, prior to adoption of the Constitution; *free, independent*, and *sovereign* nations. The South was operating under correct theory, but it failed to abide by the rules of that theory. Among nations, diplomatic personnel might be expelled for good cause, but normally, confiscation of assets does not follow. Secession was something new, radical, and revolutionary. It would take time and patience to get used to the idea. The last secession of States was 74 years before, and the seccession of 1776 from Great Britain had been 85 years.

The secession of 1776 was quite different however. It really was radical and revolutionary. Those patriots of 1776 knew they were, in effect, declaring war on the Mother Country at the same time they were declaring their independence. This secession of 1861 was mild in comparison to the action of their fathers. This secession was legal, no question about it. This secession needed no *Declaration of Independence* to justify separation. The Mother Country in this case, the Union of States, had all agreed they could freely leave the Union, just as they had freely joined. All States come into the Union as equals, and on equal terms. If Virginia or New York had reserved the right to leave the Union, every other State automatically reserved the same equal right.

On December 20, 1861, South Carolina declared her independence of the then existing Union, nullified her ratification of the Constitution of May 23, 1788, and assumed the same independence she had earlier declared with 12 sister Colonies on July 4, 1776. She "resumed" her sovereignty, as Virginia had so well framed it when she ratified the Constitution June 25, 1788.

Ten more States declared their independence, adopted a new Constitution very similar to the old one, and elected Jefferson Davis, former Senator from Mississippi, their new President. In comparison to the 13 Colonies of 1776, in declaring their independence from Great Britain, the eleven Southern States which declared independence in 1860-61, had a far stronger legal case, should the merits of each declaration, or secession, be put before a court of law.

Abraham Lincoln had promised, "blood will not flow unless the government's hand is forced." There is no reason to doubt that Lincoln would have been as good as his word, for the record shows he was a man of character, prior to his becoming President. This is not to say, however, that Lincoln was the man of greatness we are taught to believe in our elementary school textbooks. He proved as President in prosecuting the Civil War that the Constitution under extraordinary circumstances is not necessarily a barrier to tyranny. He was willing to subvert and ignore the Constitution to successfully prosecute the war. Lincoln tore the Constitution to shreds!

Friday, April 12, the South opened fire, and started the war. The next day, Major Anderson surrenders his small force, but sleeps within the walls of Fort Sumter that night. Sunday, April 14, Anderson evacuates the Fort and General Beauregard takes possession. April 15 President Lincoln asks for 75,000 volunteers to "put down the rebellion," and the previously fragmented North solidifies sentiment behind Lincoln, because the rebels "attacked and shot down our flag." Two days later, April 17, Virginia joins the first seven seceding states in declaring her independence of the Union.

But here, "a fly enters the legal ointment." Not for the South, but for the North. And because the North won the war, it was allowed to slide by. But it is there for our generation to draw upon as a precedent. In addition to already sufficient historical precedents which the South had to draw upon, cited above, our generation has the precedent of the abuse of the Constitution, and the inconsistency and hypocrisy of the North in the case of Virginia when she seceded from the Union.

When Virginia passed her ordinance of secession June 17, there was turmoil and great dissatisfaction all over the state. Numerous meetings were held by groups of people, and less than a month later, May 13, 1861, delegates from 25 counties met at Wheeling and called a convention to meet June 11.

Representatives from 40 counties attended, declared their own independence from Virginia, took measures for the establishment of a provisional government and elected Francis H. Pierpont Governor.

On July 2, a "Legislature" met and elected representatives to the United States Senate, which representatives were admitted to that body. This action was approved by the people of these renegade counties October 24, and delegates were also elected to a convention which met at Wheeling on November 26 to frame a constitution. This constitution was adopted May 3, 1862.

On May 13, the "Legislature" of the "Restored Government of Virginia" gave its consent to the formation of a new State. The act of admission was approved by President Lincoln, December 31, 1862, to take effect upon the insertion of a clause providing for gradual emancipation of the slaves. These Western Counties of the State of Virginia, which State had declared her independence and seceded from the Union, declared their own independence from Virginia and seceded from their Mother State, and these counties were formally admitted into the Union as the 35th State, said counties being 48 in number at the time of admission.*

Should secession of one or more States in the 1990's or beyond prove necessary in order to retain the Constitution as the Supreme law of the land in part of the presently constituted United States, the judiciary put its stamp of approval on this secession of counties from Virginia. A suit was brought by Virginia to recover Berkeley and Jefferson counties and was settled in favor of West Virginia (1871).

In 1866, a year after the end of the Civil War, Virginia demanded payment of $15,000,000, claiming this sum had been West Virginia's share of the state debt before the secession. In 1915, 49 years later, the U.S. Supreme Court declared the debt to be $12,393,929 plus interest, and ordered its payment. Collection was finally accomplished in 1939.

If it was illegal, or unlawful, or without constitutional provision for seven or eleven States to secede from the Union, how could it be legal, lawful, or within the Constitution for

---

* Note. Two more counties were officially added later by a Supreme Court decision. Va. vs. W. Va, 78 U.S. 39 (December, 1870). W. Virginia has 55 counties in 1993. A complete historical review of how it happened is not relevant to the main point.

some 48 counties to secede from Virginia? Lincoln and the Congress justified this action "as a war measure."

This being the case, we better be on guard for any future war in which the United States may be involved. The President has ample and numerous precedents in our history to justify any desired trampling on the Constitution. If Abraham Lincoln could, in effect, abolish the Constitution on a number of occasions, as pretended "war measures," what might far lesser men of character do in the late 20th century, or early 21st century?

The main war cry of Abraham Lincoln was "We must hold the Union together." And, "the union inseparable, inviolate, and forever." Lincoln and the Congress had to stir emotions to fever pitch and maintain that emotional high for the duration of the bloody and costly war, for that was the only thing they had to go on, except for the attack on Fort Sumter. Lincoln had no lawful or historical basis for prosecuting the Civil War and forcing seceding States back into the Union. ...except for Fort Sumter.

Lincoln and the Congress sacrificed some 620,000 men in a cause they said was unlawful and unjust in the case of eleven *free, independent* and *sovereign* States. For Lincoln and Congress to turn right around in the very middle of the act, in the very middle of the Civil War and say, in effect, "Bless you 48 counties for seceding from Virginia. We recognize your secession and your independence of Virginia."

Such blatant hypocrisy. Such outrageous inconsistency. But such a powerful precedent should one or more States decide to secede from the United States at any time in the future.

Whether the greater crime here was hypocrisy and inconsistency, or conspicuous and unblushing violation of the Constitution is difficult to discern.

The Constitution says in language plain enough for an average 10-year-old to understand: "New states may be admitted by the Congress into this union; but *no new State shall be formed or erected within the jurisdiction of any other State*; nor any state be formed by the junction of two or more States, *or parts of States, without the consent of the Legislatures of the States concerned* as well as of the Congress. Article IV, Section 3, Paragraph 1. Emphasis added.

President Lincoln and the Congress maintained throughout the war that secession was illegal, therefore, Virginia never left the Union, and she was never at any time out of the Union. Why then was the Constitution so blatantly violated? As a member of the Union, Virginia could not have part of her territory taken away from her and have that territory recognized as a new State.

Virginia, without her consent, had stolen; "lawfully" plundered from her as a sovereign State, some 24,000 square miles of land mass. Whether under the laws of fraud, treaties, contracts, the laws of nations, or some other form of agreement between parties, Virginia should have the right to this day, to recover her lost land if her people chose to do so. Should the courts deny her the right to recover, except for the Statute of Limitations, to be consistent, the Court would also have to rule that Virginia, at the time of the admittance of West Virginia into the Union, had seceded from the Union. Only if Virginia was officially out of the Union on June 20, 1863, could West Virginia be allowed, according to the Constitution, to join the Union. If Virginia was actually out of the Union, the courts might then with reason, say, "We recognize the secession of 48 counties from the independent and sovereign nation of Virginia, and we further recognize them as the new State of West Virginia in the United States of America."

Virginia could not be in the Union and at the same time out of the Union. The North could not, with a straight face, say the secession of Virginia and 10 other States was unlawful, and 10 months or 10 years later say the secession of 48 counties from Virginia was lawful.

None of the "conventions" of delegates, or "conventions of the people" or "legislatures" which led up to the admittance of West Virginia into the Union, even by the greatest stretch of the imagination, could be considered lawful or constitutional bodies with authority to act for and in behalf of the people of Virginia. The Congress and President Lincoln vainly grasped for some appearance of acting in compliance with the Constitution, but West Virginia to this day, is an unlawful member of the Union!

The twisted reasoning, the mental contortions, distortions and wrenching of the politicians of the 1860's in attempting to constitutionally justify the admittance of West Virginia as a separate State is a lesson from which the corrupt congresses of our own generation might learn, as enemies close in on the deadline to entirely abolish any pretense of honoring the Constitution as the Supreme Law of the land.

From the "first Wheeling Convention," with delegates from only twenty-six of the 55 counties that were later included in West Virginia, until the final vote of the "legislature" which gave it's consent to Congress to separate 48 counties from Virginia and make them a new State, never was there a representative body with the authority to act on behalf of the people of Virginia.

More than two-thirds of the counties in Virginia were total non-participants. And in the counties which became the new State, there was much non-participation, sometimes through neglect, sometimes by design.

Concerning the June "convention" in Wheeling: "The number of counties actually represented is thirty-four...Several of the delegates escaped from their counties at the risk of their lives, while others are still detained at home by force or menace against them or their families and property." Address at the Second Convention, Wheeling, June 25, 1861: West Virginia Legislative Handbook, 1916, pp. 275-276, quoted in Constitutional Problems under Lincoln by James G. Randall, 1926, p. 443.

"It was from the counties near Pennsylvania and Ohio that the active separationists came, while in contrast to this, a continuous group of counties covering about half the area of the new State had no participation in the convention which passed the 'Wheeling ordinance,' but were in spite of this fact, included in West Virginia as ultimately defined. The people had no opportunity, county by county, to determine whether they would adhere to Virginia or join the new commonwealth;

but their fate was determined by the whole vote cast within the boundaries indicated by the convention. McGregor states that this plan was adopted to avoid 'certain rejection in at least two thirds of the counties.' " Disruption of Virginia, pp. 235-236. Ibid p. 443.

"Little is said in the various histories of West Virginia as to the actual membership of this reorganized legislature, but light on this subject may be obtained from the rather inaccessible journals of the various sessions." Ibid 450.

This is speaking of the extra session of the legislature in July, 1861 in which only thirty counties, represented by twenty-nine delegates, of a total number of counties in Virginia at that time of 149. Yet this "legislature", without even close to a pretended quorum, was pretending to act for the State of Virginia.

When the West Virginia bill for admission of the new State into the Union was discussed in Congress, not everybody was willing to go along with this blatant violation of the Constitution. Some felt that this precedent might be followed in other seceding States. Crittenden of Kentucky refused to accept the idea that old Virginia no longer existed. He said that after the war, Virginia would be restored to the Union, and that it should be "restored whole," not divided. "Those forming the State," he said, "were the same as those consenting to its erection."

"It is the party applying for admission consenting to the admission. That is the whole of it." Ibid 455, quoting from Congressional Globe, December 9, 1862, 37th Congress, 3 session, p. 47.

Thaddeus Stevens made one of the clearest and more honest statements. He was not fooled by the notion that the State was being admitted "in pursuance of the Constitution." He apparently considered secession treason, yet nevertheless, as far as the State corporation was concerned, secession was a valid act and governed the State. He said West Virginia could not be admitted to the Union as a Constitutional measure but "under our absolute power which the laws of war give us in the circumstances in which we are placed, I shall vote for this bill upon that theory, and upon that alone, for I will not stultify myself by supposing that we have any warrant in the Constitution for this proceeding." Ibid p. 50.

When the West Virginia bill was presented to President Lincoln, he consulted with members of his Cabinet and asked for written opinions from each member.

Secretaries Seward, Chase and Stanton favored the separation of West Virginia. Seward argued that the United States could not recognize secession and must recognize loyalty, speaking of the eleven Confederate States, so far as secession was concerned, and the loyalty of parts of Virginia. "But secession was not so bad," he might have added, "that we cannot recognize just a little secession," like some 48 counties seceding from Virginia. Seward held the "restored government" was "incontestably the State of Virginia." *Lincoln,* by Nicolay and Hay, Vl, 300-301. One can picture Secretary Seward mentally stomping his feet and pounding the table as he insistently proclaimed his untenable hypothesis.

Secretary Chase, in arguing that the "Provisional Legislature" of the proposed new State of West Virginia was the only "true and lawful" legislature of Virginia, mentioned the fear of some that the case of West Virginia would form a precedent and involve "the necessity of admitting other States under the consent of extemporized legislatures assuming to act for whole States though really representing no significant part of their territory." He said such apprehensions were groundless as no parallel cases existed in any other State. Chase's words expose the fact that to admit West Virginia as a new State, was recognized as a bad precedent. Nevertheless, as this precedent is not likely to be repeated, "Let us go ahead."

Secretary Stanton claimed: "The measure is sanctioned by the legislature of the State within whose jurisdiction the new State is formed...I have been unable to perceive any point on which the act...conflicts with the Constitution." Stanton Papers, X, No. 52066, quoted by Randall, p. 458.

The Cabinet was equally divided with Secretaries Welles, Blair and Attorney General Bates taking the negative side.

"Welles could not close his eyes to the fact that the

organization claiming to be the State of Virginia was nothing more than a provisional government, and that it was 'composed almost entirely of...loyal citizens...beyond the mountains.' While admitting that a temporary recognition of this government might be proper, yet he said, 'When...this loyal fragment goes farther, and...proceeds...to erect a new State within the jurisdiction of the State of Virginia, the question arises whether this proceeding is regular, right, and in honest faith, conformable to...the Constitution.'" Ibid 458. Quoted from Nicolay and Hay, Lincoln, Vl, 304-06.

He continued, "The requirements of the Constitution are not complied with, as they in good faith should be, by Virginia, by the proposed new State, nor by the United States." Ibid 458, quoted from Diary of Gideon Welles, 1, 191. (Dec. 4, 1862)

Secretary Blair, "It is well known that the elections by which the movement (for separation) has been made did not take place in more than a third of the counties of the State." He considered the dismemberment highly irregular and "unjust to the loyal people in the greater part of the State, who were held in subjection by rebel armies" and whose consent was not obtained. Ibid 458-459.

Edward Bates' view was especially important as his was the official opinion of the Attorney General. "Bates contended that States must exist before they can be admitted into the Union. Congress, he said, has no power to make States, for a free American State can be made only by its own people. The duty of the United States toward the faithful element in Virginia, as he saw it, was to restore Virginia to the Union as she was before the insurrection. The restored government was merely a provisional government intended as a patriot nucleus. No real 'legislature of Virginia' according to his view, had consented to the separation." Ibid 459.

Bates' unofficial and confidential statements on the subject were as plain as words can tell. He wrote in his diary of "a few reckless radicals who manage those helpless puppets (the straw Governor and Legislature of Virginia) as a gamester manages his marked cards. I have warned one member of

W.V. of the fate preparing for his misbegotten, abortive State. These Jacobins, as soon as they get by the Alexandria juggle, and anti-slavery Constitution for Virginia, will discover that West Virginia was created without authority—and then, having no further use for the political bantling, will knock the blocks from under and let it slide..." Bates wrote, the West Virginia bill was precipitately passed with "the most glaring blunders" because its sponsors feared discussion and dreaded "any revival among the M.C.s of a sense of justice and decency." Ibid 459-460, quoting from MS. Diary of Edward Bates, Dec. 15, 1864; Oct. 12, 1865.

President Lincoln justified this unconstitutional monstrosity with equally twisted reasoning. He said no legal consideration is ever given to those who do not choose to vote, and in this case those who did not vote were not merely neglectful of their rights but in rebellion against the Government.

For those of us who were brought up with Lincoln as one of our greatest Presidents and a national hero, it is difficult to comprehend his reasoning. Can dead men vote? Union loyalists, as well as rebels in the rebel controlled parts of Virginia were not given the opportunity to vote. Was Lincoln suggesting free Union elections should have been held throughout the entire, and largely rebel controlled, State of Virginia?

"Can this government stand," Lincoln asked, "if it counts those against it the equals of those who maintain loyalty?" If so, then he thought that their treason enhanced the constitutional value of the disloyal. "Without braving these absurd conclusions," he said, "we cannot deny that the body which consents to the admission of West Virginia is the Legislature of Virginia."

The admittance of West Virginia into the Union is an Alice in Wonderland story.

Everything about it is backwards and upside down. It makes one wonder how in the world the Constitution has managed to survive, even as the pretended law of the land, for over 200 years.

The Supreme Court (case mentioned above, *Va. vs. W.*

Chapter 6

Va., 78 U.S. 39,) was being asked to make a decision concerning which State had jurisdiction over the two counties of Jefferson and Berkeley. The Court, probably with a sigh of relief, was not asked to make a decision regarding the constitutionality of the entry of West Virginia into the Union. The Court ruled in favor of West Virginia regarding the two counties, and one might erroneously draw the conclusion, therefore, that the Court was also ruling on the lawfulness, or constitutionality, of West Virginia's entry into the Union, and that in fact, the Court approved of the torturous rationalizations of the politicians.

In filing her action with the Court, Virginia, for whatever reason, acquiesced in the separation of her 48 counties. Virginia's own judiciary conceded the legality both of the new State and of the "restored government" of Virginia. Apparently Virginia assumed she was faced with a fait accompli, and "what difference does it make?" And she simply conceded.

Therefore, the Supreme Court found it unnecessary to rule on any direct challenge of the constitutionality of the process of separation. Like any unjust act, corporate, state, individual or otherwise, if it is not challenged, it will stand. Injustice wins by default without a fight.

If Virginia had sought a ruling in the matter, it is most difficult to conceive that the Supreme Court would have put its stamp of approval on this most unsightly can of worms, the acceptance of West Virginia as our 35th State.

Note: An interesting quirk concerning the date of entry of West Virginia. Most sources say West Virginia entered the Union June 20, 1863. One encyclopedia, at least, says it was June 19.

On April 20, 1863, President Lincoln issued a proclamation declaring West Virginia to be admitted into the Union, to take effect in 60 days. Sixty days would be June 19. Two months would be June 20.

To accurately comply with the proclamation, June 19 would be the correct date.

In a letter to the author of December 11, 1992 signed by Ken Hechler, Secretary of State of West Virginia, he says:

"I studied for my Ph.D. at Columbia University under two great historians, Allan Nevins and Henry Steele Commager, and served as a combat historian in the U.S. Army in World War II, so am doubly interested in your question.

"The Lincoln Proclamation specifically states 'after sixty days,' and it is for this reason that when you count the 10 days in April, 31 days in May, the 'after 60 days' does not begin until midnight on June 19. June 19 must have expired before the 'after 60 days' begin—meaning that the birthday is June 20, 1863."

This seems to settle the matter "officially." However, according to the reasoning of Mr. Hechler, we are apparently assuming Abraham Lincoln signed his Proclamation at precisely "midnight" at the end of the day April 19. If he signed it one minute before midnight, or at any other time of day on April 19, "after 60 days" would require the official entry of West Virginia into the Union to be June 19. It is interesting that Mr. Hechler would fail to note the necessity of an assumption of midnight being the precise moment Lincoln's signature was affixed to his Proclamation, in order to make the case for June 20, being the date of admission. Lincoln's signature at any other moment, a most likely probability, would make June 19 the proper date of admission.

At least one encyclopedia lists June 19 as the day of Union entry...The New International Encyclopaedia, published by Dodd, Mead & Company, copyright 1904.

Chapter 7

Lincoln and the North—
As guilty as the South

This cloud on the official date of entry is a fitting climax to the unlawful entry of West Virginia into this Union of States.

During the Civil War, the North routinely jailed many people without filing charges against them, kept them in jail for awhile and let them go. Many Southern sympathizers, activists, military personnel and politicians were accused and jailed as traitors and for lesser crimes such as rebellion against constituted authority.

But a very strange thing happened at the end of the war. General Robert E. Lee, commander of Southern forces, surrendered with some 28,000 Confederate troops on April 9, 1865, at Appomattox Court House, Virginia. The commander of the Northern army, General Ulysses S. Grant, and Lee, cordially sat down together and discussed the terms of Grant's proposal to accept surrender.

Grant wrote out the terms which allowed officers and men to go back to their homes if they would agree not to take up arms against the United States "until properly exchanged." The officers would be allowed to keep their side arms, their personal horses, and baggage.

On reading Grant's terms, Lee commented: "There is one thing I would like to mention. The cavalrymen and artillerists own their own horses in our army. Its organization in this respect differs from that of the United States. I would like to understand whether these men will be permitted to retain their horses?" General Grant replied, "You will find that the terms as written do not allow this. Only the officers are permitted to take their private property."

Lee read over the second page of the letter again, and then said: "No, I see the terms do not allow it; that is clear." It was obvious to Grant that this grand old gentleman, 16 years his senior and former Superintendent of West Point, greatly desired that all of his men be allowed to keep their horses. Without giving Lee time to make a direct request, the magnanimous Grant said: "Well, the subject is quite new to me. I did not know that any private soldiers owned their animals, but I think this will be the last battle of the war...and I take it that most of the men in the ranks are small farmers, and as the country has been so raided by the two armies, it is doubtful whether they will be able to put in a crop to carry themselves and their families through the next winter without the aid of the horses they are now riding, and I will arrange it in this way..." Everybody kept their horses.

Lee replied: "This will have the best possible effect upon the men. It will be very gratifying and will do much toward conciliating our people."

The Southern army and the Union prisoners they held were in a starving mode with no food, and Grant made arrangements to feed 25,000 men for that was the best estimate, for the moment, of the number of men under Lee's command.

"This done, each officer and man will be allowed to return to his home, not to be disturbed by the United States authorities so long as they observe their paroles (their agreement not to fight) and the laws in force where they may reside."

What about all the trials for war crimes and for being traitors, for rebellion? In war there are atrocities on both sides. General Sherman in his "march to the sea" through Atlanta, and later in taking Columbia, South Carolina, along with many in his army, would surely be judged guilty of war crimes by an unbiased jury, had the South won the war. The South certainly had its share of men who were bloodthirsty and liked to kill "just to watch men die." But why had General Grant not been instructed to write in provisions for trying war criminals? Why did trials for war crimes not follow the war?

By the 26th of May, all Confederate forces had been surrendered by their various generals, and the terms were essentially the same as those given to General Lee.

Following the war Alexander H. Stephens, Vice President of the Southern Confederacy for the duration of the war wrote two volumes titled: *"A Constitutional View of the Late War Between the States; its causes, character, conduct and results."* Though Stephens rationalized about who was responsible for starting the war, and vainly attempted to reason that it was really the fault of the North which caused the South to fire the first shots at Fort Sumter, his work is one of the foremost constitutional analyses of the war.

He dedicated the second volume to "The memory of those whose lives in the late War between the States were sacrificed, either in battle, in hospital, in prison, or elsewhere—in defence of the sovereign right of local self-government, on the part of the peoples of the several states of the Federal Union; and in defence of those principles upon which that Union was established..." His dedication was accomplished at Liberty Hall, Crawfordsville, Georgia on the 26th of April, 1870.

In this second volume on page 659 he writes:

> In this connection it must be borne in mind, that nothwithstanding all that was said about the *treason* of the Confederates, about "traitors," about the "Insurrection," and the "Atrocious Rebellion," so-called, the authorities at Washington have not yet put that question in issue before the Judicial Tribunals. Immediately after the surrender, as we have seen, numerous arrests were made of high Confederate, as well as State Officials, but as yet not a single one of these has been put upon trial.

Concerning Stephens himself he wrote: "I was arrested on the 11th of May, was taken to Fort Warren, Boston Harbor, as is known, and was discharged on parole the 13th of October thereafter. It affords me pleasure to state that during the whole of that period of five months and two days, I was treated with the utmost respect and kindness by all, both officers and men, who had charge of me; or at least with the utmost respect and kindness consistent with their duties in obedience to orders from superiors..."

After detailing some of his jail time, Mr. Stephens continued: "As I was discharged, so were all the other Confederate and State officials who had been arrested, discharged after an imprisonment more or less prolonged without any criminal accusation being even lodged against them for their participation in the war, except for Mr. Davis."

Mr. Davis, as President of the Confederacy, and the one who was responsible for giving the order to bombard Fort Sumter initiating the war, would most certainly be the most worthy person deserving of trial and conviction for treason.

Concerning Jefferson Davis, Stephens continued: "As to Mr. Davis, it is true, after the infamous charge upon which he was arrested—that is, of complicity in the assassination of Mr. Lincoln—was proven to have had no foundation whatever, except the perjury of suborned witnesses, a formal Bill of Indictment for Treason in the matter of Secession and the War, was brought in against him. This has not yet been tried, though he has continuously demanded a trial, and urged it in the most earnest manner. His late enlargement on bail, without a trial (through the unexampled generosity and magnanimity of Mr. Horace Greeley, Gerrit Smith, Augustus Schell, H.F. Clark, Aristides Welsch, of New York, David J. Jackman, of Pennsylvania, and others, in becoming sureties for his appearance to answer the charge when the Government shall be ready to proceed with it,) may be considered as settling the question that the officials at Washington do not intend to allow that point on the principle involved in the issue, decided by the arbitrament of arms, to come before the Judicial Forum for decisions and adjudication there. An arbitrament on the Arena of Reason, Logic, Truth, and Justice they have thus far eschewed and avoided so that the great fact is to be borne in mind, that up to this time, nothing really affecting this "Cornerstone" of our Federal Institutions, as Governor Brown styled the principle in his reply to General Sherman has, as yet, been definitely settled, except the abandonment of an attempt to maintain it by a resort to arms." Ibid p. 663-664.

The following is a news item of that day. "Fortress Monroe, May 11, 1867: A large crowd was at the steamboat landing at an early hour. Mr. Davis left Fortress Monroe after two years' imprisonment. . .

"After the execution of the bail bond, a Richmond paper of the next day continued, amongst many other exceedingly interesting incidents attending the whole scene, the following:

"The release of Mr. Davis was now ordered; Gen. Burton and Dr. Cooper went forward and tendered him their warm congratulations. The example of these officers was followed by a host of personal friends and a scene of unbounded enthusiasm and excitement prevailed.

"A shout which could not be repressed, and which shook the granite walls to their foundations, went up from the excited throng, and amidst the exultant chorus, Mr. Davis descended the stairs shaking hands right and left as he passed, and entering the carriage which was brought him to the courtroom, returned to the hotel, where he spent some time in receiving the congratulations of the hosts of friends who availed themselves of the opportunity to express their joy and gratitude at his release." Ibid 663.

Two years' confinement, but no trial for the greatest "traitor" of them all? What was going on here? Could Alexander Stephens be right? Was the Union afraid to try anybody for treason or war crimes? What was there to fear? Had the North not won the war?

Though President Lincoln had done many constitutionally questionable things during the course of the war, if he had lived, there is little question he would have treated the South much differently, and much better than it was treated during reconstruction under leadership of some of the radical Republicans.

In spite of his shortcomings in regard to sustaining the Constitution under the extraordinary stresses of a civil war, President Lincoln was a man of character and had many fine qualities. His magnanimous nature is well demonstrated in this Civil War newspaper account.

"President Lincoln and Jeff Davis."
"General Sherman says he asked President Lincoln explicitly when at City Point, whether he wanted him to capture Jeff Davis or let him escape, but the President gave him no reply except a story about a temperance lecturer, who one day, after a long ride in the hot sun, stopped at the house of a friend and was regaled with lemonade. His host insinuatingly asked if he wouldn't like the least drop of something stronger to brace up his nerves after the exhausting heat and exercise?

"'No,' replied the lecturer. 'I couldn't think of it; I'm opposed to it on principle. But,' he added, with a longing glance at the black bottle that stood conveniently at hand, 'if you could manage to put in a drop unbeknownst to me, I guess it wouldn't hurt me much.'

"'Now, General,' said Mr. Lincoln in conclusion, 'I'm bound to oppose the escape of Jeff Davis, but if you could manage to let him slip out unbeknownst like, I guess it wouldn't hurt me much.'" Ibid 634.

The fact that the United States failed; no, refused, to follow through after the war with criminal trials for both the President and Vice President of the 11-State Confederacy, or any other leaders, is not because United States leaders felt compassion toward their Southern brethren, except perhaps for President Lincoln, who was assasinated only 5 days after the surrender of General Lee. In fact Northern leadership displayed not a drop of compassion during reconstruction of the South. Reconstruction rather, displayed pent up hatred and vindictiveness. It was implemented in blatant violation of the Constitution, and over the veto of Lincoln's successor, President Andrew Johnson.

With the benefit of this generation's 20/20 hindsight, it is glaringly apparent why the victorious Union did not try anybody for treason or other war crimes. It was *fear*. *Fear*, that if Jefferson Davis and Alexander Stephens were allowed to defend themselves in a prolonged trial by a jury of their peers, the jury would find them not guilty of anything except attempting to uphold the Constitution. *Fear*, that in open court, in months long trials, all the lawful arguments for the right of States to secede from the Union would receive the stamp of approval from a 12-member jury of the "common man." *Fear*, that the whole purpose the United States had for allegedly conducting the war, "to preserve the Union," would be found by a lawfully assembled jury, to have no basis in fact, in law, in history, nor in sentiment of the average citizen.

No doubt, a jury would have found the South negligent and reckless and irresponsible in firing on Fort Sumter and in destroying Federal property, but even here, nobody could be tried for murder, for there were no casualties, miraculously, in the assault.

If a jury would have found Jefferson Davis and Alexander Stephens innocent because the cause which they championed, *secession*, was lawful and just, chaos and rioting in the North might have made the Los Angeles riots and anarchy of 1992, look like a Sunday School picnic.

An acquittal of Stephens and Davis by a jury would have put the lie to the whole foundation and excuse for the war. The North would have been confronted with explaining to 22,000,000 people why they had allowed 360,000 of their fathers, brothers and sons to be sacrificed in such an ignoble and unworthy cause of putting down a "rebellion" which was now ruled to be officially lawful and justified.

Trials for traitors was far too risky. The matter must never be allowed to go before a possibly unbiased jury. A judge? That might be okay. But a jury of 12 honest men? Never! The risk was too great.

Lock the "traitors" up, most certainly! Let things cool down. Let the dust settle. Let everybody's passions subside. Stall. "Stonewall." But no trials! "Ever!"

The fact that the United States conducted no trials for war crimes after the Civil War is powerful evidence the North knew the weakness of their legal position in arguing against Southern Secession. It shows the North knew their official "doctrine" was without merit; it was untenable. It was irresponsible and unreasonable.

The Civil War did accomplish something good, of course. It freed the slaves. But it mangled historical precedent and distorted the Constitution beyond recognition on a number of occasions.

It gave us the coerced and conceived in fraud, Fourteenth Amendment to the Constitution, which even at this late date, should be challenged by the States in the Supreme Court, or abolished and superceded by amending it out of the Constitution. The Fourteenth Amendment and numerous precedents based on it, continues to haunt us, and is used as a powerful weapon by groups such as The American Civil Liberties Union (ACLU) to stalk and destroy liberties, otherwise protected in the Constution. It is used extensively to justify pointing The Bill of Rights "cannon" at the States, as well as at the Federal government for which the Founders exclusively intended them. There is nothing wrong with the States having The Bill of Rights operational within their boundaries, but to have an arm of the Federal Government, the Judiciary, make the declaration, does great violence, not only to the theory and concept of State's Rights, but it advances the theory that *the agent is greater than the principal,* which can never be.

It is only through the advancement of this fraud, *the agent is greater than the principal,* that those in power will be able to give us the *New World Order*, for once the concept of a one-world government is understood by *the people*; the *States*, one by one, will never go along, and the one-worlders know it. Washington, as our agent, if *the people* can be kept asleep long enough, will sell us out to the New World Order, and in our ignorance, it is hoped, *the people* will not object too strenuously.

Chapter 8

Secession—Historical Precedents

Should the necessity arise, as a last resort, for *the people* to assume their right to *total sovereignty*, and demand that their *first agent*, the *State*, secede from or *dissolve and abolish* their *second and inferior agent*, the Federal government, the five arguments listed above are more than sufficient to establish their right to do so.

But let us consider very briefly, for the subject could fill volumes, secession and separation in other nations.

Less than 39 years after the end of the Civil War, which the Union fought "to preserve the Union," the Union of the United States of America conspired with a small contingent of Latin Americans to have Panama secede from the Mother country, Columbia, located at the extreme North end of South America. Proof, once more, that history and Thomas Jefferson were right; that any group of like-minded people have the lawful right to separate themselves from a larger...or smaller... group when their differences become so great they can no longer live in peace with each other.

At the end of the nineteenth century world leaders wanted to build a canal connecting the Pacific and Atlantic oceans through that narrow neck of land connecting North and South

America. It was determined that such a canal should run through either Nicaragua or that part of Colombia known as Panama.

The Panama Canal Company was organized under the laws of France and preliminary work was begun to run the canal through Panama in 1881. Unforeseen difficulties were encountered and the work, after years of effort and expenditures, came to a halt.

In 1899 President McKinley was authorized to appoint a commission of competent engineers and others to appraise the feasibility of a canal somewhere from Nicaragua to Columbia. In June, 1902, Congress authorized the President to purchase the property and franchises of the Panama Canal Company for $40,000,000, provided good title could be secured from Colombia.

After long negotiation with Colombia, about six months, a treaty was signed.

In January, 1903, the treaty was introduced in the United States Senate for ratification. A few senators opposed it, particularly Senator Morgan of Alabama, who favored a canal route through Nicaragua, and the Fifty-seventh Congress ended without action on the canal.

An extra session of the Senate was called on March 5. After some two weeks of debate, a vote was taken on March 18, and the treaty was ratified by a vote of 73 to 5.

The treaty called for the payment of $10,000,000 in gold to Colombia and $250,000 annually.

On June 20, 1903, the Colombian Senate met for the purpose of considering the treaty. The Colombian Senate objected to the provision in the treaty placing the canal strip under the joint guaranty of the United States and of Colombia, which was said to be an abdication of sovereignty by Colombia and, therefore, unconstitutional. It was also thought the price was too low. Colombia rejected the treaty.

In October, 1903, the Colombian Secretary of State tried to reopen negotiations in Washington to change the treaty to provide greater compensation and recognition of Colombian sovereignty over the canal. Washington would not reconsider the treaty. By now, the United States had other plans, which would completely go around the Colombian government.

President Theodore Roosevelt was well aware of Panamanian willingness to revolt against Colombia in order to gain for themselves the benefits that would result from construction of a canal. Armaments were smuggled into Panama at such a rate that it was not long before the Panamanians were armed and ready. Roosevelt did not intend to allow a successful Colombian counterattack, and he sent ships of the U.S. Navy to cruise Panamanian waters with orders to prevent the landing of Colombian troops.

A more pro-American view puts it this way. "The failure of the treaty created great dissatisfaction in Panama and on November 4, 1903, Panama declared itself an independent republic." The New International Encyclopaedia, second edition, Volume XVII, 1926.

Under a treaty of 1846 with Colombia, the United States was allowed to maintain free transit across the Isthmus. Under "rights" of this treaty President Roosevelt directed the commanders of the warships Nashville and Marblehead to prevent Colombian troops from coming ashore to put down this "revolution" of secession.

The United States did not lose any time in concluding a treaty with this new *free, independent* and *sovereign* nation of Panama, which treaty we signed on November 18, 1903, only two weeks after independence was declared. The United States Senate ratified the treaty on February 23, 1904 and *guaranteed* the independence of Panama.

In the treaty, the *Republic of Panama* granted to the United States in perpetuity, the use, occupation and control of an area of land 10 miles in width. The United States was granted all the powers which it would exercise "as if" it were the sovereign of the territory.

Panama was paid the same as we had offered Colombia. $10,000,000 in gold and $250,000 annually beginning in nine years.

After Panama seceded, Colombia sent General Rafael Reyes, a special ambassador, to try to negotiate the consent of the United States to allow Colombia to reannex Panama to Colombia. He said Colombia would not only ratify the same treaty we had signed with Panama, but would consent to even more liberal terms. The United States refused the General's proposals. Neither would Panama agree to assume a proportion of Colombian debt which Colombia claimed had been incurred on behalf of Panamanian citizens.

In August, 1914, the Panama Canal was opened to shipping. Actual construction had taken seven years. The total cost was $336,650,000.

The American conscience remained troubled over the part we played in the secession of Panama from Colombia, and in 1921 the United States ratified a treaty with Colombia agreeing to pay her $25,000,000 for the loss of Panama.

Panama was a Province, or State; a part of Colombia. Panama was, legally, more a part of Colombia, than California, New York or Minnesota, or any one of the other 50 States are part of the United States of America. Each of the 50 States is sovereign, except for limited delegation of power.

Colombia was embittered for years against the United States. She said we "stole" Panama. We said we simply recognized Panama as a new nation according to the wishes of her people. We simply recognized the right of that people to go their own way in spite of the central government which governed them. We claimed the right of Panama to secede was lawful and legal, and we had the muscle to back it up.

Panama had no rights so clearly defined as the 50 States have under their constitutional contract with their central government. Panama had nothing on her side like the legal argument of Virginia, in which she reserved the "right to resume her sovereignty" at her own discretion. Yet, the United States recognized Panama as a new sovereign nation. How can the United States ever claim one or more of the 50 States cannot lawfully secede from the Union of the 1990's?

Should Virginia, or any other State in the late 20th century decide to secede from the United States, on what legal theory could the United States government proceed in arguing the States have no right to leave the Union? There is no such theory which could be sustained in a court of law.

The Panama Canal Zone is 10 miles wide and consists of a total area of 648 square miles. In 1978 the United States, under the administration of President Jimmy Carter, negotiated a new treaty with Panama, in which we gave the canal away over a period of years. At that time the Canal was valued at some $10 billion, and without the constitutional requirement that the U.S. House of Representatives concur in disposing of U.S. property, the Senate and Jimmy Carter gave away this strategic and valuable piece of real estate to Panama. Panama will gradually take over, but by December 31, 1999, this 648 square miles, including the Canal itself, will be handed over to Panama. The Panama Canal Zone could be lawfully recovered by the United States if *the people* willed it, but that is another story.

* * * * * *

Now let us consider our acquisition of the lone star State, Texas.

The secession of Texas from Mexico is another fascinating part of U.S. history. Texas belonged to Mexico, but a "handful" of Texas residents agreed to a "Declaration of Independence." Against the wishes of Mexico, the United States "annexed" Texas by accepting her as the 28th State of the Union.

A convention of colonists met at Washington-on-the-Brazos, March 2, 1836, and declared Texas an independent nation. David G. Burnett was made provisional President and Sam Houston was put in command of the Texas army. The entire population of Texas at this time was only around 30,000. A constitution was ratified in September, 1836, and Houston was elected President, in the first national election in the new Republic. A proposal that Texas become part of the United States also won a large majority. But Northern objection to admission of a probable slave state prevented Statehood at that time.

The new Republic of Texas was recognized by the United

States, France, Great Britain and Holland, among others, but Mexico continued to claim possession. Mexico attempted several times to "repossess" Texas with unsuccessful military expeditions.

In early 1845, the U.S. Congress passed a resolution favoring the annexation of Texas. A special session of the Texas Congress voted their acceptance of the U.S. resolution. Texas officially entered the Union as a State on December 29, 1845.

Mexico had never relinquished its claim to Texas, and the U.S. action of accepting Texas into the Union precipitated the Mexican War of 1846-1848.

The United States army captured Mexico City on September 14, 1847. By the Treaty of Guadalupe Hidalgo, February 2, 1848, Mexico gave up its claim to Texas and also ceded to the United States other western lands for $15,000,000.

The whole point of this brief review of Texas history is, long before Texas became a State, The United States, as well as other nations, recognized the *secession* of Texas from Mexico by a mere handful of her residents whose total amounted to some 30,000 people covering a land area of hundreds of thousands of square miles.

If Texas' *secession* was recognized in 1836, why was it not recognized in 1861, and why should it not be recognized in the l990's, if *the people* of Texas should decide separation from the United States is best for them? The fact is, there is *no legal reason* which would prevent such secession.

The main reason Texas did not gain Statehood in the United States years before she did was because her admission was bound up in the question of slavery. Northerners did not wish to bring new slave States into the Union. The long term goal, like that of their fathers, was to eventually eliminate slavery, not increase it. Nevertheless, for the purposes of establishing the historical lawfulness of secession the facts are clear. The United States sanctioned and approved the secession of Texas from Mexico, a short time after a few "radicals" declared their independence. We officially recognized Texas as a new and independent nation of the earth. So did other major powers.

Chapter 8

Part of the other Western territory given up by Mexico in the Guadalupe Hidalgo Treaty was California. Whether California was received by coercion or purchase, or both, as new United States territory, we will not speculate. What is important to point out is that little more than 19 months before the 1848 treaty with Mexico a number of Americans near Sacramento, California rebelled against Mexican authority in the Bear Flag Revolt and proclaimed California an independent republic. This was June 14, 1846. On July 7, Commodore John Drake Sloat captured Monterey and proclaimed California a possession of the United States. Two days later, Captain John Montgomery of the U.S. Navy occupied San Francisco. On August 13, Commodore Robert F. Stockton and Army Captain John Fremont took Los Angeles. Colonel Stephen Kearney seized Santa Fe, which was a Mexican trading center, then moved into Southern California. By the end of 1846, whether or not the "Declaration of Independence" had been recognized by Mexico, California had been taken by conquest.

The point again is, the United States obviously recognized the *Declaration of Independence* of June 14, and quickly moved to "assist" the "rebels" in making valid the independence of California. We might even speculate that high American officials had a little something to do with the June 14 declaration.

It must be admitted however, in gaining Texas and California from Mexico, and in the secession of Panama from Colombia, American politicians of 150 years ago, were clever enough to match the best we are able to produce and send to Washington in the 20th century. We made it look good by coughing up $15,000,000 to Mexico, and many years after the fact, $25,000,000 to Colombia.

This is not to imply that Mexico's hands were any cleaner than those of the United States. General, and Dictator of Mexico, Antonio Lopez de Santa Anna, commander of the force which stormed the Alamo after a 13-day siege, was a cruel tyrant who gave Americans much justification for our "payback" of his cruelty. Out of about 180 men defending the Alamo, all but five had been killed, and these five were captured. On the orders of Santa Anna, the five were killed in cold blood. He did allow three women, two children and a negro boy to live.

In March, close to the time the Alamo was taken by Santa Anna, two parties, one under Johnson and the other under Grant, were captured by Mexicans. Prisoners were taken and then killed, as in the Alamo. Fannin's command, which had been in possession of the Goliad fortress, surrendered and these were all massacred. Nearly 500 Texans met their death.

"Remember the Alamo" became the cry of Texans, when some six weeks later they again met Santa Anna, and this time, he was captured. He was released when he all too gladly signed a "treaty," which was subsequently rejected by Mexico, granting independence to Texas or promising to do what he could for the independence of Texas.

* * * * * *

Most of the following commentary on secession is taken directly from the Encylopedia Americana, under *secession*, written by Henry B. Parkes, Author of The American Experience.

In the ancient world, the northern Israelite tribes successfully seceded from the Davidian kingdom after the death of Solomon in 933 B.C and founded the separate kingdom of Israel, which eventually became known as "The lost Ten Tribes" as they were absorbed by various conquerors. In 5th century Greece, a number of cities attempted to secede from the League of Delos, dominated by Athens, but they were held in subjection. Rome showed statesmanship in preventing the secession of Italian cities in 91-88 B.C. by granting citizenship to their inhabitants.

Among the numerous instances of successful secession in the modern world were Belgium's separation from the kingdom of the Netherlands by armed rebellion in 1830 and Norway's peaceful break with Sweden in 1905. In Latin America, secession, successful or attempted, has been frequent. Notable examples were the secession of Venezuela and Ecuador from Gran Colombia in 1830, and of Panama from

Colombia in 1903.

Of worldwide significance has been the demand of colonial peoples for the right to secede from the empires of European powers. Before the 20th century, such secession was accomplished only by force, as in the case of the American colonies held by Britain and Spain. The British conceded self-government to southern Ireland in 1922 only after failing to crush an Irish rebellion, but after 1945 they accepted the partial or complete secession of various Asian and African peoples. (Volumes could be written on these secessions, some peaceful, some bloody.) The Dutch yielded to the secession of Indonesia in 1949. After the French had unsuccessfully fought rebellion in Indochina, the government in 1958, recognized a general right of secession for colonial dominions; yet France struggled to hold on to Algeria through more than seven years of warfare, until 1962. (And rightly so, as communist agitation, not the voice of the people was the force behind this rebellion.) Portugal continued to resist independence movements in its overseas provinces. The Soviet Union, immediately after its 1917 revolution, accepted the secession of Poland, Finland, and the Baltic states. But it disallowed such rights in subsequent years and reincorporated the Baltic states in 1940. (This was with the famous pact of Joseph Stalin with Adolph Hitler as both dictators thought to outmaneuver each other in their desire to expand the empire.)

Except for the continued process of the breakup of colonial empires, secession in the second half of the 20th century has largely meant the dissolution of states and federations relatively newly constituted in relation to the history of nations. Examples include the peaceful end of the West Indian Federation (Jamaica and Trinidad-Tobago) in 1962 and the withdrawal of Singapore from Malaysia in 1965; the bloody, unsuccessful secessionist movements in Katanga province, (again communist inspired) the Congo (communist inspired) later Zaire, in 1960 and in Biafra, Nigeria, in 1969; and the equally disastrous, but successful, secession of Bangladesh from Pakistan in 1971.

End of Encyclopedia Americana commentary.

The Unravelling of the Soviet Union

In his first speech as President of Czechoslovakia, Vaclev Havel discussed life under communism. "The worst thing is that we live in a contaminated moral environment. We had all become used to a totalitarian system and accepted it as an unchallengeable fact and thus helped to perpetuate it."

Many Americans currently live under the same illusion, that Washington with its IRS, Federal Reserve System, millions of employees sucking up taxpayer dollars, and control of State governments with the carrot of Federal handouts and accompanying controls is unchallengable.

Compared to the task of challenging the Soviet system internally, the American people should be able to accomplish rather easily the restoration of the Constitution in the tradition of the Founding Fathers even if it means temporarily dissolving the Union, as was done in the Soviet Union. Then after eliminating all the excess federal baggage and debt we have managed to accumulate, the individual States can put it all back together again, assuming we can settle a few major differences which divide us. Failing that, the 50 States could still join in a military pact to protect the nation from foreign aggression.

President Franklin Roosevelt attempted to appease Joseph Stalin and the Soviet Union, as Britain's Chamberlain attempted to appease Adolph Hitler. It didn't work as any ten-year-old who has dealt with a neighborhood bully might have known it would not work. Stalin, in his Red Army Day speech of February 9, 1946, finally exposed his iron fist inside the velvet glove by declaring the United States and its allies as the new enemy.

Nevertheless, over the decades since then, the United States has appeased and often fed the Soviet Bear. One could make a powerful case that the entire cold war with the Soviet Union has been a fraud, a sham, both sides being controlled and manipulated by sinister and unseen hands of great power and influence working behind the scenes. Such a case has been made by many authors, but that is beyond the scope of this work.

The Cold War went on for decades until the United States finally elected Ronald Reagan as President. Mr. Reagan admonished the Soviets to "tear down this wall" referring to the Berlin Wall, bringing hope to the captive nations who now realized they might have a powerful Western leader as a champion of their cause. Reagan began a military buildup which the weak Soviet economic system would not match, and the built-in self-destructing empire began to come apart.

Communism, or socialism, are not in harmony with the desires of human nature to be free and independent. When a person works, his incentive is to be able to keep what he earns for the benefit of himself and his family, not for the benefit of the State. Socialism fights against this tendency of human nature.

Yet, the most astute observers among us were surprised, if not shocked, with the rapid turn of events beginning with the fall of the Berlin Wall in November 1989.

The former Soviet Union was made up of 15 "Republics," or States. The three Baltics, Latvia, Lithuania and Estonia were the first three to *secede* from the Union.

Gorbachev saw the writing on the wall and recognized the impossibility of saving Communism in central and eastern Europe by military means, but he had no intention of allowing the Baltic states or the Soviet republics their independence. He, nor anybody else, dreamed such a thing was possible, perhaps in our lifetime. Gorbachev hoped to save the U.S.S.R. through reform, and with that which had always worked before, repression.

In December, 1990, the foreign minister, Shevardnadze resigned. He was concerned about Gorbachev's appointment of Communist hardliners. He, Aleksandr Yakovlev and other reformers joined the opposition with Boris Yeltsin, President of the largest Soviet republic, Russia.

By the summer of 1991, demonstrations in support of Yeltsin and in defiance of Gorbachev were common in Moscow. And the name of Leningrad was changed back to its old name of St. Petersburg.

On August 19, 1991, Gorbachev's hardliners turned against him and attempted to seize power. But the people in Moscow stood between Soviet tanks and the Russian Parliament Building protecting Boris Yeltsin from capture and possible death. Through it all, Yeltsin was in support of Gorbachev and the coup failed.

After all this, Gorbachev still defended communism and reaffirmed his belief in Marxism-Leninism. Nevertheless, since that failed coup, we have witnessed the *secession* of the remaining 12 Soviet States, one rapidly following another, until there was no Soviet Union over which Gorbachev could preside. He resigned as Premier, when in fact, the entire Soviet Union had dissolved out from under him as each Soviet State declared its independence, seceded, and became an *independent, free*, and *sovereign* nation.

President George Bush, and quiet behind the scenes forces, were not pleased with the breakup of the Soviet Union. Though the United States had always advocated the Soviet Union should grant independence to the Baltic States because they had been unlawfully absorbed through the secret protocol of August 23, 1939, George Bush stalled as long as he could from recognizing their newly declared independence, although the United Sates finally recognized the *secession* of these new nations. We did not wish to have to deal with the 12 other Soviet Republics as single units either, but we found we had little choice.

Nobody would have ever dreamed it, but the secessions of the Soviet Union were accomplished with relatively little bloodshed in some of the States, none in others.

Historical precedent, and the eternal truths set down by Thomas Jefferson in our own *Declaration of Independence*, have triumphed before our very eyes since the shattering world events of 1989, when *the people* of various nations decided they had had enough of government telling them how to live their lives.

If it is not already past due, it appears it is just about time for 250,000,000 Americans to resurrect Thomas Jefferson and The Declaration of Independence. It is time to follow the example of Eastern Europe and the Soviet Union, and get rid of an arrogant and liberty stifling Federal monstrosity which stretches its grasping tentacles from Washington, D.C. to smother the 50 States in statism and socialism.

It is not too late! It is never too late! Washington must be made to understand that we will; we are determined to uphold the Constitution of the United States, even if it means dissolving the Union, or individual States separating themselves from the Union so the citizens in that State can uphold the Constitution if they have to do it by themselves.

And such a dissolution can, and should be accomplished with calm, reason, negotiation and peace. Bloodshed would be stupid and wasteful. If we should decide we cannot live together in peace, we should part, with all sides giving their blessing to the others, and simply agree to disagree. Divorce is never the end of the world. Neither is secession.

Should secession of one or more States come, or should 38 States get together and dissolve the Union, a great many loose ends would have to be worked out. A peaceful divorce of man and wife still must be worked out and negoiated, at least if there are any assets involved. In the case of the United States government being dissolved by the States, billions of dollars in assets would have to be equitably distributed among the 50 States, probably based on population. This is on the assumption that the "divorce" was to be permanent. But, more likely than not, there would be a "remarriage" of the States, or at least, most of them. A new Union would very likely adopt a Constitution similar to the one we have, except we might refine it in a few places.

With 200 years of experience we have learned it is too easy for the Congress, the President and the Judiciary to usurp undelegated powers. In "*a more perfect union*" we only need to fine tune the Constitution; not rewrite it.

Even without the threat of a New World Order destroying the Constitution, it looks like our best course is to dissolve the Federal government and start over from the base of 50 independent, free and sovereign States.

Chapter 9

The Kentucky and Virginia Resolutions

Two of the most powerful documents which make very clear the nature of the government of the United States are the Kentucky and Virginia Resolutions, written by, perhaps, the two foremost experts on the Constitution among the Founders of our nation, Thomas Jefferson and James Madison.

In the early years of our Republic, that which the Constitution had been so carefully written to avoid, the concentration of power into a Central government and the elimination of any powers in that Central government, except those which were specifically delegated, was already starting to get out of hand.

Alexander Hamilton, who had done the nation great service on many occasions, was not a great defender of the "strict constructionist" view of the Constitution. Hamilton became the Secretary of the Treasury in the Administrations of George Washington, and had great influence with Washington. He and Washington had come a long way together. Early in the Revolutionary War, Hamilton had distinguished himself in the military. On March 1, 1777, he was made a lieutenant colonel and aide-de-camp on the staff of George Washington.

It was Hamilton, James Madison and John Jay who wrote

the Federalist Papers in their efforts to convince New Yorkers to ratify the Constitution, and which essays became a major standard for the judiciary to later rule on the meaning of the Constitution and the intent of its writers.

But as Washington's Secretary of the Treasury, he had an undue amount of influence in arguing for implied powers in the Constitution as he convinced Washington to go along with a United States Bank. Hamilton was among the old Nationalists who were inclined toward "consolidation" of the States into a single government. They gradually stole for themselves the name Federalists, who had been for, and won, in the framing of the Constitution, independence and sovereignty for the States. As these Federalists gained power, they succeeded in electing John Adams President in 1796. Hamilton was one of the foremost Federalists, and as such, he and Thomas Jefferson had become political enemies.

Barely over a year into the Administration of President John Adams, the Federalists succeeded in passing a series of statutes called the *Alien and Sedition Acts*. These acts were occasioned in large measure by the desire of the Federalists who were in power to stifle some of the more enthusiastic criticism of their opposition, and discourage, perhaps even silence, some of their potential rivals, particularly a number of newspaper editors who did not necessarily seem to care whether their stories were based on fact, rumor, or falsehood, with intent to deceive.

According to the Encyclopedia International, the Alien and Sedition Acts were four statutes passed by Congress in 1798, "designed to crush the opposition of the pro-French Jeffersonian Republicans to the anti-French policies of the Federalist administration."

Thomas Jefferson, it should be recalled, was the Vice President in the John Adams administration. These acts had many restrictions on freedom of speech and of the press. They were allegedly intended to protect the country in time of war, but it appears the main intent was to curb the growing strength of the Republican party led by Thomas Jefferson and James Madison. There was, no doubt, at least some basis for the

Federalists passage of these acts, other than their political alarm at growing "strict constructionist" opposition.

These four acts of Congress were: the Naturalization Act, passed June 18,1798; The Act Concerning Aliens, June 25, 1798; the Act Respecting Alien Enemies, July 6, 1798, and the Act for the Punishment of Certain Crimes, the Sedition Act, July 14, 1798.

Two of these, the Act Concerning Aliens, and the Act for the Punishment of Certain Crimes, were largely responsible for this period in our history being called by many, the "Reign of Terror." The Naturalization Act raised the term of residence required before naturalization from 5 to 14 years. This was clearly meant to weaken the Republican party, as most naturalized citizens were drawn to it. Under the Act Concerning Aliens, the president was given the power to order out of the country all aliens he thought to be "dangerous" to the security of the United States.

Republicans denounced the Alien Enemies Act unconstitutional on three counts: as a deprivation of trial by jury, as an illegal usurpation of the authority of the Federal government over aliens, and as an unwarranted extension of the powers of the executive. The Republicans claimed resident aliens were wholly within the jurisdiction of the states, and the Federal government had no right to touch their persons or property. In the South, it was felt the President had been given the authority to deport slaves.

The Sedition Act actually had some very strong constitutional protections in it. The House of Representatives inserted provisions by which truth was admitted as a defense in cases of slander and libel, and proof of malicious intent was required. An outstanding provision of this bill was *the jury was permitted to determine questions of law*, as well as of fact. Though the jury had always had this power, and still does, citizens can never have too much protection against their own government by having all points of law concerning rights, spelled out as clearly as possible. Limits were also fixed upon the amount of fines and terms of imprisonment that could be imposed.

In the actual execution of the law, these safeguards proved

to be of little protection. Judges and juries were usually biased against defendants and judges' rulings often prevented truth from being an effective defense. As a result, predictions of the Republicans proved accurate, that the Sedition Act would be used to destroy freedom of speech and of the press. Under the provisions of this Act, "the publishing or printing of any false, scandalous, or malicious writings to bring government, Congress, or the president into contempt or disrepute, excite popular hostility to them, incite resistance to the laws of the United States, or encourage hostile designs against the United States, were declared a misdemeanor." Americana Encyclopedia.

A Republican congressman from Vermont was convicted of sedition, sentenced to four months in jail and fined $1,000. Perhaps only a dozen people were convicted of violating this law, but some of these were leading Republican journalists.

The Alien Act expired on June 25, 1800; the Sedition Act, March 3, 1801, the day before the next president was to take office, which was March 4 in those days. By the short duration of these Acts, and the fact the Sedition Act was to expire along with the current term of President John Adams, we get more than a glimpse of the political nature of these Acts. And the Naturalization Act was repealed by the Jeffersonian Republicans under the administration of Thomas Jefferson in 1802.

The Alien and Sedition Acts produced one good effect. In opposition to them and other Federal usurpations which were already creeping into this new experiment in liberty, two States officially passed resolutions opposing these Acts, and at the same time, clearly spelled out the nature of the State and Federal governments. This was all made quite clear in accumulated historical documents in the forming of the Union, but these resolutions added further clarification.

Kentucky passed a set of opposing resolutions November 16, 1798. The author was he who had also written the Declaration of Independence more than 22 years before, Thomas Jefferson, and who, in two more years, would be elected President of the United States. Jefferson's authorship was kept secret at the time, for he was after all, the current Vice

President of the United States. The Federalists then in power, might have felt the Vice President should have more loyalty to the sitting President, and not quite so much to principles of the Constitution.

Virginia passed her resolutions addressing the same subject on December 24, 1798. Their author was the equally eminent constitutional scholar, James Madison, "the father of the Constitution," also a President to be. He it was who was the receiver of a trunk full of books which Thomas Jefferson sent to him from France, leading up to the meeting of the Constitutional Convention of 1787. These books covered everything on history and governments Jefferson could lay his hands on after he replaced Benjamin Franklin as the United States representative to France.

The resolutions will here be quoted in full. Emphasis will be added by the author in italics.

The Kentucky resolutions by Thomas Jefferson

"1. Resolved, That the several States composing the United States of America, are not united on the principle of unlimited submission to their General Government; but that, by a compact under the style and title of a Constitution *for* the United States, and of Amendments thereto, they constituted a General Government for special purposes, delegated to that Government certain definite powers, reserving each State to itself, the residuary mass of right to their own self-government; and that whensoever *the general government assumes undelegated powers, its acts are unauthoritative, void, and of no force*:"

Comment by the author. This correct view of the early Fathers over several decades, was gradually overcome and the judiciary has been allowed to become the final arbiter between the States and the Federal government. The Founders failed to put into the Constitution a viable way of resolving conflict between two sovereigns, the States and their artificial sovereign. Should the Union be dissolved and we start over again, the new Constitution should have a provision for such conflicts, wherein say, a *Super Supreme Court*, or some sort of *council* of the 50 *states*, could resolve differences and also be the final arbiter over jurisdiction if a State believed the Supreme Court was assuming jurisdiction without justification. Such a Council, or Super Court might make binding decisions by, perhaps a simple majority of 26 States. Whatever, some sort of State agent needs to be established, other than the Supreme Court, to decide conflicting State and Federal jurisdiction and sovereignty.

As the Founders argued, however, on more than one occasion, the present system of allowing the Supreme Court to make binding decisions regarding jurisdiction, or be the arbiter of last resort on conflicts of sovereignty, has a built in bias against the States. The Supreme Court is disqualified, or should be disqualified, from making such decisions because of its built in conflict of interest. It is one of the three branches or partys which are agents, being asked to decide if its own *principal* has sovereignty over it, an absurd position.

The Supreme Court and the Federal judiciary are "married" to the Executive and Legislative branches. Each of the three branches, it must be assumed, will have the interest of the other two first and foremost, when any one of its partners is challenged by an outsider. If the Founders thought this outsider, the States, by virtue of being the *principal* and the *creator* of its artificial agent, would always maintain the supreme power and authority, history has proven them wrong.

Under our judicial system plaintiffs or defendants who believe the judge, or potential jury member may be biased against them, or have a personal conflict of interest which would give a personal benefit to the judge or jurors by ruling against them, provisions are made to have the judge disqualified from hearing the case and potential biased jurors are dismissed.

No such protection is provided for the 50 States.

Roe vs. Wade is a prime example. The Supreme Court should have ruled that it lacked jurisdiction to even make a decision. Abortion is a State issue, and the arguments regarding it should have been allowed to go no higher than the Supreme

Court in each of the States. The States make their own laws unless it can clearly be shown that the State is in some sort of violation of the Constitution in relation to another State or individual or corporation. We could reduce the load of cases which go to the Supreme Court if we had some sort of Council with authority to decide, first of all, if it has jurisdiction, and second if the issue involved State Sovereignty vs. Federal Sovereignty.

Continuing with the Kentucky resolutions: "that to this compact each State acceded as a State, and is an integral party, its co-States forming, as to itself, the other party: that *the government created by this compact, was not made the exclusive or final judge of the extent of the powers delegated to itself; since that would have made its discretion, and not the constitution, the measure of its powers*; but that, as in all other cases of compact among *powers having no common judge, each party has an equal right to judge for itself*, as well of infractions as of the mode and measure of redress.

"2. Resolved, That the Constitution of the United States, having delegated to Congress a power to punish treason, counterfeiting the securities and current coin of the United States, piracies, and felonies committed on the high seas, and offences (sic) against the law of nations, and no other crimes whatsoever; and it being true, as a general principle, and one of the amendments to the Constitution having also declared, that 'the powers not delegated to the United States by the Constitution, nor prohibited by it to the States, are reserved to the States respectively, or to the people,' (tenth amendment) therefore the act of Congress, passed on the 14th day of July, 1798, the Sedition Act as also the act passed by them on the 27th day of June, 1798, entitled 'An act to punish frauds committed on the Bank of the United States,' (and all their other acts which *assume to create, define, or punish crimes, other than those so enumerated in the constitution,) are altogether void, and of no force; and that the power to create, define, and punish such other crimes is reserved, and of right, appertains solely and exclusively to the respective states, each within its own territory.*

"3. Resolved, That it is true as a general principle, and is also expressly declared by one of the amendments to the Constitution, that 'the powers not delegated to the United States by the Constitution, nor prohibited by it to the States, are reserved to the States respectively, or to the people;' and that no power over the freedom of religion, freedom of speech, or freedom of the press being delegated to the United States by the Constitution, nor prohibited by it to the States, all lawful powers respecting the same did of right remain, and were reserved to the States or the people: that thus was manifested their determination to retain to themselves the right of judging how far the licentiousness of speech, and of the press may be abridged without lessening their useful freedom, and how far those abuses which cannot be separated from their use should be tolerated, rather than the use be destroyed. And thus also they guarded against all abridgment by the United States of the freedom of religious opinions and exercises, and retained to themselves the right of protecting the same, as this State, by a law passed on the general demand of its citizens, had already protected them from all human restraint or interference. And that in addition to this general principle and express declaration, another and more special provision has been made by one of the amendments to the Constitution, which expressly declares, that 'Congress shall make no law respecting an establishment of religion, or prohibiting the free exercise thereof, or abridging the freedom of speech, or of the press:' thereby guarding in the same sentence, and under the same words, the freedom of religion, of speech, and of the press: insomuch, that whatever violated either, throws down the sanctuary which covers the others, and that libels, falsehood, and defamation, equally with heresy and false religion, are withheld from the cognizance of Federal tribunals. That, therefore the act of Congress of the United States passed on the 14th day of July, 1798, intituted (sic, to give a name or title) 'An Act in addition to the act instituted an Act for the punishment of certain crimes against the United States,' which does abridge the freedom of the press, is not law, but is altogether void, and of no force.

"4. Resolved, That alien friends are under the jurisdiction

Chapter 9

and protection of the laws of the State wherein they are: that no power over them has been *delegated to the United States*, nor prohibited to the individual States, distinct from their power over citizens. And it being true as a general principle, and one of the amendments to the Constitution, having also declared that 'the powers not delegated to the United States by the Constitution, nor prohibited by it to the States, are reserved to the States respectively, or to the people,' the act of the Congress of the United States, passed on the 22nd day of June, 1798, entitled 'An Act concerning aliens,' which assumes powers over alien friends, *not delegated by the Constitution, is not law, but is altogether void, and of no force.*

"5. Resolved, That in addition to the general principle, as well as the express declaration, that powers not delegated are reserved, (the fourth time already, Jefferson has brought up or quoted the tenth amendment) another and more special provision, inserted in the Constitution from abundant caution, has declared that 'the migration or importation of such persons as any of the States now existing shall think proper to admit, shall not be prohibited by the Congress prior to the year 1808:' that this Commonwealth does admit the migration of alien friends described as the subject of the said act concerning aliens: that a provision against prohibiting their migration is a provision against all acts equivalent thereto, or it would be negatory, that to remove them when migrated, is equivalent to a prohibition of their migration, and is, therefore, contrary to the said provision of the Constitution, *and void*.

"6. Resolved, That the imprisonment of a person under the protection of the laws of this Commonwealth on his failure to obey the simple *order of the President to depart* out of the United States, as is undertaken by said act intituled 'An Act concerning aliens,' is contrary to the Constitution, one amendment to which has provided that 'no person shall be deprived of liberty without due process of law;' and that another having provided that 'in all criminal prosecutions, the accused shall enjoy the right to public trial, by an impartial jury, to be informed of the nature and cause of the accusation, to be confronted with the witnesses against him, to have compulsory process for obtaining witnesses in his favor, and to have the assistance of counsel for his defence,' the same act, undertaking to authorize the President to remove a person out of the United States who is under the protection of the law, on his own suspicion, without accusation, without jury, without public trial, without confrontation of the witnesses against him, without hearing witnesses in his favor, without defence, without counsel, is contrary to the provision also of the Constitution, is therefore *not law, but utterly void, and of no force*. That transferring the power of judging any person who is under the protection of the laws from the courts to the President of the United States, as is undertaken by the same act concerning aliens, is against the article of the Constitution which provides that 'the judicial power of the United States shall be vested in courts, the judges of which shall hold their offices during good behavior,' and that the said *act is void* for that reason also. And it is further to be noted, that this transfer of judiciary power is to that magistrate of the General Government who already possesses all the Executive, and a negative on all Legislative powers. (The veto of the President).

"7. Resolved, That the construction applied by the General Government (as is evidenced by sundry of their proceedings) to those parts of the Constitution of the United States which delegate to Congress a power 'to lay and collect taxes, duties, imposts and excises, to pay the debts and provide for the common defence and general welfare of the United States,' and 'to make all laws which shall be necessary and proper for carrying into execution the powers vested by the Constitution in the Government of the United States, or in any department or officer thereof,' goes to the destruction of all limits prescribed to their power by the Constitution; that words meant by the instrument to be subsidiary only to the execution of limited powers, ought not to be so construed as themselves to give unlimited powers, nor a part to be so taken as to destroy the whole residue of that instrument, that the proceedings of the General Government under color of these articles, will be a fit and necessary subject of revisal and correction at a time of greater tranquility, while those specified in the preceding resolutions call for immediate redress.

"8. Resolved, That a Committee of conference and correspondence be appointed who shall have in charge to communicate the preceding resolutions to the Legislatures of the several States; to assure them that this commonwealth continues in the same esteem of their friendship and union which it has manifested from that moment at which a common danger first suggested a common union, that it considers union for *specified National purposes*, and particularly to those specified in their late Federal compact, (the Constitution) to be friendly to the peace, happiness and prosperity of all the States, that faithful to that compact, according to the plain intent and meaning in which it was understood and acceded to by the several parties, *it is sincerely anxious for its preservation*, that it does also believe that to take from the States all the powers of self-government and transfer them to a general and consolidated government, *without regard to the special delegations and reservations solemnly agreed to in that compact*, is not for the peace, happiness or prosperity of these States; and that therefore, this commonwealth is determined, as it doubts not its co-States are, tamely to submit to undelegated, and consequently unlimited powers in no man or body of men on earth, that in cases of an abuse of the delegated powers, the members of the General Government, being chosen by the people, a change by the people would be the constitutional remedy, *but where powers are assumed which have not been delegated, a nullification of the act is the rightful remedy.*"

Comment by author. Nullification in our history was the formal suspension by a State, within its territorial jurisdiction, of a law of the United States. This theory appears to have, for the first time, been put forth in the Kentucky resolutions. Under this theory, because the Constitution created a compact or merely an agreement or contract among independent and sovereign States, and as in other cases of compact, each party had a right to judge for itself of infractions and of the mode of redress. The resolutions of 1799 went even further and declared that a nullification by the State sovereignties of all unauthorized acts done under pretended authority of the Constitution was the rightful remedy in cases of infraction.

The Virginia Resolutions written by James Madison did not go so far, but also correctly characterized the Union as a compact and called upon the other States to join her in declaring the Alien and Sedition laws null and void. No action was actually taken by any of the other States.

In 1809, the Pennsylvania government ordered out the militia to resist a Federal Court order. After the enactment of the Embargo Act, several of the New England States resorted to various means of judicial construction or evasion to nullify the carrying out of this Act of Congress. The Hartford Convention of 1814, which was made up of leaders who vigorously opposed the war of 1812 with Great Britain, had much of the nullification spirit within it. In several States the operation of Federal enlistment statutes were not effective because State governments refused to comply with the requirements. Oh, that we had such a spirit of resistance in our own day, when Washington dictates State highway speeds, seat belt laws, educational standards, etc. etc. ad nauseum!

While serving in the office of Vice President of the United States in 1828, John C. Calhoun prepared a paper for use of the South Carolina Legislature entitled *The South Carolina Exposition*. Although Calhoun was an advocate of slavery, he was, nevertheless, one of our greatest statesmen when it came to understanding and defending the Constitution. He wrote: "The United States is not a union of the people, but a league or compact between sovereign states, any of which has the right to judge when the compact is broken and to pronounce any law to be null and void which violates its conditions."

Calhoun resigned the vice presidency in 1832 and was elected Senator from South Carolina. In the Senate he overcame and put down the arguments of another great Senator and master orator, Daniel Webster in Webster's attempt to show the United States was a "consolidated" government of the people themselves, and therefore, the Union was indissoluble. As mentioned previously, Webster in later years came around, more or less, to the views of Calhoun.

In The South Carolina Exposition, Calhoun argued that the States were sovereign, that the Federal government was their agent, and whenever a sovereign State was convinced that its agent was misusing the powers delegated to it, it was the right of that State to suspend such powers. Calhoun said the suspension of Federal powers could only be accomplished through a convention of the people, not by a mere State Legislature. After a State nullified a Federal statute, such nullification would stand, unless and until three-fourths of the States met in a national convention and declared the suspended act of Congress a valid and reasonable law.

Calhoun was on the right track, but such a process would be far too cumbersome, and is not a reasonable approach. Some sort of *super court* established on a permanent basis would be a better way.

In 1830, after the publication of The South Carolina Exposition, Senator Robert Y. Hayne of South Carolina, in a grand debate with Daniel Webster made a powerful defense of the nullification doctrine, but unlike Calhoun, he argued the formal act of suspension could be made by the Legislature, as agent of *the people*.

On November 24, 1832, the South Carolina Legislature passed an ordinance declaring the tariff acts of 1828 and 1832 null and void, because they went beyond the powers the States had delegated to the United States. President Andrew Jackson denied the possibility of nullification being a peaceful remedy and talked Congress into passing the Force Bill, but only after the introduction of Senator Henry Clay's compromise tariff bill which would gradually reduce tariffs by 1842 to no more than 20%. On March 15, 1833, South Carolina repealed its nullification ordinance, but three days later she nullified the Force Act, the enforcement of which was now moot.

In the compromise reducing tariffs, and South Carolina's actions regarding nullification, both sides claimed victory.

Nullification as a constitutional and peaceful remedy against oppression was no longer asserted. Its weaknesses are obvious to the layman. It is not good theory and was rightfully abandoned. Nevertheless, its foundation of State's rights and sovereignty are rock solid. As the doctrine of nullification was gradually abandoned as unsound constitutional theory, secession came more to the forefront and by the time of the Civil War was widely accepted as sound doctrine.

Returning to the Kentucky resolutions. "That every State has a natural right in cases not within the compact, (casus non foederis,) to nullify of their own authority all assumptions of power by others within their limits; that without this right, they would be under the dominion, absolute and unlimited, of whosoever might exercise this right of judgment for them, that nevertheless, this commonwealth, from motives of regard and respect for its co-States, has wished to communicate with them on the subject, that with them alone it is proper to communicate, they alone being parties to the compact, and *solely authorized to judge in the last resort of the powers exercised under it, Congress being not a party, but merely the creature of the compact, and subject as to its assumptions of power to the final judgement of those by whom, and for whose use itself and its powers were all created and modified*, that if the acts before specified should stand, these conclusions would flow from them; that the General Government may place any act they think proper on the list of crimes, and punish it themselves whether enumerated or not enumerated by the Constitution as cognizable by them: that they may transfer its cognizance to the President, or any other person who may himself be the accuser, counsel, judge and jury, whose suspicions may be the evidence, his order the sentence, his officer the executioner, and his breast the sole record of the transaction, that a very numerous and valuable description of the inhabitants of these States being, by this precedent, reduced as outlaws to the absolute dominion of one man, and the barrier of the Constitution thus swept away from us all, no rampart now remains against the passions and the powers of a majority in Congress to protect from a like exportation, or other more grievous punishment, the minority of the same body, the legislatures, judges, governors and counselors of the States, nor their other peaceable inhabitants who may venture to reclaim the constitutional rights and liberties of the States and people, or who for other causes good or bad, may be obnoxious to the views, or marked by the suspicions of the President, or be thought dangerous to his or their election, or other interests, public or personal, *that the friendlless alien has indeed been selected as the safest subject of a first experiment,* but the citizens will soon follow, or rather has already followed, for already has a sedition act marked him as its prey, that these and successive acts of the same character, unless arrested at the threshold, necessarily drive these States into revolution and blood, and will furnish new calumnies against republican government, and new pretexts for those who wish it to be believed that man cannot be governed but by a rod of iron; that it would be a dangerous delusion were a confidence in the men of our choice to silence our fears for the safety of our rights, that *confidence is everywhere the parent of despotism—free government is founded in jealousy and not in confidence;* it is jealousy and not confidence which prescribes limited Constitutions, *to bind those whom we are obliged to trust with power*; that our Constitution has accordingly fixed the limits to which, and no further, our confidence may go; and let the honest advocate of confidence read the Alien and Sedition Acts, and say if the Constitution has not been wise in fixing limits to the government it created, and whether we should be wise in destroying those limits. Let him say that the Government is, if it be not a tyranny, which the men of our choice have conferred on our President, and the President of our choice has assented to, and accented over the friendly strangers to whom the mild spirit of our country and its laws have pledged hospitality and protection, that the men of our choice have more respected the bare suspicions of the President than the solid right of innocence, the claims of justification, the sacred force of truth, and the forms and substance of law and justice. *In questions of power, then let no more be heard of confidence in man, but bind him down from mischief by the chains of the Constitution*. That this Commonwealth does therefore call on its co-States for an expression of their sentiments on the acts concerning aliens, and for the punishment of certain crimes herein before specified, plainly declaring whether these acts are or are not authorized by the Federal compact. And it doubts not that their sense will be so announced as to prove their attachment unaltered to limited government, whether general or particular. And that the rights and liberties of their co-States will be exposed to no dangers by remaining embarked in a common bottom with their own. That they will concur with this Commonwealth in considering the said acts as so palpably against the Constitution as to amount to an undisguised declaration that the compact is not meant to be the measure of the powers of the General Government, but that it will proceed in the exercise over these States, of all powers whatsoever—that they will view this as seizing the rights of the States and consolidating them in the hands of the General Government with a power assumed to bind the States, not merely as the cases made Federal, (casus foederis,) but in all cases whatsoever, by laws made, not with their consent, but by others against their consent, that this would be to surrender the form of government we have chosen, and live under one deriving its powers from its own will, and not from our authority; and that the co-States, recurring to their natural right in cases not made Federal, will concur in declaring these acts void, and of no force, and will each take measures of its own for providing that neither these acts, nor any others of the General Government not plainly and intentionally authorized by the Constitution, *shall be exercised within their respective territories.*

"9. Resolved, That the said committee be authorized to communicate by writing or personal conferences, at any times or places whatever, with any person or persons who may be appointed by any one or more co-States to correspond or confer with them, and that they lay their proceedings before the next session of Assembly."

Jefferson's Complete Works, volume 9, page 464.

******

Chapter 9

The Virginia Resolutions

December 24, 1798. Author, James Madison.

In the Virginia House of Delegates,

"Resolved, That the General Assembly of Virginia, doth unequivocally express a firm resolution to maintain and defend the Constitution of the United States, and the Constitution of this State against every aggression either foreign or domestic, and that they will support the Government of the United States in all measures warranted by the former.

"That this Assembly most solemnly declares a warm attachment to the Union of the States, to maintain which it pledges its powers, and that for this end, it is their duty *to watch over and oppose every infraction of those principles which constitute the only basis of that union*, because a faithful observance of them can alone secure its existence and the public happiness.

"That this Assembly doth explicitly and peremptorily declare that it views the powers of the Federal Government, as resulting from the compact to which the States are parties, as limited by the plain sense and intention of the instrument constituting that compact as no further valid than they are authorized by the grants enumerated in that compact; and that, in case of a deliberate, palpable, and dangerous exercise *of other powers, not granted by the said compact, the states who are parties thereto, have the right and are in duty bound, to interpose, for arresting the progress of the evil*, and for maintaining, within their respective limits, the authorities, rights, and liberties, appertaining to them.

"That the General Assembly doth also express its deep regret, that a spirit has, in sundry instances, been manifested by the Federal Government, to enlarge its powers by forced constructions of the constitutional charter which defines them, and that indications have appeared of a design to expound certain general phrases (which, having been copied from the very limited grant of powers in the former Articles of Confederation, were the less liable to be misconstrued) so as to destroy the meaning and effect of the particular enumeration which necessarily explains and limits the general phrases, *and so as to consolidate the States by degrees into one sovereignty*, the obvious tendency and inevitable result of which would be to transform the present Republican system of the United States into an absolute, or at best, a mixed monarchy.

"That the General Assembly doth particularly protest against the palpable and alarming infractions of the Constitution in the two late causes of the "Alien and Sedition Acts," passed at the last session of Congress; the first of which exercises a power nowhere delegated to the Federal Government, and which by uniting Legislative and Judicial powers to those of Executive, subverts the general principles of free government, as well as the particular organization and positive provisions of the Federal Constitution; and the other of which acts exercises in like manner, a power not delegated by the Constitution, but on the contrary, expressly and positively forbidden by one of the amendments thereto; a power, which more than any other, ought to introduce universal alarm because it is leveled against the right of freely examining public characters and measures, and of free communication among the people thereon, which has ever been justly deemed, the only effectual guardian of every other right.

"That this State, having by its Convention which ratified the Federal Constitution, expressly declared that among other essential rights, 'the liberty of conscience and the press cannot be cancelled, abridged, restrained, or modified by any authority of the United States,' and from its extreme anxiety to guard these rights from every possible attack of sophistry and ambition having, with other States, recommended an amendment for that purpose, which amendment was, in due time, annexed to the Constitution, it would mark a reproachful inconsistency and criminal degeneracy if an indifference were now shown to the most palpable violation of one of the rights thus declared and secured, and to the establishment of a precedent which may be fatal to the other.

"That the good people of this Commonwealth, having ever felt and continuing to feel the most sincere affection for their brethren of the other States, the truest anxiety for establishing and perpetuating the union of all, and the most scrupulous fidelity to that Constitution, which is the pledge of mutual friendship, and the instrument of mutual happiness; the General Assembly doth solemnly appeal to the like dispositions in the other States, in confidence, that they will concur with this Commonwealth in declaring, as it does hereby declare, that the acts aforesaid are unconstitutional, and that the necessary and proper measures will be taken by each for cooperating with this State in maintaining unimpaired the authorities, rights, and liberties, reserved to the States respectively, or to the people.

"That the Governor be desired to transmit a copy of the foregoing resolutions to the Executive authority of each of the other States, with a request that the same may be communicated to the legislature thereof, and that a copy be furnished to each of the Senators and Representatives representing this State in the Congress of the United States."

The original copy of these resolutions was deposited in the office of the General Assembly. Also recorded in Elliot's Debates, 1861 edition, Volume IV, p. 528-529.

The Democratic Party of the United States repeated, in its successful canvass in 1856, subsequently electing James Buchanan President, the declaration made in numerous previous political contests, that it would "faithfully abide by and uphold the principles laid down in the Kentucky and Virginia resolutions of 1798, and in the report of Mr. Madison to the Virginia Legislature in 1799, and that it adopts those principles as constituting one of the main foundations of its political creed." The messages and papers of Jefferson Davis and the Confederacy, edited and compiled by James D. Richardson, Volume 1, p. 69. (1966.)

It seems apparent that the principles of the Kentucky and Virginia resolutions were maintained by, perhaps, overwhelming majorities of the people for many decades in all the States of the Union, especially in the elections of Thomas Jefferson and James Madison as the next two Presidents who each served two terms. Jefferson became President at the very next election, and Madison followed him eight years later.

After 200 years, we have strayed far from the governmental principles laid down by these two great defenders of liberty. It is hoped that this work will help renew curiosity and investigation into the history and theory of our Constitution, and cause patriots and all who love freedom, to vigorously renew their efforts to curb the tyranny and secret combinations of darkness and amorality, which are threatening to destroy the great bulwark of liberty we inherited from our fathers.

The Kentucky and Virginia resolutions were transmitted to the executives of the other States to be given to members of their respective Legislatures. Responses were made by Delaware, Rhode Island, Massachusetts, New York, Connecticut, New Hampshire and Vermont. None were sympathetic, but the major reason, we might speculate, was refusal to accept the practical application of the theory of nullification. This is understandable. If the States each decided which laws it would or would not honor, chaos would likely result, or at least, Congress, it seems, could not command much respect for any statute it passed. Nullification would certainly cause Congress and the President to weigh very carefully the effects on the States of any bills passed.

With the advantage of learning from our own history, we see nullification is not sound theory. Getting out of the Union if a State is not happy with the actions of its agent, is perfectly sound, but as long as a State chooses to remain in the Union, nullification destroys much of what is sought to be attained by uniting in the first place.

Secession, or Union dissolution, by three-fourths of the States may be the only possible viable remedy left to us, but if possible, and if we have time, we need to establish some sort of *super court* to settle our "high level" differences regarding sovereignty and jurisdiction. This might best be achieved by a constitutional amendment. Failing this, after dissolving the Union, in reorganizing Union again, the new Constitution could provide for such a super court, or *Council of States*.

As the replies of the responding States to the Kentucky and Virginia resolutions were not what had been hoped, Kentucky passed further resolutions on February 22, 1799, which were a reassertion of the principles expressed in the first resolutions. In Virginia, the replies of the States were referred to a special committee of which James Madison was chairman. The report of the committee, drafted by Madison, can be found in Madison's Writings by G. Hunt, Vol. Vl, or Elliots Debates, 1861 ed. Vol. IV, p 544.

Madison's report on the Virginia Resolutions is an outstanding thesis on constitutional theory, but is too long to be included in this work. But we will consider this report briefly.

Referring to the Constitution, Madison says. "If the powers granted be valid, it is solely because they are granted, and if the granted powers are valid, because granted, all other powers not granted, must not be valid.

"The resolution having taken this view of the Federal compact, proceeds to infer, 'That in case of a deliberate, palpable, and dangerous exercise of other powers not granted by the said compact, the States who are parties thereto, have the right and are in duty bound to interpose for arresting the progress of the evil, and for maintaining within their respective limits, the authorities, rights, and liberties appertaining to them.'

"It appears, to your committee to be a plain principle, founded in common sense, illustrated by common practice, and essential to the nature of compacts—that where resort can be had to no tribunal superior to the authority of the parties, the parties themselves must be the rightful judges in the last resort, whether the bargain made has been pursued or violated. The Constitution of the United States was framed by the sanction of the States, given by each in its sovereign capacity. It adds to the stability and dignity, as well as to the authority of the Constitution, that it rests on this legitimate and solid foundation. The States, then being the parties to the constitutional compact, and in their sovereign capacity, it follows of necessity that there can be no tribunal above their authority to decide, in the last resort, whether the compact made by them be violated, and consequently, that as the parties to it, they must themselves decide in the last resort, such questions as may be of sufficient magnitude to require their interposition...

"It must be a case not of a light and transient nature, but of a nature dangerous to the great purposes for which the Constitution was established. It must be a case, moreover, not obscure or doubtful in its construction, but plain and palpable...

"If the deliberate exercise of dangerous powers, palpably withheld by the Constitution, could not justify the parties to it in interposing even so far as to arrest the progress of the evil, and thereby to preserve the Constitution itself, as well as to provide for the safety of the parties to it, there would be an end to all relief from usurped power, and a direct subversion of the rights specified or recognized under all the State Constitutions, as well as a plain denial of the fundamental principle on which our independence itself was declared.

"But it is objected that the Judicial authority is to be regarded as the sole expositor of the Constitution in the last resort, and it may be asked for what reason the declaration by the General Assembly, supposing it to be theoretically true, could be required at the present day and in so solemn a manner.

"On this objection it might be observed: first, that there may be instances of usurped power which the forms of the Constitution would never draw within the control of the Judicial department; secondly, that if the decision of the Judiciary be raised above *the authority of the sovereign parties to the Constitution*, the decisions of the other departments not carried by the forms of the Constitution before the Judiciary, must be equally authoritative and final with the decisions of that department. But the proper answer to the objection is that the resolution of the General Asembly relates to those great and extraordinary cases, in which all the forms of the Constitution may prove ineffectual against infractions dangerous to the essential rights of the parties to it. The resolution supposes that dangerous powers not delegated, may not only be usurped and executed by the other departments, but that *the Judicial department also may exercise or sanction dangerous powers beyond the Constitution*; and consequently, that the ultimate right of the parties to the Constitution to judge whether the compact has been dangerously violated, must extend to violations by one delegated authority, as well as by another; *by the Judiciary, as well as by the Executive, or the Legislative.*

"However, true it may be that the Judicial department is, in all questions submitted to it by the forms of the Constitution, to decide in the last resort, this resort must necessarily be deemed the last in *relation to the authorities of the other departments of the Government, not in relation to the rights of the parties to the Constitutional compact, from which the Judicial as well as the other departments hold their delegated trusts. On any other hypothesis the delegation of Judicial power would annul the authority delegating it*; and the concurrence of this department *with the others in usurped powers*, might subvert forever, and beyond the possible reach of any rightful remedy, the very Constitution which all were instituted to preserve."

How farseeing were the observations of Mr. Madison! Could he have been any more accurate in describing the "Warren Court" and others which, from the decisions they handed down, we must conclude the judiciary conspired with Congress and the Executive to weaken the Constitution?

Just a few more gems from Madison's report. "Money cannot be applied to the general welfare, otherwise than by an application of it to some particular measure, conducive to the general welfare...An appropriation of money to the general welfare would be deemed rather a mockery than an observance of this consitutional injunction."

If Mr. Madison could only be here now and see how far out of shape the Judiciary and the Congress have twisted the General Welfare clause of which he here speaks.

"But it is not the inconclusiveness of the general reasoning in this passage which chiefly calls the attention to it. It is the principle assumed by it, *that the powers held by the States are given to them by the Constitution of the United States; and the inference from this principle that the powers supposed to be necessary, which are not so given to the State Government, must reside in the government of the United States.*"

Is this not the attitude of Congress and the Executive and most of the Federal bureaucracy today? Is it not absurd to say, "and Congress allowed *the states* to do such and such?" Or, "Congress will allow the States, or allow *the people*,"to do anything?

The bureaucratic and political thinking in America today is so twisted and fouled up, regarding the nature of constitutional government, it may not be possible to straighten it out except with the drastic action of secessions or Union dissolution so we can start all over again with a new and unentangled government.

Education and the morals of the people are the keys, but the imminent destruction of the Constitution does not appear to give us time for much more educational effort, and the moral decline of the nation is on a downhill run and gaining momentum every day. In this respect, Hollywood is doing its best to see if it can corrupt the nation's morals faster than Washington, New York and San Francisco.

It is as if there is a race between them to see which can first bring down the wrath of God on the United States of America, and destroy the Constitution along with our heritage of freedom. It would seem that only Satan himself could be more effective and efficient than these meccas of amorality and corruption, in mocking God and inviting his wrath to smite America, once the light of the world.

Only time will tell whether we will allow evil to overwhelm us, or a remnant with the help of God, will preserve liberty and some sort of moral society for the generation which follows ours.

Chapter 10

The Constitution is a revokable charter.

The nature of the government of the United States is easy to understand. The States created something which did not exist before; the Central, or Federal government for uniting the *free, sovereign, and independent states*. The States created an *agent* to act on their behalf under certain, and very specific circumstances. An agent cannot be, and never is, more powerful than the principal for which it acts. The agent is at all times under the direction of its principal. Under the laws of contract and Power of Attorney, the principal can at any time recall all delegated powers. In the case of an agent being some type of corporate structure, or some other type of artificial "person," such as the Federal government of the United States, the principal at all times retains the power and authority to dissolve the corporate charter and recall all delegated powers.

In the case of the "corporate charter" of the United States, which is the Constitution, the charter itself specifies the authority or conditions for dissolution, abandonment, or the making of the charter null and void under Article V, the amending process.

The Constitution is a contract, or as the Founders often

styled it, a Compact among the States. It is also a treaty, as it was an agreement among nine original *free, independent, and sovereign nations,* recognized as such by the powers of the earth at the time the contract was adopted.

No treaty, compact, contract, or any other type of agreement in the history of man, was seriously considered to be perpetual, or indissoluble. It is absurd to argue, or contend, that one generation might lawfully bind a future generation, or that fathers might bind their children by declaring contracts they make "perpetual" or "indissoluble." Especially, should the fathers attempt to bind their children with the excesses and extravagance they enjoyed, and then telling the children they must pay for those excesses, which are manifested in debt the fathers knew could never be paid, so great were they as prodigals. It would be just as absurd to argue that the fathers could bind their children to a certain form of government, no matter how good and benevolent.

Whether an Assembly, Congress, Legislature, Executive, Judiciary, Corporation, an individual, or a generation, none have the authority, the right or the power, to bind or hold accountable without consent, its later equal. The judiciary, generally speaking, does a fairly decent job of following precedent, but on the other hand, the Supreme Court of the United States has reversed its peers of the past on numerous occasions. As the skeptic has correctly observed, the Constitution "is what the Supreme Court says it is."

For one generation to attempt to bind the next generation to its debt, as the preceding generation did to us, and which we are now doing to our children, is fraudulent, immoral and unconscionable. There is no legal obligation to pay it, and certainly no moral obligation. Children do, of course, have an option to pay the debt of their fathers if they choose, if the debt is not impossibly large. But in our case, our children will likely write it off unless the New World Order or some other form of overpowering government has them so intimidated they dare not resist.

A law, constitution, or debt can lawfully and morally, be repealed or cancelled; or confirmed by him, or those who follow, who had no choice, or took no part in the burden, which was unjustly foisted upon them.

In the case of the United States Constitution, several generations have adopted and accepted it as their own, but our generation, or the next, might choose to discard it. If that should be the choice, there is nothing wrong or illegal about it. It might be foolish, it might be unwise, it might be for better or for worse, but we have just as much right to choose our form of government as did our fathers.

And our fathers made a wonderful choice in establishing the United States. But when politicians and judges twist the Constitution into a grotesque socialistic form which would barely be recognizable by the Founders, we may have to dissolve the artificial government created by it, and start over again.

These truths are so obvious and simple it is hardly necessary to amplify them, but let's consider one example.

Let's say ten of us know where there is a rich gold deposit, and we raise a million dollars by putting up $100,000 each. We incorporate under the laws of the State of Nevada, and in the corporate charter we specify that the company will enter into no other enterprise except the mining of gold. The company hits it rich and makes millions.

After 50 years, the original ten investors are dead and their children have control of the stock. The gold mine is still profitable, but the children decide they want to diversify and get into coal and oil, utilizing the same corporate structure. They can honor their fathers' desire, or they can change the corporate charter to suit their own will. Or if they choose, they can completely abolish the charter of their fathers and incorporate a brand new company in Nevada, or any other state or country for that matter. It would be foolish to think one can establish a charter in perpetuity or make it irrevocable to the next generation.

Wise children learn from their fathers. They adopt and hang onto that which is good. They discard that which proves of little worth.

The Founding Fathers learned their lesson in this respect.

With the best of intentions they declared the Articles of Confederation to be "perpetual" in four different places. In less than a decade, they discarded, abandoned, and quietly "forgot" such foolish declarations as perpetual or indissoluble. Finding they had made fools of themselves with what appeared at the time to be great, noble and affectionate declarations of loyalty and fidelity, they abandoned all such pretentions when they adopted their *new Constitution*, which left out entirely any phrase implying perpetuity.

Our Fathers, of course, hoped for a lasting and strong Union, but they made no pretensions of it being perpetual or indissoluble. It was well understood that just the opposite was possible, for after the nine filled the requirement of Union with the adoption of the Constitution by New Hampshire on June 21, 1788, those nine allowed Virginia to enter as the tenth State with specific reservations that she might withdraw from the Union and "resume" her sovereignty if she chose to do so. New York, the eleventh State to join, and Rhode Island, waiting almost two years before joining, likewise made the same reservations, that they could *leave the Union or secede* if they "found it necessary to their happiness."

The United States government is similar to the relationship established by a *Power of Attorney*. A principal delegates certain, usually limited authority, to another person or perhaps in the case of a parent and child the parent might assign a General Power of Attorney, wherein no matter what the child does in behalf of the parent, it will be binding on the parent. Unless of course, the child acts in behalf of the parent in a fraudulent manner, the parent, or principal, might not be bound. In any case, the principal at all times retains the right to cancel and bring to an end, with proper notification, his assigned power of attorney. No court of law would recognize a two or three hundred year old power of attorney as binding several generations later. It would be binding only to the extent, that those it attempted to bind, voluntarily chose to be bound.

So it is with the 50 States of the United States. They are bound so long as they voluntarily choose to be bound. For over

200 years, we have found the contract to be of benefit, more or less, in securing the protection and happiness of *the people*. But if *the people* decide our Union no longer brings happiness and domestic tranquility, there is no reason to continue an unhappy Union.

The 50 States are principal in relation to the Federal government. The State governments themselves are mere agents of the *real principals*, *the people* and citizens of the 50 States.

The people at all times have, and do retain all power to govern themselves. This assertion is founded in logic, common sense, the Constitution, history, precedent and Supreme Court decisions of the United States. If the Peoples' agents of government get much more out of hand; if their agents of government attempt to destroy the corporate charter, the Constitution, and attempt to reverse the roles of power, establishing government as the principal and *the people* as agents of government, and the States as agents of Washington; if the courts continue to cooperate with atheistic and humanist attempts to remove all values from our society, and all references to deity in the classroom and numerous other areas, then it is time to dissolve the corporate charter, declare the contract null and void, and go our separate ways in peace.

That would be revolution. But there is no reason it should have to be accomplished through bloodshed. Such revolution should be just as peaceful and calm as the revolution of 1788 when our fathers quietly destroyed the government under the Articles of Confederation, and established a truly revolutionary and untried form of "corporate charter," the Constitution *for* the United States of America.

Murderers, rapists, thieves and other assorted criminals cannot live in peace in a society of law abiding people. That's why we lock them up. Neither can those who believe the black man is inferior and only fit to be a slave, live in peace with those who believe all men should have equal rights. Neither can those who believe abortion is right, live with those who believe it is murder. Those who seriously attempt to live by a high moral code will find it difficult to live in peace with those who believe anything goes, or "if it feels good, do it."

Separation is the most viable solution to major differences, is it not?

Virginia, New York and Rhode Island, and perhaps other later States reserved the right to leave the Union. Therefore, every other State automatically acquired the same priviledge.

When a new state is admitted to the Union, it comes in with all the powers of sovereignty and jurisdiction which pertained to the original States. Such powers may not be diminished, impaired, or taken away by any conditions or stipulations later put into statute by Congress. All States come into the Union upon an equal footing, regardless of the limitations upon the previous territorial government. This doctrine of "equal footing" does not rest on any express provision of the Constitution, but on what is considered and has been held by the Supreme Court to be the general character and purpose of the union of the States, as established by the Constitution. We are a union of political equals. All of this is well established in the following cases, as well as many others which could be cited.

Virginia vs. West Virginia, 246 US 565, 62 L. Ed 883, 38 S Ct 400; *Hawkins vs. Bleakly*, 243 US 210, 61 L. Ed 678, 37 S Ct 255; *United States vs. Utah*, 283 US 64, 75 L. Ed 844, 51 S Ct 438; *Brewer-Elliott Oil & Gas Co. vs. United States*, 260 US 77, 67 L Ed 140, 43 S Ct 60; *McCabe vs. Atchison, T. & S.F.R. Co*. 235 US 151, 59 L. Ed 169, 35 S Ct 69; Ex parte Webb, 225 US 663, 56 L. Ed 1248, 32 S Ct 769; *Kansas vs. Colorado*, 206 US 46, 51 L. Ed 956, 27 S Ct 655.

We will quote from one case which is illustrative of the equality of the States once accepted into the Union; a Supreme Court decision of 1911, *Coyle vs. Smith*, 221 U.S. 559; 31 S. Ct. 688; 551. Ed. 853. Mr. Justice Lurton delivered the opinion of the Court: ..."The plain deduction from this case is that when a new state is admitted into the Union, it is so admitted with all of the powers of sovereignty and jurisdiction which pertain to the original states, and that such powers may not be constitutionally diminished, impaired, or shorn away by any conditions, compacts, or stipulations embraced in the act under which the new state came into the Union, which would not be valid and effectual if the subject of congressional legislation after admission..."

It being well established then, that all States entered the Union as equals, that if Virginia, New York and Rhode Island, and perhaps others, such as Wisconsin, entered the Union specifically reserving their sovereign right to again leave the Union and *resume* full sovereignty, all 50 States have the same right, whether or not they were as careful as those mentioned in putting those rights down in black and white in their documents of ratification.

Common sense tells us, that should one or more of the 50 States decide to exercise their lawful option of seceding from the Union, that many loose ends would have to be taken care of properly, and it would take time. Military bases, national parks, a State's share of Federal debt, legitimate debt not owned by the Federal Reserve System. Many things would need to be set in order and negotiated between the United States and the newly sovereign, free and independent seceding nation, or nations.

If only one or two States decided they wished to leave the Union, those States would probably wish to contract with the United States for military protection, the main reason for having a Central government in the first place. Just like Japan and Germany have relied on the United States for over 40 years as their military protectors. We have provided said protection at bargain basement rates, allowing them to put the saved billions into their economies, enabling them to more effectively and efficiently compete with us. If California were to secede and then pay back to the United States for military protection, the same low percentage of their gross domestic production which is paid by Germany and Japan for their national defense, and keep the balance she currently pays to Uncle Sam, California might well tell the world, "you haven't seen anything yet," as her economy took off.

If the 50 States could, say for 3-5 years, rid themselves of the Federal albatross with which they are shackled, and eliminate the Federal drag on the national economy caused by the siphoning away from the States of 1.5 trillion dollars annually, America might get back on her feet and rebuild her crumbling infrastructure.

After a three to five year demonstration that the only real reason we need the Federal government is for national defense, and we have returned to prosperity never known before in America, we might, or might not, want to again join in Union. We might discover we could get along just as well, or better than we do now, by treaties between the States regulating commerce and other problems as they arose. And the 50 States might establish some sort of super court, or arbitration panel to settle differences peacefully.

To some, secession, or Union dissolution, will sound foolish, radical and unrealistic. But the way we are headed in America, it may not be too long before these proposals start to look pretty good. Just knowing they are a lawful option, should be a comfort. But to work, the groundwork must be laid ahead of time, in preparation for the crisis.

When a State enters the Union, it is pledged to the other States to support the Constitution. A State carved out of a former territory, as most of the Western and Midwestern States were, gains title of every species of property owned by the territory upon its admission to the Union, unless otherwise declared by Congress at the time of admission. Certain conditions, and withholding of massive tracts of lands in the Western States by Congress is still a question which has not been satisfactorily settled under the doctrine of equality of the States, a very powerful argument for Union dissolution in itself, as far as some Western States are concerned.

The Constitution is a voidable contract at the option of any one or all of the parties to it, the 50 States. It is void as to the wrongdoer, but voidable as to the wronged party. This is especially the case, in the case of the States, in which they established no remedy other than secession for blatant or inexcusable violations of the contract, or right out fraud on the part of the agent. Black's Law Dictionary lists a case illustrating voidable contract as: *Depner vs. Joseph Zukin Blouses*, 13 Cal. App 2d 124, 56 P. 2d 574, 575.

Numerous examples of Federal constitutional fraud might

be cited. The entrance of West Virginia into the Union in 1863 is a prime example. The conspiracy of the Judiciary in United States Supreme Court decisions, in conjunction with their brothers in the Executive and Congress, have practically torn the Constitution to shreds in a number of cases. We will discuss two of these, Texas vs. White and *Knox vs. Lee*. The court in these cases apparently felt compelled to join in and sanction the fraud of their fellow Executive and Legislative brethren, rather than take the hard and correct course of upholding the Constitution. These two decisions, and others, have contributed mightily to the current pitiful condition of Constitutional law in America.

Other major frauds our more recent fathers allowed to be perpetrated against *the people* and *the States* are the Fourteenth and Sixteenth Amendments. The precedents established by the courts under these two fraudulently adopted amendments are numerous and have done grave damage to the Constitution. Both these amendments need to be challenged by a State directly in the Supreme Court to show they were never lawfully ratified and should, therefore, be abolished along with all the precedents established under them.

Bill Benson and J. "Red" Beckman published an outstanding account titled *The Law That Never Was*, showing that three-fourths of the States never ratified the Sixteenth Amendment in a lawful and legal manner. They spent many months pouring over the certified copies of ratification documents the States submitted to Congress. The copies Congress sent to the States were altered by some of the States prior to being sent back to Congress, and these were counted in making up the three-fourths needed to ratify new amendments. Any alteration, even moving of a comma is not proper, for even such a minor change can potentially change the meaning of a phrase or a sentence. If these changes had been challenged at the time, or even today, an honest Court would have to rule the 16th Amendment invalid, null and void. Alterations of an amendment by a State might, at best, be called a counter proposal. Out of this Frankenstein fraud has grown the Internal Revenue Service which is the great intimidator of most of the American people; at least for those who file.

The 14th Amendment's constitutionality is also highly questionable. It's apparent objective was most praiseworthy; to make the black man equal as a citizen. But such a high objective should have been accomplished, nevertheless, by lawful means.

The Congress of 1866 got so wound up in wreaking vengeance on the South, they left little doubt that they were operating by the law of the jungle, not the Constitution. *Might makes right*, and the *end justifies the means*. The radical Republicans led by the fire breathing Thaddeus Stevens would, if they could, make the South pay for their rebellion to the last penny. No punishment was too great. President Johnson and the Supreme Court were able to exert limited influence in maintaining constitutional order, but Congress quickly overrode the veto, and even passed legislation to take jurisdiction away from the Supreme Court, so the Court could not overrule the blatantly unconstitutional reconstruction legislation.

The 13th Amendment, proclaimed valid on December 18, 1865, freed the slaves. That required the ratification of 27 States, as there were then 36 States in the Union. Nebraska came into the Union March 1, 1867. Thereafter, it would take at least 28 States to adopt a constitutional amendment.

The 14th Amendment made black men full-fledged citizens of the United States, among other things.

By a concurrent resolution of Congress adopted July 21, 1868, it was declared to have been ratified by "three-fourths and more of the several States of the Union." On July 28, 1868, the Secretary of State, William Seward declared the 14th Amendment "apparently" ratified by 30 States, "being more than three-fourths."

Apparent or not, we might safely say the 14th Amendment was improperly ratified by February 18, 1870, for that was the day Texas became the 33rd State to ratify, at least according to Congress. There were two reasons why the Secretary of State had some "apparent" confusion in this whole matter. First, New Jersey was the fourth State to ratify on September

11, 1866. But on March 24, 1868, four months before Congress announced ratification by three-fourths of the States, counting that of New Jersey, she rescinded her ratification for the second time, this time over the governor's veto.

Oregon was the 5th State to ratify on September 19, 1866, but according to Dr. Martin Larson, quoting from *The Hundred Years Hoax*, by Patrick Henry Omlor, "the House of Representatives of Oregon formally repudiated the aforesaid ratification because of the fraud involved therein, within 2 1/2 weeks—namely, on October 6." Although such action is indicative of strong sentiment, it would not be effective in disqualifying Oregon as a ratifying State without the other legislative body of the State concurring, even though done in such a short period of time. Oregon did, however, officially rescind her ratification on October 15, 1868, too late to stop the steamroller tactics of Congress. For even discounting the rescissions of New Jersey and Ohio, which rescinded her ratification January 15, 1868, 28 States would have sent up "acceptable" certifications by July 21, 1868.

Virginia became the 31st State to ratify the 14th Amendment, Mississippi the 32nd, January 17, 1870, Texas, the 33rd, February 18, 1870. By this time, even subtracting the rescinding States, we could safely say the 14th Amendment had been "improperly" ratified...except for one other "minor" problem.

Four of the ratifying States which had been counted by Congress on July 21, 1868, were coerced. Any first year law student knows that any agreement, contract, compact, etc. which is forced upon a party, coerced by threat, intimidation, or in any other manner agreed to because of fear, or without free will is invalid, null and void, and of no force or effect in a court of law. To be binding, contracts or agreements must be entered into by free choice.

In addition to New Jersey, Ohio and Oregon rescinding their ratifications, thus putting themselves by precedent, by law, by reason and logic, in the same position as if they had never ratified in the first place, four other States which Congress counted, right out rejected the 14th Amendment.

These were North Carolina, December 14, 1866, Louisiana, February 6, 1867, South Carolina, December 20, 1866, and Georgia November 9, 1866.

Take away these seven States and we have only 23, five States short of the necessary three-fourths.

Now let's include Virginia, Mississippi, and Texas, making the total being counted by Congress through February 18, 1870, 33 States. But now, we must again subtract Virginia, which rejected the Amendment the first time around, January 9, 1867, and Texas, which rejected it October 27, 1866. This gives us one more valid ratification making 24 States, still four short.

A fascinating story might be told about the rejection of the 14th Amendment by three other States. The rejections of these three were "quietly" accepted by the Congress, unlike the rejections of those noted above. Delaware, on February 8, 1867, Maryland, March 23, 1867, and Kentucky, January 8, 1867. Why were these three States not coerced into changing their votes like North Carolina, Louisiana, South Carolina and Georgia? The political answer jumps out at us. These three States did not attempt secession. They were at least nominally loyal to the Union and fought with the North.

But this makes a difference when taking action according to law? Are we a government of law, or a government of men? The Constitution is supposed to make us a government of law! As still relatively free men, we best be extremely cautious. Our history is filled with government of men, not of laws, and we best be on our guard continually, for men are no different today than they were a hundred, or a thousand years ago.

Delaware finally ratified the 14th Amendment on February 12, 1901!

Maryland, April 4, 1959.

California, which had never done anything at all, ratified May 6, 1959.

Kentucky, March 18, 1976. (This is not a typo)

By the time Delaware ratified in 1901, the Union had 45 States and it would have taken 34 States to make the 14th Amendment part of the Constitution.

How were some of the States which rejected the 14th Amendment coerced into saying they accepted it? Congress divided the Confederate States into five military districts and governed by martial law. And the South was told they would not be allowed back into the Union with representatives in Congress, and all other State rights, unless, and until, they ratified the 14th Amendment.

Like allowing the entrance of West Virginia into the Union as the 35th State, with pretensions of adhering to the Constitution, Washington liked to, if possible, give the appearance of being law abiding, especially on something of such great significance, an Amendment to the Constitution. On the other hand, "if we find it impossible to even pretend we are within the law, we'll do it anyway. *The people* are too damn dumb to know what's going on." Besides, "everything we do for the people is for their own good, they just don't know it."

On December 18, 1865, the Secretary of State proclaimed the 13th Amendment as having been ratified by 27 States, constituting three-fourths. Congress accepted, for the purpose of this amendment, the ratifications of Southern States. The ratifying Legislatures were lawfully constituted assemblies. But a year later, more or less, these rebel Legislatures in rejecting the 14th Amendment, were no longer worthy of recognition. Without the South, there would have been no 13th Amendment. But in rejecting the 14th Amendment, the radical Congress declared these governments illegal. But are politicians supposed to be consistent? If the Southern states did what they were told, they were counted for the purpose of amending the Constitution. If they refused to obey the radical Congress, they were not counted and were ruled by martial law.

The outlaw congressional Republicans of 1866-68 got their 14th Amendment, with which the courts are still struggling trying to figure out what it means, and more often than not, using it in a way to twist out of shape The Bill of Rights, and foist on the Nation social legislation to fit the personal bias of liberal judges.

Is it ever too late to correct a wrong? To go back and do

something right?

Congress should rewrite the 14th Amendment and resubmit it to the States. If 38 States wish to adopt it, fine. If not, it should be abolished. It has never been a legitimate and lawful part of the Constitution. Much of it was outdated and obsolete within a few years after adoption. It is a cluttering mishmash forced on us by a vengeance minded and mean spirited bunch of radical rabble rousers who are long dead, and couldn't have cared less about the harvest their children would have to reap because of their hatred and malice. It is an invalid law, trailing numerous invalid and unlawful precedents. Like a contorted monster, it needs to be destroyed.

If Congress won't initiate the action, this is just one more reason for 38 States to take the bull by the horns and abolish Congress and the entire Constitution, including the 14th Amendment. Then we will be able to make a fresh start without the chains of the 1860's generation suppressing our liberties.

Chapter 11

The Supreme Court
"The Constitution means what we say it means"

What evidence do we have for the position of Abraham Lincoln and the North who contended secession from the union was unconstitutional? Lincoln, and those who came after him contended the unconstitutionality of secession, but were willing themselves to unconstitutionally force upon the nation the new State of West Virginia, the 14th Amendment, martial law, Southern reconstruction and the blatantly unconstitutional, legal tender laws. Under these laws the North issued $450,000,000 in paper money which allowed them to successfully prosecute the Civil War.

We will briefly look at one of the legal tender cases to come before the Supreme Court, but merely as an example to show how treacherous and protective the Supreme Court can be in protecting its peers and brethren in the Executive and Legislative branches of the Federal government. Once those brethren have taken unconstitutional actions which have become cement hard, and would be difficult to reverse without a great deal of political fallout, the court usually goes along.

In deciding the issues of secession legality, and the constitutionality of the legal tender laws, the political consequences for many in power, had the Court ruled on the side of justice, right and truth, might have been rather unpleasant. Abraham Lincoln instead of being remembered as one of our national heroes might have gone down in history as a constitutional tyrant along with many of the radical Republicans of that time. Until doing the research to write this book, the author had always held Lincoln to be right up there with Washington and Jefferson, and even yet, is willing to give Lincoln the benefit of the doubt often times, for no President ever had to contend with Union turmoil like Lincoln faced on inauguration day. But his greatness appears to be sustained by martyrdom and exaggeration of Northern historians.

The Supreme Court has ruled on the issue of secession only indirectly. An actual case in which the merits and lawfulness of secession itself has never been brought before the Court. The leading case appears to be *Texas vs. White*, 7 Wallace, 700, U.S. Reports, Volume 74, (1869). Other cases are *Hickman vs. Jones*, 9 id. 197; *Hanauer vs. Doane*, 12 id. 342; *Knox vs. Lee*, id. 457; *Hanauer vs. Woodruff*, 15 id. 439; *Cornet vs. Williams*, 20 id. 226; *Sprott vs. United States*, id. 459.

Knox vs. Lee was a major legal tender case, but is one of the cases commonly cited as showing the illegality of secession, though secession is a minor and insignificant portion of the case.

The same is true in *Texas vs. White*. The Court was forced to make a decision on the legality of secession, merely incidentally, in order to reach an opinion on the real issue concerning bonds issued to Texas by the Federal government. If the Court had presented to it at any time, even the evidence outlined and inexpertly put together in this brief, can there be any doubt that an honest court would have ruled that the South was right? Not a case regarding slavery, but regarding her right to leave the Union?

Knowing then, the Supreme Court has never had a brief such as this work placed before it, on which it was asked to make a decision on secession, let us consider the reasoning of the Court with the limited knowledge and background we must assume it had at its disposal when ruling against the

Chapter 11

legality of secession.

Without a second thought, if we have ever thought about it at all, most Americans assume the question of whether one or more of the states of the Union may legally secede from the Union was effectively and permanently answered on the field of battle in the Civil War. Four years after the war ended, the Supreme Court found itself under the necessity of deciding, incidental to reaching a decision on the main point of a case, whether the Southern States had at any time during the period of secession been actually out of the Union. The case was *Texas vs. White*.

During the time of this case, there was still great turmoil as the South was still in a state of poverty, and the radical Republicans were in the process of reconstructing the Southern States "with a vengeance." Great hatred was in evidence in both North and South.

These were the facts: In 1850 the United States agreed to give the State of Texas $10,000,000 in 5% bonds in settlement of certain boundary claims. Texas had come into the Union December 29, 1845, as the 28th State. Half of these bonds were held in Washington and half were delivered to the State, made payable to the State, or bearer, and redeemable after December 31, 1864. They were dated January 1, 1851. Texas passed a law providing that the bonds should not be negotiable in the hands of any holder until after the endorsement by the governor of Texas.

Texas joined the Confederacy as the last of the seven seceding States prior to the beginning of the Civil War. In 1862 the State legislature repealed the act requiring the endorsement of the bonds by the governor and created a military board to provide for the expenses of the war, empowering the board to use any bonds then in the State Treasury for this purpose to a limit of $1,000,000.

In early 1865, this board negotiated a contract with White and others for the transfer of some of the bonds for military supplies. None of these bonds was endorsed by the governor of the State. Immediately upon the end of the war, and while the State was still unreconstructed or unrestored to its former normal status as a member of the Union, the governor of Texas brought suit to get the bonds back and to stop White and the other defendants from receiving payment for the bonds from the Federal government. The suit was brought by Texas in the Supreme Court of the United States as an original action under Article III, Section 2, Paragraph 2 of the Constitution which says: "In all cases...in which a State shall be party, the supreme court shall have original jurisdiction."

The first thing the Supreme Court had to decide was whether or not Texas, at the time of bringing the suit, was legally a State of the Union. If Texas was not a State, the Supreme Court could not take "original" jurisdiction and hear the case.

Jurisdiction was accepted and the Chief Justice, the Honorable Salmon Portland Chase, delivered the opinion of the court.

..."If, therefore, it is true that the State of Texas was not at the time of filing this bill, or is not now, one of the United States, we have no jurisdiction of this suit, and it is our duty to dismiss it..."

Continuing after discussing the rebellion and secession of Texas:

"Did Texas, in consequence of these acts, cease to be a State? Or, if not, did the State cease to be a member of the Union?

"It is needless to discuss at length, the question whether the right of a State to withdraw from the Union for any cause regarded by herself as sufficient, is consistent with the Constitution of the United States.

"The Union of the States never was a purely artificial and arbitrary relation." Here is where the honorable justices begin a dishonest rationalization in attempting to build a case against secession, for the statement is totally false, even to a layman. Just a little knowledge of our history proves just the opposite. The United States is in fact, a *purely artificial* creation of nine States who *arbitrarily* adopted a Constitution, which brought into existence something which did not exist before June 21, 1788. Prior to the Constitution, an equally arbitrary and artificial Union existed under the Articles of Confederation.

The Court: "It began among the Colonies and grew out of common origin, mutual sympathies, kindred principles, similar interests, and geographical relations. It was confirmed and strengthened by the necessities of war, and received definite form, and character, and sanction from the Articles of Confederation. By these the Union was solemnly declared to 'be perpetual.' And when these Articles were found to be inadequate to the exigencies of the country, the Constitution was ordained 'to form a more perfect Union.' It is difficult to convey the idea of indissoluble unity more clearly than by these words. What can be indissoluble if a perpetual Union, made more perfect, is not?"

Either the honorable Justice Chase and his brethren are abysmally ignorant of our own history during 1787-1790, when the Articles of Confederation were unceremoniously abandoned, and the Constituion held together by an *outlaw government* from June 21, 1788, until Rhode Island entered the Union, May 29, 1790, or they are simply dishonest in attempting to justify prosecution of the Civil War by Abraham Lincoln and the Northern radical Republicans. The Court refers to the perpetuity of the Union under the Articles of Confederation, but fails to mention the failure of this perpetuity and the dropping of four of the thirteen perpetual States when New Hampshire joined eight sister States in a new Union, which this time around, makes no mention or pretense to perpetual union.

The court brings up the *Preamble* to the Constitution in attempting to justify the position they are going to take, which says the Constitution is proposed, and it was in fact, adopted "to form a more perfect Union." Yes, because the old Union was so imperfect and unworkable, it was felt almost anything would be an improvement. But the preamble in no way implies perpetuity, nor does it lay any groundwork for arguing the Constitution was merely a continuation, or an amended form of the Articles of Confederation. There is no implication of continuity in history, showing any kind of pretended transition from a government under the Articles of Confederation to one under the Constitution. One government came to an end. A brand new government was begun. One died. A new one was born. Nine States *seceded* from four States, a reversal of the normal secession, when a smaller group breaks off from a larger. And for almost two years, it was wondered if the last of the thirteen States, Rhode Island, would ever come into this *new Federation of Nations*. When she finally did, it was whisker close; 34 for joining, 32 against.

The court makes a true observation when it said: "...without the States in union, there could be no such political body as the United States..." and cites, County of Lane vs. The State of Oregon, Texas Reports of the Committee (Library of Congress), 45.

But it strays from the truth again: "...The Constitution, in all its provisions, looks to an indestructible Union, composed of indestructible States." We expect to hear such gibberish from snake oil salesmen, but not Supreme Court Justices.

"When, therefore, Texas became one of the United States, she entered into an indissoluble relation. All the obligations of perpetual union, and all the guaranties of republican government in the Union attached at once to the State. The act which consummated her admission into the Union was something more than a compact."

Oh? How sir? Please tell us! We have already discussed compact, and it is a contract, an agreement between parties, a treaty. How sir, can the Constitution be more than these? It cannot, if we may be so bold as to disagree with the honorable justices. Who shall we believe sir? This court, or James Madison, George Washington and other Statesmen who actually wrote the document which you are allegedly attempting to interpret? They specifically said the Constitution was a compact between independent States.

When you say the Constitution is "something more than a compact," you go on and say, "it was the incorporation of a new member into the political body. And it was final." Personally sir, if His Honor will not be too offended, your gibberish sounds more like meaningless rhetoric meant to obscure, rather than enlighten and establish truth.

The Court continues: "...The union between Texas and the other States was as complete, as perpetual, and as indissoluble as the union between the original States. There was no place for reconsideration, or evocation, except through revolution, or through consent of the States."

Sir, please do not find me in contempt, but would you mind telling us where anything of this nature is found in the Constitution, in the Philadelphia debates when the Constitution was being written, or in the State Convention debates when the States were deciding whether or not to adopt the Constitution? Or in that authoritative guide written by Hamilton, Jay and Madison, the Federalist papers? Where does it say there is no place for reconsideration or revocation? If it will not displease His Honor, may we suggest just the opposite is true, if His Honor will please refer to the documents of Virginia, New York and Rhode Island in which they certified their ratifications of the Constitution, wherein they specifically reserved to themselves the right to withdraw from the Union? If His Honor is not familiar with these, we apologize, for counsel should have made them available to the Court, and no doubt would have done so, had this case been one of directly deciding the lawfulness of secession.

And are you suggesting, Your Honor, when you say "revolution," that revolution must be by blood, or the kind of revolution which took place with the adoption of the Constitution? And when you say a State may leave the Union "with consent of the States," where does it say that, sir, in the Constitution? Are you referring to Article V, under the amendment power? Are you now suggesting that, well,...perhaps,... maybe,...the Union is not necessarily perpetual, or well, necessarily indissoluble, after all?

The Court: "Considered therefore as transactions under the Constitution, the ordinance of secession, adopted by the convention and ratified by a majority of the citizens of Texas, and all the acts of her legislature intended to give effect to that ordinance, were absolutely null. They were utterly without operation in law. The obligations of the State as a member of the Union, and every citizen of the State, as a citizen of the United States, remained perfect and unimpaired. It certainly follows that the State did not cease to be a State, nor her citizens to be citizens of the Union. If this were otherwise, the State must have become foreign, and her citizens foreigners..."

And now comes the undisguised and unvarnished truth as to why the Court felt compelled apparently, to find against lawful secession. The truth seems to be the same as that which suppressed any Union prosecutions of Confederate "traitors" following the Civil War, except here in the Supreme Court, with only one and a final hearing, and on a case which is only indirectly considering secessionist evidence, the powers behind the scenes only have to convince a mere five men who are "intelligent enough" to understand the possible consequences of an adverse ruling on the secession issue.

If the Union would have dared try "traitors" for "treason," such prosecutions would have had to take place numerous times, presenting evidence to numerous juries who would be impossible to control or who would, necessarily, accept the judges interpretation of the law. To place the question of lawful secession before numerous uncontrolled juries was quite different than placing the question indirectly before the Supreme Court who were men intelligent enough to see that in this question of secession, suppression of truth was not only justified, it was absolutely essential and necessary to the peace and conscience of the nation; at least, to the conscience of the victors, the States which stayed in the Union and gave their blessing to suppressing the rebellion by sacrificing 360,000 of their loved ones to the holy cause of preserving the Union.

Surely the Supreme Court would not let down their brethren in the Congress, and their martyred President, Abraham Lincoln, by even for a moment considering the Southern secessions were lawful. That would mean 360,000 Northern lives had been sacrificed in vain, while at the same time, the North had *murdered* 260,000 Confederates who, after all, had been merely defending their homeland against aggression. An adverse ruling by the Supreme Court, or by juries if the Union had dared place the issue before juries, would have meant the

South was right, not only lawfully, but morally, and the North was wrong.

Their Honors under the Honorable Justice Chase betrayed their acute awareness of these issues, if not their own predetermined conclusion to rule against the South regardless of the evidence in this remarkable admission, should they find the South had lawfully seceded: "*the war must have ceased to be a war for the suppression of rebellion, and must have become a war for conquest and subjugation.*"

Exactly, Your Honor. That's why you felt compelled to sustain a lie. Oh, that men, not only of integrity and honor and competence, might be sustained as judges to this high Court, but men of uncompromising courage and conviction. But alas, it is not to be. Men are men, and all have the weaknesses of the flesh to contend with. Only a few dare rule against powerful peers.

The Court: "Our conclusion therefore is, that Texas continued to be a State, and a State of the Union, notwithstanding the transactions to which we have referred."

To show further this case was decided by politics, not the desire to establish justice and truth, we will quote extensively from the Honorable Justice Robert Cooper Grier, who dissented, along with Justices Samuel F. Miller, and Noah H. Swayne.

Justice Grier, in dissenting.

"I regret that I am compelled to dissent from the opinion of the majority of the court on all the points raised and decided in this case.

"The first question in order is the jurisdiction of the court to entertain this bill in behalf of the State of Texas.

"The original jurisdiction of this court can be invoked only by one of the United States. The Territories have no such right conferred on them by the Constitution, nor have the Indian tribes who are under the protection of the military authorities of the govenment.

"Is Texas one of these United States? Or was she such at the time this bill was filed, or since?

"This is to be decided as a *political fact,* not as a *legal fiction.* This court is bound to know and notice the public history of the nation.

"If I regard the truth of history for the last eight years, I cannot discover the State of Texas as one of these United States. I do not think it necessary to notice any of the very astute arguments which have been advanced by the learned counsel in this case, to find the definition of a State, when we have the subject treated in a clear and common sense manner by Chief Justice Marshall, in the case of *Hepburn Dundass vs. Ellxey.* (2 Cranch, 452)..." The case is short, and is quoted in full by Justice Grier before going on.

"Now we have here a clear and well defined test by which we may arrive at a conclusion with regard to the questions of fact now to be decided.

"Is Texas a State, now represented by members chosen by the people of that State and received on the floor of Congress? Has she two senators to represent her as a State in the Senate of the United States? Has her voice been heard in the late election of President? Is she not now held and governed as a conquered province by military force? The act of Congress of March 2nd, 1867, declares Texas to be a 'rebel State,' and provides for its government until a legal and republican State government could be legally established. It constituted Louisiana and Texas the fifth military district, and made it subject, not to the civil authority, but to the 'military authorities of the United States.'

"It is true that no organized rebellion now exists there, and the courts of the United States now exercise jurisdiction over the people of that province. But this is no test of the State's being in the Union; Dacotah is no State, and yet the courts of the United States administer justice there as they do in Texas. The Indian tribes, who are governed by military force, cannot claim to be States of the Union. Wherein does the condition of Texas differ from theirs?

"Now, by assuming or admitting as a fact the present status of Texas as a State not in the Union politically, I beg leave to protest against any charge of inconsistency as to judicial opinions heretofore expressed as a member of this court, or silently assented to. I do not consider myself bound to express any opinion judicially as to the constitutional right of Texas to exercise the rights and privileges of a State of this Union, or the power of Congress to govern her as a conquered province, to subject her to military domination, and keep her in pupilage. I can only submit to *the fact* as decided by the political position of the government, and I am not disposed to join in any essay to prove Texas to be a State of the Union, when Congress have decided that she is not. It is a question of fact only.

"*Politically*, Texas is not a State in this Union. Whether rightfully out of it or not is a question not before the court."

It sounds a little like the Warren Commission which was authorized to bring in the *official* verdict on the assasination of President John F. Kennedy. The decision was made prior to the "investigation" being conducted, and before the "facts" were presented. There is little doubt that the alleged killer of the President, Lee Harvey Oswald, was a setup, a patsy, a scapegoat, to cover the dark machinations of those high in our own government, who for whatever reason, wished the President dead. The facts were not important. The investigation headed by Earl Warren, the Chief Justice of the Supreme Court, was designed to cover up the truth, from all appearances, not discover and shed light on the truth. So it appears with the Chief Justice of 1868. Whether or not he was a "hired gun," we will never know. But it is easy to know he was wrong in attempting to rationalize the illegality of secession.

Justice Grier continues: "Now, whether we assume the State of Texas to be judicially in the Union (though actually out of it) or not, it will not alter the case. The contest now is between the State of Texas and her own citizens. She seeks to annul a contract with the respondents, based on the allegation that there was no authority in Texas competent to enter into an agreement during the rebellion. Having relied upon one fiction, namely, that she *is* a State in the Union, she now relies upon a second one, which she wishes this court to adopt, that she was not a State at all during the five years that she was in rebellion. She now sets up the plea of *insanity*, and asks the court to treat all her acts made during the disease as void...

"The ordinance of secession was adopted by the convention on the 18th of February, 1861, submitted to a vote of the people, and ratified by an overwhelming majority. I admit that this was a very ill-advised measure. Still it was the sovereign act of a sovereign State, and the verdict on the trial of this question, 'by battle' (Prize Cases, 2 Black, 673) as to her right to secede, has been against her. But that verdict did not settle any question not involved in the case. It did not settle the question of her fight to plead insanity and set aside all her contracts made during the pending of the trial with her own citizens, for food, clothing, or medicines....She cannot, like the chameleon, assume the color of the object to which she adheres, and ask this court to involve itself in the contradictory positions that she is a State in the Union and was never out of it, and yet not a State at all for four years, during which she acted and claims to be 'an organized political body,' exercising all the powers and functions of an independent sovereign State. Whether a State de facto or de jure, she is estopped from denying her identity in disputes with her own citizens. If they have not fulfilled their contract, she can have her legal remedy for the breach of it in her own courts."

Right on Your Honor! You did your best, and even in a losing cause, your arguments are there for our generation to draw upon to add to the cumulative and overwhelming amount of evidence in favor of a people to separte themselves from another if there is no way they can get along in peace

* * * * * *

It takes big money to fight a war. And if the people of a nation are not convinced the war is just even though it starts out as a popular cause, it will be difficult to sustain over a long period of time. For *the people* must carry an increased tax burden, and at the same time send their sons and fathers into battle, many to be killed.

But during the Civil War, somebody came up with a brilliant scheme. Whether it was Abraham Lincoln, somebody in his Cabinet, or some Congressman, it would be difficult to say. And it was probably not really a new idea, for Congress had played around with it to some degree in the past.

More money was badly needed and "high" interest was demanded if it was to be borrowed. The Constitution said nothing but gold and silver should be the nation's money, so even the government couldn't just print it. At least not until the Civil War, Abraham Lincoln and the radical Republicans.

If paper money could simply be declared "legal tender" by an act of Congress, and the people would allow the government to get away with it, perhaps an unlimited supply could be printed. Prices might rise, as a result of the inflation a rapid increase in the money supply would cause, but the people would be "too damn dumb to ever figure out what was causing it."

Lincoln and the Congress might conspire together to subvert the Constitution in this manner, but would the Supreme Court go along?

What the heck! Nothing ventured, nothing gained.

Thus, almost a year into the Civil War, and Congress having already shown its willingness to join Lincoln in subverting the Constituion "in these extraordinary times of stress," Congress authorized the first issue of paper "legal tender," February 25, 1862 in the amount of $150,000,000. It felt good, so another $150,000,000 was authorized July 11, 1862. Nobody seemed to mind too much and this was so easy, without the requirement of hassling *the people* quite so much with higher taxes to slaughter our rebel brothers. "It will take a long time before this issue ever makes it to the Supreme Court, and it feels so darn good, let's do it once more." March 3, 1863, one final printing was ordered for another $150,000,000.

This $450,000,000 was issued interest free and circulates to this day as *United States notes*, if you ever come across one which has not been hoarded and hidden by the Federal Reserve System. Though this issue of "greenbacks" was another obvious violation of the Constitution, "the war will be over before the matter reaches the Supreme Court."

If good can be said to have come out of these issues of greenback money, at least they have not drawn interest which must be paid by the American taxpayer, in contrast to the interest the American people are forced to pay to the privately owned Federal Reserve System. Every Federal Reserve Note we carry in our wallets or purses, is drawing interest from American taxpayers.

Modern day patriots have been heard to praise Lincoln for this interest free issue of money, but on the contrary, Lincoln set a precedent which would eventually result in the Federal Reserve System being established in 1913. Under this system the politicians have discovered a "free money tree," and nobody knows where the escalating debt it has allowed us to create, is going to take us. We do know the interest alone on the debt is rapidly approaching the point at which, not even the entire income tax collected by the IRS will be sufficient to pay it.

Lincoln's three issues of non-interest bearing greenbacks has, it is true, saved the United States tens of billions of dollars in interest the last 130 years. But at what cost? The Lincoln precedent led to the elimination of gold and silver backing of our money and credit which the Founders so wisely wrote into the Constitution as the lawful requirement. The Constitution still requires gold and silver backing of our money, but we allow the politicians to ignore it. If Lincoln and the 1860's Congress had honored the Constitution, and did not create the $450,000,000 out of thin air, the Civil War might have come to an abrupt end. If Lincoln had attempted to tax this money from the American people of the North, they might well have said, "no way," and refused to both fight and be heavily taxed.

As the Civil War was winding down, everybody knew the day of reckoning was approaching when the Supreme Court would be challenged to decide whether Lincoln and Congress had constitutionally acted within their delegated powers in issuing the greenbacks.

One cannot be certain, but it appears President Lincoln was looking to the future when in the Fall of 1864, he had the opportunity to appoint a new Chief Justice to the Supreme Court. His former, until a short time before, Secretary of the Treasury, Salmon Portland Chase, had overseen the issuance of the greenbacks and had carried a heavy load in overseeing the nation's money supply during the war. Relations between Chase and Lincoln had become strained, but after Lincoln had been renominated as the Republican candidate for President in 1864, Chase supported the nomination. Lincoln nominated Chase to be the new Chief Justice, and he was confirmed December 6, 1864.

If Lincoln thought Chase would side with him on the greenback issue, he would have been disappointed had he lived.

Two preliminary skirmishes came before the Court in the cases of *Bronson vs. Rodes*, 7 Wallace, 229, and *Butler vs. Horwitz*, 7 Wallace, 258, in 1868. A year later, in the Fall of 1869, the first cast questioning the constitutionality of the Legal Tender Acts themselves, came before the Supreme Court, in *Hepburn vs. Griswold*, 8 Wallace 603.

With the depreciation of the paper money issued under them, the Legal Tender Acts were being more and more violently attacked by banks, mortgage holders, large and small creditors alike, and in general, by all who "opposed legalized cheating." On the other side was the debtor class, including particularly, the powerful railroad magnates who were constructing railroads all over the country on borrowed capital. Kind of like our inflation of the 1970's when speculators borrowed heavily with the expectation of paying the debt back with cheaper dollars.

In 1869, the Supreme Court was only authorized eight members. In the first conference on *Hepburn vs. Griswold*, the Court was divided four to four. Justices Miller, Swayne, Davis, and Grier upheld the Acts as constitutional. Chief Justice Chase was joined in opposition by Nelson, Clifford and Field. Justice Grier was 76 years old. An inconsistency in his position was pointed out to him in the discussion, and he was honest enough to switch. The next week the other Justices took the extraordinary action of sending a message through Justice Field, "that it was their unanimous opinion that he ought to resign." James Ford Rhodes, History of the United States, 1850-1877, Vol. 6, p. 262-63.

As a result, Justice Grier did resign and on February 7, 1870, the Court handed down the decision declaring the Acts unconstitutional. Chief Justice Chase wrote the opinion, being joined by Clifford, Nelson and Field. Justices Miller, Swayne, and Davis dissented.

The decision affected the Acts only in so far as they applied to contracts entered into prior to the Acts, not after, but Chief Justice Chase left the definite impression he thought they were, as a whole, unconstitutional. He thought the authority of Congress to issue paper money was not one of its delegated powers. He thought no act, even during time of war, could be necessary or proper if it impaired the obligation of contracts.

This case should have settled the question, and the United States should have had no more paper money as legal tender.

But the last had not been heard from Congress. Congress and the newly inaugurated President Ulysses Grant were getting along quite well. Grant having been, of course, the Commander of Union forces at the end of the war. On April 10, 1869, Congress increased the seats on the Supreme Court from eight to nine, to take effect from (sic) the first Monday of December, 1869. (Stat. at Large, 44) Edwin M. Stanton was appointed to fill the new vacancy, but died before he could take his seat. *Hepburn vs. Griswold* was decided in conference November 27, 1869, but was not officially handed down until February 7, 1870, six days after the resignation of Justice Grier on February 1. With Grier gone, there were now two vacancies on the Court to be filled by President Grant.

He nominated two able lawyers who were connected with railroad interests as attorneys, stockholders, and directors. They were William Strong of Pennsylvania and Joseph P. Bradley. Bradley was attorney for, and a director of, the United Railway Companies of New Jersey, a corporation with a large bonded debt. Strong had been chief counsel for the Philadelphia and Reading Railroad before taking a seat on the Supreme Court of Pennsylvania in 1857. He had resigned that seat in 1868 to return to his practice with the railroad.

Congress and the President were not going to take the *Hepburn vs. Griswold* decision lying down. Paper money had too many political possibilities to be exploited, to give up on the matter after only a single Court decision.

Both new Justices were quickly confirmed. William Strong took his seat on February 18, 1870. Joseph P. Bradley on March 21, 1870.

Only four days after the confirmation of Bradley, the government, in the person of Attorney General Hoar, moved to take up in the Supreme Court two Legal Tender cases, *Latham vs. United States* and *Deming vs. United States*, 12 Wallace, 529, which were somewhat different than *Hepburn vs. Griswold*. Mr. Hoar did not agree, for there was no record, but the Chief Justice prevailed in saying these cases had been disposed of with an order under the previous decision, *Hepburn vs. Griswold*.

Not long afterward the Court was presented with a Legal Tender case known as *Knox vs. Lee*, 12 Wallace, 457. The Court's opinion in this case is over 220 pages.

On May 1, 1871, by a five to four vote, the Court overturned its own decision of only a little more than a year before. Chief Justice Chase, Nelson, Clifford, and Field, as they had done the year before, held the Legal Tender Acts unconstitutional.

But this time they were in the minority. The two new Justices, Strong and Bradley, joined the former minority of three, Swayne, Miller and Davis and reversed *Hepburn vs. Griswold* and held the Legal Tender Acts constitutional in regard to all contracts whether made before or after the Acts became law.

Some said President Grant packed the Court with his two nominees whose far-reaching decision set the precedent which has brought us to the point today, where the gold and silver requirement for the nation's money written in the Constitution, is something of which Americans are almost totally ignorant. Paper money is all they know. And the inflation which is caused by the ability of the government to print, therefore, unlimited amounts of money, is not understood by one in a thousand.

The Founders wrote in the gold and silver clauses to limit the government's ability to print money. But once again, we see the Constitution means what judges say it means. Change the judges, and you can change the meaning. And if the people are too busy to notice, or too corrupt to care, liberty is nibbled away, until one day we wake up and find the liberty we took for granted has somehow disappeared.

The *Knox vs. Lee* case is made part of this treatise as it is one referenced by the courts as a precedent against secession. But its real thrust is the Legal Tender Acts. Reference was also thought desireable as we now quote from Justice Strong who delivered the opinion of the court. Strong and Bradley were the two new appointees of President Grant.

Justice Strong: "The controlling questions in these cases are the following: Are the acts of Congress, known as the legal tender acts, constitutional when applied to contracts made before their passage; and secondly, are they valid as applicable to debts contracted since their enactment? These questions have been elaborately argued, and they have received from the court that consideration which their great importance demands. It would be difficult to over estimate the consequences which must follow our decision. They will affect the entire business of the country, *and take hold of the possible continued existence of the Government...*" Emphasis added.

Here is the tipoff that regardless of the Constitution, the court was going to rule that paper money was legal, otherwise, the consequences could be so far reaching, "the government itself, the United States might cease to exist." How absurd. There was going to be great "pain" no matter which way the court ruled. In the entire 220 pages of this opinion and argument, nowhere did Justice Strong mention his personal biases and ties with the railroads or other huge creditor classes who stood to gain immeasurably by the decision he was handing down.

"...If it be held by this court that Congress has no constitutional power, under any circumstances or in any emergency, to make treasury notes a legal tender for the payment of all debts (a power confessedly possessed by every independent sovereignty other than the United States), the government is without those means of self-preservation which, all must admit may, in certain contingencies, become indispensable, even if they were not when the acts of Congress now called in question were enacted..."

Who does His Honor think he and his four brethren are? Are their minds more brilliant? Are their experiences in the practical application, and day to day living with the results of government paper money, greater than the combined wisdom and intellect of the 39 statesmen giants who signed the Constitution? Do these five consider themselves to be more qualified than the hundreds of others who voted in thirteen State conventions to adopt the wisdom of the 39 and make this Nation different than other independent sovereignties, by limiting the evils of paper money, by specifically setting in concrete, they had supposed, the requirement that nothing except gold and silver should act as the Nation's money?

The arrogance and hypocrisy of these five justices is overwhelming. Never mind whether the nation's Founders were right or wrong about gold and silver; regardless of that, gold and silver were set in concrete in the Constitution, and the only lawful way it could be changed was by amending it. Only with the consent of three-fourths of the States could gold and silver be removed as backing for the nation's currency. But five outlaws dressed in black robes defied the Founders, defied *the people*, and defied the Supreme Law of the land. And there was nothing anybody could do about it.

The Founders greatest fears had come to pass. A Supreme Court running wild. They didn't make the Constitution perfect. They should have established some sort of Super Court which was controlled directly by the States themselves. To be called into session on just such rare occasions as this when the Supreme Court was running amok, or when there was a serious question as to its jurisdiction in questions concerning sovereignty of *the people*, and the limited sovereignty *the people* had delegated to their agents, the States and Federal government.

"...It is also clear that if we hold the acts invalid as applicable to debts incurred, or transactions which have taken place since their enactment, our decision must cause, throughout the country, great business derangement, widespread distress, and the rankest injustice..."

Your Honor, let's just be honest please! What you really mean is *"the Constitution be damned!* We are going to save the railroads and other debtors millions of dollars by allowing them to pay back their creditors in depreciated paper money, rather than in gold, or in money backed by gold. So it will cause widespread distress, and the rankest injustice as well, on the other side, by defrauding those who have loaned money." But that's okay. Lenders are rich. They can afford it. "And stop bringing up the damned Constitution in this court."

Injustice? Distress? Business derangement? These are all irrelevent, Your Honor! The question before the court is...pardon me sir for mentioning it again...whether Abraham Lincoln and the Congress of 1862-63 violated the Constitution by making paper money Legal Tender in payment of debts, private transactions and business. Please, Your Honor, this case is setting a monumental precedent for generations to come. Might we stay strictly with the issue?

"...The debts which have been contracted since February 25th, 1862, constitute, doubtless, by far the greatest portion of the existing indebtedness of the country. They have been contracted in view of the acts of Congress declaring treasury notes a legal tender, and in reliance upon that declaration. Men have bought and sold, borrowed and lent, and assumed every variety of obligations contemplating that payment might be made with such notes. Indeed, legal tender treasury notes have become the universal measure of values. *If now, by our decision, it be established that these debts and obligations can be discharged only by gold coin; if, contrary to the expectation of all parties to these contracts, legal tender notes are rendered unavailable, the Government has become an instrument of the grossest injustice; all debtors are loaded with an obligation it was never contemplated they should assume; a large percentage is added to every debt, and such must become the demand for gold to satisfy contracts, that ruinous sacrifices, general distress, and bankruptcy may be expected. These consequences are too obvious to admit of question...*"

Yes sir, Your Honor. We understand. Your mind is made up. Your ruling is to be based on irrelevancies, not the law, not the Constitution. When things get a little difficult in society, when wars come along, if there is a national emergency, or even a natural disaster, you simply cannot be bothered by law. Expediency must be the order of the day. Maybe we can go along with the Constitution on minor stuff, but on questions of major importance, it is simply too restrictive. Okay your Honor, we understand your point.

"...And there is no *well-founded* (emphasis added) distinction to be made between the constitutional validity of an act of Congress declaring treasury notes a legal tender for the payment of debts contracted after its passage and that of an act making them a legal tender for the discharge of all debts, as well those incurred before as those made after its enactment..."

In other words, Your Honor, you mean this court is throwing out as bad law and a bad decision, the ruling of *this very court* made only 14 months ago in *Hepburn vs. Griswold?* "Well...yes, sonny, but don't be so blunt about it, or we'll find you in contempt."

"...There may be a difference in the effects produced by the acts, and in the hardship of their operation, but in both cases the fundamental question, that which tests the validity of the legislation is, can Congress constitutionally give to treasury notes the character and qualities of money? Can such notes be constituted a legitimate circulating medium, having a defined legal value? If they can, then such notes must be available to fulfill all contracts (not expressly excepted) solvable in money, without reference to the time when the contracts were made. Hence it is not strange that those who hold the legal tender acts unconstitutional when applied to contracts made before February, 1862, find themselves compelled also to hold that the acts are invalid as to debts created after that time, and to hold that both classes of debts alike can be discharged only by gold and silver coin."

We will end this tirade of a tyrant with one more sentence he uses as he quotes Chief Justice Marshall who sat on the Court from 1801 until his death in 1835. Marshall was a "midnight" appointment of President John Adams, taking the oath of office February 4, 1801, just one month prior to the new President, Thomas Jefferson, taking office. Marshall is said to be the greatest Justice who ever sat on the Supreme Court, but he was a strong Federalist who believed in expanding Federal powers and taking them to their constitutional limits. For this, he was often at odds with Presidents Jefferson and James Madison who were strict constructionists.

Strong quoting Marshall in *Fletcher vs. Peck* (6 Cranch, 87): "It is not on slight implication and vague conjecture that the legislature is to be pronounced to have transcended its powers and its acts to be considered void. The opposition between the Constitution and the law should be such that the judge feels a clear and strong conviction of their incompatibility with each other."

Then, Your Honor, I presume we are to take it, the court feels these Legal Tender Acts which you just said have monumental implications of injustice and distress, are on the other hand, of "slight implication," and you have no "clear and strong conviction of their incompatibility," with the Constitution?

Your Honors,...please! Just tell it like it is. Since you plan to disregard the Constitution in your momentous and historic decision, just tell us in plain English: *"The Constitution means what we say it means."*

Just to make sure we understand your reasoning, Your Honor. You say this case has "monumental implications" yet it only has "slight implications." On this basis then, we can agree white is black, up is down, one can get so hot he is cold, good is evil, and wrong is right. Okay. Thank you kind sirs.

By the way sir, your personal interests in railroad debt is not having any influence on your decision in this case, is it? Good. We were hoping your personal integrity would not cause you to be biased in any manner. But, sir. Shouldn't some of the good Justices have disqualified themselves in this case, because they stand to personally gain immensely financially, with the decision you are handing down.

"That's about enough out of you, sonny. You either keep your mouth shut or you're headed for the slammer."

Chapter 12

Jurisdiction
State vs. Federal

Most people do not realize when they refer to the United States, there are three different meanings. Black's Law Dictionary defines it this way: UNITED STATES. This term has several meanings. It may be merely the name of a sovereign occupying the position analogous to that of other sovereigns in family of nations, it may designate territory over which sovereignty of United States extends, or it may be a collective name of the states which are united by and under the Constitution. *Hooven Allison Co. vs. Evatt*, U.S. Ohio, 324 U.S. 652, 65 S.Ct. 870, 880, 89 L.Ed.1252.

In other words there are three separate definitions, or kinds of United States.

1. The United States as formed by the States under the Constitution. This is our Federal Government with three separate and equal branches, the Executive, the Legislative and the Judicial. This is an artificial entity, or corporate type structure established by the States to represent them as a single unit in dealings with foreign nations, to arbitrate differences between the States, or between citizens of different States, and regulate commerce with foreign nations and between the States.

2. The United States is that physical territory over which

exclusive jurisdiction is exercised which includes all territory, or land mass and water, which is not within the boundary of a State. This includes the District of Columbia, American Samoa, Guam, the Northern Mariana Islands, Puerto Rico, and the Virgin Islands. It also includes federal property within the boundaries of States which have been ceded by a State to the federal government, such as "forts, magazines, arsenals, dock yards, and other needful buildings." Article 1, Section 8, Clause 17, United States Constitution. The federal government can lawfully exercise jurisdiction over these relatively small parcels of land mass, water, and, of course, the open seas, where jurisdiction is not claimed by a foreign nation. Both one and two are *Federal United States*.

3. The United States, or 50 States united, consisting of 50 separate, independent, and sovereign States, except for the limited and specific powers delegated to that United States known also as the Federal government, to act as their joint agent. Each of the 50 States retain the right to prosecute all criminal cases in State courts when crimes are committed within State boundaries, unless the crime is committed on territory which has actually been ceded to the Federal United States by one of the States, or the crime is committed, perhaps, on Indian land. These 50 separate States which have united themselves with a contract, or trust, into a temporary, or permanent, confederation, the choice being that of each individual State, retain the legal status of dormant, legal, 50 separate nations, equal to any other nation of the earth if they should decide to secede from each other or break the constitutional alliance or compact. They then would be equal to England, Germany, Japan, France or Italy, or any other nation. These 50 are under contract with each other. The contract is the Constitution. The 50, actually 38 of the States, could dissolve the contract and they would automatically eliminate the first two of the above definitions of United States. All territory now constituted as Federal would revert to ownership of the 50 States, and each State would revert to the same status as the first 13 States when they declared their independence from England on July 4, 1776, until nine joined

in the present compact under the Constitution on June 21, 1788. These States would continue to exist independently as nations even if there was no United States under the first two definitions.

This chapter was submitted to the author by Mr. Wayne Veldon Ault, residing in Tucson, Arizona. Mr. Ault, though not an attorney, submitted this as a brief in federal court on behalf of a friend of his. The friend actually filed it Pro Se, or as his own attorney.

The brief makes a powerful case for the release of prisoners, specifically the friend of Mr. Ault, who had been imprisoned under the Drug Abuse Prevention and Control Act of 1970. Thousands, if not tens of thousands of men are serving time in federal prison who have been convicted under this blatantly unconstitutional Act of Congress. It is to be hoped the federal court, or the Supreme Court on appeal, will overturn this law and free these thousands of prisoners. Many, perhaps most, deserve to be doing time, but not under a law which is in violation of the Constitution. If Congress can get away with unlawfully persecuting one element of society, they can, and will persecute, and have prosecuted, other less heinous individuals and groups of American citizens...and aliens, as time passes.

The point is, we either have a Constitution which is the Supreme Law, or we don't. If we do, let's honor it, and force an already out-of-control Congress to also honor it. The States are perfectly capable of prosecuting and punishing crime including the prosecution of those who illegally sell and distribute narcotics. When the States allow, or worse, invite federal intervention within State boundaries, or more accurately, within State jurisdiction, they are playing the part of fools.

In our present state of affairs, State governments and most of our people seem to have little understanding of how decades of allowing federal intervention in criminal and civil matters of the States, has set so many unconstitutional precedents. It has become so commonplace, that now it will be almost impossible to restore Constitutional balance without the drastic, some will say radical, steps of either dissolving the Union in order to start over, or for the States to go their separate ways and leave a corrupt and outlaw central government to work its will on those sister States who are willing to sink with it into bankruptcy and anarchy, finally, to repeat the history of the dark ages with the super rich ruling with a rod of iron, while the masses will live in poverty and under conditions little different than slavery.

If defense lawyers will start arguing lack of jurisdiction in thousands of federal prosecutions, we might have a chance to restore the Constitution as Supreme Law and avoid more drastic actions. For this purpose, defense attorneys are encouraged to use and copy the following brief, not only in federal drug prosecutions, but in numerous other cases where there is no constitutional jurisdiction. If the federal government is challenged on jurisdiction, first of all, in every case it brings improperly, we might have a chance to put our government house in order.

If defense lawyers will wake up and start informing juries of their right, and their duty, to judge the law under which prosecution is brought, not just the facts of a case, in spite of the judges instructions, this too will discourage numerous unjust federal prosecutions...and persecution...of tax rebels, religious "cultists;" and others who presidents and congressmen put on "hit lists."

In the early decades of our Republic, juries did, in fact, judge both the law and the facts in civil and criminal cases. Finally with the Sparf decision of 1895, and since, we have allowed the judiciary to misinform the jury, telling the jury members, he, the judge, will instruct them on the law; their only duty is to judge the facts.

For an outstanding essay on the right and power of the jury, write and ask for Citizens Rule Book, $1.00 to Liberty Library, 300 Independence Ave., SE, Washington, D.C. 20003. Also see *State of Georgia vs. Brailsford*, et al, 3 Dall. 1, 1794. U.S. vs. Dougherty, 473 F 2d 1113, 1139, 1972. *U.S. vs. Moylan*, 417 F 2d 1006, 1969.

The remainder of this chapter is that which came to the author from Mr. Ault except for a few very slight changes. This outstanding brief should prove to be worth thousands of dollars in time saved doing research for any attorney who wishes to use it contesting federal jurisdiction.

If the courts refuse to honor lawful jurisdiction of the States as outlined in this brief, there will be little choice for us, if we wish to retain freedom, other than to dissolve our Union or secede from it.

UNITED STATES DISTRICT COURT
DISTRICT OF MASSACHUSETTS

United States of America	)	
	)	
Plaintiff	)	
vs.	)	Civil No. 1993
John Doe and	)	
John Q. Public	)	or Criminal No. 1993
	)	
Defendants	)	

The Drug Abuse Prevention and Control Act, 21 U.S.C., section 801, et. seq., generally provides a list of controlled substances by schedules and a method for supplementing the names of other drugs to those schedules. It requires importers, manufacturers, distributors, pharmacists and physicians who manufacture, distribute or dispense controlled substances to become licensed for such activity. These licenses are subject to revocation, and parties violating the Act can be criminally punished.

The United States Constitution contains no express provision permitting Congress to control the practice of medicine within the States of the Union; indeed, in *Linder vs. United States*, 268 U.S. 5, 45 S.Ct. 446 (1925), the Supreme Court stated:

> "Obviously, direct control of medical practice in the states is beyond the power of the federal government," 268 U.S., at 18.

The only possible method by which Congress could control the drug distribution system within the States would be by means of its power over interstate commerce. A federal license simply does not confer any authority to perform the licensed activity within the jurisdiction of a State; see License Tax Cases, 72 U.S. (5 Wall.) 462 (1866); *United States vs. DeWitt*, 76 U.S. (9 Wall) 41 (1870); *Patterson vs. Kentucky*, 97 U.S. 501 (1879); and *Reagan vs. Mercantile Trust Co.*, 154 U.S. 4 13 , 14 S. Ct. 1060 (1894).

Before 1936, the Supreme Court construed Congressional control over interstate commerce in a highly limited fashion; see *Hammer vs. Dagenhart*, 247 U.S. 251, 38 S.Ct. 529 (1918); *Bailey vs. Drexel Furniture Co.*, 259 U.S. 20, 42 S.Ct. 449 (1922); *Hill vs. Wallace*, 259 U.S. 44, 42 S.Ct. 453 (1922); *United Mine Workers of America vs. Coronado Coal Co.*, 259 U.S. 344, 42 S.Ct. 570 (1922); *United Leather Workers' International Union vs. Herkert & Meisel Trunk Co.*, 265 U.S. 457, 44 S.Ct. 623 (1924); *Industrial Ass'n. of San Francisco vs. United States*, 268 U.S. 64, 45 S.Ct. 403 (1925); *Levering vs. Garrigues Co.*, 289 U.S. 103, 53 S.Ct. 549 (1933); *Railroad Retirement Board vs. Alton R. Co.*, 295 U.S. 330, 55 S.Ct. 758 (1935); *A.L.A. Schecter Poultry Corp. vs. United States*, 275 U.S. 495, 55 S.Ct. 837 (1935); *United States vs. Butler*, 297 U.S. 1, 56 S.Ct. 312 (1936); and *Carter vs. Carter Coal Co.*, 298 U.S. 238, 56 S.Ct. 855 (1936). But, since the Great Depression, the Supreme Court has expanded Congressional interstate commerce powers to the point where such control encompasses that which affects interstate commerce; see *Heart of Atlanta Motel. Inc. vs. United States*, 379 U.S. 241, 85 S.Ct. 348 (1964); and *Katzenbach vs. McClung*, 379 U.S. 294, 85 S.Ct. 377 (1964). Nonetheless, whatever power Congress possesses over interstate commerce, whenever it desires to exercise its interstate commerce powers it must, by clear, statutory language, base the act upon such Congressional power. Failing such clearly expressed connection with interstate commerce, the act cannot be one having a constitutional foundation based on that power; see *United States vs. Steffens* (The Trade-Mark Cases), 100 U.S. 82 (1879).

We contend that the "jurisdiction of the United States" extends only over Washington, D.C., the federal enclaves within the States, in the territories and insular possessions of the United States, on the "high seas", and in the remainder of the areas described in 18 U.S.C., section 7. We further contend that, generally, all federal legislation applies only within the jurisdiction of the United States. By construing the express language of the Drug Abuse Prevention and Control Act in the light of inherent limitations on Congressional power, we strenuously assert that this act applies solely within the jurisdiction of the United States and not within the jurisdiction of the State of Texas, or any other State, which claims jurisdiction over all within borders, excluding federal enclaves; see T.C.A., section 4-1-101.

We anticipate that the government herein will contend that the act in question is based on the power of Congress to control interstate commerce, such argument being based upon 21 U.S.C., section 801, which is the only place alluding to Congressional interstate commerce powers in the entire act. However, we argue that such "findings" in section 801 merely state "truisms", and section 801 fails to base the provisions of the act on interstate commerce powers. *Further, the case law dealing with preambles to legislative acts holds that preambles cannot confer powers or expand the operative provisions of an act.* Here, this drug control act has no operative provision (especially the criminal provisions) based on interstate commerce; this being the case, the act in question is one which applies only within the jurisdiction of the United States, but not within the jurisdiction of any of the 50 States.

To fully comprehend the significance of our argument, it is essential to discuss hereafter at length the case law which defines the jurisdiction of the United States. Thereafter, we will treat herein the case law which demonstrates the insignificance of preambles in legislative acts. We will conclude by showing that the act in question has no statutory relation to interstate commerce and has application only within the jurisdiction of the United States, and not within the jurisdiction of any of the 50 States.

FEDERAL JURISDICTION

In the United States, there are two separate and distinct jurisdictions, such being the jurisdiction of the States within their own territorial boundaries and the other being federal jurisdiction. A third jurisdiction is county government whose enforcement powers come under authority of the Sheriff. Under threat of criminal prosecution, county governments can require federal and state officials to comply with and honor county ordinances.[1] Broadly speaking, state jurisdiction encompasses the legislative power to regulate, control and govern real and personal property, individuals and enterprises within the territorial boundaries of any given State. In contrast, federal jurisdiction is extremely limited, with the same being exercised only in areas external to state legislative power and territory. Notwithstanding the clarity of this simple principle, the line of demarcation between these two jurisdic-

---

1. County jurisdiction is not an issue here, but for more information, write to: Box Elder County Commission
01 South Main
Brigham City, Utah 84302-2599
Ask for Ordinance No.s 178, 179, 180 and 181, cost $5.00. These Ordinances are powerful in forcing federal officials to comply with County law. Section 3 of Ordinance 178 says: "Violations of this Ordinance shall place liability upon the federal official or officials responsible for making and implementing any decision which fails to comply with this Ordinance." Violations are made a criminal matter. The Ordinances were passed and adopted April 21, 1992.
Catron County, Reserve, New Mexico 87830 was the first County in the United States to begin asserting power in the people, and warning federal officials they WILL comply with County Law or face criminal prosecution; that Catron County would take no more Federal coercion or intimidation. Catron County has shown the way for over 100 Counties in eight Western States which are currently in the process of instituting "County Home Rule."
Further information and lecturer/teacher/speakers are available from:
National Federal Lands Conference
P. O. Box 847
Bountiful, Utah 84011

Chapter 12

tions and the extent and reach of each has become somewhat blurred, due to popular misconceptions and the *efforts expended by the federal government to conceal one of its major weaknesses*. Only by resorting to history and case law can this obfuscation be clarified and the two distinct jurisdictions be readily seen.

The original thirteen colonies of America were each separately established by charters from the English Crown. Outside of the common bond of each being a dependency and colony of the mother country, England, the colonies were not otherwise united. Each had its own governor, legislative assembly and courts, and each was governed separately and independently by the English Parliament.

The political connections of the separate colonies to the English Crown and Parliament descended to an unhappy state of affairs as the direct result of Parliamentary acts adopted in the late 1760's and early 1770's. Due to the real and perceived dangers caused by these various acts, the First Continental Congress was convened by representatives of the several colonies in October, 1774, the purpose of which was to submit a petition of grievances to the British Parliament and Crown. By the Declaration and Resolves of the First Continental Congress, dated October 14, 1774, the colonial representatives labelled these Parliamentary acts of which they complained as "impolitic, unjust, and cruel, as well as unconstitutional, and most dangerous and destructive of American rights," and the purpose of which were designs, schemes and plans "which demonstrate a system formed to enslave America." Revolution was assuredly in the formative stages absent conciliation between the mother country and colonies.

Between October, 1775, and the middle of 1776, each of the colonies separately severed their ties and relations with England, and several adopted constitutions for the newly formed States. By July, 1776, the exercise of British authority in any and all colonies was not recognized in any degree. The capstone of this actual separation of the colonies from England was the more formal Declaration of Independence. The legal effect of the Declaration of Independence was to make each new State a separate and independent sovereign over which there was no other government of superior power or jurisdiction. This was clearly shown in *M'Ilvaine vs. Coxe's Lessee*, 8 U.S. (4 Cranch) 209 (1808), where it was held:

> "This opinion is predicated upon a principle which is believed to be undeniable, that the several states which composed this Union, so far at least as regarded their municipal regulations, became entitled, from the time when they declared themselves independent, to all the rights and powers of sovereign states, and that they did not derive them from concessions made by the British king. *The treaty of peace contains a recoqnition of their independence, not a grant of it.* From hence it results, that the laws of the several state governments were the laws of sovereign states, and as such were obligatory upon the people of such state, from the time they were enacted," 4 Cranch, at 212.

And a further expression of similar import is found in *Harcourt vs. Gaillard*, 25 U.S. (12 Wheat.) 523 (1827), where the Court stated:

> "There was no territory within the United States that was claimed in any other right than that of some one of the confederated states; therefore, there could be no acquisition of territory made by the United States distinct from, or independent of some one of the states.
>
> "Each declared itself sovereign and independent, according to the limits of its territory.
>
> "[T]he soil and sovereignty within their acknowledged limits were as much theirs at the Declaration of Independence as at this hour," 12 Wheat., at 526, 527.

Thus, unequivocally, in July, 1776, the new States possessed all sovereignty, power, and jurisdiction over all the soil and people in their respective territorial limits.

This condition of supreme sovereignty of each State over all property and persons within the borders thereof continued notwithstanding the adoption of the Articles of Confederation. In Article II of such Articles, it was expressly stated:

> "Article II. Each state retains its sovereignty, freedom, and independence, and every power, jurisdiction and right, which is not by this confederation expressly delegated to the United States, in Congress assembled."

As the history of the confederation government has shown, each State was indeed sovereign and independent to the degree that it made the central government created by the confederation fairly ineffectual. These defects of the confederation government strained the relations between and among the States and the remedy became the calling of a constitutional convention.

The representatives which assembled in Philadelphia in May, 1787, to attend the Constitutional Convention met for the primary purpose of improving the commercial relations among the States, although the product of the Convention produced more than this. But, no intention was demonstrated for the States to surrender in any degree the jurisdiction so possessed by the States at that time, and indeed the Constitution as finally drafted continued the same territorial jurisdiction of the States as existed under the Articles of Confederation. The essence of this retention of state jurisdiction is embodied in Article I, Section 8, Clause 17 of the U.S. Constitution, which reads as follows:

> "To exercise exclusive legislation in all cases whatsoever, over such district (not exceeding ten miles square) as may, by cession of particular States, and the acceptance of

Congress, become the Seat of the Government of the United States, and to exercise like authority over all places purchased by the consent of the legislature of the State in which the same shall be, for the erection of forts, magazines, arsenals, dock yards, and other needful buildings."

The reason for the inclusion of this clause in the Constitution was and is obvious. Under the Articles of Confederation, the States retained full and complete jurisdiction over lands and persons within their borders. The Congress under the Articles was merely a body which represented and acted as agents of the separate States for external affairs, and had no jurisdiction within the States. This defect in the Articles made the Confederation Congress totally dependent upon any given State for protection, and this dependency did, in fact, cause embarrassment for that Congress. During the Revolutionary War, while the Congress met in Philadelphia, a body of mutineers from the Continental Army surrounded the Congress and chastised and insulted the members thereof. The governments of both Philadelphia and Pennsylvania proved themselves powerless to remedy the situation, and the Congress was forced to flee first to Princeton, New Jersey, and finally to Annapolis, Maryland.[2] Thus, this clause was inserted into the Constitution to give jurisdiction to Congress over its capital, and such other places as Congress might purchase for forts, magazines, arsenals, and other needful buildings wherein the State ceded jurisdiction of such lands to the federal government. Other than in these areas, this clause of the Constitution did not operate to cede further jurisdiction to the federal government, and jurisdiction over unceded areas remained within the States.

While there had been no real provisions in the Articles

---

2. See *Fort Leavenworth R. Co. vs. Lowe*, 114 U.S. 525, 529, 5 S. Ct. 995 (1885).

which permitted the Confederation Congress to acquire property and possess exclusive jurisdiction over such property, the above clause filled an essential need by permitting the federal government to acquire land for the seat of government and other purposes from certain of the States. Such possessions were deemed essential to enable the United States to perform the powers conveyed by the Constitution, and a cession of lands by any particular State would grant exclusive jurisdiction of such lands to Congress. Perhaps the most cogent reasons and explanations for this clause in the Constitution were set forth in Essay No. 43 of The Federalist:

> "The indispensable necessity of complete authority at the seat of government carries its own evidence with it. It is a power exercised by every legislature of the Union, I might say of the world, by virtue of its general supremacy. Without it not only the public authority might be insulted and its proceedings interrupted with impunity, but a dependence of the members of the general government on the State comprehending the seat of the government for protection in the exercise of their duty might bring on the national councils an imputation of awe or influence equally dishonorable to the government and dissatisfactory to the other members of the Confederacy. This consideration has the more weight as the gradual accumulation of public improvements at the stationary residence of the government would be both too great a public pledge to be left in the hands of a single State, and would create so many obstacles to a removal of the government, as still further to abridge its necessary independence. The extent of this federal district is sufficiently circumscribed to satisfy every jealousy of an opposite nature. And as it is to be appropriated to this use with

the consent of the State ceding it; as the State will no doubt provide in the compact for the rights and the consent of the citizens inhabiting it; as the inhabitants will find sufficient inducements of interest to become willing parties to the cession; as they will have had their voice in the election of the government which is to exercise authority over them; as a municipal legislature for local purposes, derived from their own suffrages, will of course be allowed them; and as the authority of the legislature of the State, and of the inhabitants of the ceded part of it, to concur in the cession will be derived from the whole people of the State in their adoption of the Constitution, every imaginable objection seems to be obviated.

"The necessity of a like authority over forts, magazines, etc., established by the general government, is not less evident. The public money expended on such places, and the public property deposited in them, require that they should be exempt from the authority of the particular State. Nor would it be proper for the places on which the security of the entire Union may depend to be in any degree dependent on a particular member of it. All objections and scruples are here also obviated by requiring the concurrence of the States concerned in every such establishment."

Since the time of the ratification and implementation of the present U.S. Constitution, the U.S. Supreme Court and all lower courts have had many opportunities to construe and apply the above provision of the Constitution. And the essence of all these decisions is that the States of this nation have exclusive jurisdiction of property and persons located within their borders, excluding such lands and persons residing thereon which have been ceded to the United States.

Perhaps one of the earliest decisions on this point was *United States vs. Bevans*, 16 U.S. (3 Wheat.) 336 (1818), which involved a federal prosecution for a murder committed on board the war ship, Independence, anchored in the harbor of Boston, Massachusetts. The defense complained that only the state had jurisdiction to prosecute and argued that the federal Circuit Courts had no jurisdiction of this crime supposedly committed within the federal government's admiralty jurisdiction. In argument before the Supreme Court counsel for the United States admitted as follows:

> "The exclusive jurisdiction which the United States have in forts and dock yards ceded to them, is derived from the express assent of the states by whom the cessions are made. It could be derived in no other manner, because without it, the authority of the state would be supreme and exclusive therein," 3 Wheat., at 350, 351.

In holding that the State of Massachusetts had jurisdiction over the crime, the Court held:

> "What, then, is the extent of jurisdiction which a state possesses?
> "We answer, without hesitation, the jurisdiction of a state is co-extensive with its territory, co-extensive with its legislative power," 3 Wheat., at 386, 387.
> "The article which describes the judicial power of the United States is not intended for the cession of territory or of general jurisdiction. ... Congress has power to exercise exclusive jurisdiction over this district, and over all places purchased by the consent of the legislature of the state in which the same shall be, for the erection of forts, magazines, arsenals, dock yards, and other needful buildings.

> "It is observable that the power of exclusive legislation (which is jurisdiction) is united with cession of territory, which is to be the free act of the States. It is difficult to compare the two sections together without feeling a conviction, not to be strengthened by any commentary on them, that in describing the judicial power, the framers of our constitution had not in view any cession of territory, or, which is essentially the same, of general jurisdiction," 3 Wheat., at 388.

Thus, in *Bevans*, the Court established a principle that federal jurisdiction extends only over the areas wherein it possesses *the power of exclusive legislation*, and this is a principle incorporated into all subsequent decisions regarding the extent of federal jurisdiction. To hold otherwise would destroy the purpose, intent and meaning of the entire U.S. Constitution.

The decision in Bevans was closely followed by decisions made in two state courts and one federal court within the next two years. In *Commonwealth vs. Young*, Brightly, N.P. 302 (Pa., 1818), the Supreme Court of Pennsylvania was presented with the issue of whether lands owned by the United States for which Pennsylvania had never ceded jurisdiction had to be sold pursuant to state law. In deciding that the state law of Pennsylvania exclusively controlled this sale of federal land, the Court held:

> "The legislation and authority of Congress is confined to cessions by particular states for the seat of government, and purchases made by consent of the legislature of the state, for the purpose of erecting forts. The legislative power and exclusive jurisdiction remained in the several states, of all territory within their limits, not ceded to, or purchased by, Congress, with the assent of the state legislature, to prevent the

collision of legislation and authority between the United States and the several states," Id., at 309.

A year later, the Supreme Court of New York was presented with the issue of whether the State of New York had jurisdiction over a murder committed at Fort Niagara, a federal fort. In *People vs. Godfrey*, 17 Johns, 225 (N.Y., 1819), that court held that the fort was subject to the jurisdiction of the State since the lands therefore had not been ceded to the United States. The rationale of its opinion stated:

> "To oust this state of its jurisdiction to support and maintain its laws, and to punish crimes, it must be shown that an offense committed within the acknowledged limits of the state, is clearly and exclusively cognizable by the laws and courts of the United States. In the case already cited, Chief Justice Marshall observed, that to bring the offense within the jurisdiction of the courts of the union, it must have been committed out of the jurisdiction of any state, it is not (he says,) the offence committed, but the place in which it is committed, which must be out of the jurisdiction of the State," 17 Johns., at 233.

The case relied upon by this court was *U.S. vs. Bevans*, supra. At about the same time that the New York Supreme Court rendered its opinion in Godfrey, a similar fact situation was before a federal court, the only difference being that the murder committed in the case occurred on land which had been ceded to the United States. In *United States vs. Cornell*, 25 Fed.Cas. 646, No. 14, 867 (C.C.D.R.I., 1819), the court held that the case fell within federal jurisdiction, describing such jurisdiction as follows:

> "But although the United States may well purchase and hold lands for public purposes,

> within the territorial limits of a state, this does not of itself oust the jurisdiction or sovereignty of such State over the lands so purchased. It remains until the State has relinquished its authority over the land either expressly or by necessary implication.
>
> "When therefore a purchase of land for any of these purposes is made by the national government, and the State Legislature has given its consent to the purchase, the land so purchased by the very terms of the constitution ipso facto falls within the exclusive legislation of Congress, and the State jurisdiction is completely ousted," Id., at 648.

Almost 18 years later, the U.S. Supreme Court was again presented with a case involving the distinction between State and Federal jurisdiction. In *New Orleans vs. United States*, 35 U.S. (10 Pet.) 662 (1836), the United States claimed title to property in New Orleans likewise claimed by the city. After holding that title to the subject lands was owned by the city, the Court addressed the question of federal jurisdiction and stated:

> "Special provision is made in the Constitution for the cession of jurisdiction from the States over places where the federal government shall establish forts or other military works. And it is only in these places, or in the territories of the United States, where it can exercise a general jurisdiction," 10 Pet., at 737.

In *New York vs. Miln*, 36 U.S. (11 Pet.) 102 (1837), the question before the Court involved the attempt by the City of New York to assess penalties against the master of a ship for his failure to make a report as to the persons his ship brought to New York. As against the master's contention that the act was unconstitutional and that New York had no jurisdiction in the matter, the Court held:

> "If we look at the place of its operation, we find it to be within the territory, and therefore, within the jurisdiction of New York. If we look at the person on whom it operates, he is found within the same territory and jurisdiction," 36 U.S., at 133.
>
> "They are these: that a State has the same undeniable and unlimited jurisdiction over all persons and things within its territorial limits, as any foreign nation, where that jurisdiction is not surrendered or restrained by the Constitution of the United States. That, by virtue of this, it is not only the right, but the bounden and solemn duty of a State, to advance the safety, happiness and prosperity of its people, and to provide for its general welfare, by any and every act of legislation which it may deem to be conducive to these ends; where the power over the particular subject, or the manner of its exercise is not surrendered or restrained, in the manner just stated. That all those powers which relate to merely municipal legislation, or what may, perhaps, more properly be called internal police, are not thus surrendered or restrained; and that, consequently, in relation to these, the authority of a State is complete, unqualified and exclusive," 36 U.S., at 139.

Some eight years later, in *Pollard vs. Hagan*, 44 U.S. (3 How.) 212 (1845), the question of federal jurisdiction was once again before the Court. This case involved a contest of the title to real property, with one of the parties claiming a right to the disputed property via a U.S. patent; the lands in question were situated in Mobile, Alabama, adjacent to Mobile Bay. In discussing the subject of federal jurisdiction, the Court held: "We think a proper examination of this subject will show that the United States never held any municipal sovereignty, jurisdiction, or right of soil in and to the territory of which Alabama or any of the new States were formed," 44 U.S., at 221.

> "[B]ecause the United States have no constitutional capacity to exercise municipal jurisdiction, sovereignty, or eminent domain within the limits of a State or elsewhere, except in the cases in which it is expressly granted," 44 U.S., at 223.
>
> "Alabama is therefore entitled to the sovereignty and jurisdiction over all the territory within the limits, subject to the common law," 44 U.S., at 228, 229.

The single most important case regarding the subject of federal jurisdiction appears to be *Fort Leavenworth R. Co. vs. Lowe*, 114 U.S. 525, 5 S.Ct. 995 (1885), which sets forth the law on this point fully. There, the railroad company property which passed through the Fort Leavenworth federal enclave was being subjected to taxation by Kansas, and the company claimed an exemption from state taxation. In holding that the railroad company's property could be taxed, the Court carefully explained federal jurisdiction within the States:

> "The consent of the states to the purchase of lands within them for the special purposes named, is, however, essential under the constitution to the transfer to the general government, with the title of political jurisdiction and dominion. Where lands are acquired without such consent, the possession of the United States, unless political jurisdiction be ceded to them in some other way, is simply that of an ordinary proprietor. The property in that case, unless used as a means to carry out the purposes of the government, is subject to the legislative authority and control of the states equally with the property of private individuals," 114 U.S., at 531.

Thus, the cases decided within the 19th century clearly disclosed the extent and scope of both State and federal jurisdiction. In essence, these cases, among many others, hold that the jurisdiction of any particular State is co-extensive with its borders or territory, and all persons and property located or found therein are subject to such jurisdiction; this jurisdiction is superior. Federal jurisdiction results only from a conveyance of state jurisdiction to the federal government for lands owned or otherwise possessed by the federal government, and thus federal jurisdiction is extremely limited in nature. And there is no federal jurisdiction if there be no grant or cession of jurisdiction by the State to the federal government. Therefore, federal territorial jurisdiction exists only in Washington, D.C., the federal enclaves within the States, and the territories and insular possessions of the United States.

The above principles of jurisdiction established in the last century continue their vitality today with only one minor exception. In the last century, the cessions of jurisdiction by States to the federal government were by legislative acts which typically ceded full jurisdiction to the federal government, thus placing into the hands of the federal government the troublesome problem of dealing with and governing scattered, localized federal enclaves which had been totally surrendered by the States. With the advent in this century of large federal works projects and national parks, the problems regarding management of these areas by the federal government were magnified. During the last century, it was thought that if a State ceded jurisdiction to the federal government, the cession granted full and complete jurisdiction. But, with the ever increasing number of separate tracts of land falling within the jurisdiction of the federal government in this century, it was obviously determined by both federal and state public officers that the States should retain greater control over these ceded lands, and the courts have acknowledged the constitutionality of varying degrees of state jurisdiction and control over lands so ceded.

Perhaps one of the first cases to acknowledge the proposition that a State could retain a degree of jurisdiction over property ceded to the federal government was *Surplus Trading Co. vs. Cook*, 281 U.S. 647, 50 S.Ct. 455 (1930). In this case, a state attempt to assess an ad valorem tax on army blankets located within a federal army camp was found invalid and beyond the state's jurisdiction. But, in regards to the proposition that a State could make a qualified cession of jurisdiction to the federal government, the Court held:

> "[T]he state undoubtedly may cede her jurisdiction to the United States and may make the cession either absolute or qualified as to her may appear desirable, provided the qualification is consistent with the purposes for which the reservation is maintained and is accepted by the United States. And, where such a cession is made and accepted, it will be determinative of the jurisdiction of both the United States and the state within the reservation," 281 U.S., at 651, 652.

Two cases decided in 1937 by the U.S. Supreme Court further clarify the constitutionality of a reservation of any degree of state jurisdiction over lands ceded to the jurisdiction of the United States. In *James vs. Dravo Contracting Company*, 302 U.S. 134, 58 S.Ct. 208 (1937), the State of West Virginia sought to impose a tax upon the gross receipts of the company arising from a contract which it had made with the United States to build some dams on rivers. One of the issues involved in this case was the validity of the state tax imposed on the receipts derived by the company from work performed on lands to which the State had ceded "concurrent" jurisdiction to the United States. In the Court's opinion, it held that a State could reserve and qualify any cession of jurisdiction for lands owned by the United States; since the State had done so here, the Court upheld this part of the challenged tax notwithstanding a partial cession of jurisdiction to the U.S. A similar result occurred in *Silas Mason Co. vs. Tax Commission of State of Washington*, 302 U.S. 186, 58 S.Ct. 233

(1937). Here, the United States was undertaking the construction of several dams on the Columbia River in Washington, and had purchased the lands necessary for the project. Silas Mason obtained a contract to build a part of the Grand Coulee Dam, but filed suit challenging the Washington income tax when that State sought to impose such tax on the contract proceeds. Mason's argument that the federal government had exclusive jurisdiction over both the lands and such contract was not upheld by either the Supreme Court of Washington or the U.S. Supreme Court. The latter Court held that none of the lands owned by the U.S. were within its jurisdiction and thus Washington clearly had jurisdiction to impose the challenged tax; see also *Wilson vs. Cook,* 327 U.S. 474, 66 S.Ct. 663 (1946).

Some few years later in 1943, the Supreme Court was again presented with similar taxation and jurisdiction issues; the facts in these two cases were identical with the exception that one clearly involved lands ceded to the jurisdiction of the United States. This single difference caused directly opposite results in both cases. In *Pacific Coast Dairy vs. Department of Agriculture of California*, 318 U.S. 285, 63 S.Ct. 628 (1943), the question involved the applicability of state law to a contract entered into and performed on a federal enclave to which jurisdiction had been ceded to the United States. During World War II, California passed a law setting a minimum price for the sale of milk, which law imposed penalties for sales made below the regulated price. Here, Pacific Coast Dairy consummated a contract on Moffett Field, a federal enclave within the exclusive jurisdiction of the United States, to sell milk to such federal facility at below the regulated price. When this occurred, California sought to impose a penalty for what it perceived as a violation of state law. But, the U.S. Supreme Court refused to permit the enforcement of the California law, holding that the contract was made and performed in a territory outside the jurisdiction of California and within the jurisdiction of the United States, a place where this law didn't apply. Thus, in this case, the existence of federal jurisdiction was the foundation for the ruling. However, in

Penn Dairies vs. Milk Control Commission of Pennsylvania, 318 U.S. 261, (63 S.Ct. 17 (1943), an opposite result was reached on almost identical facts. Here, Pennsylvania likewise had a law which regulated the price of milk and penalized sales of milk below the regulated price. During World War II, the United States leased some land from Pennsylvania for the construction of a military camp; since the land was leased, Pennsylvania did not cede jurisdiction to the United States. When Penn Dairies sold milk to the military facility for a price below the regulated price, the Commission sought to impose the penalty. In this case, since there was no federal jurisdiction, the Supreme Court found that the state law applied and permitted the imposition of the penalty. Thus, these two cases clearly show the different results which can occur with the presence or absence of federal jurisdiction.

A final point which must be made regarding federal jurisdiction involves the point as to when such jurisdiction ends or ceases. This point was considered in S.R.A. vs. Minnesota, 327 U.S. 558, 66 S. Ct. 749 (1946), which involved the power of a State to tax the real property interest of a purchaser of land sold by the United States. Here, a federal post office building was sold to S.R.A. pursuant to a real estate sale contract, which provided that title would pass only after the purchase price had been paid. In refuting the argument of S.R.A. that the ad valorem tax on its equitable interest in the property was really an unlawful tax on U.S. property, the Court held:

> "In the absence of some such provisions, a transfer of property held by the United States under state cessions pursuant to Article I, Section 8, Clause 17, of the Constitution would leave numerous isolated islands of federal jurisdiction, unless the unrestricted transfer of the property to private hands is thought without more to revest sovereignty in the states. As the purpose of Clause 17 was to give control over the sites of governmental operations to

the United States, when such control was deemed essential for federal activities, it would seem that the sovereignty of the United States would end with the reason for its existence and the disposition of the property. We shall treat this case as though the Government's unrestricted transfer of property to non-federal hands is a relinquishment of the exclusive legislative power," 327 U.S., at 563, 564.

Thus, it appears clearly that once any property within the exclusive jurisdiction of the United States is no longer utilized by that government for governmental purposes, and the title or any interest therein is conveyed to private interests, the jurisdiction of the federal government ceases and jurisdiction once again reverts to the State.

The above principles regarding the distinction between State and federal jurisdiction continue through today; see *Paul vs. United States*, 371 U.S. 245, 83 S. Ct. 426 (1963), and *United States vs. State Tax Commission of Mississippi*, 412 U.S. 363, 93 S. Ct. 2183 (1973). And what was definitely decided in the beginning days of this Republic regarding the extent, scope, and reach of each of these two distinct jurisdictions remains unchanged and forms the foundation and basis for the smooth workings of state governmental systems in conjunction with the federal government. Without such jurisdictional principles which form a clear boundary between the jurisdiction of the States and the United States, our federal governmental system would have surely met its demise long before now.

In summary, jurisdiction of the States is essentially the same as that possessed by the states which were leagued together under the Articles of Confederation. The confederated States possessed absolute, complete and full jurisdiction over property and persons located within their borders. *It is hypocritical to assume or argue that these States, which had absolved and banished the centralized power and jurisdiction of the English Parliament and Crown over them by the*

Declaration of Independence, would shortly thereafter cede comparable power and jurisdiction to the Confederation Congress. They did not and they closely and jealously guarded their own rights, powers and jurisdiction. When the Articles were replaced by the Constitution, the intent and purpose of the States was to retain their same powers and jurisdiction, with a small concession of jurisdiction to the United States for lands found essential for the operation of that government. However, even this provision did not operate to instantly change any aspect of state jurisdiction, it only permitted its future operation wherein any State, by its own volition, *should choose to cede jurisdiction to the United States.*

By the adoption of the Constitution, the States jointly surrendered *some 17 specific* and well defined powers to the federal Congress, which related strictly to external affairs of the States. *Any single power, or even several powers combined, do not operate in a fashion as to invade or divest a State of its jurisdiction. As against a single State, the remainder of the States under the Constitution have no right to jurisdiction within the single State absent its consent.*

The only provision in the Constitution which permits jurisdiction to be vested in the United States is found in Article I, Section 8, Clause 17, which provides the mechanism for a voluntary cession of jurisdiction from any State to the United States. *When the Constitution was adopted, the United States had jurisdiction over no lands within the States*, possessing jurisdiction only in the lands encompassed in the Northern Territories. Shortly thereafter, Maryland and Virginia ceded jurisdiction to the United States for Washington, D.C. Cession progressed thereafter, the States at various times ceded jurisdiction to federal enclaves within the States. Today territorial jurisdiction of the United States is found only in those ceded areas, which encompass Washington, D.C., the federal enclaves within the States, and such territories and possessions which are now owned by the United States.

The above conclusion is not the mere opinion of the petitioner of this brief, but it is likewise the opinion of the United States government itself.

Chapter 12   341

In June 1957, the government of the United States published a work entitled *Jurisdiction Over Federal Property Within The States: Report of the Interdepartmental Commission on the Study of Jurisdiction Over Federal Areas Within the States, Part II*, which report is the definitive study on jurisdiction therein, the Committee stated:

> "The Constitution gives express recognition to but no means of Federal acquisition of legislative jurisdiction—by State consent under Article 1, section 8, clause 17....Justice McLean suggested that the Constitution provided the sole mode for transfer of jurisdiction, that if this mode is not pursued, no transfer of jurisdiction can take place." Id., at 41.
>
> "It scarccey needs to be said that unless there has been a transfer of jurisdiction (l) pursuant to clause 17, a Federal acquisition of land with State consent, only by cession from the State to the Federal Government, unless the Federal Government has reserved jurisdiction upon admission of the State, the Federal Government possesses no legislative jurisdiction over any lands within a State, such jurisdiction being for exercise of the State, subject to non-interference by the State in Federal functions," Id., at 45.
>
> "The Federal Government cannot, by unilateral action on its part, acquire legislative jurisdiction over any area within the exterior boundaries of a State," Id., at 46.
>
> "On the other hand, while the Federal Government has power under various provisions of the Constitution to define, and prohibit as criminal, certain acts or omissions *occurring anywhere in the United States*, it has no power to punish for various other crimes, jurisdiction over which is retained by the states under our

Federal State system of government, unless such crime occurs on areas as to which legislative jurisdiction has been vested in the Federal Government," Id., at 107.

Thus, from an abundance of case law, buttressed by this lengthy and definitive government treatise on this issue, the "jurisdiction of the United States" is carefully circumscribed and defined as a very precise portion of America. The United States is one of the 51 jurisdictions existing on this continent, excluding Canada and its provinces.

FEDERAL CRIMINAL JURISDICTION

It is a well established principle of law that all federal "legislation applies only within the *territorial jurisdiction of the United States* unless a contrary intent appears"; see *Caha vs. United States*, 152 U.S. 211, 215, 14 S. Ct. 513 (1894); *American Banana Company vs. United Fruit Company* 213 U.S. 347, 357, 29 S. Ct. 511 (1909); *United States vs. Bowman*, 260 U.S. 94, 97, 98, 43 S.Ct. 39 (1922); *Blackmer vs. United States*, 284 U.S. 421, 437, 52 S. Ct. 252 (1932); *Foley Bros. vs. Filardo*, 336 U.S. 281, 285, 69 S.Ct. 575 (1949); *United States vs. Spelar*, 338 U.S. 217, 222, 70 S. Ct. 10 (1949); and *United States vs. First National City Bank*, 321 F.2d 14, 23 (2nd Cir., 1963). And this principle of law is expressed in a 27 number of cases from the federal appellate courts; see *McKeel vs. Islamic Republic of Iran*, 722 F.2d 582, 589 (9th Cir., 1983) (holding the Foreign Sovereign Immunities Act as territorial); *Meredith vs. United States*, 330 F.2d 9, 11 (9th Cir., 1964) (holding the Federal Torts Claims Act as territorial); *United States vs. Cotroni*, 521 F.2d 708, 711 (2nd Cir., 1975) holding federal wiretap laws as territorial); *Stowe vs. Devoy*, 588 F.2d 336, 341 (2nd Cir., 1978); *Cleary vs. United States Lines Inc.*, 728 F.2d 607, 609 (3rd Cir., 1984) (holding federal age discrimination laws as territorial); *Thomas vs. Brown & Root. Inc.,* 745 F.2d 279, 281 (4th Cir., 1984) (holding same as Cleary, supra); *United States vs. Mitchell*, 553

F.2d 996, 1002 (5th Cir., 1977) (holding marine mammals protection act as territorial); *Pfeiffer vs. William Wrigley Jr. Co.*, 755 F.2d 554, 557 (7th Cir., 1985) (holding age discrimination laws as territorial); *Airline Stewards & Stewardesses Assn. vs. Northwest Airlines. Inc.*, 267 F.2d 170, 175 (8th Cir., 1959) (holding Railway Labor Act as territorial); *Zahourek vs. Arthur Young and Co.*, 750 F.2d 827, 829 (l0th Cir., 1984) (holding age discrimination laws as territorial); *Commodities Futures Trading Comm. vs. Nahas*, 738 F.2d 487, 493 (D.C. Cir., 1984) (holding commission's subpoena power under federal law as territorial); *Reves vs. Secretary of H.E.W.*, 476 F.2d 910, 915 (D.C. Cir., 1973) (holding administration of Social Security Act as territorial); and *Schoenbaum vs. Firstbrook*, 268 F. Supp. 385, 392 (S.D.N.Y., 1967) (*holding securities act as territorial*). But because of statutory language, certain federal drug laws operate extra-territorially; see *United States vs. King*, 55. F. 2d 833, 851 (9th Cir., 1976). The United States, meaning the Federal Government has territorial jurisdiction only in Washington, D.C., the federal enclaves within the States, and in the territories and insular possessions of the United States. *However, it has no territorial jurisdiction over non-federally owned areas inside the territorial jurisdiction of the States within the American Union. And this proposition of law is supported by literally hundreds of cases.*[3]

As a general rule, the power of the United States to criminally prosecute is, for the most part, confined to offenses committed within "its jurisdiction". This is born out simply by examination of Title 18, U.S.C. Section 5 thereof defining the

---

[3] Counsel has prepared a list containing the cites to and summaries of approximately 400 cases supportive of this proposition; its length, 90 pages, precludes incorporation herein.

[4] The statutory definition of "United States" as expressed in this section 5 is identical to the constitutional definition of this term; see *Cunard S. S. Co. vs. Mellon*, 22 U.S. 100, 43 S. Ct. 504 (1923), which deals with the definition of "United States" as used in the 18th Amendment. Section 802 (26) of the act in question likewise defines the "United States" in jurisdictional terms.

term "United States" in clear jurisdictional terms.[4] *Section 7 contains the fullest statutory definition of the "jurisdiction of the United States."* The U.S. District Courts have jurisdiction of offenses occurring within the "United States" pursuant to Title 18, U.S.C., section 3231.

Examples of this proposition are numerous. In *Pothier vs. Rodman*, 291 F. 311 (lst Cir., 1923), the question involved whether a murder committed at Camp Lewis Military Reservation of Washington was a federal crime. Here, the murder was committed more than a year before the U. S. acquired a deed for the property in question. Pothier was arrested and incarcerated in Rhode Island and filed a habeas corpus petition seeking his release on the grounds that the Federal courts had no jurisdiction over an offense not committed in U.S. jurisdiction. The First Circuit agreed that there was no federal jurisdiction and ordered his release. But, on appeal to the U.S. Supreme Court, in *Rodman vs. Pothier*, 264 U.S. 399, 44 S. Ct. 360 (1924), that Court reversed; although agreeing with the jurisdictional principles enunciated by the First Circuit, it held that only the federal court in Washington State could hear that issue. In *United States vs. Unzeuta*, 35 F.2d 750 (8th Cir, 1929), the Eighth Circuit held that the U.S. had no jurisdiction over a murder committed in a railroad car at Fort Robinson, the state cession statute being construed as not including railroad rights-of-way. This decision was reversed in *United States vs. Unzeuta*, 281 U.S. 138, So S.Ct. 284 (1930), the court holding that the U.S. did have jurisdiction over the railroad rights-of-way in Fort Robinson. In *Bowen vs. Johnson*, 97 F.2d 860 (9th Cir., 1938), the question presented was whether jurisdiction over an offense prosecuted in federal court could be raised in a petition for habeas corpus. The denial of Bowen's petition was reversed in *Bowen vs. Johnston*, 306 U.S. 19, 59 S.Ct. 442 (1939), the Court concluding that such a jurisdictional challenge could be raised in a habeas corpus petition. But, the Court then addressed the issue, found that the U.S. both owned the property in question and had a state legislative grant ceding jurisdiction to the United States, thus there was jurisdiction in the United States to prosecute

Bowen. But, if jurisdiction is not vested in the United States pursuant to statute, there is no jurisdiction; see *Adams vs. United States*, 319 U.S. 312, 63 S.Ct. 1122 (1943).

And the lower federal courts also require the presence of federal jurisdiction in criminal prosecutions. In *Kelly vs. United States*, 27 F. 616 (D. Me., 1885), federal jurisdiction of a manslaughter committed at Fort Popham was upheld when it was shown that the U.S. owned the property where the offense occurred and the state had ceded jurisdiction. In *United States vs. Andem*, 158 F. 996 (D.N.J., 1908), federal jurisdiction for a forgery offense was upheld on a showing that the United States owned the property where the offense was committed and the state had ceded jurisdiction of the property to the U.S. In *United States vs. Penn*, 48 F. 669 (E.D.Va., 1880), since the U.S. did not have jurisdiction over Arlington National Cemetery, a federal larceny prosecution was dismissed. In *United States vs. Lovely*, 319 F.2d 673 (4th Cir., 1963), federal jurisdiction was found to exist by U.S. ownership of the property and a state cession of jurisdiction. In United States vs. Watson, 80 F.Supp. 649 (E.D.Va., 1948), federal criminal charges were dismissed, the court stating as follows:

> "Without proof of the requisite ownership or possession of the United States, the crime has not been made out," 80 F.Supp., at 651.

In *Brown vs. United States*, 257 F. 46 (5th Cir., 1919), federal jurisdiction was upheld on the basis that the U.S. owned the post office site where a murder was committed and the state had ceded jurisdiction; see also *England vs. United States*, 174 F.2d 466 (5th Cir., 1949); *Krull vs. United States*, 240 F.2d 122 (5th Cir., 1957); *Hudspeth vs. United States*, 223 F.2d 848 (5th Cir., 1955); and *Gainey vs. United States*, 324 F.2d 731 (Sth Cir., 1963). In *United States vs. Townsend*, 474 F.2d 209 (5th Cir., 1973), a conviction for receiving stolen property was reversed when the court reviewed the record and learned that there was absolutely no evidence disclosing that the defendant had committed this offense within the jurisdiction of the United States. And in *United States vs. Benson*, 495 F.2d 475 (5th Cir., 1974), in finding federal jurisdiction for a robbery committed at Fort Rucer, the court stated:

> "It is axiomatic that the prosecution must always prove territorial jurisdiction over a crime in order to sustain a conviction therefor," 495 F.2d, at 481.

In two Sixth Circuit cases, *United States vs. Tucker*, 122 F. 518 (W.D. Ky., 1903), a case involving an assault committed at a federal dam, and *United States vs. Blunt*, 558 F.2d 1245 (6th Cir., 1977), a case involving an assault within a federal penitentiary, jurisdiction was sustained by finding that the U.S. owned the property in question and the state involved had ceded jurisdiction. In *In re Kelly*, 71 F. 545 (E.D.Wis., 1895), a federal assault charge was dismissed when the court held that the state cession statute in question was not adequate to convey jurisdiction of the property in question to the United States. In *United States vs. Johnson*, 426 F.2d 1112 (7th Cir., 1970), a case involving a federal burglary prosecution, federal jurisdiction was sustained upon the showing of U.S. ownership and cession. And cases from the Eighth and Tenth Circuits likewise require the same elements to be shown to demonstrate the presence of federal jurisdiction; see *United States vs. Heard*, 270 F.Supp. 198 (W.D.Mo., 1967); *United States vs. Redstone*, 488 F.2d 300 (8th Cir., 1973); *United States vs. Goings*, 504 F.2d 809 (8th Cir., 1974) (demonstrating loss of jurisdiction); *Hayes vs. United States*, 367 F.2d 216 (l0th Cir., 1966); *United States vs. Carter*, 430 F.2d 1278 (l0th Cir., 1970); *Hall vs. United States*, 404 F.2d 1367 (l0th Cir., 1969); and *United States vs. Cassidy*, 571 F.2d 534 (l0th Cir., 1978).

Of all the circuits, the Ninth Circuit has addressed jurisdictional issues more than any of the rest. In *United States vs. Bateman*, 34 F. 86 (N.D.Cal., 1888), it was determined that the United States did not have jurisdiction to prosecute for a murder committed at the Presidio because California had never ceded jurisdiction; see also *United States vs. Tully*, 140

F. 899 (D.Mon., 1905). But later, California ceded jurisdiction for the Presidio to the United States, and it was held in *United States vs. Watkins*, 22 F.2d 437 (N.D.Cal., 1927), that this enabled the U.S. to maintain a murder prosecution; see also *United State vs. Holt,* 168 F. 141 (W.D.Wash., 1909), *United States vs. Lewis*, 253 F. 469 (S.D.Cal, 1918), and *United States vs. Wurtzbarger*, 276 F. 753 (D.Or., 1921). Because the U.S. owned and had a state cession of jurisdiction for Fort Douglas in Utah, it was held that the U.S. had jurisdiction for a rape prosecution in *Rogers vs. Squier*, 157 F.2d 948 (9th Cir., 1946). But, without a cession, the U.S has no jurisdiction; see *Arizona vs. Manypenny*, 445 F.Supp. 1123 (D.Ariz., 1977).

The above cases from the U.S. Supreme Court and federal appellate courts set forth the rule that in criminal prosecutions, the government, as the party seeking to establish the existence of federal jurisdicton, must prove U.S. ownership of the property in question and a state cession of jurisdiction; this same rule manifests itself in state cases. State courts are courts of general jurisdiction and in a state criminal prosecution, the state must only prove that the offense was committed within the state and a county thereof. If a defendant contends that only the federal government has jurisdiction over the offense, he, as proponent for the existence of federal jurisdiction, must likewise prove U.S. ownership of the property where the crime was committed and state cession of jurisdiction.

Examples of the operation of this principle are numerous. In Arizona, the State has jurisdiction over federal lands in the public domain, the state not having ceded jurisdiction of that property to the U.S.; see *State vs. Dykes* 114 Ariz. 592, 562 P.2d 1090 (1977). In California, if it is not proved by a defendant in a state prosecution that the state has ceded jurisdiction, it is presumed the state does have jurisdiction over a criminal offense; see *People vs. Brown*, 69 Cal. App. 2d 602, 159 P.2d 686 (1945). If the cession exists, the state has no jurisdiction; see *People vs. Mouse,* 203 Cal. 782, 265 P. 944 (1928). In Montana, the state has jurisdiction over property if it is not proved there is a state cession of jurisdiction to the U.S.; see *State ex rel Parker vs. District Court*, 147 Mon. 151,

410 P.2d 459 (1966); the existence of a state cession of jurisdiction to the U.S. ousts the state of jurisdiction; see *State vs. Tully*, 31 Mont. 365, 78 P. 760 (1904). The same applies in Nevada; see *State vs Mack*, 23 Nev. 359, 47 P. 763 (1897), and *Pendleton vs. State*, 734 P.2d 693 (Nev., 1987); it applies in Oregon (see *State vs. Chin Ping*, 91 Or. 593, 176 P. 188 (1918) and *State vs. Aguilar*, 85 Or.App. 410, 736 P.2d 620 (1987)); and in Washington (see *State vs. Williams*, 23 Wash. App. 694, 598 P. 2d 731 (1979))

In *People vs. Hammond*, 1 Ill.2d 65, 115 N.E.2d 331 (1953), a burglary of an I.R.S. office was held to be within state jurisdiction, the court holding that the defendant was required to prove existence of federal jurisdiction by U.S. ownership of the property and state cession of jurisdiction. In two cases from Michigan, larcenies committed at a U.S. post office which were rented were held to be within state jurisdiction; see *People vs. Burke*, 161 Mich. 397, 126 N.W. 446 (1910) and *People vs. Van Dyke*, 276 Mich. 32, 267 N.W. 778 (1936); see also *In re Kelly*, 311 Mich. 596, 19 N.W.2d 218 (1945). In *Kansas City vs. Garner*, 430 S.W.2d 630 (Mo App 1968), state jurisdiction over a theft offense occurring in a federal building was upheld, and the court stated that a defendant had to show federal jurisdiction by proving U.S. ownership of the building and a cession of jurisdiction from the state to the United States. A similar holding was made for a theft at a U.S. missile site in *State vs. Rindall*, 146 Mon. 64, 404 P.2d 327 (1965). In *Pendleton vs. State*, 734 P.2d 693 (Nev., 1987), the state court was held to have jurisdiction over a D.U.I. committed on federal lands, the defendant having failed to show U.S. ownership and state cession of jurisdiction.

In *People vs. Gerald*, 40 Misc. 2d 819, 243 N.Y.S.2d 1001 (1963), the state was held to have jurisdiction of an assault at a U.S. post office since the defendant did not meet his burden of showing presence of federal jurisdiction; and because a defendant failed to prove title and jurisdiction in the United States for an offense committed at a customs station, state jurisdiction was upheld in *People vs. Fisher*, 97 A.D. 2d 651,

469 N.Y.S. 2d 187 (A.D. 3 Dept., 1983). The proper method of showing federal jurisdiction in state court is demonstrated by the decision in *People vs. Williams*, 136 Misc. 2d 294, 518 N.Y.S. 2d 751 (1987). This rule was likewise enunciated in *State vs. Burger*, 33 Ohio App. 3d 231, 515 N.E. 2d 640 (1986), in a case involving a D.U.I. offense committed on a road near a federal arsenal.

In *Kuerschner vs. State*, 493 P.2d 1402 (Okl. Cr. App., 1972), the state was held to have jurisdiction of a drug sales offense occurring at an Air Force Base, *the defendant not having attempted to prove federal jurisdiction* by showing title and jurisdiction of the property in question in the United States; see also *Towry vs. State*, 540 P. 2d 597 (Okl. Cr. App., 1975). Similar holdings for murders committed at U.S. post offices were made in *State vs. Chin Ping,* 91 Or. 593, 176 P.1 188 (1918), and in *United States vs. Pate*, 393 F.2d 44 (7th Cir., 1968). Another Oregon case, *State vs. Aquilar*, 85 Or. App. 410, 736 P.2d 620 (1987), demonstrated this rule. And finally, in *Curry vs. State*, 111 Tex. Cr. 264, 12 S.W. 2d 796 (1828), it was held that, in the absence of proof that the state had ceded jurisdiction of a place to the United States, the state courts had jurisdiction over an offense.

Therefore, in federal criminal prosecutions, the government must prove the existence of federal jurisdiction by showing U.S. ownership of the place where the crime was commited and a cession of jurisdiction. If the government contends for the power to criminally prosecute for an offense occurring outside "its jurisdiction", it must prove an extraterritorial application of the statute in question as well as a constitutional foundation supporting the same. Absent this showing, no federal prosecution can be commenced for offenses committed outside "its jurisdiction."

With the above limits of "federal jurisdiction" in mind, it is now necessary to consider the precise statutory language of the act in question to determine whether it applies solely within the jurisdiction of the United States. Analysis of the operative sections of the act, particularly the sections at issue herein, clearly reveals that there is nothing which indicates that the act applies anyhere but within U.S. jurisdiction; there simply is no statutory language expressly stating that the act applies "extrajurisdictionally". Further, the sections of this act at issue totally fail to mention or refer to "interstate commerce" or otherwise connect the provisions of this act to Congressional interstate commerce powers. This is particularly apparent from a review of section 841, which is similarly deficient. While section 841 mentions nothing in reference to "interstate commerce," it must be noted that in other criminal acts, Congress statutorily bases such acts upon its "interstate commerce" powers; see 18 U.S.C., sections 659, 660, 842, 844, 875, 922, 1231, 1301, 1343, 1365, 1761, 1951, 1952, 1953, 1962, 1992, 2101, 2251, 2312, 2314, 2316, 2317, 2421, 2422 and 2423. The only part of the act mentioning interstate commerce in any fashion is the preamble, section 801. Such being the case, it becomes necessary to determine whether this "preamble" may operate to expand the act itself to encompass interstate commerce.

THE INSIGNIFICANCE OF PREAMBLES

It is common for legislative acts to contain a part known as a "preamble", which is simply a clause inserted into a legislative enactment to explain the reasons for the adoption of any given act. Outside of demonstrating the legislature's motive in adopting a particular statute, the preamble has no other real purpose as it has been repeatedly held that the preamble is not a part of the law. A substantial body of case law demonstrates this rule of statutory construction.

Perhaps the most frequently cited case enunciating the rule that preambles are not a part of the law is *Yazoo & M.V.R. Co. vs. Thomas*, 132 U.S. 174, 10 S.Ct. 68 (1889). Here, the Mississippi legislature incorporated the railroad in question by a special act, which contained a preamble declaring that the railroad was a "work of great public importance", to "be encouraged by legislative sanction and liberality." The act provided that the railroad would be exempt from taxation for 20 years "from the completion of said railroad to the Mississippi River." However, other general laws of Mississippi taxed those parts of railroads in operation and generating a profit. Here, the Yazoo railroad began building its railroad and put the completed portions into operation before extending the line to the Mississippi River. Under other general laws of Mississippi, taxes were laid on the railroad for those portions which Yazoo was operating, but the company challenged the taxes as unlawful, asserting that it was exempt under its charter from such taxation. The company premised its argument on those parts of the preamble of the act chartering the corporation mentioned above and the part thereof which indicated that the Mississippi legislature wanted "to induce the investment of capital in the construction, maintenance and operation of such a railroad" by providing an exemption from taxation. Both the Mississippi Supreme Court and U.S. Supreme Court rejected this argument built upon the preamble, the latter Court stating:

> "But, as the preamble is no part of the act, and cannot enlarge or confer powers, nor control the words of the act, unless they are doubtful or ambiguous, the necessity of resorting to it to assist in ascertaining the true intent and meaning of the legislature is in itself fatal to the claim set up," 159 U.S., at 188.

Here, the Yazoo railroad's attempt to expand the meaning and interpretation of the statute by resorting to the preamble was held impermissible according to the above cited rule of construction.

In *State ex rel. Berry vs. Superior Court*, 92 Wash. 16, 159 P. 92 (1916), an extremely interesting problem regarding a preamble was before the Supreme Court of the State of Washington. Here, Washington law permitted legislative acts to be adopted via initiatives and referenda by the voters. The initiative in question here had a long and glorious preamble to justify the act in question, and opponents of the measure sought to have the court strike the preamble of the measure on the grounds that it had no legal effect and constituted nothing more than arguments in favor of the act. The Washington Supreme Court agreed and ordered that the preamble be struck from the initiative. The Court held:

> "Both in England and in this country it was at one time a common practice to prefix to each law a preface or preamble stating the motives and inducement to the making of it; but it is not an essential part of the statute, and is now generally omitted. It is not only not essential and generally omitted, but it is without force in a legislative sense, being but a guide to the intentions of the framer. As such guide, it is often of importance. In this sense it is said to be a key to open the understanding of a statute. The preamble is properly referred to when doubts or ambiguities arise upon the words of the enacting part. It can never enlarge. It is no part of the law....If it is no part of the law, proponents have no constitutional right to propose it as a law," 159 P., at 96.

A large number of state courts have likewise concluded that preambles are not a part of the law; see *Crisp vs. Head*, 187 Ga. 20, 199 S.E. 219 (1938). In *City of New Orleans vs. Administrators of Tulane Educational Fund*, 193 La. 297, 190 So. 560 (1939), a preamble was held incapable of limiting or controlling the application of a statute. In *State vs. Crane Hook Oil Storage Co.*, 41 Del. 194, 18 A.2d 427 (1941), and *State ex rel. Arn vs. Consumers Co-op. Assn.*, 163 Kan. 324, 183 P.2d 423 (1947), identical holdings were made. In *Reeves vs. Adam Hat Stores*, 303 Ky. 633, 198 S.W. 2d 789, 791 (1946), that court held that a "preamble is not generally considered as an essential part of a legislative act and cannot confer or enlarge its powers." Other cases holding similarly are *Sunshine Dairy vs. Peterson*, 13 Or. 305, 193 P. 2d 543 (1948); *Hammond vs. Frankfeld*, 194 Md. 487, 71 A.2d 482 (1950); *Thompson* vs. Wallin, 301 N.Y. 476, 95 N.E.2d 806 (1950); *May's Drug Stores vs. State Tax Comm.*, 242 Iowa 319, 45 N.W.2d 245 (1950); *Gibson vs. State*, 204 Md. 423, 104 A.2d 800 (1954); *National Can Corp. vs. State Tax Comm. of Maryland*, 220 Md. 418, 153 A.2d 287 (1959); *Jasper vs. Commonwealth*, 375 S.W.2d 709 (Ky. App., 1964); *James vs. Orange Savings & Loan Assn.*, 195 So.2d 183 (La. App., 1967); *Ederer vs. Board of Zoning Appeal,* 18 Ohio Misc. 143, 248 N.E.2d 234 (1969); *Chambers Lumber Co. vs. Martin,* 112 Ga. App. 826, 146 S.E.2d 529 (1965); *Idaho Comm. on Human Rights vs. Campbell*, 95 Idaho 215, 506 P.2d 112 (1973); *Hobbs vs. State*, 451 N.E.2d 356 (Ind.App., 1983); *Haven vs. County of Ogle*, 116 Ill.App.3d 80, 451 .E.2d 612 (1983); *Commercial Fisheries Entry Comm. vs. Apokedak*, 680 P.2d 486 (Alaska, 1984); and *PRB Enterprises. Inc. vs. South Brunswick Planning Board*, 205 N.J. Super. 225, 500 A.2d 732 (1985).

The federal courts follow the same rule. In *In re American States Public Service Co.*, 12 F.Supp. 667, 681 (D.Md., 1935), that District Court stated in regards to preambles:

> "It cannot enlarge or confer powers, or control the words employed in the provisions of the act itself."

And another District Court, in *In re Camden Shipbuilding Co.*, 227 F.Supp. 751, 7S3 (D.Me., 1964) held as follows:

> "First, where, as here, the language of a statute is plain and unambiguous, courts may not properly resort to the preamble of the act as an aid in its construction."

In *Hughes Tool Company vs. Meier*, 486 F. d 593 (10th cir., 1973), the issue before the court involved the application of the State of Utah's "long-arm" statute for service of process. The preamble of this act clearly indicated that the long-arm statute could only be invoked by state citizens to serve process on non-residents. Here, Hughes Tool Company was a Delaware chartered corporation having its principal office in Texas and was transacting business in Utah at the time of the accrual of its claim against others transacting business there who were also non-residents. Hughes Tool initiated suit and utilized Utah's long-arm statute to serve process. In response, the defendants attacked the use of the long-arm statute by Hughes Tool arguing that the statute itself, based upon the preamble, could only be used by citizens of Utah and not another non-resident. In rejecting this argument, the following was stated regarding the insignificance of the preamble:

> "It is, therefore, neither essential nor controlling in the construction of the Act where the operative sections are clear and unambiguous (cites omitted)," 486 F.2d 596.

Thus, the court held that the preamble of the act, which appeared to limit the use of the act only to state citizens, did not control the operation of the statute so that it could not be used by non-citizens.

The operation of this rule regarding the insignificance of preambles was considered in *Association of American Railroads vs. Costle*, 562 F.2d 1310 (D.C.Cir., 1977). Here, Congress adopted noise abatement legislation applicable to interstate rail carriers. The preamble of the act indicated a Congressional purpose to apply the act to "major noise sources", yet the act itself provided for a broader application to "the equipment and facilities of surface carriers engaged in interstate commerce by railroad." The act granted rule making authority to the Administrator of EPA who eventually formulated certain noise abatement rules applicable solely to locomotives and railcars and not to other "equipment and facilities." For reasons known only by the Railroad Association, the acts of the Administrator were challenged because he failed to promulgate regulations for all "equipment and facilities." The Administrator of EPA defended his position by arguing that the act, pursuant to the preamble, addressed itself only to "major noise sources" and this justified the limited regulations he had so promulgated. Following the rule that preambles are insignificant, the court rejected EPA's argument and stated:

> "The EPA argument based on the language in the preamble is based on an erroneous perception of the operation and significance of such language. A preamble no doubt contributes to a general understanding of a statute, but it is not an operative part of the statute and it does not enlarge or confer powers on administrative agencies or officers. Where the enacting or operative parts of a statute are unambiguous, the meaning of the statute cannot be controlled by language in the preamble. The operative provisions of statutes are those which prescribe rights and duties and otherwise declare the legislative will .... We find the reference to 'the equipment and facilities' in Section 17 (a)(1) to be unambiguous and, therefore, do not look to the preamble for guidance as to the legislative intent," 562 F.2d 1316.

In *National Wildlife Federation vs. Marsh*, 721 F.2d 767 (llth Cir., 1983), the facts involved compliance with statutes and regulations applicable to federally funded projects for local improvements. Here, efforts were being taken to construct a lake near the City of Alma, Georgia, with HUD funding. Objections to this project were based on an argument that it failed to "principally benefit" persons of low or moderate income, a goal stated in the preamble of the act in question. In addressing this point, the Court cast aside consideration of the preamble by stating:

> "It is clear from the face of the statute that no explicit principal benefit requirement is statutorily imposed. 'Principally benefiting' is explicitly made the primary goal of the statute,

not a requirement. Preambles to statutes do not impose substantive rights, duties or obligations," 721 F.2d at 773.

In *Jurgensen vs. Fairfax County Virginia*, 745 F. 2d 868 (4th Cir., 1984), reliance upon a preamble was also rejected as a grounds to construe the operation of a statute. In this case, an employee of a police department sued for what he contended was a civil rights violation committed in his demotion. Here, Jurgensen provided to reporter Bob Woodward of Watergate fame an internal report concerning the police department for which he worked. This act caused Jurgensen's demotion and he sued the county for violating his civil rights. He claimed that his act of disclosing the internal report concerning the department was lawful based upon the preamble of the Virginia Freedom of Information Act. In refusing to accept this particular argument, this court cited several of the above authorities and held:

> "This reasoning, based as it is on the language in the preamble, rests on what has been correctly described as 'an erroneous perception of the operation and significance of such language' .... If 'the operative sections [of a section] are clear and unambiguous,' the preamble of the statute is 'neither essential nor controlling in the construction of the Act'," 745 F.2d, at 885.

The rules which can be condensed from cases on the point dealing with preambles to legislative acts can be succinctly stated. First, the preamble itself is not the law or any part of the enactment in question, and is not necessary for an enactment. Secondly, it cannot serve to either limit or extend the operation of the act in question. Thirdly, it cannot confer or enlarge powers as expressed in the act. Finally, the only purpose of a preamble is to aid construction only in the event that the act in question is ambiguous.

By applying the above rules of statutory construction

regarding legislative preambles to the act in question, it becomes clear that the provisions thereof at issue herein, particularly section 841, have force only within the jurisdiction of the United States. Since, as a matter of law, section 801 cannot supply the "interstate commerce" foundation for the act itself, and since the provisions at issue are not themselves based on Congressional interstate commerce powers, the only place these provisions can apply is within U.S. jurisdiction.

The Preamble to the Constitution of the United States begins: "We, the people of the United States..." These words are referred to over and over by those who would make our Republic into a Democracy. "Consolidationists" from the beginning have, in vain, attempted to use these words in the Preamble to try to convince us the States are a consolidation into a single Union, and that the Federal government is the all-powerful head of a single, consolidated into one, Union.

Until the former Vice President, later Senator John Calhoun, educated him regarding this matter, even the brilliant Senator Daniel Webster had argued for a consolidated Union.

The motivation of those arguing consolidation was, or is, if the United States is a single consolidated mass, or a single body, then it is impossible for one or more states to leave the Union. Secession becomes unlawful. One part of a body cannot separate itself without the consent of the rest of the body. This was the basis for the position of Abraham Lincoln in saying States cannot secede from the Union.

As shown conclusively above by case law, Preambles are not law. They are like a table of contents of a book. We could eliminate the Preamble to the Constitution and it would not change in the slightest, the Constitution itself.

The United States is a Republic, not a Democracy. The Preamble, in spite of liberals, socialists, and one-worlders protesting, cannot be cited to change the United States into the democracy they would like us to become, nor can it be cited as evidence that the States are no longer sovereign, independent and free nations, except for the temporary and limited delegation of power they allow the Federal government to exercise in their behalf.

SUMMARY OF LIMITS OF CONGRESSIONAL POWERS

Most people do not perceive that Congress possesses legislative power derived from two places within the U.S. Constitution. All readily admit that Article I, Section 8 of the Constitution contains the delegated powers. But, another place which provides substantial legislative power for Congress is found in Article IV, section 3, clause 2 which provides that Congress can *enact needful rules and regulations to govern its territory and property.* Within "its territory", Congress possesses legislative power similar to that possessed by a State legislature within any State of the Union. But, how much power does Congress possess within the States of the Union? To answer this question, it is necessary to review a number of cases on this point.

The U.S. Supreme Court has on many occasions struck down acts of Congress which invaded State jurisdiction. In the License Tax Cases, 72 U.S. 462 (1866), the Supreme Court held that Congress could not authorize the conduct of business within the States in order to tax that business. In *United States vs. DeWitt*, 76 U.S. 41 (1870), the Court held that a certain penal regulation in a tax act could not be enforced in a state. In *United States vs. Fox*, 94 U.S. 315 (1877), the Court held that the United States could not receive property via a testamentary devise contrary to state law.

In *United States vs. Fox*, 95 U.S. 670 (1878), a penal statute remotely related to bankruptcy laws was held inapplicable in the States. In *Patterson vs. Kentucky*, 97 U.S. 501 (1879), the Court held that U.S. patent laws conferred no superior rights within the States. In *United States vs. Steffens*, 100 U.S. 82 (1879), federal trademark legislation unconnected with "interstate commerce" was held inapplicable inside the States. In *Baldwin vs. Franks*, 120 U.S. 678, 7 S.Ct. 656 (1887), certain penal, federal civil rights legislation was held unenforceable "within a state". In *Ex parte Burrus*, 136 U.S. 586, 10 S.Ct. 850 (1890), and *De La Rama vs. De La Rama*, 201 U.S. 303, 26 S.Ct. 485 (1906), the Court held that domestic relations matters were solely state concerns. In *Reagan vs. Mercantile Trust Co.*, 154 U.S. 413, 14 S.Ct. 1060 (1894), it was held that federally created corporations engaged in business in the States were subject to state laws. In *Keller vs. United States*, 213 U.S. 138, 29 S.Ct. 470 (1909), it was held that Congress could not exercise police powers within the States. In *Coyle vs. Smith*, 221 U.S. 559, 31 S.Ct. 688 (1911), it was held Congress could not dictate to a state where to locate its state capitol. In *Hammer vs. Dagenhart*, 247 U.S. 251, 38 S.Ct. 529 (1918), and *Bailey vs. Drexel Furniture Co.*, 259 U.S. 20, 42 S.Ct. 449 (1922), the Court held that Congressional attempts to regulate and control manufacturing activities in the States were unconstitutional; see also *Ill vs. Wallace*, 259 U.S. 44, 42 S.Ct. 453 (1922). In *United Mine Workers of America vs. Coronado Coal Co.*, 259 U.S. 344, 42 S.Ct. 570 (1922), the Court held that Congress could not regulate coal mining in the States. In *Linder vs. United States*, 268 U.S. 5, 45 S.Ct. 446 (1925), it was held that Congress could not regulate the practice of medicine in the States. In *Industrial Ass'n. of San Francisco vs. United States,* 268 U.S. 64, 45 S.Ct. 403 (1925), the construction industry was deemed to be inherently of local concern and beyond Congressional powers. In *Indian Motocycle Co. vs. United States*, 283 U.S. 570, 51 S.Ct. 601 (1931), the Court held that Congress could not impose a sales tax on items sold to state and local government. Before the advent of Social Security, a statutorily mandated retirement system applicable to interstate carriers was held unconstitutional in *Railroad Retirement Board vs. Alton R. Co.*, 295 U.S. 330, 55 S.Ct. 758 (1935). The case of *Hopkins Fed. S. & L. Ass'n. vs. Cleary*, 296 U.S. 315, 56 S.Ct. 235 (1935), stands for the proposition that Congress cannot *"federalize" state financial institutions over objection from the State*. The cases of *A.L.A. Schecter Poultry Corp. vs. United States*, 295 U.S. 495, 55 S.Ct. 837 (1935), *Panama Refining Co. vs. Ryan*, 293 U.S. 388, 55 S.Ct. 241 (1935), and *Carter vs. Carter Coal Co.*, 298 U.S. 238, 56 S.Ct. 855 (1936), emasculated most of the *National Industrial Recovery Acts* in part on the grounds of *invasion of reserved powers of the*

States. In *United States vs. Butler*, 297 U.S. 1, 56 S.Ct. 312 (1936), the Court held that Congress had no direct power to regulate agricultural production within the States. Finally, in *Oregon vs. Mitchell*, 400 U.S. 112, 91 S.Ct. 260 (1970), it was held that Congress could not dictate voter qualifications to the States.

Perhaps the greatest power of Congress to enact legislation applicable within the jurisdiction of the States is its power to control interstate commerce, and every lawyer and judge is familiar with the case precedence elucidating the breadth of this power. Before 1936, the Supreme Court construed Congressional control over "interstate commerce" in a highly limited fashion; see cases cited immediately above. But since the Great Depression, Congress has enacted legislation to expressly control activity *"affecting" interstate commerce*, and the Court has sanctioned such legislation and held it constitutional; see *Heart of Atlanta Motel, Inc. vs. United States*, 379 U.S. 241, 85 S.Ct. 348 (1964); and *Katzenbach vs. McClung*, 379 U.S. 294, 85 S.Ct. 377 (1964). But, insofar as the question raised herein is concerned, the question is not one dealing with the limits of "interstate commerce" powers of Congress, but how Congress bases its legislation upon this Constitutional power.

In *United States vs. Steffens*, 100 U.S. 82 (1879), the Supreme Court was required to determine the constitutionality of certain statutes proscribing fraudulent use of trademarks. Here, Congress had adopted certain legislation regarding trademark registration in 1870, and it supplemented that legislation in 1876 by an act making it penal to fraudulently use a registered trademark.[5] In this case, parties from New York and Ohio, indicted for alleged violations of this latter act, challenged the constitutionality of such legislation. The Court in its decision noted that Congress had no constitutional authority regarding trademarks and the protection of trade-

---

5. This legislation is an Act of August 14, 1876, 19 Stat. 141, ch. 274.

marks, such being the case, the act in question could have a constitutional foundation only if it was based on Congressional power over "interstate commerce." But the problem with the act in question arose from the fact that nothing in the act itself mentioned interstate commerce. Addressing this deficiency, the Court stated:

> "[T]here still remains a very large amount of commerce, perhaps the largest, which, being trade or traffic between citizens of the same State, is beyond the control of Congress.
>
> "When, therefore, Congress undertakes to enact a law, which can only be valid as a regulation of commerce, it is reasonable to expect to find on the face of the statute, or from its essential nature, that it is a regulation of commerce with foreign nations, among the several States, or with the Indian Tribes. If it is not so limited, it is in excess of the power of Congress. If its main purpose be to establish a regulation applicable to all trade, to commerce at all points, especially if it is apparent that it is designed to govern the commerce wholly between citizens of the same State, it is obviously the exercise of a power not confided to Congress," 100 U.S., at 96, 97.

Since this trademark law did not limit its operation to "interstate commerce," it was held unconstitutional.

A similar question was presented to the Court in *Illinois Central Railroad Company vs. McKendree,* 203 U.S. 514, 27 S.Ct. 153 (1906). Here, Congress adopted an act to suppress cattle diseases, and made the act applicable to cattle shipped in "interstate commerce"; the act also permitted the Secretary of Agriculture to implement regulations for enforcement of the Act. Pursuant to this authority, the Secretary promulgated a regulation which established a "quarantine district" in the southern portion of the continental U.S., and prohibited shipments of cattle from the quarantine district to points outside and north thereof. In this case, the railroad company shipped infected cattle from a part of the State of Tennessee in the quarantine district to a point in Kentucky outside the district. These cattle then infected other cattle, the owner of whom sued for damages. The railroad company's contention that the regulations were unconstitutional prevailed in the Supreme Court, where the Court stated:

> "We think the defendant was right in the contention that, if the act of February 2, 1903, was constitutional, and rightfully conferred the power upon the Secretary of Agriculture to make orders and regulations concerning interstate commerce, there was no power conferred upon the Secretary to make regulations concerning intrastate commerce, over which Congress has no control," 203 U.S., at 527.
>
> "The terms of order 107 apply to all cattle transported from the south of this line to parts of the United States north thereof. It would, therefore, include cattle transported within the state of Tennesee from the south of the line as well as those from outside that state; there is no exception in the order, and in terms it includes all cattle transported from the south of the line, whether within or without the state of Tennessee .... But the order in terms applies alike to interstate and intrastate commerce," 203 U.S., at 528.

It was because the regulation in question was not limited to interstate commerce and was broader than such and encompassed intrastate commerce that it was found unconstitutional.

In *Howard vs. Illinois Central Railroad Company*, 207 U.S. 463, 28 S.Ct. 141 (1908), the Supreme Court found unconstitutional a Congressional act which regulated both intrastate and interstate commerce. Here, Congress adopted legislation ("Employers' Liability Act") which denied the defense of contributory negligence in tort actions by employees against employers who were common carriers in "interstate commerce." In this wrongful death action, the railroad challenged the constitutionality of the act, arguing that its scope covered both intrastate and interstate commerce in that it attached liability to interstate carriers regardless of whether the employee concerned or the accident in question were similarly involved in interstate commerce. In holding this act unconstitutional, the Court held:

> "The act, then, being addressed to all common carriers engaged in interstate commerce, and imposing a liability upon them in favor of any of their employees, without qualification or restriction as to the business in which the carriers or their employees may be engaged at the time of the injury, of necessity includes subjects wholly outside of the power of Congress to regulate commerce," 207 U.S., at 498.
>
> "As the act thus includes many subjects wholly beyond the power to regulate commerce, and depends for its sanction upon that authority, it results that the act is repugnant to the Constitution," 207 U.S., at 499.

The case of *Hill vs. Wallace*, 259 U.S. 44, 42 S.Ct. 453 (1922), is very similar to *United States vs. Steffens*, supra, in that the act in question was also devoid of an "interstate commerce" foundation. Here, Congress enacted legislation to tax certain transactions involving futures contracts and to regulate boards of trade, but the act contained nothing within it basing the act on Congressional interstate commerce powers. Members of the Board of Trade of Chicago challenged the constitutionality of this act, arguing that Congress had no innate authority of its own to regulate boards of trade and that the only power of Congress to enact such legislation would be its interstate commerce powers with which this act was totally unconnected. The Supreme Court agreed and held the act unconstitutional.

The lesson of the above cases is clear. *United States vs. Steffens* and *Hill vs. Wallace*, supra, stand for the proposition that if Congressional legislation can be valid only under the power of Congress to regulate interstate commerce, the statute itself must express its relationship to interstate commerce; in the absence of such statutory expression, the act is not one based on Congressional interstate commerce powers. The cases of *Illinois Central Railroad Company vs. McKendree* and *Howard vs. Illinois Central Railroad Company*, supra, demonstrate that certain acts statutorily connected to "interstate commerce" can be unconstitutional if they are overbroad and encompass both intrastate and interstate commerce.

The act in question cannot be based on Congressional interstate commerce powers for the above reasons. First, no section thereof contains the words "interstate commerce" or words of similar meaning; from the face of these statutes, there is no statutory expression that any of them are related to "interstate commerce." Secondly, assuming that the preamble can legally supply the "interstate commerce" foundation for these sections, still these sections would cover all drug transactions, whether such transactions were involved in "interstate commerce, whether such transactions "affected" interstate commerce, whether such transactions were within the "de minimis" rule, or whether the transactions were not within the "de minimis" rule and were purely intrastate. Thus, being overly broad, if this act is indeed connected to "interstate commerce," it is unconstitutional on the basis of being overly broad and encompassing acts beyond the power of Congress to control.

All will readily admit that Congress can adopt legislation to regulate and control "interstate commerce" and all which "affects" interstate commerce. But, it is equally true that there is a boundary or limit to Congressional power to regulate those activities which "affect interstate commerce." Simply stated, acts "affecting interstate commerce" do not include all human activity, and there is a sizeable amount of human activity which is neither "interstate commerce" or acts "affecting" interstate commerce. It is the "de minimis" rule which describes and defines the outer boundary of the power of Congress to regulate activities "affecting interstate commerce." To fall within this rule, an act must have some minimal effect on interstate commerce. An act which does not minimally affect interstate commerce is outside the scope of this Congressional power.

There exists a line of cases clearly demonstrating just some of the acts which are beyond and outside the "de minimis" rule. In *United States vs. Critchley,* 353 F.2d 358 (3rd Cir., 1965), a union official was indicted for a Hobbs Act violation, the facts being based upon the defendant making a complaint against a roofing company for the sole purpose of soliciting a bribe. His conviction was reversed on the grounds that this act was not one which affected interstate commerce, and there was no other evidence offered to show an interference or obstruction of interstate commerce. In *Houchin vs. Thompson*, 438 F.2d 927 (6th Cir., 1970), at issue was whether certain workers in a commercial office building were covered by the provisions of the Fair Labor Standards Act. The court found that these workers were not engaged in activities "affecting interstate commerce", so they were not covered by the act. Regarding the "de minimis" rule, the Court stated:

> "Where some inconsequential incident of interstate commerce happens to result from the general conduct of a fundamentally intrastate business, the rule of de minimis is applicable and the Act does not apply," 438 F.2d, at 928, 929.

In *National Labor Relations Board vs. Clark*, 468 F.2d 459 (5th Cir., 1972), an attempt was being made to subject a nursing home in Alabama to federal labor laws. Here, the only nexus of the home to "interstate commerce" was a $1,700 purchase of supplies from a company whose main office was in Atlanta, Georgia; but, it was not shown how these supplies were shipped to the nursing home. Regarding the "de minimis" rule, the Court stated:

> "In passing the National Labor Relations Act, Congress intended to provide the Board with the fullest jurisdictional power constitutionally permissible under the Commerce Clause .... If intrastate activity has more than a de minimis effect on interstate commerce, it affects commerce within the meaning of the Act," 468 F.2d, at 466.

The Court concluded here that there was no evidence showing that the home's activities affected interstate commerce.

In *United States vs. Merolla*, 523 F.2d 51 (2nd Cir., 1975), a conviction under the Hobbs Act was reversed upon showing that the underlying facts of the case demonstrated no "effect" upon interstate commerce. The defendant in this case had contracted with the victim to build a car showroom for an automobile dealership, but when work on the showroom was jeopardized, the defendant beat the victim and extorted money and property from him. Nonetheless, under the facts of this case, the Court held that there was not a sufficient jurisdictional nexus in the facts to support a Hobbs Act conviction.

In *United States vs. Elders*, 569 F.2d 1020 (7th Cir., 1978), Elders' conviction under the Hobbs Act was reversed also on the basis that the facts involved in the case showed no "de minimis" connection to interstate commerce. In essence, Elders, an employee of a municipality, sought and obtained a series of "kickbacks" or bribes from a tree trimming company engaged in work for the city. In its opinion, the Court summarized the requirements for a federal interstate commerce prosecution as follows:

> "In each case, however, a nexus has been

required between the extortionate conduct and interstate commerce in order to establish federal jurisdiction. That nexus may be de minimis ... but it must nonetheless exist," 569 F.2d, at 1023, 1024.

A federal indictment was dismissed in *United States vs. Mennuti*, 639 F.2d 107 (2nd Cir., 1981), on the grounds that the conduct of the defendants' in the case had no "de minimis" effect on interstate commerce; the facts involved the bombing of a residential home. In another attempted bombing case, convictions were reversed on the grounds that the events of which the government complained had no minimal connection to interstate commerce; see *United States vs. Monholland*, 607 F.2d 1311 (10th Cir., 1979). And in *United States vs. Voss*, 787 F.2d 393 (8th Cir., 1986), it was held that an attempted arson of a home, even though potentially held for commercial activity, involved no "de minimis" connection with interstate commerce; see also *Gramercy 222 Residents Corp. vs. Gramercy Realty Assoc.*, 591 F.Supp. 1408 (S.D.N.Y., 1984).

The sum and substance of the above cases is that the maximum constitutional reach of Congressional interstate commerce powers extends to regulating activities "affecting interstate commerce." The above cases are just a few instances of conduct and acts which do not affect interstate commerce, and are therefore beyond congressional power. And there are many more countless acts encountered in everyday life which are obviously beyond the control of Congress under the Commerce Clause. Congressional attempts to control these manifold acts outside this power would be unconstitutional.

If the preamble to this drug act is relied upon to provide the "interstate commerce" foundation for its provisions, a serious constitutional problem is immediately evident. The preamble's finding is that all drug transactions affect interstate commerce, regardless of the "de minimis" connection of any particular transaction to interstate commerce. The fallacy of the preamble consists in the fact that it arbitrarily and unconstitutionally applies to all such transactions, thus encompassing those being purely intrastate and beyond the de minimis" rule. This analysis leads to the logical conclusion that, if the preamble provides the constitutional foundation for this act, then the act is unconstitutional.

When necessary, courts are required to construe Congressional enactments in a fashion so that they are constitutional. The only way that the provisions of this act can survive all constitutional challenges is to hold that it has force and application only within the jurisdiction of the United States.

SUMMARY

It is one thing for Congress to intend to do something in a legislative enactment, and it is quite another for it to express that intent in the act itself.[6] If Congress fails to manifest its intent in plain, statutory language; if it fails to clothe that intent with statutory garments, then its intent means precious little and cannot control clear statutory language.

Review of the Drug Abuse Prevention and Control Act from section 802 to the end of the act clearly reveals that no provision thereof is based on Congressional interstate com-

---

6. In *Smietanka vs. First Trust & Savings Bank*, 257 U.S. 602, 42 S. Ct. 223 (1922), at issue was whether the income of a trust having unborn beneficiaries was taxable and the trustee thereof was required to file an income tax return for the trust. Although there was evidence in this respect regarding the intent of Congress, the statute itself failed to manifest this intention. The Court held:

> "It may be that Congress had a general intention to tax all incomes whether for the benefit of persons living or unborn, but a general intention of this kind must be carried into language which can be reasonably construed to effect it. Otherwise the intention cannot be enforced by the courts. *The provisions of such acts are not to be extended by implication,*" 257 U.S., at 606.

merce powers. Such being the case, it is clear that, standing alone, these provisions could only apply within the jurisdiction of the United States, in its narrow definition. It is only by considering section 801 that an argument could be made that this act embodies the exercise by Congress of its control over interstate commerce. But, section 801 merely states facts constituting "truisms" that drug traffic is indeed in interstate commerce; but it fails to expressly state that the provisions of the act itself are based on these powers. Further, the provisions of sections 802, et seq., are clear and unambiguous; by themselves, they apply only within "its jurisdiction." Consideration of section 801 only creates ambiguity; does it mean that Congress is only exercising control over interstate commerce which occurs within the jurisdiction of the United States? *Why is the definition of "United States" in section 802 (26) a jurisdictional definition?*

By considering the inherent limitations on the powers of Congress, the case law dealing with the "jurisdiction of the United States," the law regarding "preambles", the rules of statutory construction and the language of the act itself, it is clear that this act only applies to that drug traffic which occurs within the jurisdiction of the United States. It has no application to events which occur within the jurisdiction of any one of the 50 States.

It is our hope that this outstanding brief and citation of case law clearly defining the extremely limited jurisdiction of the Federal agent, or the Federal United States, will inspire many criminal defense attorneys to make lack of Federal jurisdiction their first line of defense.

For example, it seems the conviction of the two police officers in the Los Angeles "Rodney King" trial, might be overturned on appeal. First, because there was no Federal jurisdiction; second, because the secondal under which the conviction was attained, was a violation of all four police officers double jeopardy protections under the Fifth Amendment which says;...nor shall any person be subject for the same offence (sic) to be twice put in jeopardy of life or limb." Unnecessary police force, or police brutality on any citizen, black white, or any other color, cannot be tolerated, but the second trial of these four white policemen was Federal grandstanding to appease many in the black community, along with many white politicians who care only about the black vote; whose compassion is feigned and who couldn't care less about real human rights. The same applies to most of the feigned compassion of the media corps. There is big money in violence and brutality stories.

If David Koresh and his followers who burned to death in Waco, Texas were abusing children, or violating gun laws, which is doubtful, considering we all have a Constitutional right to keep and bear arsm, for self-protection, as well as for protection against tyrannical government; if Koresh was violating law, Texas is big enough to handle its own law enforcement without the interference of Federal agents. How did Federal agents and the attorney general of the United States get jurisdiction at Waco, Texas?

Was Waco, Texas just another planned and drawn out Federal/liberal/media scam in the continuing and never-ending war to get Americans to give up their guns?

How about the Los Angeles riots after the first "Rodney King" acquittal of the four policemen? Was this another planned demonstration to convince Americans "we've got to do something about guns?

And the assault by hundreds of Federal Marshalls and other agents against the Randy Weaver Family in Northern Idaho in the Summer of 1992; where they shot a mother with babe in arms and a teenage son and his dog? In this case why did the liberal Democrat governor of Idaho, Cecil Andrus invite Federal troops into Idaho? Is Idaho law enforcement so weak, it dare not attempt the arrest of a single man who alledgedly had committed a minor gun law violation? Did the governor really need the assistance of Federal agents with helicopters and heavy military hardware? Perhaps Idaho is strapped for tax dollars and the governor wished to save Idaho taxpayers money by allowing taxpayers nationwide to pay the tab.

Which religious group, family, or "cult" is next on the list?

Which of us is the next Federal target?

When Adolph Hitler came to power in Germany, the German people, perhaps, grumbled a little, but they nevertheless allowed Hitler and his "Brown Shirts" to gradually increase the tempo of terror and tyranny against individuals and small groups, until nobody dared to oppose him. Are these recent assaults on American citizens by our own government, the beginning of a nazi Germany-like tyranny in the United States? In Northern Idaho and Waco, Texas, are the assaults of the Bureau of Alcohol, Tobacco and Firearms (BATF) akin to Hitler's initial advances against the people in Germany when he was "testing the water" to see how far the German people would allow him to go?

Is our Federal government "testing the water," and sending up "trial balloons" to see how much we will allow them to abuse us? Are they testing to see if they can totally ignore the Constitution with an eye to soon scrapping it altogether?

Will more Wacos be allowed by states other than Texas, Idaho and California? In the "land of the free" Americans are intimidated and fearful of anything Federal. Even the State Legislatures and governors! Are there any men of courage left who dare to stand and say **"No More"**?

If there are none holding elective office now, who dare challenge Federal monster, we better start electing men of courage, integrity, knowledge and understanding, before the opportunity to do so is taken from us.

Today we stand idly by because we are not personally affected while the Federal government attacks and pesecutes "cults" and "white supremacists," or "skin heads;" or people who have "too many" guns which they "might" convert to automatic weapons; or people who wish to home school their children to keep them out of morally corrupt and drug infested and violent public schools. Tomorrow, as with Hitler, it is going to be you and me. Tomorrow, when the monster gets a little bolder, the practicing Christian, of whatever denomination, will be the targets of terror, burning and looting.

Chapter 13

Model Ultimatum Resolution to dissolve the Union. Resolution of secession.

New York became the 11th State to adopt the Constitution and join the new Union of States July 25, 1788. Many of our Fathers "kept their fingers crossed" until Virginia and New York joined the new Confederation of Nations for they were two of the largest and most powerful, and without them some felt the new Union might not survive very long.

Alexander Hamilton, John Jay and James Madison wrote 85 essays we now know as The Federalist Papers, largely to convince the people of New York to ratify the Constitution and join the *new revolution* against the Articles of Confederation.

Ten Nations had already revolted and seceded from the government under the Articles.

Even after months of this writing and great debate among the people and the politicians, the delegation of New York Representatives barely agreed to adopt the Constitution and abandon the Articles of Confederation by a vote of 30 yeas, and 27 nays. Those voting not to join, and even some of those voting yea, were apprehensive about giving the Federal government too much power. They feared exactly what we have been experiencing in America since the 1930's beginning with The New Deal under President Franklin Delano Roosevelt. They feared Federal usurpations of undelegated powers such as took place in the administration of President Abraham Lincoln during the Civil War, and from time to time ever since.

Alexander Hamilton was a brilliant man, and even though many of us who revere the Constitution look on Hamilton as a scoundrel in some ways, nevertheless, we must give him much credit for his help in convincing his countrymen to adopt the Constitution and give the proposed "new experiment in government" a fair try.

In the New York debates, one of Hamilton's arguments went like this. He said: "Sir, the most powerful obstacle to the members of Congress betraying the interest of their constituents, is the State Legislatures themselves, who will be standing bodies of observation, possessing the confidence of the people, jealous of Federal encroachments, and armed with every power to check the first essays of treachery. They will institute regular modes of inquiry. The complicated domestic attachments which subsist between the State Legislators and their electors, will ever make them vigilant guardians of the people's rights. Possessed of the means and the disposition of resistance, the spirit of opposition will be easily communicated to the people, and under the conduct of an organized body of leaders, will act with weight and system. Thus it appears, that the *very structure of the Confederacy* affords the surest preventions from error, and the most powerful checks to misconduct."

In Federalist No. 28, Hamilton shows the great confidence he and others of our Fathers had in the State governments in keeping their new Frankenstein Monster under control. He assured his countrymen: "It may safely be received as an axiom in our political system that the State governments will, in all possible contingencies, afford complete security against invasions of the public liberty by the national authority. Projects of usurpation cannot be masked under pretenses so likely to escape the penetration of select bodies of men, as of the people at large. The legislatures will have better means of information. They can discover the danger at a distance; and possessing all the organs of civil power and the confidence of the people, they can at once adopt a regular plan of opposition, in which they can combine all the resources of the community. They can readily communicate with each other in the different States, and unite their common forces for the protection of their common liberty."

Yes sir, Mr. Hamilton! Right on! That is exactly what we hope to accomplish in writing this book. The State Legislatures can, and must, put the boys in Washington on notice that their fun and games with the liberties and resources of *the states* and *the people* is *over*. That 38 of these States have taken all the abuse, double-talk and triple-speak, usurpation and intimidation, we are going to take, and that very shortly, we are going to *fire the whole rotten bunch* and *dissolve the Union* if they don't get it together. What Principal ever puts up with a rotten and corrupt Agent who is continually conspiring to become master and superior to his master who created him? Only fools and illiterate or ignorant Principals would allow the Washington masquerade to continue as our generation has done.

But we cannot entirely blame ignorant State Legislatures and an ignorant generation. Tyrants have had almost 6,000 years of practice in attempting to gain control of the entire planet. Only in our day has all this experience and learning given modern Pharaohs and Caesars the ability to "gain the whole world, yet lose their own souls," as Jesus Christ seemed to prophesy. Holy Bible, Matthew 16:26.

In a previous writing., Hamilton said: "...the State legislatures, who will always be not only vigilant but suspicious and jealous guardians of the rights of the citizens against encroachments from the federal government, will constantly have their attention awakened to the conduct of the national rulers and will be ready enough, if anything improper appears, to sound the alarm to the people, and not only to be the *voice*, but, if necessary, the *arm* of their discontent." Federalist No. 26.

Mr. Fisher Ames expressed the same sentiment as Hamilton

in the debates of the Massachusetts Convention. He said: "Too much provision cannot be made against a consolidation. The state governments represent the wishes, and feelings, and local interests of the people. They are the safeguard and ornament of the Constitution; they will protract the period of our liberties; they will afford a shelter against the abuse of power, and will be the natural avengers of our violated rights." Elliot's Debates 2:46.

James Madison had this to say: "I may say, with truth, that there never was a more economical government in any age or country, nor which will require fewer hands or give less influence...From the chief officers to the lowest, we shall find the scale preponderating so much in favor of the states, that, while so many persons are attached to them, it will be impossible to turn the balance against them. There will be an irresistible bias towards the state governments." Ibid 3:258-59.

Mr. Increase Sumner joined Mr. Ames in the Massachusetts debates: "But some gentlemen object further, and say the delegation of these great powers will destroy the state legislatures; but I trust this never can take place, for the general government depends on the state legislatures for its very existence." Ibid 2:63

Again, Mr. Hamilton in comparing powers to be retained by the States and those to be delegated to the Federal agent. "If we compare the nature of their different powers, or the means of popular influence which each possesses, we shall find the advantage entirely on the side of the states...The aggregate number of representatives through the states may be two thousand. (In 1993 the total number of Legislators of the 50 States is over 7,400). The personal influence will, therefore, be proportionately more extensive than that of one or two hundred men in Congress. (In 1993 it is 535; 100 in the Senate and 435 in The House of Representatives). The state establishments of civil and military officers of every description, infinitely surpassing in number any possible correspondent establishments in the general government, will create such an extent and complication of attachments, as will ever secure the predilection and support of the people. Whenever, therefore, Congress shall meditate any infringement of the state constitutions, the great body of the people will naturally take part with their domestic representatives. Can the general government withstand such a united opposition? Will the people suffer themselves to be stripped of their privileges? Will they suffer their legislatures to be reduced to a shadow and name? The idea is shocking to common sense." Ibid 304.

Yes, Mr. Hamilton, sir! If you could only have forseen this day of your great grandchildren, you and the rest of our Fathers would be more than shocked if you could see how these "bastions of liberty," the State Legislatures, are turned into cowards, toads and bootlicks; mere messenger boys, many of which are as corrupt as their Federal agents in Washington. Nevertheless, your words give us renewed hope that even if we can discover only a few hundred honest and patriotic State Legislators, we might yet get our Washington agent under control when we point out to them what great confidence you and the other Fathers placed in them for the safe-guarding of our liberties. And when we remind them of the tremendous power they have to get rid of and fire the bulliesof Washington.

Mr. Hamilton: "The people have an obvious and powerful protection in their state governments. Should anything dangerous be attempted, these bodies of perpetual observation will be capable of forming and conducting plans of regular opposition. Can we suppose the people's love of liberty will not, under the incitement of their legislative leaders, be roused into resistance, and the madness of tyranny be extinguished at a blow?" Ibid 2:253.

One last word from Mr. Hamilton. These words are on a different but related subject. "There is no position which depends on clearer principles than that every act of a delegated authority, contrary to the tenor of the commission under which it is exercised, is void. No legislative act, therefore, contrary to the Constitution, can be valid. To deny this would be to affirm that the deputy is greater than his principal; that the servant is above his master; that the representatives of the people are superior to the people themselves; that men acting by virtue of powers may do, not only what their powers do not authorize, but what they forbid." Federalist Papers, 78.

These are great self-evident truths. But that which Hamilton imagined to be impossible is happening in America today. Only by acting through the Legislatures of each of our States, can we the people put our national government's house in order. We the people have all the power legally, and in theory, but we can most effectively act through the legislatures.

We the people do not wish to willy nilly take up arms and head for the hills or worse yet, organize small bands and begin resisting by force of arms. That's the way to die or permanently be put away in prison. It may come to that in the end of our once great Republic, but we have not even begun to exhaust our legal remedies by getting our elected representatives in the State legislatures to act to preserve law and order and the Constitution. After we give our State Representatives an opportunity to take on the Federal government, or go to work to elect the right Representatives who *will*, there should be no need for the radical action of bloodshed. If all else fails, yes, then bloodshed may become necessary, for as Winston Churchill noted, "it is better to perish than live as slaves." But a moral and god-fearing people will only resort to bloodshed when all other remedies have proven to be futile.

The American people have not even tried to apply the proper remedy because they are ignorant of our history and the structure of our State and Federal governments, and this ignorance, of course, is by design of those who would enslave us.

With all the brilliance of our Founding Fathers, they failed to see our day, when Congress, through the *power of the purse*, and using our nation's own credit against us, would intimidate and control the legislatures of the States. They failed to see our day when our State legislators, governors, and attorneys general, would remain so ignorant of the very structure of our government that they would allow Congress to nearly destroy the Constitution; that they would let Congress spend this nation into bankruptcy and run up a debt so gigantic that generations to come, to infinity, will not be able to pay it.

Ladies and gentlemen; my fellow Americans; the time has arrived when the governors and legislatures of at least 38 States, must surely exert all the sovereignty which is, and always has been, held by each of the 50 States. It is time to solemnly analyze State relationship to, and beneflts of, maintaining the Federal structure. It is time to ask ourselves, is the Federal government worth its cost, both economically and in lost freedoms, both to individuals and to the agent States? It is time to question why the States created the Federal government in the first place. Was not the Federal government created essentially for purposes of national defense and to regulate commerce between the States?

Hamilton stated the proposition succintly: "The principal purposes to be answered by union are these—the common defense of the members; the preservation of the public peace, as well against internal convulsions as external attacks; the regulation of commerce with other nations and between the States; the superintendence of our intercourse, political and commercial, with foreign countries." Federalist Papers, No. 23.

Ladies and gentlemen of the 50 State legislatures, we ask you, isn't our common agent, the Federal government, far more the tyrant than the servant? Do any of us really believe the Federal government any more; do we really believe our new President, Bill Clinton, will have any impact, or even has any intent or desire, in getting the Federal deficit under control? Is it not plain that the Constitution is hanging by a thread? That Washington, rather than honoring and sustaining the Constitution, is destroying it? Is it not time you ladies and gentlemen of the State legislatures admit, "the emperor is wearing no clothes" and get America back to her Godly Heritage and put Washington in its place?

How many of us as individuals having appointed an agent for some specific purpose, or having given power of attorney to somebody to act in our behalf, would tolerate such an agent not only representing us poorly, but in fact, actively working to use our own authority to either destroy or bankrupt us? Our agent, Washington, has nearly bankrupted us with admitted debt of some 4.2 trillion dollars, and perhaps, four or more times that amount in unfunded future obligations, with no end in sight. Would we allow, personally, an agent to borrow not only against every asset we own, but against all probable future assets of ourselves, our children and our grandchildren to infinity? Yet we are allowing our mere agent to do this to our children.

The Founders of America were fearful that what is happening to America, would, in fact, one day overtake their best efforts at preserving liberty for themselves and for us.

In preparation for that day when the nature of man would again threaten the destruction of liberty, they gave us tools by which we might, without bloodshed, reclaim liberty in its full flower. Hamilton thought the State legislatures were one of the main tools, and so they are. But they must be awakened and reminded of who they are. They must be reminded they are the *Principals*, that Washington is only an *Agent*, and even at that, an artificial agent little different than a private or public corporation which can be dissolved at the whim of a majority of the stockholders.

Unlike a corporation, we all have agreed under Article V of the Constitution, that by a vote of three-fourths, we can dissolve the Federal Charter. Under corporate law or if we were to accept and adopt the common assumption that we are a Democracy, a mere majority could dissolve the Union. But we are a Republic, not a Democracy; a government of laws, not a government of the whims of men. So lawfully, it will take three-fourths of the States acting together to dissolve the Federal "corporation," though we need not rely on Article V to do so. We must rely on the precedent of New Hampshire, June 21, 1788, and inherent rights of principals.

We do not advocate dissolution of the Union, if it can possibly be avoided. But it will be wise, indeed, to prepare ahead of time, and give an ultimatum to Washington that unless it straightens out its act, we will in fact, not only seriously consider such a radical proposal, we will actually carry it out.

Publicity and national recognition that the States actually have such power, will have a very sobering effect on the entire Federal establishment. Most will be astonished that such a proposal is lawfully possible. If a few States actually start working toward dissolving the Union, this will give 535 Congressmen, nine Supreme Court justices, and one President some powerful incentive to shape up and straighten out the mess they have created in this country.

If we can't get 38 States to act together, perhaps one or more of the better managed states will have to act alone and begin withdrawing from the Union one by one. If America is determined to spend herself into chaos and economic slavery, it is wisdom for a minority of States to abandon a sinking ship and save freedom and opportunity within the borders of indivldual states.

The following **model Ultimatum Resolution** is only a suggested form. The only essential ingredients on which 38 States should agree are the precise items which will trigger automatically, the dissolution of the Federal Union. One of the main items is the arbitrary figure chosen by the author of a national debt reaching $6,000,000,000,000, perhaps some four years away. But that figure might be more, or less, depending on the collective wisdom of the State legislatures.

Items other than those specified by the author might be included as triggers to dissolution. Leaders in each State will, of course, consult beforehand, so that all 38 States agree on what will, or will not, trigger a dissolution of the Union.

Introduction to the Model Ultimatum Resolution

The proposed Ultimatum Resolution which follows is a document for not only consideration, but, we believe, urgent action by the legislatures of at least 38 of the 50 states comprising the United States. "Congress, you will honor and obey the Constitution or we will withdraw our authority for you to act as our agent."

In essence, our federal government is the agent of all state governments. The states are the creator and the federal government is the creature. It is axiomatic, or self evident, that the creature cannot exceed the creator. The agent cannot exceed the authority granted by its principal. Any attempt to do so is "ultra vires," or without authority, and a usurpation of power.

Thus, if the federal government no longer obeys the will of the states, and is continually in violatlon of the contract of agency, each state is free to withdraw its support of the federal government and select, or create, another agent to carry out the collective will of the states.

During 1993, the model Ultimatum Resolution will be mailed to every legislator in each of the 50 states, to each of the 50 governors and the 50 attorneys general, to each member of Congress, to each of the nine supreme court justices and to the President, William Jefferson Clinton, and selected news media.

The current national debt is about 4.2 trillion dollars and we are adding to this at the rate of some 300 billion a year, which will probably under the administration of President Clinton, escalate to 400 and 500 billion dollars annually. We might anticipate we have some four years before the debt will hit the arbitrary six-trillion-dollar figure in the Resolution, at which point the Union would be dissolved should this plan be successful.

There are several reasons for putting forth an Ultimatum Resolution by the States:

1. It is the only idea anybody has advanced which can actually stop the United States from probable self-destruction, wherein the people and the states can take charge and over-

power Washington and the runaway Congress.

2. By widely distributing this plan and getting legislators in a few states to go to work to implement it, it will quickly get the attention of the entire federal establishment. Should it appear the plan has the remotest chance of being successful, it will have a very sobering effect on Washington, and Congress will suddenly get serious about controlling the extravagant spending spree we have been on for 60 years.

3. It will make unnecessary the calling of a Constitutional Convention for the alledged purpose of getting the States to pass a Balanced Budget Amendment to the Constitution. Congress would ignore a Balanced Budget Amendment anyway, even if we should pass one, just as they are now ignoring most of the Constitution. If Congress knows the States are serious about dissolving the Union at the trigger point of a six-trillion-dollar national debt, we can safely bet that Congress *will* get spending under control before the debt hits that "magic" figure or some other arbitrary figure which 38 states might decide to adopt.

4. Wide publicity of a plan to have the States dissolve the Union will be an extremely valuable and powerful educational tool, which will wake up thousands of politicians, some of them, we might assume, who are reasonably honest, along with waking up millions of Americans as to the actual structure of our state and national governments.

5. By simply setting forth an actual proposal to dissolve the Federal Union, or, failing that, a proposal that one or more states acting independently should sever the ties of union by declaring their independence, will cause many of our 7,400 plus state legislators of the 50 states to be astonished as they suddenly realize that such drastic remedies are not only possible, but absolutely lawful and historically sound. We hope to instill in them the sense that they are the only hope for saving the Constitution; that unless they act, America is going the way corrupt governments have always gone; that America is going down as she succumbs to corruption, immorality, godlessness, anarchy and finally tyranny—unable to be governed except at the hands of an intellectual elite who will rule

as did the ancient pharaohs, with a rod of iron, and who think of themselves not as men but as gods.

6. By bringing to the forefront the possibility of Union dissolution, we put on notice the entire federal establishment, the President, Congress, and the Judiciary that *we the people*, and each of the 50 states, have taken all the abuse, monetary nonsense, intimidation, usurpation of undelegated powers, and phony bureaucratic compassion with taxpayer dollars, that we intend to take. We turn on the lights for a Congress and President gone mad with power and grandeur, and bring them down to earth so they realize their smallness and understand that they truly are public servants, not kings or gods. We cause Congress to reassess its role as a mere *agent* of *the people* and *the states*. That if Congress persists in bankrupting the nation and ignoring the constitutional contract, they will, at last, realize they are going to be put out of business by the States acting in unison.

We wish to make our 50 state legislatures aware of their enormous power--that they actually hold the destiny of the United States in their hands and that if they choose to do so, they can lawfully eliminate the Washington bully and place these 50 States in the same position held by the original 13 States as free, sovereign, and independent nations. Many state legislators will suddenly realize how they have been played for fools, and how they have been deceived into believing the lie that they must "go along to get along" with Washington. Few of them realize the Founding Fathers placed great confidence in the state legislatures to protect the rights of the people from the federal government, but these proposals will help awaken them to their duty and their right to stand up to the federal establishment and either put it in order or dissolve it.

When the welfare checks, the Social Security checks and other "entitlement" checks start bouncing, or become worthless because of hyper-inflation, blood is going to flow in the streets of America. And under present federal policy that day cannot be delayed very many more years. We hope an Ultimatum Resolution and possible or actual dissolution of the Union will prevent such bloodshed.

Struggling young families will eventually realize how the older generation is ripping them off by forcing them to contribute to a Social Security "trust fund" which does not exist except in the figment of federal imagination; when the young people organize to resist this fraud we call Social Security, realizing there is going to be nothing in the alleged trust fund when they reach retirement age, nobody can predict the result. We can only hope that bloodshed will not come about.

Thomas Jefferson warned that "The tree of liberty must, from time to time, be watered with the blood of patriots and tyrants." We hope these proposals will prevent the bloodshed which appears to be imminent if we allow the federal government to continue on its present course.

The bloody history of mankind is getting close to being repeated in America. It appears that the only possibility of preventing historical repetition is to either convince 38 states to dissolve the Union and start over, or to separate ourselves, one by one, according to state boundaries. If neither of these two actions are successful, bloodshed and anarchy in the streets of America appear to be inevitable.

It is with great admiration and respect for our Founding Fathers, and eternal devotion to our beloved United States Constitution, that we hereby set forth a:

Model Ultimatum Resolution
to be introduced for debate and passage in the
legislature of each of the 50 states

* * * * * *

WHEREAS, our Pilgrim Fathers chose to secede from the Church of England and flee to the American wilderness early in the spring of 1620 during the week of Passover, to attain freedom in a new land and to escape the coercion and compulsory welfare of a state religion that was set up by British politicians to hide the tyranny of a feudal government; and,

WHEREAS, more than half of our Pilgrim forebears died during that first harsh winter after their exodus to this new land, after sharing equally with each other their meager food supplies—without any federal food subsidies; and,

WHEREAS, despite such awesome tests of faith during that first winter after our Pilgrim Fathers seceded from the British empire, every Pilgrim survivor elected to remain on the sacred new soil where their kindred dead were buried and valiantly refused to return to the British empire when the Mayflower departed from Plymouth on the 6th of April, 1621; and,

WHEREAS, ten years later our Puritan and Protestant Fathers chose to secede from the mighty British empire and separate themselves from the orthodox religion early in the spring of 1630 during the week of Passover, and boarded the Arbella and 16 other ships, led by their Pastor, John Winthrop; and,

WHEREAS, our Pilgrim, Puritan and Patriot Fathers did only that which they saw their ancient Fathers do when they seceded from the wicked world order to establish the Kingdom of God within their own families; and,

WHEREAS, our Fathers voted to declare their economic independence from Great Britain in Philadelphia on the 6th of April, 1776, and to send forth emissaries to deal directly with foreign nations, after which they set forth their reasons for separation and listed their grievances against the mother country; and,

WHEREAS, our Fathers held certain truths to be self-evident, among which are "Governments are instituted among men, deriving their powers from the consent of the governed," and "that whenever any form of government becomes destructive of these ends, it is the right of the people to alter or to abolish it, and to institute new government, laying its foundation on such principles, and organizing its powers in such form, as to them shall seem most likely to effect their safety and happiness;" and,

WHEREAS, following their formal Declaration of Independence of July 4, 1776, our Fathers formed a 13-nation Confederation under a contract, or charter, they called the Articles of Confederation, wherein they agreed to be bound in perpetual union and if any amendments or changes in these Articles were to be made, such must be by unanimous consent of all 13 nations; and,

WHEREAS, the Articles of Confederation, with experience, were discovered to be weak and ineffective in providing peace, happiness and domestic tranquility, therefore, our Fathers determined to meet in Philadelphia in May 1787 for the specific purpose of revising the Articles of Confederation; and,

WHEREAS, after some four months, on September 17, 1787, they signed, not a revision or amendments to the Articles of Confederation, but a totally new proposal of confederation, a compact, contract, treaty or alliance between nations, which they called a Constitution for the United States of America, and which on the 28th of September, Congress sent a copy of said Constitution to each of the 13 free, independent and sovereign nations which were allied under the Articles of Confederation, including Rhode Island, which had refused to send delegates to Philadelphia; and,

WHEREAS, this proposal to unite under this Constitution, like the Declaration of Independence of 1776, was a document of secession, wherein, upon the adoption of the proposed Constitution by a mere nine of the 13 nations, states, or little republics (Article VII), the nine were declared to be joined in a new Union, these nine, in effect, declaring their secession or separation from the remaining four. This in spite of the existing and continuing compact between the 13 that all were joined in Union perpetually, and unanimous consent must be obtained to change or amend their agreement, and, most certainly would unanimous consent be required to *abandon* the Articles of Confederation, or dissolve the existing Union which was established under them, if nations were held to the same standard of law under contracts or treaties as individuals, which they are not; and,

WHEREAS, only nine of thirteen nations, less than three-fourths, formed a new government under the Constitution, abandoning four who could choose to also join or remain outside as sovereign and independent nations, these nine eventually becoming 50, delegated to their new agent which they called a Federal Government, certain *very limited* and specific powers, retaining all other powers to themselves, or to their people. These states gave their new agent the responsibility and authority to unite them against foreign invaders, act as an arbiter among themselves when differences arose, and regulate commerce between themselves and foreign nations; and,

WHEREAS, these states as *principals*, creating an artificial corporate structure to act as their agent, formally reserved to themselves the right to freely leave, or abandon, their new creation, just as they had abandoned the old Union under the Articles of Confederation; and,

WHEREAS, Virginia, the tenth nation to join the new confederation on June 25, 1788, said in her official ratification:

". . . in the name and in behalf of the people of Virginia, declare and make known, that the powers granted under the Constitution, being derived from the people of the United States, *may be resumed by them whensoever the same shall be perverted to their injury or oppression. . .;*" and,

WHEREAS, New York, the eleventh Nation to join on July 25, 1788 said: **"That the powers of Government may be re-assumed by the people, whensoever it shall become necessary to their happiness...;"** and,

WHEREAS, Rhode Island, the thirteenth to join, remained outside as an independent nation for almost two years, finally joining May 29, 1790, declared:

"That the powers of government may be resumed by the people whensoever it shall become necessary to their happiness;" and,

WHEREAS, these formal declarations were superfluous and unnecessary to the States as sovereign principals, nevertheless our Fathers understood well the tendency for governments to usurp undelegated powers, and they wished it clearly understood that if or when their mutual agent should somehow get out from under their control, they could simply walk away, or abandon their creation to die a natural death, or to survive as the remaining agent of those sister States who wished to remain in the confederation; and,

WHEREAS, our Fathers embarrassed themselves by saying four times in the Articles of Confederation that they were a confederation in "*perpetuity*," and a short time afterward abandoning that Union to die quietly, they said nothing of perpetuity in the new Constitution, for they had realized that such indiscretion and folly was a contradiction of their own declaration of July 4, 1776, and in establishing this new "experiment in government," they knew it was possible the experiment might not work and again, they might choose to let their federal agent die a natural death; and,

WHEREAS, under Article V of the Constitution our Fathers agreed that three-fourths of the States could amend the Constitution, and that, in fact, three-fourths of the States could abolish the Constitution and thereby automatically call an end to the alliance of states, thus ending the life of all three branches of the federal government—the Executive, the Legislative and the Judicial. All agencies functioning under the Constitution would cease to exist, including the Internal Revenue Service, the Central Intelligence Agency, OSHA, MSHA, FDA, TVA, FBI, SS, SSI, foreign aid, the Federal Reserve System, a private corporate agent of an agent of an agent, and along with it approximately 75% of the national debt, or over $3 trillion, along with numerous other federal agencies, and about 3.1 million federal employees; and,

WHEREAS, in recent decades the federal agent has attempted, and largely succeeded, in reversing roles with its

Principal, the States, telling them what they can and cannot do, and threatening to withhold "federal monies" from states which do not comply with federal laws and regulations, and usurping undelegated powers from the states and the people, until now the people fear, rather than respect and revere, their own government and are burdened with taxes some 67 times greater than those placed on our Fathers by Great Britain; and,

WHEREAS, our agent, some three decades ago, took prayer out of the public schools, and refused to further allow our children to be taught about God, values, morality, or religion in the schools, which has caused our law enforcement agencies to be overwhelmed with crime, our jails and prisons filled to overflowing, our unmarried children to become sexually active and pregnant by the millions, venereal disease and AIDS to flourish, murder and rape to be rampant to where many dare not walk our streets after dark, and with pretended lawfulness of a supreme court decision assuming undelegated jurisdiction, we have slaughtered some 30,000,000 of our unborn children. Child abuse, sodomy, and pornography are commonplace. Greed and litigiousness have taken over and we scramble, lobby, and fight each other to "get our share" of "federal" dollars which is nothing more than our own money and credit coming back to us with numerous strings attached; and,

WHEREAS, it is now plain to everybody that the agent created by our Fathers on June 21, 1788, when New Hampshire became the ninth state to ratify the Constitution, has grown into an uncontrollable monster which, if we do not get control of it, or destroy it, will destroy its own creators through bankrupting them, merging them into a one-world government wherein the United Nations Charter will replace the Constitution, or we will die by our own hand through moral corruption, crime and anarchy; and,

WHEREAS, should two-thirds of the several states call a Convention for proposing the abolishment of the Federal Government, under Article V of the Constitution, it is highly unlikely that Congress would comply with said Article and faithfully call such a Convention of States, for should such a proposal be sent out to the States and three-fourths of them ratified the proposal to abolish Congress, the Executive and federal Judiciary, and dissolve the Union, 535 congressmen, nine supreme court justices and one president would be out of a job, and would automatically lose all of their lucrative pensions, perks, emoluments and grandeur of high public office; and

WHEREAS, our Fathers said it was right for the People to change or abolish governments when it was for their happiness, or when government becomes the tyrant rather than the protector, and every July 4, we honor our Fathers as heroes and patriots for their secession from Great Britain in 1776, and nine states for abolishing the Articles of Confederation, and thereby, dismantling and destroying an existing Union of States as nine states seceded from four, giving us our present Constitution which we hold high as the Supreme Law of our land; and,

WHEREAS, three-fourths of the States have the power to abolish the federal government under authority of Article V; and,

WHEREAS, the federal government is no longer a servant, but has outlived its usefulness and become the master, and an agent tyrant, trampling not only the rights of individual citizens, but the rights of the very states themselves and usurping the rightful and reserved powers of the states; and,

WHEREAS, should such be the desire of 38 states, said states have the right and power ***inherently,*** without regard to Article V, and without consulting or relying on Congress to call a Convention of States, when requested to make such a call by two-thirds, or 34 states; three-fourths of the states can, as Principals, without consulting their agent, do as they please, including abolishing the federal agent by dissolving the Charter which established said agent. It would be absurd to hold that one's agent could stop the Principal from doing whatever the Principal feels is right, especially when the agent is a mere artificial corporate creation of less than three-fourths of the principals; and,

WHEREAS, if this Union were truly a democracy as the politicians and media almost universally contend that it is, but which it is not because it is a republic, in theory, being governed by law, not by citizen majority; but if a democracy, a mere majority of 26 states, rather than 38, would have the power to dissolve the Union and eliminate the entire federal government; and,

WHEREAS, relying on the precedents of our Fathers whom we love and honor as patriots brave and God-fearing men, as wise in the ways of government as any men who ever lived, we, the legislature of the State of _____, of the United States of America, do

NOW THEREFORE RESOLVE that when, or if, Congress allows the national debt to reach six trillion dollars, ($6,000,000,000,000)

OR if Congress by way of treaty, resolution or otherwise,

OR should the President of the United States by way of Executive Order or in any other fashion, attempt to abolish or in any way make the Constitution of the United States ineffective, or null and void;

UPON THE HAPPENING of any event set forth herein, the State of _____ when joined by 37 of her sister states, being three-fourths of the States of the Union, hereby declare the United States government to be in violation of its Constitutional authority, and the Federal Confederacy and Union are hereby *dissolved*, and without further power to act on behalf of the States;

WITH EACH of the 50 States of this Union resuming the same sovereignty, independence and freedom, and assuming that same condition in which the 13 original States of America placed themselves from July 4, 1776, through June 21, 1788, when nine of these 13 formed the Union currently in place.

BE IT FURTHER RESOLVED, that immediately upon dissolution of the Union, representatives of the 38 states, along with representatives of the other 12 states, should they choose, shall meet in the City of _____, in the State of _____, for the purpose of dividing and selling the assets currently controlled by the government of the United States. All such assets shall be sold or otherwise equitably distributed, and the proceeds divided between the 50 States according to the population of citizens of each state as of the last census prior to dissolution.

BE IT FURTHER RESOLVED, that the military forces of

the United States shall at all times, remain in place until treaty arrangements are negotiated between all states wishing to participate in mutual alliance for our common protection from potential aggression, foreign or domestic. All present military commanders and field personnel shall remain in place and be paid according to the negotiations worked out among the participating states.

BE IT FURTHER RESOLVED, that the Constitution, insofar as it is applicable to the states, shall continue to be the Supreme Law of the individual states, and all individual rights and liberties guaranteed therein, and within the Bill of Rights, shall be maintained in each of the 50 nations, until each nation, by a vote of a majority of its own citizens, shall change or amend it.

NOW LET IT BE NOTED, that the Constitutional Union of these 50 States, under the original plan of our Founding Fathers enabled us to become the most powerful, prosperous, wealthy and free people on the earth, in spite of the interference, intimidation, violations and usurpations of the federal agent and its apparent deliberate attempts to muzzle, hamper, slow down and destroy much of the private industry of these States, causing such to leave our borders and establish themselves in foreign lands; however, Union with an obedient agent in the beginning proved to be most desirable; and

IT IS THEREFORE the desire of the State of _____, as soon as practical after dissolving the federal government, that one or more new confederations should be formed under a Constitution substantially similar to that which presently binds us together;

EXCEPT THAT during the last 204 years, we know from sad experience that it is in the nature of almost all men as soon as they receive a little authority, as they suppose, they will immediately begin to exercise unrighteous dominion by exceeding their authority as agents to act for their principals; and

THEREFORE, it may need to be that some changes are in order to better control the tendency of human rulers to usurp undelegated authority and powers.

BE IT FURTHER NOTED, that it is the desire of the legislature of this state that this *Ultimatum Resolution* shall be debated and considered in every legislature of our 49 sister states, and if ratified as a joint resolution of a state's legislature, an executed original shall be delivered to:

_____, the Attorney General of the State of _____, who is commanded to hold, as agent, each and every *Ultimatum Resolution* submitted to him.

IF AT LEAST 38 states so submit these *resolutions*, and should any of the above listed conditions take place, he is authorized and commanded to immediately serve copies of all 38 *Ultimatum Resolutions* on the Executive, Legislative, and Judicial bodies of the United States Government, and the United States Government in all of its various branches shall be declared to be *dissolved*, and each of the 50 States shall be restored to the same sovereign, independent and free status enjoyed by them before they created their federal agent, and each State shall become a new and separate nation of the former United States of America.

* * * * * *

This Ultimatum Resolution was jointly written by the author and:

Tom Wood
Attorney at Law
Suite 285
7050 South Union Park Center
Midvale, Utah 84047
Telephone 801-561-2200

April 6, 1993
Salt Lake City, Utah

* * * * * *

Permission is granted, and you are encouraged, to reprint the Model Ultimatum Resolution and the Introduction to the Model Ultimatum Resolution for wide distribution.

The following is a suggested outline for a formal *Declaration of Independence* from the United States of America which might be accomplished by any one of the 50 States acting independently. Some might choose to call such a declaration an *Ordinance of Secession*, or an *Ordinance of Separation*.

Should any one or more of the 50 States of the 1990's choose to declare their independence from the United States, the lawful basis for doing so is greater than that of our Fathers when they did the same with their Mother Country, Great Britain, July 4, 1776. And the risk of bloodshed today is far less than that encountered by our Fathers. In America, under the Constitution which merely created an artificial *agent* for the benefit of the *principal*, the States remain members of the Union, or may leave it, at their pleasure.

The Federal government was created out of nothing to act as an *agent* and *servant* of nine *independent, sovereign, and free nations*. They were later joined by 41 more States, equal in every way to the original nine.

These 50 Nations which we call States, are only temporarily bound together as long as each believes union to be advantageous to them, and for the benefit and happiness of their respective people. The Union is secured by a contract we call the Constitution which we might also call a trust, an alliance, or treaty. No contract is permanent, except at the option of each succeeding generation. One generation cannot lawfully, or morally bind following generations without their consent.

In forming the present temporary Union of Nations, at least three, Virginia, New York and Rhode Island, reserved to themselves the right in their official documents of ratification to leave the Union just as freely as they joined, should each ever decide union was no longer to the advantage or happiness of their people. As equals, therefore, each of the 50 States now constituting the Union, retain the lawful right to leave the Union, with or without citing specific reasons for doing so. Courtesy and diplomacy, however, calls for notification of all affected parties and the reasons for separation.

Had Virginia, New York and Rhode Island failed to formalize their right to leave the Union, they nevertheless retained, and do retain inherently, the right to leave and separate themselves from their sister States. This is well established under the laws of nations and numerous historical precedents as outlined in this book.

In the alternative, each of the 50 States have the right to leave the Union under the laws of *contract*, which holds that when one party to a contract violates the contract, the other party, or parties, are, at their option, released from further obligation under the contract. The harmed party can simply declare the contract null and void and no longer of any effect.

A third legal remedy for a State wishing to leave the Union is found under the law of *agency*. Each of the 50 States is legally a *principal*. Each delegated certain specific powers to an artificial *agent* of their own creation which we call the Federal government which we divided into three separate branches equal to each other, but not equal with the *principal* creators. Under the laws of agency, if an agent acts in a manner which is harmful, or works to the disadvantage of the principal, or deliberately attempts to bankrupt or destroy the principal, the principal at all times, at his pleasure, retains the right to terminate, or to make null and void the contract of agency.

It is common knowledge among legislators, leaders and *the people*, that the Federal government is constantly acting in violation of the constitutional contract and has been doing so from almost the very beginning. In recent decades the violations and usurpations of undelegated authority have been increasing rapidly until at the present time these violations are so commonplace and so conspicuous that our people who wish to breathe the clean air of freedom find the violations and abuses have reached an intolerable level.

The government of the United States is not only ignoring the Constitution to the detriment of *the people*, but to the detriment of the very State governments themselves. A free people can no longer tolerate an out-of-control Washington monster which is running amok with imagined grandeur and pretended power which it only retains with the trembling and fearful acquiescence of State governments who have lost the historical perspective of who they are; that they are the *principals* and retain all power if they choose to exercise it. It has become obvious that the advantages of the States being united under the Constitution are no longer sufficient that this Union should continue.

The disadvantages of Union far outweigh the advantages and unless the *prinicpals* quickly bring back discipline and control of the federal *agent*, and cause the *agent* to serve only in the limited capacity to which it was assigned, a state may _____ find that in order to keep its citizens, their children and grandchildren from being placed under economic bondage of a spiraling national debt, and for many other reasons, it is to their advantage and happiness to separate from her sister states who still believe union has more advantages for them than it has disadvantages.

* * * * * *

The following is a proposal; a suggested form which might be followed or altered to suit the pleasure of a particular State which might decide separation from the United States will be to its benefit. Prior to the adoption of a 1990's Declaration of Independence by any one of the 50 States, it will be well to review the hallowed and honored Declaration of our Fathers done July 4, 1776, which begins:

"When in the course of human events, it becomes necessary for one people to dissolve the political bands which have connected them with another and to assume among the powers of the earth the separate and equal station to which the laws of nature and of nature's God entitle them,..."

* * * * * *

A Declaration of Secession

A Declaration and joint resolution of the Senate and House of Representatives of the State of _____, July 4, 1995?

  WHEREAS in order to be free and practice their religious beliefs, our first Fathers came from the Old World landing at, and founding Jamestown, Virginia on May 14, 1607. A separate group of our Fathers established the second permanent settlement on this continent at Plymouth, Massachusetts, December 21, 1620, again leaving the Mother Country in order to be free, believing the national church to be so corrupt that separation from it was the only moral course for them to follow; and
  WHEREAS, on July 4, 1776, our Fathers declared themselves to be thirteen *free, sovereign, and independent nations*, and in their official declaration said; "that whenever any form of government becomes destructive...it is the right of the people to alter or to abolish it, and to institute new government...;" and,
  WHEREAS, thereafter our Fathers joined these thirteen Nations into a Union under a Charter they called the Articles of Confederation, declaring some four times that said confederation should be in perpetuity and that change in the Charter could only be done by unanimous consent of all thirteen; and,
  WHEREAS, the said perpetual Union only lasted from March 1, 1781, through June 21, 1788, when New Hampshire became the ninth State to declare itself a member of a new and separate Union under a Constitution *for* the United States, Article VII thereof; thus nine of the Nations separated, or seceded from four sister Nations; and,
  WHEREAS, three of the remaining four, when eventually joining the new Union under the Constitution, these four also officially abolishing the old *perpetual union* under the Articles of Confederation, namely, Virginia, New York and Rhode Island, though not necessary to preserve an inherent right, officially declared in their documents of ratification, that they retained the right to freely leave this new Union, just

as all had freely left the old Union under the Articles of Confederation, and to *resume their sovereignty*; and,

WHEREAS, abuses, violations and usurpations under the new Constitution quickly began to take place, Alexander Hamilton arguing for "implied powers" of the Federal Agent under the Constitution, and in 1798 Congress passing the blatantly unconstitutional Alien and Sedition Acts, which resulted in Thomas Jefferson, the same who wrote The Declaration of Independence, writing in opposition thereto, a thesis showing the unconstitutionality of these Acts of Congress, said thesis becoming known as The Kentucky Resolutions, and being officially adopted by the Legislature of Kentucky. Also in opposition to these Acts, James Madison, the "Father" of the Constitution wrote the Virginia Resolutions; and

WHEREAS, the Federal Agent grossly violated the constitutional contract when, while prosecuting the War Between The States from 1861-1865, allegedly to *preserve the Union*, saying secession of a State was illegal and not allowed under the Constitution, the Federal Agent under the administration of Abraham Lincoln, allowed 48 counties of Virginia to secede from their Mother State and join the Union as the 35th State of West Virginia, June 20, 1863, in the middle of the war. Thus West Virginia, consisting of 55 present counties, and taking some 38% of the land mass of Virginia away from her without the consent of the Legislature thereof as required by the constitutional contract, Article IV, Section 3, remains an outlaw entry into the Union of States to this day; and

WHEREAS, in order to prosecute the "Civil War" Congress and the President conspired to create $450,000,000 in "greenbacks," or paper money, out of nothing, and violate with impunity the contract which says; "No State shall...make any thing but gold and silver coin a tender in payment of debts...," Article 1, Section 10, and if the *Principal*, the States, being barred from making unbacked paper a legal tender, obviously so was the Agent, namely Congress and the President, also barred; and,

WHEREAS, the third arm of Agency, the Supreme Court

in *Knox vs. Lee*, 12 Wallace 457, (May 1871) after the first two arms of the Federal Agent had "packed the Court" with two new justices for the purpose, going so far as to actually increase the total number from eight to nine justices, reversed the decision of its own brothers of only a year before in *Hepburn vs. Griswold*, 8 Wallace 603, and ruled that regardless of the Constitution saying otherwise, something other than gold and silver; paper backed by nothing, could be used in payment of debts; and,

WHEREAS, this original elimination from and violation of the contract, of silver and gold as backing for our money and credit system, has brought us to the verge of national bankruptcy and economic chaos, as well as a national debt so large and spiraling, that it will soon be impossible to pay the interest thereon, and our children to future infinity will be enslaved by, and be unable to pay this debt, created largely out of nothing and by using the very credit of the States; and,

WHEREAS, the Federal Agent, with passing years, finds it more and more convenient, and finding little resistance from its Principals, not only ignores the gold and silver clause of the contract, but ignores and violates more arrogantly with each passing year, the Commerce and General Welfare Clauses, and has reached the point of usurpations where it even presumes the authority to legislate a mandatory "Motor-Voter" law which allows citizens in each State to register to vote when they get a driver's license, said Act being passed by the U.S. Senate March 17, 1993, by a 62-37 vote; this knowing full well they are violating and abusing the Supreme Law of the Land, having no authority to tell the Principals in what manner to register their own citizens. This and thousands of other reversals of the roles of Principal and Agent is absurd and contrary to every form of contract law, and is contrary to the common sense of any ordinary, average intelligence, human being; and

WHEREAS, the Federal Agent has pretended the Principals added the 14th and 16th Amendments to the Constitution, and has arbitrarily and fraudulently declared said Amendments are part of the contract, untruthfully saying that three-fourths of the States had ratified them, and has by these acts alone proven itself unworthy of further trust and that its authority as Agent for the States should be relinquished to the Principals. In the alternative, these Amendments not having been ratified by three-fourths of the States as required by the contract, should be declared by the Principals to be invalid, null and void, and not binding as law within the boundaries of each of the Sovereign States; and

WHEREAS, the Federal Agent was created out of nothing by the Principal, the States, for the purpose of protection from foreign aggressors, to regulate commerce between themselves and foreign nations, and to act as an arbiter in grievances between themselves, and no longer functions efficiently or effectively under the limited delegation of authority allowed, and pretends itself to have inherently, the authority of the creator, meting out to its Principals certain "rights, and privileges," and especially money, along with numerous qualifying conditions and controls; and,

WHEREAS, the violations of the contract being too numerous to list, numbering in the thousands over the past 200 years, and because of these violations the Principals, at their option, having the right to declare the contract, the Constitution, null and void and of no effect, thus eliminating any further federal agency, and even without said violations, these States by the laws of nations and historical precedents, have the inherent right, as well as having specifically reserved the right, to leave the Union of these States, *we*, hereby giving notice to the Federal Agent and the other 49 Principal sister States, that the Great State of_____ finds the current and numerous violations of the Contract, and especially finding the national debt to be an unbearable burden on ourselves and our children, and declaring these accumulating abuses by the Federal Agent to be no longer tolerable, this State,

NOW THEREFORE RESOLVES, that when, or if, Congress allows the national debt to reach six trillion dollars, ($6,000,000,000,000) or should Congress by way of treaty, resolution or otherwise, or should the President of the United States by way of Executive Order or in any other fashion, attempt to abolish or in any way make the Constitution of the United States ineffective, or null and void; in either case, this State hereby revokes the agency it granted under that contract, alliance, trust or treaty we call the Constitution of the United States, and immediately resumes that same sovereignty, independence and freedom established by the original 13 Nations from the time they declared their independence July 4, 1776, through June 21, 1788, when New Hampshire became the ninth State which lawfully established the Constitution which still binds the 50 States in a confederacy of independent Nations.

BE IT FURTHER RESOLVED, that this State recognizes its responsibility to pay its pro-rated share of the national debt, but to also share in the pro-rated assets of all common property, and for this purpose we demand an independent audit by a large and established certified public accounting firm which shall be agreeable to all parties, who will determine the gross value of all common assets currently controlled by the Federal United States. This State agrees to pay all of its prorated legitimate debt, but refuses to pay any portion of the alleged debt owed to The Federal Reserve System which this State declares is debt contracted in fraud, and is therefore, no debt at all. All debts owing to individuals, corporations and foreign nations, this State agrees to pay its prorated share after the audit, assuming the amount of legitimate debt surpasses the value of the common assets.

BE IT FURTHER RESOLVED, that this State desires to continue commerce with her former sister Nations and will, by treaty, formalize the necessary agreements to efficiently and effectively accomplish peaceful and on-going commercial enterprise between us and all other foreign nations.

BE IT KNOWN, that this State desires to remain under the protection of the military forces of the United States currently in place, and will pay its fair share, pro-rated costs of such protection. This protection shall be only against foreign aggressors and at the specific invitation of the Legislature of the State of _____, or in the case of actual attack, by the Executive Officer of this State. This State will continue to furnish its own internal police forces and law enforcement agencies and will rely on its own Supreme Court as the Court of finality.

BE IT ALSO KNOWN, that this State recognizes that its separation from the long and profitable association with its sister States, casts a shadow of sadness over the entire Union, and that it is the desire of this State to rejoin her former sisters as soon as practicable in a new Union, if and when it is determined a new corporate entity is bound down by sufficient chains to keep its limited delegations of authority within the meaning and intent of any new proposed Constitution.

BE IT FURTHER RESOLVED, that until that happy and anticipated day of *reunion* shall arrive, the State of _____ declares itself to be a *free, sovereign*, and *independent nation* of the earth, resuming all authority and powers formerly delegated to the United States of America.

DONE on this, the ____ day of _____ 199___, in the capital city of _____, in the State of _____.

This *Declaration of Independence* shall be immediately hand delivered to the President of The United States, the Vice President in his capacity as the presiding officer of the United States Senate, the Speaker of The House of Representatives and shall be sent by registered mail, return receipt requested to each of the 49 governors of our former sister States and to the Heads of State of every foreign nation on the earth. In notifying Heads of State, this is a mere diplomatic courtesy, and for the purpose of seeking their official recognition of the status of this State of _____ as a Nation in existence since July 4, 1776, but as released from her former confedederate Union with the other 49 American Nations.

* * * * * *

"Come out of her, my people, that ye be not partakers of her sins, and that ye receive not of her plagues.

For her sins have reached unto heaven, and God hath remembered her iniquities." The Holy Bible. Book of Revelation: 18:4-5

"Wherefore come out from among them, and be ye separate, saith the Lord, and touch not the unclean thing;and I will receive you." Ibid, II Corinthians 6:17.

If nothing comes of these proposals of *Union dissolution or secession*, other than widespread national debate, the very discussion will, perhaps, temper and slow down the federal juggernaut as it continues to grind the Constitution into powder.

These may be a little ahead of their time, but as the federal usurpations and abuse of our people become worse and more blatant, and as federal arrogance no longer even pretends to be adhering to constitutional law, many will remember these *Resolutions* and realize, after all, the States can take out the federal government if they don't wait until the last minute; if they don't wait until the federal government hands down its own ultimatum to the States, demanding either submission to *The New World Order* and the new *One World Government*, or elimination of resisters by, perhaps, our own armed forces, unlawfully integrated by the President into the ranks of the One World United Nations forces.

Should a single State adopt either a Declaration of Secession or Union Dissolution, that State will be doing the nation an invaluable service as it will focus attention on the fact that Washington, D.C. and all of its power brokers actually have no power at all, except at the pleasure of the States.

That the people should even be thinking of such "radical" and unheard of ideas, will go a long way in giving Congress some incentive to straighten out the Washington mess and stop thinking only of how they can best feather their own nests and maintain themselves in office.

Serious national consideration of these drastic proposals appears to be the only hope we have of avoiding national bankruptcy, chaos and anarchy. If the States do not assume control, take command, and either discipline or destroy the Washington monster, America the beautiful is going down.

Historians will write as they did of Rome: "The Rise and Fall of The Great American Empire. The richest and most powerful nation which ever existed."

This song is dedicated to our children.

THE SONG OF ACCLAMATION

We want the Bell of Liberty,
Ringing for us once more.
We want our 50 States to be,
Sovereign, independent and free.
We want the USA to rise,
Peaceful and clean again.
We want our country guided by,
God-fearing, honest men.

Those who serve with all their verve,
To help our economy,
Who'll do the job and help build up,
The Public's treasury.
Only that *one* of destiny,
Our need will satisfy.
This is the cry for you and me,
"PRESERVE OUR LIBERTY"

This song was written by Erlinda Duce. She is the wife of Roy Duce. Erlinda is a Canadian citizen, of Phillipine parentage. She completed her studies in the United States. Any requests for the music to the song will be forwarded to her by writing to:

The Committee of 50 States
4808 Quailbrook Circle
Salt Lake City, Utah 84118

Chapter 14

Conclusion.
What You Can Do

After 200 years, the United States is deteriorating into a socialist and tightly controlled society just like most governments have done before us. Liberty brings prosperity and wealth. Wealth brings apathy and corruption. Apathy and corruption again bring tighter controls and loss of liberty. Tyranny and dictatorship take over, and the cycle starts all over again. When the people finally tire of tyranny, they throw off their chains by revolution, which normally can only be accomplished by the shedding of blood. Then they again enjoy the fruits of liberty for a season.

That's history folks. That's the way it is. That's the way it is going to be again, unless we are bright enough to do that which other generations have been unwilling to do; that is, learn from history and stop repeating it over and over.

At this moment in time, with a new President, Bill Clinton, assuming office, we have a strong socialist and a believer in consolidation of government power, replacing another President, George Bush, who believed the same things.

Both men were put in power by behind the scenes power brokers who, for decades, have been working to dismantle the Constitution and eliminate American sovereignty in a one-world government. These powerful one-worlders are very close to reaching their goal under the New World Order.

There appears to be only one way of stopping this juggernaut. That is to have the individual States of the Union, in unison we hope, individually if necessary, to proclaim, manifest, and reclaim that sovereignty and independence they have retained since July 4, 1776. Then in official State Resolutions of the State Legislatures, announce to Washington, the rest of the Nation and the world, and particularly to the insiders who plan to take over our government, that should an attempt to abolish the Constitution come about, rather than allow such to happen, these States will dissolve the government of the United States. They will resume their original and total sovereignty, and until the "dust settles," govern themselves with their own already functioning State governments, and establish relations with each other by treaty.

This is a grand and earth-shaking concept, at least in our generation. But if it is the only way to maintain liberty under the Constitution; if it is the only way to fire, and send packing, an arrogant Congress, and inefficient Federal bureaucracy, why stand we here idle? Let liberty loving Americans in each of the 50 States convince their respective State Legislatures to pass resolutions similar to the one proposed in chapter 13 of this book.

There is no new unexplored continent to which we can flee as did our fathers. There is no place on the planet where those who wish to be left alone by government can go to make a new home, where they can establish a new Nation as did our fathers.

This is the place liberty must make its stand. History is looking to us, the few, but the mighty in spirit and love for liberty, to preserve that which was given to us by our fathers. If we succeed in our own revolution against tyrannical government, our children will thank us as we initially thanked the Founders of the United States.

However that may be, only these 50 States stand between one world government and liberty as we have known it under the Constitution. Only we, the few, the remnant, who understand what is really going on in the fast-paced countdown to Armageddon; only we stand in the way of those who will rule with a rod of iron and the slave master's whip, all the people on earth, unless we stop them. Nobody else, except God, can do it.

Perhaps no other government on earth has the structure which will allow its people to take charge of their own destiny in accordance with law like we have, without violent and bloody revolution.

And if we, the remnant, the few, the patriots, the inheritors of and the lovers of real freedom; if we do not give up, thinking it is all over, we can preserve the Constitution and liberty for ourselves and for our children. For, though the odds appear to be greatly against us, and the enemy appears to be all-powerful and unbeatable, we can beat him. We can win because we are in the right; because the law and precedent and history are all on our side; and most of all, because God is on the side of those who stand for freedom and He will bless our efforts as he did those of our fathers when with the hurricane, He sank the ships of the British fleet in Boston Harbor.

Speaking of our own day, immediately preceding the Second Coming of Christ, we have the promise of the Lord: "Wherefore, he will preserve the righteous by his power, even if it so be that the fulness of his wrath must come, and the righteous be preserved, even unto the destruction of their enemies by fire. Wherefore, the righteous need not fear; for thus saith the prophet, they shall be saved, even if it so be as by fire." Book of Mormon, 1 Nephi 22:17

It is the conviction of the auhor that the Constitution of the United States was inspired by Deity. That God spoke to the minds of our fathers who wrote it at Philadelphia in 1787. It is, therefore, logical that God will help preserve it as long as there is a remnant who are determined to serve him and do their fair share to help Him.

Only by default can we lose. Only by giving up. And our efforts only need to be small in comparison with those of our fathers who had to pay in blood and treasure. Our effort requires no blood, and little treasure, in comparison to that expended in war, and little risk. We just have to reach out and reclaim that which has always belonged to us. We just have to cancel out the "Power of Attorney," our Fathers temporarily gave to an artificial "person," the "corporation" of the United States, chartered by the Constitution. We just have to recall, or give notice of cancellation of powers we temporarily delegated to our Federal *agents*. We just have to remind ourselves that *agents* cannot presume anything; they cannot assume authority which the *principal* has not specifically delegated.

This book needs to be put into the hands of every governor and attorney general and every legislator in each of the 50 States. We need to have at least one key individual in every State to see that this is done. In handling this, it would be best to have a person of some influence transmit the book to these leaders so they will be encouraged to actually read it. If you feel you have no influence in this regard, you can send a donation to the Committee of 50 States to help buy these books for distribution to these leaders, then to students, community leaders, policemen and others. It will be helpful if you let the Committee know what you are doing in your State.

In the meantime, the Committee of 50 States will, assuming funding becomes available, begin a coordinated national effort to personally contact all of the governors, attorneys general, and every legislator in each of the 50 States, to try to convince them to cooperate with us in setting up a barrier to the New World Order, and to further federal usurpation.

If the barrier is established before the fact; if 38 States will, in unison, give notice of their intent to dissolve the Union, rather than accept the chains of the New World Order, this very action will probably be sufficient to stop the New World Order. They cannot take over without destroying the Constitution. If at least 38 States give notice they are standing by the Constitution at all hazards, the New World Order cannot beat us. They would be ineffective if they attempt to turn the U.S. Army against the people of 38 or more States. Army commanders are sworn to uphold the Constitution.

If world leaders can get United Nations troops in large numbers established on American soil before we are ready, they might have a small chance of beating us. This too, however, is highly unlikely. As long as the American people have guns, United Nations forces are unlikely to be turned loose on them. If our government succeeds in getting our guns, then we will have a problem.

If the Committee is unsuccessful in getting 38 States to work together in preparation to resist the New World Order, we will be working to find State leaders, and in two years, working to help elect State leaders who will cooperate in convincing one or more States to actually secede from the Union, if and when the New World Order, at the last minute, will be forced to reveal their real intent and purposes.

At that moment, perhaps not before, will there be leaders in some States who will recognize that secession, after all, is the only possible way to preserve the Constitution within the boundaries of their State. If no governor will act until the last moment, the risk will be greatly increased, but if, even at that point in time, secession is not a brand new concept to him, it will be possible to convince him that secession is the only possible way to *save the Union.* And that it is *legal and lawful* and does not require any moral compromising.

Most State Legislatures consist of a Senate and a House of Representatives. Every voter can usually get easy access, one on one, with his two Representatives in these bodies. You can make an appointment with them, personally explain to them what they need to do, and leave with them a copy of the Ultimatum Resolution, or a copy of this book.

We hope you will do your part. To coordinate your efforts with the national committee, write to:

COMMITTEE OF 50 STATES
4808 Quailbrook Circle
Salt Lake City, Utah 84118

Appendix

Secession Declaration of South Carolina
December 20, 1861

Declaration of the immediate causes which induce and justify the secession of South Carolina from the Federal Union.

The people of the State of South Carolina, in Convention assembled, on the 26th day of April, A.D., 1852, declared that the frequent violations of the Constitution of the United States, by the Federal Government, and its encroachments upon the reserved rights of the States, fully justified this State in then withdrawing from the Federal Union; but in deference to the opinions and wishes of the other slave-holding states, she forbore, at that time, to exercise this right. Since that time, these encroachments have continued to increase, and further forbearance ceases to be a virtue.

And, now, the State of South Carolina having resumed her separate and equal place among nations, deems it due to herself, to the remaining United States of America, and to the Nations of the world, that she should declare the immediate causes which have led to this act.

In the year 1765, that portion of the British Empire embracing Great Britain, undertook to make laws for the government of that portion composed of the thirteen American Colonies. A struggle for the right of self-government ensued, which resulted, on the 4th of July, 1776, in a Declaration by the Colonies, "that they are, and of right ought to be, *free, and independent states*; and that, as free and independent States, they have full power to levy war, conclude peace, contract alliances, establish commerce, and to do all other acts and things which independent States may of right do."

They further solemnly declared, that "whenever any form of Government becomes destructive of the ends for which it was established, it is the right of the people to alter or abolish it, and to institute a new Government. Deeming the Government of Great Britain to have become destructive of these ends, they declared that the Colonies "are absolved from all allegiance to the British Crown, and that all political connection between them and the State of Great Britain is, and ought to be, totally dissolved."

In pursuance of this Declaration of Independence, each of the thirteen States proceeded to exercise its separate Sovereignty; adopted for itself a Constitution, and appointed officers for the administration of Government in all its departments—Legislative, Executive, and Judicial. For purposes of defence, they united their arms and their counsels; and, in 1778, they entered into a League known as the Articles of Confederation, whereby they agreed to entrust the administration of their external relations to a Common Agent, known as the Congress of the United States expressly declaring, in the first article, "that each State retains its sovereignty, freedom, and independence, and every power, jurisdiction, and right which is not, by this Confederation, expressly delegated to the United States in Congress assembled."

Under this Confederation, the war of the Revolution was carried on, and on the 3rd of September, 1783, the contest ended, and a definitive Treaty was signed by Great Britain, in which she acknowledged the Independence of the Colonies in the following terms:

"ARTICLE 1. His Britannic Majesty acknowledges the said United States, viz.: New Hampshire, Massachusetts Bay, Rhode Island and Providence Plantations, Connecticut, New York, New Jersey, Pennsylvania, Delaware, Maryland, Virginia, North Carolina, South Carolina and Georgia, to be *free, sovereign, and independent states*; that he treats with them as such; and for himself, his heir and successor, relinquishes all claims to the Government, propriety and territorial rights of the same and every part thereof."

Thus were established the two great principles asserted by the Colonies, namely: the right of a state to govern itself; and the right of a people to abolish a General Government when it becomes destructive of the ends for which it was instituted. And concurrent with the establishment of these

Appendix

principles, was the fact that each Colony became and was recognized by the Mother Country as a *free, sovereign and independent state.*

In 1787, Deputies were appointed by the States to revise the Articles of Confederation, and on 17 September, 1787, these Deputies recommended for the adoption of the States, the Articles of Union known as the Constitution of the United States.

The Parties to whom this Constitution was submitted, were the several Sovereign States; they were to agree or disagree, and when nine of them agreed, the Compact was to take effect among those concurring; and the general Government, as the common Agent, was then to be invested with their authority.

If only nine of the thirteen States had concurred, the other four would have remained as they then were—Separate, Sovereign States, independent of any of the provisions of the Constitution. In fact, two of the States did not accede to the Constitution until long after it had gone into operation among the other eleven; and during that interval, they each exercised the functions of an Independent Nation.

By this Constitution, certain duties were imposed upon the several States, and the exercise of certain of their powers was restrained, which necessarily implied their continued existence as Sovereign States. But, to remove all doubt, an amendment was added, which declared that the powers not delegated to the United States by the Constitution, nor prohibited by it to the States, are reserved to the States, respectively, or to the people. On 23d May, 1788, South Carolina, by a Convention of her people, passed an Ordinance assenting to this Constitution, and afterwards altered her own Constitution to conform herself to the obligations she had undertaken.

Thus was established, by Compact between the States, a Government, with defined objects and power, limited to the express words of the Grant. This limitation left the whole remaining mass power subject to the clause reserving it to the States or to the people, and rendered unnecessary any specification of reserved rights.

We hold that the Government thus established is subject to the two great principles asserted in the Declaration of Independence; and we hold further, that the mode of its formation subjects it to a third fundamental principle, namely: *the law of Compact.* **We maintain that in every Compact between two or more Parties, the obligation is mutual; that the failure of one of the contracting Parties to perform a Material part of the**

agreement, entirely releases the obligation of the other; and that where no arbiter is provided, each Party is remitted to his own judgment to determine the fact of failure, with all its consequences. Emphasis added.

In the present case, that fact is established with certainty. We assert, that fourteen of the States have deliberately refused for years past to fulfil their Constitutional obligations, and we refer to their own Statutes for the proof.

The Constitution of the United States, in its Fourth Article, provides as follows:

"No person held to service or labor in one State, under the laws thereof, escaping into another shall, in consequence of any law or regulation therein, be discharged from such service or labor, but shall be delivered up, on claim of the party to whom such service or labor may be due."

This stipulation was so material to it that without it that Compact would not have been made. The greater number of the contracting parties held slaves, and they had previously evinced their estimate of the value of such a stipulation by making it a condition in the Ordinance for the government of the territory ceded by Virginia, which now composes the States north of the Ohio River.

The same Article of the Constitution stipulates also for rendition by the several States of fugitives from justice from the other States.

The General Government, as the Common Agent, passed laws to carry into effect these stipulations of the States. For many years these laws were executed. But an increasing hostility on the part of the non-slave-holding States to the Institution of Slavery has led to a disregard of their obligations, and the laws of the General Government have ceased to effect the objects of the Constitution. The States of Maine, New Hampshire, Vermont, Massachusetts, Connecticut, Rhode Island, New York, Pennsylvania, Illinois, Indiana, Michigan, Wisconsin and Iowa, have enacted laws which either nullify the Acts of Congress or render useless any attempt to execute them. In many of these States the fugitive is discharged from the service or labor claimed, and in none of them has the State Government complied with the stipulation made in the Constitution. *The State of New Jersey, at an early day, passed a law in conformity with her Constitutional obligation; but the current of Anti-Slavery feeling has led her more recently to enact laws which render inoperative the remedies provided by her own law and by the laws of Congress.* Emphasis added. In the State of

New York even the right of transit for a slave has been denied by her tribunals; and the States of Ohio and Iowa have refused to surrender to justice fugitives charged with murder and with inciting servile insurrection in the State of Virginia. Thus the Constitutional Compact has been deliberately broken and disregarded by these non-slave-holding States, and the consequence follows that South Carolina is released from her obligation.

The ends for which this Constitution was framed, are declared by itself to be "to form a more perfect Union, establish justice, insure domestic tranquillity, provide for the common defence, promote the general welfare, and secure the blessings of liberty to ourselves and our posterity."

These ends it endeavored to accomplish by a Federal Government, in which each State was recognized as an equal, and had separate control over its own Institutions. The right of property in slaves was recognized by giving to free persons distinct political rights, by giving them the right to represent, and burdening them with direct taxes for three-fifths of their slaves; by authorizing the importation of slaves for twenty years; and by stipulating for the rendition of fugitives from labor.

We affirm that these ends for which this Government was instituted have been defeated, and the government itself has been made destructive of them by the action of non-slave-holding States. Those States have assumed the right of deciding upon the propriety of our domestic Institutions; and have denied the rights of property established in fifteen of the States and recognized by the Constitution; they have denounced as sinful the Institution of Slavery; they have permitted the open establishment among them of societies, whose avowed object is to disturb the peace and to eloign the property of citizens of other States. They have encouraged and assisted thousands of our slaves to leave their homes; and those who remain, have been incited by emissaries, books, and pictures to servile insurrection.

For twenty-five years this agitation has been steadily increasing, until it has now secured to its aid the power of the Common Government. Observing the *forms* of the Constitution, a Sectional Party has found within that article establishing the Executive Department, the means of subverting the Constitution itself. A geographical line has been drawn across the Union, and all the States north of that line have united in the election of a man to the high office of President of the United States whose opinions and purposes are hostile to slavery. He is to be entrusted with the administration of the Common Government, because he has declared that that "Government cannot endure permanently half slave, half free," and that the public mind must rest in the belief that Slavery is in the course of ultimate extinction.

This Sectional Combination for the subversion of the Constitution, has been aided in some of the States by elevating to citizenship persons, who, by the Supreme Law of the land, are incapable of becoming citizens; and their votes have been used to inaugurate a new policy, hostile to the South, and destructive of its peace and safety.

On the 4th of March next, this Party will take possession of the Government. It has announced, that the South shall be excluded from the common territory; that the Judicial Tribunals shall be made sectional, and that a war must be waged against Slavery until it shall cease throughout the United States.

The Guaranties of the Constitution will then no longer exist; the equal rights of the States will be lost. The slave-holding States will no longer have the power of Self-government, or Self-protection, and the Federal Government will have become their enemy.

Sectional interest and animosity will deepen the irritation, and all hope of remedy is rendered vain, by the fact that public opinion at the North has invested a great political error with the sanctions of a more erroneous religious belief.

We, therefore, the People of South Carolina, by our Delegates, in Convention assembled, appealing to the Supreme Judge of the world for the rectitude of our intentions, have solemnly declared that the Union heretofore existing between this State and the other States of North America is dissolved, and that the State of South Carolina has resumed her position among the Nations of the world, as a Separate and Independent State; with full power to levy war, conclude peace, contract alliances, establish commerce, and to do all other acts and things which Independent States may of right do.

Other Books

Joseph Stumph is the author of a previous book titled THE CONSTITUTION HANGING BY A THREAD, which shows how a single attorney general of just one of the 50 States can make a powerful difference in preserving the Constitution, by filing challenges directly in the U.S. Supreme Court under the *Original Jurisdiction* clause of the Constitution.

It was also published by Northwest Publishing, and is available from the publisher for $6.95 plus $1.05 postage.

Sassy Ever After World

Thank you for reading my contribution to the Sassy Ever After World!

Reviews are greatly appreciated.

For more amazing stories in the Sassy Ever After World follow us on Social Media:

MT World Press website:

http://mtworldspress.com/

MT Shared Worlds Reader Group:

https://www.facebook.com/groups/412969162428913/

MT Worlds Facebook page:

https://www.facebook.com/AlphaPNR/

email: mtwpress1@gmail.com

Made in the USA
Middletown, DE
04 July 2019